ANNUAL EDITIONS

The Family

Thirty-third Edition

W9-BRI-835

07/08

EDITOR

Kathleen R. Gilbert

Indiana University

Kathleen Gilbert is an associate professor in the Department of Applied Health Science at Indiana University. She received a B.A. in Sociology and an M.S. in Marriage and Family Relations from Northern Illinois University. Her Ph.D. in Family Studies is from Purdue University. Dr. Gilbert's primary areas of interest are loss and grief in a family context, trauma and the family, family process, and minority families. She has published several books and articles in these areas.

**Contemporary
Learning Series**

2460 Kerper Blvd., Dubuque, IA 52001

Visit us on the Internet
http://www.mhcls.com

Credits

1. **Varied Perspectives on the Family**
   Unit photo—Dynamic Graphics/Jupiter Images
2. **Exploring and Establishing Relationships**
   Unit photo—Getty Images/SW Productions
3. **Finding a Balance: Maintaining Relationships**
   Unit photo—Eyewire (Photodisc)/Punchstock
4. **Challenges and Opportunities**
   Unit photo—U.S. Air Force photo by Scott H. Spitzer
5. **Families, Now and Into the Future**
   Unit photo—Dynamic Graphics/Jupiter Images

Copyright

Cataloging in Publication Data
Main entry under title: Annual Editions: The Family. 2007/2008.
1. The Family—Periodicals. I. Gilbert, Kathleen R., *comp.* II. Title: The Family.
ISBN-13: 978–0–07–351617–2   ISBN-10: 0–07–351617–1   658'.05   ISSN 1092–4876

Thirty-third Edition

Cover image © Photodisc Collection/Getty Images and Ryan McVay/Getty Images
Printed in the United States of America   1234567890QPDQPD9876   Printed on Recycled Paper

Editors/Advisory Board

Members of the Advisory Board are instrumental in the final selection of articles for each edition of ANNUAL EDITIONS. Their review of articles for content, level, currentness, and appropriateness provides critical direction to the editor and staff. We think that you will find their careful consideration well reflected in this volume.

EDITOR

Kathleen R. Gilbert
Indiana University

ADVISORY BOARD

Kevin Alltucker
University of Oregon

Judith Bordin
California State University, Chico

Rhonda Buckley
Texas Woman's University

Sari G. Byrd
Suffolk Community College

Ellen Carpenter
Appalachian State University

Donna K. Crossman
Ohio State University

Bernard Davidson
Medical College of Georgia

William Michael Fleming
University of Northern Iowa

Andrea G. Hunter
*University of North Carolina–
Greensboro*

Dennis W. Johnson
Monterey Peninsula College

Rhonda Korol
Lyndon State College

Marcia Lasswell
California State Polytechnic University

Larry LeFlore
Texas Woman's University

Kari Morgan
University of Wyoming–Laramie

N. Catherine Norris-Bush
Carson-Newman College

Esther Onaga
Michigan State University

Hiromi Ono
Washington State University

Lauren M. Papp
University of Wisconsin–Madison

Larry Rosenberg
Millersville University

Barbara Settles
University of Delaware

Fred E. Stickle
Western Kentucky University

George F. Stine
Millersville University

James C. Stroud
Ball State University

Bahira Trask
University of Delaware

Staff

EDITORIAL STAFF

Larry Loeppke, Managing Editor
Jay Oberbroeckling, Developmental Editor
Jade Benedict, Developmental Editor
Nancy Meissner, Editorial Assistant

PERMISSIONS STAFF

Lenny J. Behnke, Permissions Coordinator
Lori Church, Permissions Coordinator
Shirley Lanners, Permissions Coordinator

TECHNOLOGY STAFF

Luke David, eContent Coordinator

MARKETING STAFF

Julie Keck, Senior Marketing Manager
Mary Klein, Marketing Communications Specialist
Alice Link, Marketing Coordinator
Tracie Kammerude, Senior Marketing Assistant

PRODUCTION STAFF

Beth Kundert, Production Manager
Trish Mish, Production Assistant
Kari Voss, Lead Typesetter
Jean Smith, Typesetter
Karen Spring, Typesetter
Sandy Wille, Typesetter
Tara McDermott, Designer
Maggie Lytle, Cover Graphics

Preface

In publishing ANNUAL EDITIONS we recognize the enormous role played by the magazines, newspapers, and journals of the public press in providing current, first-rate educational information in a broad spectrum of interest areas. Many of these articles are appropriate for students, researchers, and professionals seeking accurate, current material to help bridge the gap between principles and theories and the real world. These articles, however, become more useful for study when those of lasting value are carefully collected, organized, indexed, and reproduced in a low-cost format, which provides easy and permanent access when the material is needed. That is the role played by ANNUAL EDITIONS.

The purpose of *Annual Editions: The Family 07/08* is to bring to the reader the latest thoughts and trends in our understanding of the family, to identify current concerns as well as problems and potential solutions, and to present alternative views of family processes. The intent of this anthology is to explore intimate relationships as they are played out within the family and, in doing this, to reflect the family's evolving function and importance.

The articles in this volume are taken from professional journals as well as semiprofessional publications and popular lay publications aimed at both special populations and a general readership. The selections are carefully reviewed for their currency and accuracy. In some cases, contrasting viewpoints are presented; in others, articles are paired in such a way as to personalize more impersonal scholarly information. In the current edition, a number of new articles have been added to reflect reviewers' comments on the previous edition. As the reader, you will note the tremendous range in tone and focus of these articles, from first-person accounts to reports of scientific discoveries as well as philosophical and theoretical writings. Some are more practical and applications-oriented, while others are more conceptual and research-oriented.

This anthology is organized to address many of the important aspects of family and family relationships. The first unit takes an overview perspective and looks at varied perspectives on the family. The second unit examines the beginning steps of relationship building as individuals go through the process of exploring and establishing connections. In the third unit, the means of finding and maintaining a relationship balance—for romantic as well as for other intimate relationships—are examined. Unit 4 is concerned with crises and ways in which these can act as challenges and opportunities for families and their members. Finally, unit 5 takes an affirming tone as it looks at family strengths and ways of empowering families.

Instructors can use *Annual Editions: The Family 07/08* as a primary text for lower-level, introductory marriage and family classes, particularly when they tie the content of the readings to basic information on marriage and family. This book can also be used as a supplement to update or emphasize certain aspects of standard marriage and family textbooks. Because of the provocative nature of many of the essays in this anthology, it works well as a basis for class discussion about various aspects of marriage and family relationships.

This edition of *Annual Editions: The Family 07/08* contains *Internet References* that can be used to further explore topics addressed in the articles. These sites are cross-referenced by number in the *topic guide*.

I would like to thank everyone involved in the development of this volume. My appreciation goes to those who sent in *article rating forms* and comments on the previous edition as well as those who suggested articles to consider for inclusion in this edition. To all of the students in my Marriage and Family Interaction class who have contributed critiques of articles, I would like to say thanks.

Anyone interested in providing input for future editions of *Annual Editions: The Family* should complete and return the postage-paid *article rating form* at the end of this book. Your suggestions are much appreciated and contribute to the continuing quality of this anthology.

Kathleen R. Gilbert
Editor

Contents

UNIT 1
Varied Perspectives on the Family

UNIT 2
Exploring and Establishing Relationships

The concepts in bold italics are developed in the article. For further expansion, please refer to the Topic Guide and the Index.

The concepts in bold italics are developed in the article. For further expansion, please refer to the Topic Guide and the Index.

The concepts in bold italics are developed in the article. For further expansion, please refer to the Topic Guide and the Index.

UNIT 3
Finding a Balance: Maintaining Relationships

The concepts in bold italics are developed in the article. For further expansion, please refer to the Topic Guide and the Index.

UNIT 4
Challenges and Opportunities

Part A.   Family Violence and Chaos

The concepts in bold italics are developed in the article. For further expansion, please refer to the Topic Guide and the Index.

The concepts in bold italics are developed in the article. For further expansion, please refer to the Topic Guide and the Index.

UNIT 5
Families, Now and Into the Future

The concepts in bold italics are developed in the article. For further expansion, please refer to the Topic Guide and the Index.

The concepts in bold italics are developed in the article. For further expansion, please refer to the Topic Guide and the Index.

Topic Guide

This topic guide suggests how the selections in this book relate to the subjects covered in your course. You may want to use the topics listed on these pages to search the Web more easily.

On the following pages a number of Web sites have been gathered specifically for this book. They are arranged to reflect the units of this *Annual Edition*. You can link to these sites by going to the student online support site at *http://www.mhcls.com/online/*.

ALL THE ARTICLES THAT RELATE TO EACH TOPIC ARE LISTED BELOW THE BOLD-FACED TERM.

Abortion
14. The Abortion Wars: 30 Years After Roe v. Wade

Abuse
3. Families and Family Study in International Perspective
24. Spanking Children: Evidence and Issues
35. Hitting Home
36. The Myths and Truths of Family Abduction

Adoption
19. Adopting a New American Family
20. After the Bliss
26. The Kids Are All Right
28. Adoption by Lesbian Couples

Aging
30. The Perma Parent Trap
33. Roles of American Indian Grandparents in Times of Cultural Crisis
34. Aging Japanese Pen Messages to Posterity
39. Keeping Work and Life in Balance
40. How to Land on Your Feet

Bereavement
16. Barren
34. Aging Japanese Pen Messages to Posterity
42. Terrorism, Trauma, and Children: What Can We Do?
47. Death of One's Partner: The Anticipation and the Reality
48. The Hispanic Way of Dying: Three Families, Three Perspectives, Three Cultures

Biology
4. Gender Bender
5. What Makes You Who You Are
6. This Thing Called Love
8. Go Ahead, Kiss Your Cousin: Heck, Marry Her If You Want To
13. A New Fertility Factor
15. Brave New Babies
16. Barren

Birth defects
8. Go Ahead, Kiss Your Cousin: Heck, Marry Her If You Want To

Childcare
2. Children as a Public Good
39. Keeping Work and Life in Balance

Children
2. Children as a Public Good
15. Brave New Babies
17. Who's Raising Baby?
18. And Now, the Hard Part: That Sweet Little Thing Is About to Commandeer Your Life
23. Kaleidoscope of Parenting Cultures
24. Spanking Children: Evidence and Issues
26. The Kids Are All Right
27. What About Black Fathers?
28. Adoption by Lesbian Couples

29. Are Married Parents Really Better for Children?
31. Being a Sibling
36. The Myths and Truths of Family Abduction
41. Home Alone
42. Terrorism, Trauma, and Children: What Can We Do?

Communication
7. Great Expectations
10. New Technologies and Our Feelings: Romance on the Internet
37. Love But Don't Touch
38. For Better or Worse: Couples Confront Unemployment
50. Get a Closer Look: 12 Tips for Successful Family Interviews

Dating
8. Go Ahead, Kiss Your Cousin: Heck, Marry Her If You Want To
9. Interracial Intimacy
10. New Technologies and Our Feelings: Romance on the Internet
44. Dating After Divorce

Divorce
36. The Myths and Truths of Family Abduction
43. Marriage and Divorce American Style
44. Dating After Divorce
45. Managing a Blended Family

Emotions
7. Great Expectations
10. New Technologies and Our Feelings: Romance on the Internet
17. Who's Raising Baby?
20. After the Bliss

Family and marriage
1. The World Historical Transformation of Marriage
2. Children as a Public Good
3. Families and Family Study in International Perspective
21. Contextual Influences on Marriage: Implications for Policy and Intervention
22. Marriage at First Sight
29. Are Married Parents Really Better for Children?
32. Aunties and Uncles
45. Managing a Blended Family
46. Stepfamily Success Depends on Ingredients

Family interaction
3. Families and Family Study in International Perspective
30. The Perma Parent Trap
31. Being a Sibling
46. Stepfamily Success Depends on Ingredients
50. Get a Closer Look: 12 Tips for Successful Family Interviews
51. Examining Family Rituals

Fathers
25. Stress and the Superdad
27. What About Black Fathers?

Finances, family
3. Families and Family Study in International Perspective
21. Contextual Influences on Marriage: Implications for Policy and Intervention

Internet References

The following Internet sites have been carefully researched and selected to support the articles found in this reader. The easiest way to access these selected sites is to go to our student online support site at *http://www.mhcls.com/online/*.

AE: The Family 07/08

The following sites were available at the time of publication. Visit our Web site—we update our student online support site regularly to reflect any changes.

General Sources

AARP (American Association of Retired Persons)
http://www.aarp.org
This major advocacy group for older people includes among its many resources suggested readings and Internet links to organizations that deal with social issues that may affect people and their families as they age.

Encyclopedia Britannica
http://www.britannica.com
This huge "Britannica Internet Guide" leads to a cornucopia of informational sites and reference sources on such topics as family structure, the family cycle, forms of family organization, and other social issues.

Planned Parenthood
http://www.plannedparenthood.org
Visit this well-known organization's home page for links to information on the various kinds of contraceptives (including outercourse and abstinence) and to discussions of other topics related to sexual and reproductive health.

Social Science Information Gateway
http://sosig.esrc.bris.ac.uk/
This is an online catalog of Internet resources relevant to social science education and research. Sites are selected and described by a librarian or subject specialist.

Sympatico: HealthyWay: Health Links
http://www1.sympatico.ca/Contents/health/
This Canadian site, which is meant for consumers, will lead you to many links that are related to sexual orientation. *Sympatico* also addresses aspects of human sexuality as well as reproductive health over the life span.

UNIT 1: Varied Perspectives on the Family

American Studies Web
http://www.georgetown.edu/crossroads/asw/
This site provides links to a wealth of resources on the Internet related to American studies, from gender to race and ethnicity to demography and population studies.

Anthropology Resources Page
http://www.usd.edu/anth/
Many cultural topics can be accessed from this site from the University of South Dakota. Click on the links to find comparisons of values and lifestyles among the world's peoples.

Women's Studies Resources
http://www.inform.umd.edu/EdRes/Topic/WomensStudies/
This site provides a wealth of resources related to women and their concerns. You can find links to such topics as body image, comfort (or discomfort) with sexuality, personal relationships, pornography, and more.

UNIT 2: Exploring and Establishing Relationships

Bonobo Sex and Society
http://songweaver.com/info/bonobos.html
This site, accessed through Carnegie Mellon University, contains an article explaining how a primate's behavior challenges traditional assumptions about male supremacy in human evolution. This interesting site is guaranteed to generate much spirited debate.

Go Ask Alice!
http://www.goaskalice.columbia.edu/index.html
This interactive site of the Columbia University Health Services provides discussion and insight into a number of personal issues of interest to college-age people—and those younger and older.

The Kinsey Institute for Research in Sex, Gender, and Reproduction
http://www.indiana.edu/~kinsey/
The purpose of this Kinsey Institute Web site is to support interdisciplinary research in the study of human sexuality.

Mysteries of Odor in Human Sexuality
http://www.pheromones.com
This is a commercial site with the goal of selling a book by James Kohl. Look here to find topics of interest to nonscientists about pheromones. Check out the diagram of "Mammalian Olfactory-Genetic-Neuronal-Hormonal-Behavioral Reciprocity and Human Sexuality" for a sense of the myriad biological influences that play a part in sexual behavior.

The Society for the Scientific Study of Sexuality
http://www.sexscience.org
The Society for the Scientific Study of Sexuality is an international organization dedicated to the advancement of knowledge about sexuality.

UNIT 3: Finding a Balance: Maintaining Relationships

Child Welfare League of America
http://www.cwla.org
The CWLA is the largest U.S. organization devoted entirely to the well-being of vulnerable children and their families. This site provides links to information about such issues as teaching morality and values.

Coalition for Marriage, Family, and Couples Education
http://www.smartmarriages.com
CMFCE is dedicated to bringing information about and directories of skill-based marriage education courses to the public. It hopes to lower the rate of family breakdown through couple-empowering preventive education.

The National Academy for Child Development
http://www.nacd.org
The NACD, dedicated to helping children and adults reach their full potential, presents links to various programs, research, and resources into a variety of family topics.

National Council on Family Relations
http://www.ncfr.com
This NCFR home page leads to valuable links to articles, research, and other resources on issues in family relations, such as stepfamilies, couples, and children of divorce.

Positive Parenting
http://www.positiveparenting.com
Positive Parenting is an organization dedicated to providing resources and information to make parenting rewarding, effective, and fun.

SocioSite
http://www.pscw.uva.nl/sociosite/TOPICS/Women.html
Open this site to gain insights into a number of issues that affect family relationships. It provides wide-ranging issues of women and men, of family and children, and more.

UNIT 4: Challenges and Opportunities

Alzheimer's Association
http://www.alz.org
The Alzheimer's Association, dedicated to the prevention, cure, and treatment of Alzheimer's and related disorders, provides support to afflicted patients and their families.

Caregiver's Handbook
http://www.acsu.buffalo.edu/~drstall/hndbk0.html
This site is an online handbook for caregivers. Topics include medical aspects and liabilities of care giving.

National Crime Prevention Council
http://www.ncpc.org
NCPC's mission is to enable people to create safer and more caring communities by addressing the causes of crime and violence and reducing the opportunities for crime to occur.

Widow Net
http://www.widownet.org
Widow Net is an information and self-help resource for and by widows and widowers. The information is helpful to people of all ages, religious backgrounds, and sexual orientation who have experienced a loss.

UNIT 5: Families, Now and Into the Future

National Institute on Aging
http://www.nih.gov/nia/
The NIA presents this home page that will take you to a variety of resources on health and lifestyle issues that are of interest to people as they grow older.

We highly recommend that you review our Web site for expanded information and our other product lines. We are continually updating and adding links to our Web site in order to offer you the most usable and useful information that will support and expand the value of your Annual Editions. You can reach us at: *http://www.mhcls.com/annualeditions/*.

UNIT 1

Varied Perspectives on the Family

Unit Selections

1. **The World Historical Transformation of Marriage**, Stephanie Coontz
2. **Children as a Public Good**, Myra H. Strober
3. **Families and Family Study in International Perspective**, Bert N. Adams

Key Points to Consider

- How has marriage evolved over time? What might it look like in the future?

- What are your expectations for the family as an institution? How do personally held views of family influence policy? What might be the effect of this?

- What are your views on the changing nature of the American family? Does the change indicate that the family is "drifting apart?" Is there an alternative interpretation?

- What are some of the universalities of families that transcend culture? How do families vary across cultures? What is your comfort level with these differences?

Student Website

www.mhcls.com/online

Internet References

Further information regarding these websites may be found in this book's preface or online.

American Studies Web
http://www.georgetown.edu/crossroads/asw/

Anthropology Resources Page
http://www.usd.edu/anth/

Women's Studies Resources
http://www.inform.umd.edu/EdRes/Topic/WomensStudies/

Our image of what family is and what it should be is a powerful combination of personal experience, family forms we encounter or observe, and attitudes we hold. Once formed, this image informs decision making and interpersonal interaction throughout our lives. It has far-reaching effects: On an intimate level, it influences individual and family development as well as relationships both inside and outside the family. On a broader level, it affects legislation as well as social policy and programming.

In many ways, this image can be positive. It can act to clarify our thinking and facilitate interaction with like-minded individuals. It can also be negative, because it can narrow our thinking and limit our ability to see that other ways of carrying out the functions of family have value. Their very differentness can make them seem "bad." In this case, interaction with others can be impeded because of contrasting views.

This unit is intended to meet several goals with regard to perspectives on the family: (1) to sensitize the reader to sources of beliefs about the "shoulds" of the family—what the family should be and the ways in which family roles should be carried out, (2) to show how different views of the family can influence attitudes toward community responsibility and family policy, and (3) to show how views that dominate one's culture can influence awareness of ways of structuring family life.

In the first reading, "The World Historical Transformation of Marriage," Stephanie Coontz takes the long view of over 5,000 years of recorded history to examine the historic evolution of marriage, with results that may surprise the reader. The level of responsibility a society should take for the care and well-being of children is explored in the next reading, "Children as a Public Good." We live in an increasingly globalized world, with increasing cross-cultural exposure. This is projected to increase in the future, yet our understanding of the family has not kept pace.

The World Historical Transformation of Marriage

Stephanie Coontz

For the past several years, I have had the disconcerting but exhilarating privilege of ranging back and forth over a time span of 5,000 years in my readings on marriage and family life. In the book I am just finishing on the history of marriage, I have pushed my studies further back into the past than I have ever ventured before. But as the national cochair and press liaison for the Council on Contemporary Families, it was also my job to stay on top of the exciting new research that appears in journals. Being able to combine these two projects has helped me gain a better perspective on both the historical trends in marriage and the contemporary debates about its future.

I have spent much of my career as a historian explaining to people that many things that seem new in family life are actually quite traditional. Two-provider families, for example, were the norm through most of history. Stepfamilies were more numerous in much of history than they are today. There have been several times and places when cohabitation, out-of-wedlock births, or nonmarital sex were more widespread than they are today. Divorce was higher in Malaysia during the 1940s and 1950s than it is today in the United States. Even same-sex marriage, though comparatively rare, has been accepted in some cultures under certain conditions.

Similarly, many societies have had a very casual attitude toward what deserves recognition as a marriage. The "tradition" that marriage has to be licensed by the state or sanctified by the church is more recent than most people assume. In ancient Rome, for example, the difference between cohabitation and legal marriage was entirely subjective. It depended solely upon the partners' intent. And I am more than a little bemused when people talk about the traditional sanctity of the Christian wedding ceremony. For more than a thousand years, the Catholic church took the position that if a man and woman claimed that they had exchanged words of consent, whether in the kitchen or out by the haystack, then they were married.

In the process of writing this book, however, I have shifted my focus. I still believe that when it comes to any particular practice or variation on marriage, there is really nothing new under the sun. But when we look at the larger picture, it is clear that the social role and mutual relationship of marriage, divorce, and singlehood in the contemporary world is qualitatively different from anything to be found in the past. Almost any separate way of organizing caregiving, childrearing, residential arrangements, sexual interactions, or interpersonal redistribution of resources has been tried by some society at some point in time. But the coexistence in *one* society of so many alternative ways of doing all of these different things—and the comparative legitimacy accorded to many of them—has never been seen before.

The contemporary revolution in marriage and family life is what historians sometimes call an *overdetermined* phenomenon—something that has so many separate causes and aspects that getting rid of one, two, or even several elements of the change would not reverse it. Divorce and single parenthood have both been common in many societies in the past, but they almost never coexisted with the right of women to initiate the divorce, or the ability of so many single women to actually support themselves and their children. The extraordinary increase in the economic independence and legal equality of women has reshaped the social landscape of family life. It has put a new spin on almost every contemporary aspect of marriage (and of nonmarriage), even if some of our contemporary features superficially resemble something in the past. The rise of new forms and patterns of cohabitation has had similar far-reaching effects, as many contributors to this issue point out. And the legal gains for unmarried heterosexual and same-sex partners have challenged the ways that marriage traditionally organized people's rights and responsibilities on the basis of biology and gender.

But marriage has also been transformed by the behavior of married people who will never divorce, and by the actions of heterosexual singles who would never consider having a child out of wedlock. The reproductive revolution, for example, was pioneered by married couples eager to overcome their infertility. Yet it transformed all of the traditionally taken-for-granted relationships between marriage, sex, conception, childbirth, and parenting, allowing individuals to become parents who would never have been able to do so before. They can have those children in such bewildering combinations that a child can theoretically have five different parents (a sperm donor, an egg donor, a birth mother, and the social parents who raise the child). And that count does not reckon with any later complications introduced by divorce and remarriage!

An even more revolutionary innovation is the increasingly common option of not having any children at all. A large proportion of people who marry today will never have children, not because of infertility, but because they choose to remain childless. This is a huge change from the past, when childlessness was an economic disaster and often led to divorce even when the couple would have preferred to stay together.

The many young people who are delaying marriage until their late 20s or early 30s also contribute to the lessened role of marriage in organizing social and personal life. These young people are not necessarily antimarriage. Often, they delay marriage because they are very antidivorce. But the long period of life when they live on their own, with full access to the rights and privileges of adulthood, reduces the social weight that marriage exerts in society.

Today, unlike many periods in history, almost any heterosexual is free to marry. But marriage is no longer necessary to activate one's property rights, legal standing, public roles, and social status. The large pool of people who remain single for years but who are still allowed to assume adult roles challenges the ways that Europeans and Americans have organized social life for hundreds, if not thousands, of years. This challenge would exist even if everyone eventually married and the divorce rate dropped back to the levels of the 1950s.

The expansion of solitary living in contemporary Western societies has been staggering. In 1950, just 10% of all households in Europe contained only one person. Five decades later, one-person households made up slightly more than one quarter of all households in the United States, 30% of all British households, and 40% of all Swedish households. Greece had the lowest percentage of one-person households in Europe at the end of the 20th century. But even there, one-person households represented almost 20% of the total, twice the 1950 average for Europe as a whole.

Never before have so many people lived alone. And never before have unmarried people, living alone or in couples, had the same rights as married adults. The lessened importance of marriage in organizing people's life cycles and assumption of adult responsibilities changes the experience of all people who marry, no matter how "traditional" they hope that marriage will be.

When I look at contemporary debates about what is happening to marriage through this historical lens, I am struck by how often the "optimistic" and the "pessimistic" predictions of the future are based on what are in many ways secondary or surface fluctuations taking place above the more long-range subterranean changes in family life. In the mid-1990s, the consensus among popular commentators was that marriage was dying. The dramatic jump in the proportion of cohabiting couples between 1990 and 1996 was projected into the future, generating the forecast that marriage would be extinct in 30 years. Trends in single-mother families led to predictions of a "fatherless" America.

Then at the end of the 1990s, commentators found a number of signs that led them to hope that the pace of change in marriage arrangements and family life was slowing down and even in some cases reversing. Divorce rates fell in the United States and Britain. In the United States, young men in the 1990s expressed more support for marriage than their same-age counterparts had in the 1970s. The late 1990s saw an uptick in the number of impoverished children living with two adults instead of one. A study of more than 10,000 American high school students reported that 48% had engaged in sexual intercourse in 1997, down from 54% in 1991. Teens who did engage in sex were more likely to use condoms during the 1990s, which produced a decline in the abortion rate and in sexually transmitted diseases (Ellman, 2000; Risman & Schwartz, 2002; Thornton & Young-DeMarco, 2001).

All of this was heady news to many observers. "Abstinence: the Next Teen Thing," announced the teasers for a local television program in my area. The head of one institute aimed at restoring "traditional" American family values wrote hopefully that "after more than three decades of relentless advance, the family structure revolution in the U.S. may be over" (Blankenhorn, 2001).

In a 1997 survey of 10 European countries, demographers Anton Kuijsten and Klaus Strohmeier found several trends suggesting that the "de-traditionalization" of marriage and family life had reached its limits. They noted that countries that had lagged in family change during the 1970s and 1980s were still catching up in the 1990s, with increases in divorce rates and the age of first marriage, and decreases in male breadwinner families and birth rates. But countries that had led the way in family change during the 1970s and 1980s, they claimed, "seem to be over the hill and have started their way back" (Kuijsten & Strohmeier, 1997).

Perhaps the most excitement of all was generated by a single statistic from the United States census indicating that between 1998 and 2000, the labor force participation of women with babies dropped for the first time in a quarter century. The Census Bureau reported that as of June 2000, 55% of women with infants under 1 year old were in the work force, a decline from 59% in 1998 (Lewin, 2001). The *New York Times Magazine*, combining Census Bureau statistics with a few anecdotes about high-achieving women who quit their jobs, announced the arrival of "The Opt-Out Revolution" among working moms (Belkin, 2003). And as I write this article, I have on my desk six other media reports about how working moms are rediscovering the joys of staying home.

On closer inspection, of course, none of these trends presages any return to so-called "traditional" marriages and family life. Divorce rates have been falling, yes, but in many countries, marriage rates have been falling even more. The uptick in two-parent families among the poor turned out to be due mainly to an increase in cohabitation. The much-ballyhooed dip in working mothers with children under the age of 1 left more than 50% of such mothers still in the workforce, a much larger figure than the 30% of such moms in paid labor in the 1970s. And 72% of mothers with children above the age of 1 were in the workforce in 2002, maintaining the 100-year high reached in the late 1990s (Gerson, 2003; U.S. Census Bureau, 2003).

For those still harboring any illusion that the historical transformation of marriage had come to an end, the rash of victories for proponents of same-sex marriage in 2003 and 2004 must have come as a major shock. In 2003, Canada legalized same-sex marriage. Then, on November 18, 2003, the Massachusetts

Supreme Court ruled that the state constitution guaranteed equal marriage rights for same-sex couples. Responding to an uproar of protest from his conservative base, President Bush declared in his State of the Union Address on January 20, 2004, that the nation must "defend the sanctity of marriage." This in turn spurred the newly elected mayor of San Francisco, Gavin Newsome, to express his indignation by directing the city to start issuing marriage licenses to gay and lesbian couples on February 12. More than 3,200 couples, many of them from out of state, flocked to San Francisco to get married.

In response to the mounting controversy, President Bush endorsed a constitutional amendment prohibiting same-sex marriage. But this only incited more defiance. In New Mexico, New York, and Oregon, county clerks and commissioners also began issuing wedding licenses to gay and lesbian couples. As this issue goes to press, the controversy continues to rage.

Whatever people's feelings about same-sex marriage, everyone could see that gender norms and marriage behaviors had not stabilized after all. Commentators who had been happily predicting a return to traditional marriage immediately changed their tune. "The gays have moved in to deliver the knockout punch" to marriage, claimed Phyllis Schlaffly, who led the successful battle against the Equal Rights Amendment in the 1970s (Nieves, 2003).

The fundamentalist Protestant minister James Dobson, founder of Focus on the Family, put it even more starkly: "The institution of marriage is on the ropes," he wrote in September 2003, after the victories for same-sex marriage in Canada and the U.S. Supreme Court ruling overturning antisodomy laws. "Unless we act quickly, the family as it has been known for 5,000 years will be gone" (Dobson, 2003).

Now, it is not often that I agree with James Dobson about issues relating to marriage, and it is even more rare for me to accuse him of understatement. But the research I have been doing for my forthcoming history of marriage convinces me that Dobson is not only making an important point but also is actually underestimating just how momentous a change we are talking about.

In my view, marriage as we have known it for 5,000 years has *already* been overthrown. But it was heterosexuals, not gays and lesbians, who accomplished this revolution. The demand of gays and lesbians for legal recognition of their unions is a symptom, not the cause, of how much and how irreversibly marriage has changed.

The *Real* Traditional Marriage

For thousands of years, marriage organized people's places in the economic and political hierarchy of society. Whatever functions marriage served for the man and woman involved and for the children they produced, marriage was not primarily for their individual benefit. It was a way of raising capital, constructing political alliances, organizing the division of labor by age and gender, and deciding what claim, if any, children had on their parents, and what rights parents had in their children. Marriage served so many political, social, and economic functions that the individual needs and desires of its members (especially

women and children, its subordinate members) were secondary considerations. In fact, for most people, whether rich or poor, marriage was as much about getting in-laws as about finding a mate and having a child.

For the propertied classes, marriage was the main way of consolidating wealth, transferring property, laying claim to political power, even concluding peace treaties. When upper-class men and women married, dowry, bride wealth, or tribute changed hands, making the match a major economic investment by the parents and other kin of the couple. Even middle-class families had a huge economic stake in who married whom. Until the late 18th century, historian Margaret Hunt (1996) points out, marriage was "the main means of transferring property, occupational status, personal contacts, money, tools, livestock and women across generations and kin groups". For most men, the dowry that a wife brought was the biggest infusion of cash, goods, or land that they would ever acquire. For most women, finding a husband was the most important investment they could make in their economic future.

In the lower classes, marriage was also an economic and political transaction, but on a different scale. Instead of making an alliance with another domain to prevent war, the concerns of commoners were more immediate: "Do I marry someone with fields near my fields?" "Will my prospective mate meet the approval of the neighbors and relatives on whom I depend?" "Would these in-laws be a help to our family or a hindrance?" And because few farms or businesses could be run by a single person, the skills, resources, and tools prospective partners brought to the marriage were at least as important as their personality or attractiveness.

For all socioeconomic groups, marriage was the most important marker of adulthood and respectability. It was the primary way of organizing work along lines of age and gender. It was the main vehicle for redistributing resources to old and young—and also, contrary to contemporary romanticization of family life in the past, the main vehicle for extracting labor *from* the young.

For all of these reasons, love was considered a very poor reason to get married. It was desirable for love, or at least affection, to develop *after* marriage, and many parents allowed their children to veto a match with a partner who repelled them. But love was not the main thing that people took into account in deciding when and whom to marry. And when divorce occurred, it was more often to get a better set of in-laws or because of childlessness rather than because love had fled the home.

The Love Revolution

In the 17th century, a series of interrelated political, economic, and cultural changes began to erode the older functions of marriage and throw into question the right of parents, local elites, and government officials to limit individual autonomy in personal life, including marriage. And in the 18th century, the revolutionary new ideal of the love match triumphed in most of Western Europe and North America.

The marital ideals inaugurated in the 18th century represented a break with literally thousands of years of history. Suddenly, couples were supposed to invest more of their emotional energy in each other and their children than in their natal families, their kin, their friends, and their patrons. There was a new stress on marital companionship, intimacy, and privacy. The new ideal was a long way from the 20th century notion that men and women should be friends and lovers, but it was headed in that direction.

Contemporaries immediately recognized that this new idea threatened to radically destabilize personal life and gender relations. No sooner was the ideal of the love match and lifelong intimacy invented than people who took it seriously began to demand the right to divorce. The first demands to decriminalize homosexuality also came at the end of the 18th century, and they were raised by some of the most ardent defenders of the love match. Even in stable marriages, conservatives complained, the new values caused the couple "to be constantly taken up with each other" instead of carrying out their duties to society.

In other words, the very values that we have come to think of as traditional, the very values that invested marriage with such emotional weight in people's lives, had an inherent tendency to undermine the stability of marriage as an institution even as they increased the satisfactions of marriage as a relationship. I try to show in my forthcoming book that today's crisis of marriage was built in to the radical new marital values that so many people mistakenly believe are many thousands of years old. The same things that made marriage become such a unique and treasured personal relationship during the last 200 years paved the way for it to become an optional and fragile one.

For years, we have debated why the institution of lifelong marriage began to unravel in the 1970s. Liberals have blamed socioeconomic forces. Conservatives have pointed to value changes. But I now believe that the real question is not why things fell apart in the 1970s, but why they did *not* fall apart in the 1790s. That is what I am currently attempting to figure out in my new book.

I do not believe that marriage will disappear. However, the trends that we are seeing, not just in Europe and North America, but all over the world, suggest that marriage will never regain its monopoly over the regulation of sex, the rearing of children, the transmission of resources from the older to the younger generation, or the organization of the division of labor by gender.

In legal terms, almost all Western nations, and even some non-Western ones, have experienced a blurring of the differences between the legal responsibilities and rights of married and unmarried individuals. Unmarried individuals who behave as if they are married have many of the same rights and are subject to many of the same obligations that used to depend on possession of a marriage license. Conversely, married people who wish to part are no longer held together by legal compulsion or economic necessity. It is more possible for individuals to live on their own than ever before in history.

Scholars of marriage and family life have many names to describe the breakdown of the wall separating marriage from nonmarriage. Andrew Cherlin (2004) talks about the *deinstitutionalization* of marriage in his contribution to this issue. Legal scholars refer to the *delegalization* of marriage. French sociologist Irene Thery (1994) calls the process "*demarriage*." I

like historian Nancy Cott's (2000) suggestion that what has happened to marriage is akin to the historical disestablishment of religion. Once the state stopped conferring a whole set of special rights and privileges on one particular religious denomination, religion itself did not disappear, but many different churches and new religious groups proliferated. Similarly, once the state stopped insisting on a government-sanctioned marriage license for people to partake of the privileges and duties of parenthood or other longterm commitments, other forms of intimate relationships and childrearing arrangements proliferated, or came out from underground (Cott; Millar & Warman, 1996; Thery; Willekens, 2003).

Historians are generally reluctant to use the word revolution to describe changes in social life, because such changes usually have very deep historical roots and almost always retain tremendous continuities with the past. We are especially skeptical when it comes to issues connected with family life, because ever since ancient Egypt and classical Rome, older generations have been bemoaning the loss of older family forms or marital values and predicting disaster for the next generation.

But in my current writing project, I have become convinced that we are indeed in the middle of a world-historic transformation of marriage and family life. Things are changing so fast that it is hard to tell which new relationships and interpersonal outcomes we observe are features of a new system and which are products of the transitional period we are going through. But one thing is for sure: There will be no turning back.

For better or worse, the relationship of marriage to larger social and economic institutions has been fundamentally changed, and so have individuals' own personal experiences of marriage or nonmarriage. Our research and practice must take this as a given. In the current historical context, the appropriate question for researchers and family practitioners is not what single family form or marriage arrangement we would prefer in the abstract, but how we can help people in a wide array of different committed relationships minimize their shortcomings and maximize their solidarities.

Note

1. Stephanie Coontz teaches history at The Evergreen State College. Her new book on the history of marriage will be published by Viking-Penguin in 2005.

References

Belkin, L. (2003, October 26). The opt-out revolution. *The New York Times Magazine.*

Blankenhorn, D. (2001, October). Is the family structure revolution over? *American Values Reporter.*

Cherlin, A. J. (2004). The deinstitutionalization of American marriage. *Journal of Marriage and Family, 66,* 848-861.

Cott, N. (2000). *Public vows: A history of marriage and the nation.* Cambridge, MA: Harvard University Press.

Dobson, J. (2003, September). *Focus on the Family Newsletter.*

Ellman, I. (2000). Divorce rates, marriage rates, and the problematic persistence of traditional marital roles. *Family Law Quarterly, 34.*

Gerson, K. (2003, December 17). Working moms heading home? Not likely. *Council on Contemporary Families news release, As-*

cribe Newswire. Retrieved December 18, 2003, from **http://www.contemporaryfamilies.org.**

Hunt, M. (1996). *The middling sort: Commerce. gender, and the family in England, 1680-1780.* Berkeley: University of California Press.

Kuijsten, A., & Strohmeier, K. (1997). Ten countries in Europe: An overview. In F. Kaufmann et al. (Eds.), *Family life and family policies in Europe* (Vol. I). Oxford, England: Clarendon Press.

Lewin, T. (2001, October 19). More mothers of babies under 1 are staying home. *New York Times.*

Millar, J., & Warman, A. (1996). *Family obligations in Europe.* London: Family Policy Studies Centre.

Nieves, E. (2003, August 17). Family values groups and gay marriage. *Washington Post.*

Risman, B., & Schwartz, P. (2002). After the sexual revolution: Gender politics in teen dating. *Contexts, 1.*

Thery, I. (1994). *Demarriage.* Paris: Edition Odile Jacob.

Thornton, A., & Young-DeMarco, L. (2001). Four decades of trends in attitudes toward family issues in the United States. *Journal of Marriage and Family, 63.*

U.S. Census Bureau. (2003, October). *Fertility of American women, June 2002* (Current Population Survey).

Willekens, H. (2003). Is contemporary family law historically unique? *Journal of Family History, 28.*

Children as a Public Good

M YRA H. S TROBER

Whose responsibility are children? In twenty-first-century America, the answer too often is "their parents." Although politicians and pundits frequently make pious pronouncements calling children "our best hope," "our future," and "our nation's most valuable resource," mouthing such sentiments is a far cry from taking collective responsibility. In the current election season, one listens in vain for concrete proposals from candidates to improve the lives of children. The United States lags behind all other western democracies in providing for their needs. We have to revise the national mindset, visible on the left as well as the right, that puts sole responsibility for children in the hands of individual families, many of whom are ill-equipped to give them the care and opportunities necessary to provide for the citizens, workers, and human beings we wish to develop. Further, instead of viewing parents with professional careers as irresponsible workaholics, we should appreciate the incredibly hard work that parents do when they are simultaneously holding jobs and raising children.

Certainly, parents have primary responsibility for meeting the needs of their children; the argument here is that meeting children's needs should be a collective responsibility as well. Although parents reap the rewards of well-reared children (emotional rather than economic rewards in this day and age), children whose needs have been met confer benefits as well on society as a whole. We need to make a reality of the rhetoric that sees children as our most valuable asset.

As an economist, I argue that children must be considered a public good whose welfare and education need to be addressed collectively. In other words, it really does take a village to raise a child. A public good is one whose provision confers externalities—benefits beyond those accruing to the direct beneficiaries. Public schooling confers such externalities; the public as well as individual students and parents benefit when its citizens are literate and numerate, and when they understand the benefits of democracy. This is how the state justifies taxing the public to provide for children's schooling.

The notion that children are a private good leads to the conclusion that their economic and emotional care is the sole responsibility of their parents. This philosophy was most clearly articulated by President Richard Nixon, when he vetoed the Child Development Act of 1971: "For the Federal Government to plunge headlong financially into supporting child development would commit the vast moral authority of the National Government to the side of communal approaches to child rearing over against [sic] the family-centered approach." There was no sense that parents and the federal government might engage in a partnership for child care, no sense that there were public benefits to be gained from federal involvement in improving the child care system. Or, consider the case of the city of Fremont, California, which defeated a 1989 measure asking taxpayers to approve a $12 per year property tax levied on all residential dwelling units to pay for childcare services. An exit poll found that 88 percent of the three-fourths of the electorate that had voted against the measure agreed with the statement, "Child care should be paid for by parents, not by the whole community."

If, instead, we thought of children as public goods, we would behave far differently toward their economic and emotional needs. And we would seek collective solutions for their care. I want to spell out several critical areas in which children's needs are not being met and argue for public investment to remedy that situation. This is not a new argument on the left, but it is one rarely articulated these days.

Freedom from Poverty

What are we doing about child poverty? What are we doing about the fact (published by our own government) that 12.9 million children under the age of eighteen—17.6 percent of all children—live in poverty, that they go hungry, have inadequate clothing and shelter, and are ill-equipped for the education they need? Among white children, 14.3 percent live in poverty, but among black children, an astounding 34.1 percent are poor. Although children under eighteen represent about one-quarter of the total population, they are more than one-third of those in poverty. Similarly, in 2000, families with children under eighteen accounted for 36 percent of Americans who were homeless.

Not only does poverty affect children's economic well-being, it is also associated with poorer performance in school, in part because children in poor neighborhoods go to schools with lower per-pupil expenditures. Data from the National Assessment of Educational Progress (NAEP) indicate that in tests of children in the fourth and eighth grades, those who live in poverty (as measured by being eligible for the National School Lunch Program) score lower in several subjects as compared to better-off children. NAEP data for twelfth-grade students show that Title I Schools (those with the highest levels of poverty) have a much higher proportion of students who score below basic skill levels in reading, writing, and civics, and especially in math and science.

Let us compare children's poverty in the United States and other developed countries in the late 1990s and 2000. Data from the Luxembourg Income Study show that if we use 50 percent of median adjusted disposable income for all persons in a family as the measure of poverty, 22 percent of all U.S. children are in poverty, one of the highest percentages in the study. Among the 25 countries surveyed, the percentage of all children in poverty ranged from a low of 3 percent in Finland to a high of 24 percent in Russia. The only other country with a rate higher than 20 percent was Italy.

Living with a single mother increases children's chances of being in poverty in all the countries in the Luxembourg study. In some countries, the probabilities triple or quadruple. For example, in Finland, the probability of being in poverty in 2000 was 2 percent for children in two-parent families, but 8 percent for children with a single mother. In the United States, the probability of being in poverty in 2000 was 15 percent for children in two-parent families, but almost 50 percent for children in single-mother families.

Child Care

I won't focus here on the timeworn debate about whether mothers of young children should work outside the home. Others in this series will discuss the rhetoric and sentiments associated with the changing norms of motherhood and their intensive demands. It is enough to say that mothers are in the workforce by economic necessity and seek an income so that they can improve their lives and the lives of their families. For the vast majority of families, the division of emotional and housekeeping labor and income-producing labor between men and women is no longer an option. One could also argue that child care outside the home may offer benefits not to be found in the home—also the topic of another discussion.

But let us consider the pressing needs of families today for quality, affordable, collective child care. Depending on the ages of their children, between 55 percent and 80 percent of mothers are employed. According to the Bureau of Labor Statistics, in 1999, the labor-force participation rate of mothers with school-age children, six to seventeen, was 79 percent; among mothers with children ages three to five, it was 72 percent; among those with children under three, the rate was 61 percent. In 2000, among mothers with infants, the labor-force participation rate was 55 percent, down slightly from 59 percent two years earlier.

These figures represent a sea change from the situation in 1966, when the BLS first began publishing data on mothers' labor-force participation by age of child. In 1966, only about one-fifth of married mothers with a child under age three, and only about 40 percent of widowed and divorced mothers with children under three, were in the labor force.

The role of wives in providing for the money income needs of their families has become exceedingly important. In dual-earner families, wives provide about 40 percent of family income, and in about 25 percent of those families, wives earn more than their husbands. Moreover, in recent years, while men's average earnings have failed to grow (not even keeping up with a modest rate of inflation), women's average earnings have grown, so that the increases in average family income are attributable to women's earnings.

Because mothers now provide for their children's need for emotional and physical care *and* their need for money income (including, often, access to employer-sponsored health insurance), families face serious issues about how to meet these two sets of needs. Because children are considered a private good and child-rearing a private activity, they get little assistance from either employers or the government.

Mothers balance the needs of their children for care and income by using child-care services—either informal (unpaid) or formal (paid). A report by the Urban Institute, based on the 1999 Survey of America's Families, provides information about the primary child-care arrangements for children under the age of thirteen while the adults "most responsible for their care" (most often their mothers) were employed.

Among preschoolers, age zero to four, there were three equally prevalent types of care, which together accounted for slightly more than 80 percent of all the primary-care arrangements of preschoolers: center-based care, care by a parent, and care by a relative. Care by a parent means care by the parent who is not at the place of employment during the time of child care; in two-parent families, it generally means that the parents split shifts. In addition, 14 percent of preschoolers were cared for in family child care, and 4 percent were cared for primarily by a nanny or babysitter.

Among five-year-olds, 40 percent were cared for at centers, 19 percent by a parent, 19 percent by a relative, 11 percent in family child care, 8 percent in before- and after-school programs, and 3 percent by a nanny or babysitter. Among school-age children, ages six to twelve, 41 percent were cared for by a parent, 23 percent by a relative, 15 percent in before- and after-school programs, 10 percent by the child him or herself, 7 percent in family child care, and 4 percent by a nanny or babysitter.

A recent book by Suzanne Helburn and Barbara Bergmann underscores the problems with our current child-care system (or lack thereof). Child care in a center is expensive, and many families cannot afford it; it costs between $5,000 and $10,000 per year per child, depending on the age of the child (infant care costs more) and the geographic location. In some areas, it is even more expensive than $10,000 per year. Median household income in the United States in 2000 was $42,178; the median income for families with four persons was $62,228. Using either measure, child-care costs for two children represent a significant fraction of income.

The second (related) problem with child care is its quality. The Cost, Quality, and Childhood Outcomes Study (CQO) looked at a hundred randomly selected centers in 1993. Although it found that the majority of classrooms provided minimally adequate care, only about 25 percent of preschool care and less than 10 percent of toddler care was rated as "good" or "developmentally appropriate." The highest quality centers were run by public agencies, private schools and colleges, and employers.

Determining the quality of care in family-child-care homes is difficult, because so many are unlicensed. Studies of family-child-care homes find that their quality is more variable than that in centers. In some cases, these homes provided care on a par with centers, but particularly in unlicensed homes, care was often found to be poor. Quality control, as currently practiced, has more to do with the child's physical safety than with the emotional or educational skills of the provider or the content of the program.

The search costs of finding good quality child care are high, particularly because parents are generally not well informed about what to look for when they interview potential providers. Parents report that their primary considerations when purchasing child care are location and convenience, the hours of service provided, their child's safety and well-being, and cost. Absent public subsidies, they may not be able to spend enough to assure the high quality of their children's child care.

Policies that Would Help

Helping children in poverty requires more than simply transferring resources to them, although that is certainly important. It requires helping their parents, and particularly their mothers, earn higher incomes. Much of the research on the effects of the recent Temporary Aid to Needy Families (aka "welfare reform") legislation indicates that women are not being trained for the higher paying jobs—that is, for jobs that traditionally have been filled by men only. Women who have been on welfare need training for those jobs if they are to keep their children out of poverty. At the same time, because most poor women will continue to do women's jobs, it is important to raise their wages. In recent years, there has been little progress on the matter of pay equity (paying women the same as men for jobs requiring the same education and experience). Mothers of children in poverty are in dire need of pay equity.

There needs to be national recognition of the service that parents are providing to the society as a whole—and some kind of reimbursement for their efforts. In other countries, most notably Japan, Spain, and Italy, people have reacted to the unwillingness of employers and the government to help parents combine work with child-rearing by not having children or by having only one. The birth rates in these countries are now below replacement. Although Americans have not (yet) taken that tack, government and employers should act now to enable us to meet the emotional, physical, and economic needs of future citizens and workers.

A change in the national mindset about the value of children would lead government, private businesses, and nonprofit organizations to develop policies to assist parents in meeting their child-rearing responsibilities. We might begin by providing partially paid leave to parents during the first year after the birth of their child. We are one of the few industrialized countries that do not provide such leave.

We could also stop discriminating against part-time workers, paying them less per hour than employees who do the same work full time, and often offering them no benefits. Working part time is one of the ways that mothers balance raising chil-dren and earning money. We should stop punishing them for working part time. Legislation prohibiting discrimination against part-time workers is long overdue. It would be easy to add a prohibition against discrimination in earnings and benefits for part-time workers to the Fair Labor Standards Act. This would be expensive for employers, and so it might result in less part-time work. On balance, however, the prohibition would be beneficial. The European Union has already begun to move in this direction.

Jerry Jacobs has suggested that we deal with the extraordinary demands for long work hours for highly educated professionals and managers in certain industries by amending the Fair Labor Standards Act so that currently exempted workers are covered. If that were done, employers who wanted their professional and managerial workers to put in more than forty hours a week would have to pay time and a half for overtime and double time for weekends. Jacobs suspects, as I do, that under those circumstances, employers would get the same work done by hiring more employees and helping current employees to work more efficiently. If such a penalty for long hours were enacted, children might well get to see more of their highly educated parents and, presumably, the public interest would be better served.

Lotte Bailyn has done research on firms that have changed their professional structures to allow parents (and others) to work on more reasonable schedules. She has found that such changes produce win-win situations. Not only do employees experience reduced stress, higher morale, and a greater ability to respond to their family's needs, but employers gain increased productivity.

Finally, we must mend our child-care system so that all children who need it get quality care. Helburn and Bergmann estimate (without even considering that child-care workers need higher wages), that the United States would have to spend an additional $26 billion a year on child care. We could afford it, if we didn't spend it elsewhere—or if we stopped reducing taxes. Having a good child-care system simply requires a collective will to spend tax revenues for that purpose.

How will these changes come about? Children are one of the few groups that have not yet created a social movement to improve their situation. Such a movement may one day emerge, but one problem with childhood as a basis for a social movement is that people grow out of it rather quickly. A second problem is that children don't vote. It needs to be adults who lead the way in a movement on children's behalf. There are of course several well-known child advocacy groups, but because they have not been successful in getting Americans to change the way in which we view children, they have not been successful in winning over policymakers. Most child advocates, coming from an equity perspective, argue that treating children well is the right thing to do. This argument has had little traction in our increasingly selfish world. I argue that treating children well is the right thing to do from a self-interest perspective. Collectively meeting the needs of children enhances the well-being of each of us. To get the change we need, children should be viewed as a public good.

Sources of Statistics Cited

Ed Source, "NAEP Results Consistently Show Achievement Gaps Nationally," 2003. **http://www.edsource.org/sch_naep03.cfm**

Luxembourg Income Study, "Poverty Rates for Children by Family Type," 2000. **http://www.lisproject.org/keyfigures/ childpovrates.htm**

National Education Association, "America's Top Education Priority: Lifting Up Low-Performing Schools," February 2001. **http://www.nea.org/ lac/bluebook/priority/html**

Freya L. Sonenstein, et al., "Primary Child Care Arrangements of Employed Parents: Findings from the 1999 National Survey of America's Families," Occasional Paper No. 59. Washington, D.C.: The Urban Institute, May 2002.

U.S. Bureau of Labor Statistics, "Report on the American Workforce," 1999.

U.S. Dept. of Labor, Bureau of Labor Statistics, "Current Population Survey," 2002. Washington, D.C., U.S. Government Printing Office, 2000. **http://ferret.bls.census.gov/macro/032002/pov/new01_001.htm**

U.S. Census Bureau, Census of Population, 2000. Washington, D.C.: U.S. Government Printing Office, 2000. **http://www.census. gov/population/www/cen2000/phc-t9.html**

U.S. Census Bureau, Income 2000 (Income of Households by State). **http://www.census.gov/hhes/income/income00/statemhi.html**

U.S. Census Bureau, Current Population Reports, pp. 60–226, "Income, Poverty, and Health Insurance Coverage in the United States, 2003," Washington, D.C.: U.S. Government Printing Office, 2004. **http:// www.census.gov/prod/2004pubs/p60-226**

U.S. Census Bureau, Median Family Income for Families with Four Persons, **http://www.census.gov/hhes/income/4person.html**

U.S. Census Bureau, "Labor Force Participation for Mothers with Infants Declines for First Time," Census Bureau Reports, Press Release, October 18, 2001. **http://www.census.gov/Press-Release/ www/2001/cb01-170. html**

U.S. Dept. of Labor, Bureau of Labor Statistics, "Working in the Twenty-First Century," 1999. **http://www.bls.gov/0pub/working/home.htm**

MYRA H. STROBER is a labor economist and professor of education and business at Stanford University.

Families and Family Study in International Perspective

Many changes are occurring in the world's families. Some observers feel that the changes are destructive, whereas others see them as leading to new opportunities and understanding. Issues in international family studies include regional limitations and the various aspects of doing research cross-culturally. Knowledge regarding certain categories of families, inheritance, and the social psychology of families is incomplete. There are, however, some universals and universal or worldwide changes, including movement toward individual partner choice, more divorces, lower fertility, and greater opportunities for women.

BERT N. ADAMS
University of Wisconsin—Madison

To introduce this special issue on families from an international perspective, this article has two foci. The first is the condition of and approach to scholarly work and research on families. The second is what we do and do not know about the world's families, and how they are changing.

The world in which families exist today is one of economic globalization. It is a world of religious, racial, and economic violence. It is the world of the Internet and CNN, of mass communications, and, as Kerry Daly and Anna Dienhart (1998) reminded us, of accelerating time demands (p. 113). It is a world of migration, rural to urban and nation to nation, both voluntary and involuntary. It is a world in which millions of people living in villages and countrysides are affected by urban and industrial technology. The results of these factors were described by Michael Wallace (1998) in negative terms:

> The restructuring of the global economy has unleashed a tremendous torrent of technological and organizational changes that are leaving in their wake broken careers, disheveled families, and shattered dreams. The affluent society is being divided into winners and losers, haves and havenots, the jobbed and the dejobbed. (p. 36)

Some feel, with Wallace, that today's changes are destructive, but others do not agree. This is, after all, a world in which many people have new freedoms and opportunities. It is a world in which cross-cultural contact may result in understanding instead of conflict. And, from an academic perspective, new knowledge and insights on the part of scholars make this an exciting time to be a student of the world's families.

Although progress has been made toward understanding families in various cultures, there is much to be done. Many studies have been carried out by reputable scholars in their own societies, but only a small fraction of international family studies are truly comparative. Comparative examples are Kamerman and Kahn's (1997) book on family policies in Great Britain, Canada, New Zealand, and the United States, and Lynda Walters and colleagues' (2002) look at hidden differences in families cross-culturally. It is my intention to report on both the international study of families and families themselves. I begin with some issues in cross-cultural family studies and scholarship, then turn to some of the things that we do not know about families themselves in our changing world, and, finally, to what we do know.

Issues in Cross-Cultural Family Studies

The Committee on Family Research of the International Sociological Association (ISA) includes scholars from many of the world's societies. They have presented papers at ISA meetings and at various regional conferences, and their papers are often published in journals such as the *Journal of Comparative Family Studies (JCFS)*. In fact, journals such as the *JCFS* consist of research and discussion of families in societies around the world, yet scholarly publications on families do not equally represent the various parts of the world. Although it is hardly surprising that scholarship is dominated by knowledge of Western industrial societies, it would be well to explain the regional limitations on information about the world's families.

Regional Limitations

An obvious problem with international family research and writing is that it represents some societies more than others. Numerous productive family scholars can be found in most Western societies, and in countries such as India, Japan, and Taiwan. In addition, there is a scattering of professionals throughout the Middle East, Sub-Saharan Africa, Russia, China, and Latin America. Yet many nations, including those of North Africa and Southeast Asia, are infrequently found in recent sociological literature on families. Reasons for such omissions include communication, money, and values.

First, regarding communication, it is quite possible that family sociologists are active in Libya, Chad, Bolivia, Cambodia, and so on, but are not in touch with outside scholars. They may even publish in their own national and regional journals. For example, I have published in the *Bangladesh Journal of Sociology*, but would never have known of its existence had I not been speaking on U.S. families in Bangladesh. Now, e-mail and the Internet afford access to and information about such countries, including the professionals located there. These means of communication may eventually give rise to international contacts that go beyond those that exist today, and may bring additional countries into the circle of international scholarship.

But there is a second cause of regional limitations: money. It costs money to design research, collect data, analyze research, and get it published. Although old, value-laden anthropological reports exist, today's scholarship may be lacking because professionals are incapable of doing large-sample or survey research simply because it is too costly. Granted, collecting data in many countries, especially those of the developing world, is usually much less expensive than in the West, but it still requires money that may not be available to local scholars. Western sources of funding make cross-cultural collaboration a possibility, even when it is locally limited by fiscal constraints (I say more about such collaboration below).

A further factor may restrict research on families in certain societies: national values. A subtle but important cause of research limitation can be that strong conservative values do not allow for open, quasi-value-free analysis of families and family problems. Here we are thinking of some Muslim societies, Roman Catholic-dominated societies, communist societies, and others. It is quite possible that the "party line" restricts the freedom to collect data that would make it possible to write about "what is" instead of "what is supposed to be" in families.

Doing Research Cross-Culturally

Let us assume that one way to resolve at least a portion of the regional imbalance in knowledge of families and family change is collaboration between scholars (with funding) in economically developed societies and scholars in another part of the world. In 1974, I wrote about "Doing Survey Research Cross-Culturally" (Adams, 1974, 1999). Recently, I made another presentation on collaborative research in which I listed the following issues (notice that most of these pertain to any research in a host country, not just collaborative research).

Perhaps the most important issue is the need for a *host co-principal investigator* (P.I.), even if the expatriate scholar provides the funding. This avoids the classic form of "academic imperialism"—that is, the Western scholar collecting data and taking them "home." In addition, a local collaborator may be able to get research clearance in a timely fashion, whereas an outsider may not receive clearance for years, if at all. The local colleague is aware of local conditions, capable of finding interviewers, and able to set a pay scale commensurate with other wages in the host country. Of course, collaborative research is only completed as fast as its slowest link.

Clearance. If the country has a national or regional research council, clearance will be needed. This may require adding some questions that the council would like covered by the research. It also may mean leaving copies of the data with the council when leaving the country, and it will certainly require a report to the council when the research is completed.

Sensitivity to local conditions is crucial. This is one area where a co-P.I. and local officials can be helpful. In many societies, an area may have to be avoided because of border wars, ethnic instability, or a natural disaster. Without such awareness, research may never be approved or may be terminated in midstream.

Interviewers may be found among teachers looking for work while on vacation, or recent (but unemployed) university graduates. If multiple languages are involved, different interviewers may need to be hired for different parts of the country. Though the literature is inconsistent on this issue, the gender of the interviewers may be determined by the local P.I. Interviewer training and practice will help to resolve interviewer attitude problems that could affect the results. The interviewer must be made comfortable, especially if the questions include sexuality and perhaps cohabitation, so as to avoid influencing the results.

Sampling. It is a good idea to contact district officials before beginning. They will know whether certain areas have been over-studied, or whether the respondents will expect payment. Urban officials can also be helpful in identifying parts of a city where certain ethnic groups are located. Rural research may require a design such as sampling in various directions from a small trade center.

Translating into a local language (Kiswahili, Gujarati, or whatever) is usually necessary. One way to do this is to have a language expert translate the instrument into the local language, and another translate it back into the language of the outsider (e.g., Japanese, German, English). Discussion will help to resolve inconsistencies and language problems. For example, "spoiling the child" is an unusable phrase in most societies. In Kenya, we discovered that family "power" did not translate correctly into Kiswahili. A pretest will help to catch any further issues that arise.

The last issue in collaborative research is its *value to the country*. Even with a co-P.I. in the host society, the question remains: What good will the research do them? At the very least, as noted above, the data can be left with district officials, where they were collected. Ethnically sensitive data may require secrecy, however, because they might be used against a people. This is an ethical issue that requires thoughtful decision making by a research team.

The issues of regional limitations and collaboration are not all that restrict cross-cultural knowledge of families. In the next section, I turn from such scholarly issues to families themselves, beginning with some of the things that are *not* known or clearly understood about the world's families.

Incomplete Knowledge: What Is Not Known About Families

It has been my good fortune to edit, with Jan Trost of Uppsala, Sweden, the *Handbook of World Families*, which is being published by Sage at the end of 2004. The handbook contains chapters on 25 nations, written by 34 authors from around the world. Each chapter has background material on the society under consideration, and covers a series of subtopics on families. But the process of editing this volume has made very plain the gaps in our knowledge, not just regionally, but categorically and topically as well.

Categories

Even in less developed societies, information is likely to be most complete on urban middleclass families. This means that the following groups of people are often omitted by research designs: refugees, the oppressed, nomads, rural residents, poor urbanites, and the very rich. Let us look briefly at each of these categories.

Those families (and individuals) most likely to "fall through the cracks" of family research are refugees, either from country to country or within countries. It is simply difficult to find and sample them. Such peoples are located in southern Sudan, or may have been driven out of Rwanda, or Tibet, or Croatia. Second, oppressed nonrefugees may also be unstudied because the government keeps them isolated and inaccessible—an example being the peoples of East Timor in Indonesia. A third national category likely to be under-researched consists of nomads. These include the gypsies, or Roma people, of Europe, and the Khoi-san of the Kalahari.

Although more likely to be studied than refugees and oppressed groups, ruralites and urban poor may also be undersampled because they are harder to locate than the urban middle

class. There are, of course, degrees of rurality. For example, the peoples of the Amazon River basin are extremely difficult to get to, whereas those in the rural areas and slums of developed countries are more accessible, but still less likely to be studied.

The other category whose families are extremely difficult to study is the upper class. They are not only socially exclusive, but they have the means, financial and otherwise, to separate themselves from other classes and from those who would study them. As Blumberg and Paul (1975) said, "…the upper class has maintained itself remarkably intact, and, having done so, it is perhaps the most untouched group in American life" (p. 75). This is equally true of the upper classes of other societies.

Inheritance and Property

A few topics demonstrate the gaps in international family knowledge—first, inheritance and property. The lineal systems, patrilineal and matrilineal, have received much attention. In the 19th century, as they arrived in Africa, India, and the South Pacific, anthropologists were intrigued by the lineal passage of property down the male—or in some cases, the female—line. The norms of the patrilineage were such that only men could inherit. Even this norm has had several versions: primogeniture, ultimogeniture, undivided interest to all sons, divided interest to all sons, and, in Korea, half the property to the oldest son, and the rest divided equally among the other sons (Lee, 2004, chap. 6). In unusual circumstances, such as having no male heir, an adoption was possible, the property could be passed to a woman (or women), or there could be a community distribution.

A major change has occurred with the individualization of occupations and incomes. This has meant that property is not owned in common by kin, thus allowing for the breakup of the lineage into nuclear (or conjugal) or individual units. This is central to the dramatic worldwide changes that W. J. Goode discussed in his book *World Revolution and Family Patterns* (1963). Majid al-Haj (1995) noted that, among the Arabs in Israel, "kin economics change away from kin ownership and inheritance to a pooling of resources for individual mobility. That is, the change is from lineal property concerns to individual careers and success" (p. 326; Adams, 1999, p. 80).

Alteration in lineal inheritance and property control, however, has not been in the direction of a single new pattern. In Western societies, the passing on of property is ordinarily at the discretion of the current owner. In those societies that have recently gone through the weakening of the lineage, kin still perform economic functions, though these may not include a normative approach to inheritance. For example, Xuewen Sheng (2004) noted that in contemporary China, there are still economic exchanges and transfers, "mainly between direct relatives (parents and children), including upward and downward flow of money and materials" (p. 23). Inheritance is, of course, complicated by divorce and remarriage, issues that are discussed below. In other words, there is much left to learn about property and inheritance in both the developed and developing worlds of the 21st century.

Violence

A third family issue about which knowledge is far from complete is violence. Even in Western societies, information on elder abuse is just beginning to emerge from the shadows, and data on all forms of family violence began to appear around 1970. Today, spouse and child abuse are receiving considerable attention in the industrialized world.

There are, however, two antithetical reasons that violence has been ignored until recently in much of the world. On one hand, in normatively patriarchal societies, the beating of women and children has been taken for granted, with both men and women accepting it as normal (even normative) and undeserving of attention. On the other hand, in societies such as China and Cuba, with a communist and equalitarian ideology, the assumption has been that family violence does not occur. Roschelle, Toro-Morn, and Facio (2004) describe the situation in Cuba quite clearly:

> ...during the first twenty years of the revolutionary government there was a denial that domestic violence even existed. Cuban officials vehemently denied that Cuban women were victims of domestic violence and there were no shelters for battered women. ...Domestic violence and rape were portrayed as problems associated with capitalism. (p. 27)

In other words, in much of the world, family violence has been ignored either because it was acceptable or because it was not believed to exist. Denial is consistent with the party line mentioned earlier.

This does not mean that nothing is known about family violence in non-Western cultures. Not only does family violence exist, but it also has an ancient history in many societies. Singh (2004) put it thus: "In the Indian context women are of special concern, as they have been victims of humiliation and torture for as long as we have written records of Indian society" (p. 40). Chen and Yi (2004) added simply that "family violence has always been around in Taiwan" (p. 21).

Why does family violence occur? Ziehl (2004) noted that it may be a result of an individual pathology, sociostructural stressors, or patriarchy. Violence against women may have its roots in patriarchy, or else in men's response to women's rising status, but the specific triggering factors are multiple. In patriarchal societies, including those in which the wife moves into her husband's household, violence may result from her not living up to her wifely roles (in her husband's eyes). Singh (2004) noted that in India the range of causes varies "from not cooking on time to mismanagement of the household to neglect of children. In short, non-adherence to gender roles and responsibilities leads to violence" (p. 42). Even though alcohol may fuel the man's violence, he seldom feels guilty, and is usually able to point to some behavior on the woman's part as having caused it—perhaps even her expressing an opinion on some issue. In addition, Modo (2004) commented that Nigerian women may be beaten for reasons having nothing to do with them—perhaps a transference after a quarrel by the husband at work.

The same patriarchal conditions for wife-beating give rise to child abuse. Wife and child both may be considered servants or property. Much child abuse today is related to school behavior and success on the part of the offspring. In Turkey, for example, "disobedience, bad habits, disrespect, lying, cheating, and protest are ...causes for violence" (Nauck & Klaus, 2004, p. 27). Toth and Somlai (2004) added that in Hungary,

> physical abuse of children is related on the one hand to the parents' high expectations regarding school, i.e., a performance-oriented attitude. In other words, the parents, sensing the importance of scholastic qualifications and learning, try to squeeze the best performance out of children by abusing them physically. (p. 17)

Of course, in traditional societies, child abuse may also be caused by disrespect on the children's part, instead of laziness and school failure. An important issue is differentiating abuse from discipline. Most parents would justify their behavior by arguing that their treatment of children is the latter.

Although we may understand the causes of family violence, its prevalence is much more difficult to ascertain. There are data from the United States, Europe, China, Kenya, and elsewhere, but it is generally agreed that estimates are inaccurate at best. The reasons for inaccuracies include definitions, sampling problems, and willingness to report. Again, much is to be done in this area of family research.

Social Psychology

Briefly, another family topic about which international knowledge is uneven is the social psychology of family relations. Marital satisfaction is an important topic in Western family research, but this and other internal family issues are less frequently studied in many parts of the world. An important reason is that cross-cultural research is often based on census data or other types of structured surveys. Another reason is that the intimate workings of families, including sexuality and communication, are often very sensitive issues, and thus are difficult to get respondents to talk about.

What Is Known About the World's Families

In this section, I discuss universals and universal changes, and a few topics about which much is known regarding the world's families.

Universals

Despite a changing world with hidden variations within societies, Lynda Walters and her coauthors (2002) reminded us that

> in many respects the experience of living in a family is the same in all cultures. For example, relationships between spouses and between parents and children are negotiated; most relationships within families are still

hierarchical; the work of the home is still primarily the responsibility of the wife. (p. 448)

Financial support is provided by both spouses, but the wife's is usually seen as supplementary, conflict is damaging to children, and "individuals and families change, or develop, in predictable ways" (p. 448). But whereas all families operate within the above parameters, there are cultural differences, subcultural differences, and differences (often hidden, as Walters, Warzywoda-Kruszynska, and Gurko note) in the functioning of individual families.

Universal Cross-Cultural Changes

An important cross-cultural change described throughout the *Handbook* (Adams & Trost, 2004) and in many other places is the increase in women's education and employment outside the home. This change, however, has not resulted in gender equality. The support mechanisms, such as day care, have not been sufficiently forthcoming, equal opportunities and equal pay are not a reality, and men may not see the necessity of taking on a domestic role equal to that of women (see Mirsky & Radlett, 2000).

Besides the incomplete revolution in gendered family roles, there are other changes occurring not just in the industrialized nations, but in Africa, the Middle East, and elsewhere. Miller and Browning (2000) note that family patterns include "decreases in household size and fertility rates overall and increases in divorce and nontraditional living arrangements" (p. 302). (Incidentally, it is most interesting that one might begin with increased women's employment, increased divorce, or decreased fertility as the independent variable, and explain the other two.)

Thus far, I have introduced the cross-cultural family picture with very broad strokes. My intention now is to divide international family experiences into a few topics about which much has been written. These include (a) marriage or pairing/divorce/remarriage, (b) fertility and socialization, and (c) gender.

Marriage or Pairing/Divorce/Remarriage

The first issue in pairing concerns multiple wives, or polygyny. Patrilineal systems, such as in many Muslim and Sub-Saharan African societies, are fairly highly correlated historically with polygyny (Mburugu & Adams, 2004; Modo, 2004; Ziehl, 2004). Polygyny is a diminishing phenomenon worldwide, however. (Note that in societies in which polygyny is normative, monogamy has always predominated numerically or behaviorally.)

Another historical factor in pairing is arranged marriage, sometimes involving child betrothal (see Modo, 2004). Chen and Yi (2004) described the Taiwanese pairing process as being "characterized by the overwhelming power of parents....Marriage was a process of agreements and rituals rather than an interpersonal event, and a family-based decision rather than a personal choice" (p. 4). Singh (2004), speaking of India, stated that "even now young boys or girls seldom exercise their rights in matters of mate selection, especially in the vast rural community" (p. 19).

As with the decrease in polygyny, however, arranged marriage is slowly giving way to personal choice in urban India. Societies characterized historically by arranged marriages are likely to experience some intergenerational conflict in this area as the younger generation asserts its independence.

Marriage itself is not as universal as it was just a few decades ago. Since the 1960s, nonmarital cohabitation has replaced marriage more rapidly in Sweden than in any other country in the Western world (Trost & Levin, 2004). David de Vaus (2004), writing about Australia, said that "since the mid-1980s there has been a steady decline in the proportion of people aged 20–49 who are partnered at any given point in time" (p. 3). To this, Toth and Somlai (2004) added that in Hungary, the number of marriages per year has fallen from over 100,000 in 1948–1949 to 43,000 per year at present. In fact, Western industrial societies generally have fewer people marrying and more cohabiting today than in the recent past.

Cohabitation, said Theresa Martin (2002), has gained social visibility only in this generation in the developed world. It is far from a new basis for pairing or intimate life, however. Calling them consensual unions, Martin noted that, with the exception of the southern countries of South America (Argentina, Brazil, Chile, Uruguay), such unions have been a large minority of pairs in Latin America. "Despite their higher instability and the fact that many of them are eventually formalized, a large proportion of consensual unions are long-lived and therefore cannot be portrayed as a transient stage of the marital life cycle" (p. 49). Cohabitation is particularly widespread among the poor, for whom legalized marriage provides little obvious economic or other benefit. It is also an increasingly prevalent response to a divorce or separation.

Besides cohabitation, the other alternative to traditional marriage is living apart together. Marriage has had as one of its givens coresidence, but there is a small and increasing minority of marriages in which the couple live apart. This situation is not a separation or a predivorce. The most common term for this is "living apart together" (Levin & Trost, 1999; Trost & Levin, 2004). Schvanefeldt, Young, and Schvanefeldt (2001) called such relationships in Thailand "dual resident marriages," and described them as a married couple that "resides in two different residences, often many miles away from each other" (pp. 347–360). This, they say, is synonymous with commuter marriages in the United States, and is what Trost and Levin (and others) call living apart together. Such arrangements are efforts to keep marriage alive, while not letting it stand in the way of individual goals.

So pairing today is increasingly monogamous, even in normatively polygynous societies, but is also less likely to be a matter of legalized and coresidential monogamy than it was a few decades ago. Cohabitation, and in some cases same-sex partnering, is spreading in Western societies, and the former is a long-term characteristic of the poor in Latin American (and other) societies.

A universal change is the rise in the divorce rate in the world's nations. The most dramatic rise in the divorce rate may very well be that in Argentina, where there was an 800% increase between 1960 and 2000 (Jelin, 2004). In Australia, the increase has been 300% since 1970 (de Vaus, 2004). In China, the increase was 500% since 1978 (Sheng, 2004), and in South Korea, 600% in 30 years (Lee, 2004). Taiwan's divorce rate has not climbed as rapidly, although divorce can be traced to the early 20th century (Chen & Yi, 2004).

Dumon (2004) found it interesting that Belgium—the country in Europe that he said has the highest divorce rate—also has the most out-of-date legal procedures, having not yet adopted faultless or no-fault divorce. Forsberg (2004) claimed, however, that it is Finland and Sweden that have the highest divorce rates in the European Union.

What has caused the international increase in divorce rates? Singh (2004) noted that a portion of it (at least in India) is the change away from seeing marriage as a sacred pairing. "Marriage," he said, "is no longer held to be a 'divine match' or a 'sacred union' in the urban milieu" (p. 44). In addition, the change in families economically from producing and consuming units to simply consumers has left them with little reason to tolerate a bad marriage. In speaking of Peru, Vincent (2000) stated that the "family working in common" is disappearing, leaving couples with what she calls "more brittle bonds" (p. 168). But most of the macro-explanations focus on the societal changes noted at the outset of this article. For example, Toth and Somlai (2004) noted that the high rate of divorces in Hungary is "related to the economic, …in recent decades. Women's entry into employment on a mass scale, social and geographical mobility, and the changes in the legal background of divorce have all had an influence in this direction" (p. 19). Sheng (2004) stated the same issues in China thus: As a result of this amendment to marriage law and other social changes caused

> by the introduction of a market economy (e.g., the growing awareness of independence among women, increasing social interaction, the acceleration of employment mobility, the introducing of Western values toward marriage and divorce, etc.), China's divorce rates have increased dramatically in recent decades. (p. 21)

Beginning with the same societal factors, Jelin (2004) introduced us to the proximate or interpersonal reasons for divorces today. She called them the "socio-cultural processes linked to individuation":

> The spread of modern values of personal autonomy, free choice of a partner based on romantic love, the growing social expectation of being able to act on one's wishes and feelings—all these have their counterpart in the freedom to sever ties when there is no more love, when the costs of maintaining a conflictful relationship exceed those of severing the conjugal bond. (p. 33)

Modo (2004) stated these interpersonal reasons for urban Nigerian divorces as adultery, desertion, arson, stubbornness, lack of love, and constant beatings and batterings. The main reason for divorce in Turkey is given as "incompatibility," though this may subsume other specifics, such as infertility (Nauck & Klaus, 2004). In Taiwan, the wife may seek a divorce on the basis of the husband's extramarital affair(s) (Chen & Yi, 2004). Al-Naser (2004) added that in Kuwait, there are multiple causes for a wife divorcing her husband: refusal of the husband to maintain her, abuse, impotence, his imprisonment, disease, and his desertion.

Structural or demographic factors in divorce, according to Mozny and Katrnak (2004), include early marriage and low education, and, according to Forsberg (2004), having no children. It is also true that more divorces occur in cities than in rural areas, and according to Modo (2004), the reason is lack of urban kin care and surveillance.

Although remarriage occurs after some divorces, there are increasing numbers of divorcees who choose to cohabit instead of risking another legalized intimate relationship (see Dumon, 2004). Yet the rate of remarriage after divorce is high, indicating that those who have tired of a particular spouse are not rejecting the institution of marriage. In fact, one way to view it is that worldwide, the rates of divorce, remarriage, and cohabitation have all increased in the current generation.

Remarriages are more likely to end in divorce than are first marriages. The difference is not as great as one might expect, however, given that remarrieds are, by definition, those who have already shown their willingness to use divorce as a solution to a bad marriage. The reason that the divorce rate among the remarried is not much higher is, in all likelihood, because the remarried work very hard at succeeding the second time.

One irony about remarriage following divorce is that women with children are more likely to need and prefer to remarry, whereas those without children are more likely to be able to find a new partner because they are not carrying with them the "baggage" of children. Remarriages involving children give rise to stepfamilies. These are complex units that require relational negotiations, including with any previous spouse who still exists. Harvey (2004) put it thus: "Besides the confusion over roles and responsibilities, stepfamilies also have to work out residence, visitations to the non-custodial parent and his or her kin, and money" (p. 20).

Fertility and Socialization

Earlier in this article, I noted that reduced fertility is a world-wide change. Although this is true cross-culturally, the decline in fertility began in the developed world earlier, and has progressed further there. In many European nations, the rate of fertility is below replacement level, meaning that fewer than two children are being born per two adults. This is not just true of Western nations, however; South Korea, for example, has gone from an average family size of 5.29 in 1955 to 3.51 today (Lee, 2004). And Cuba has the lowest fertility rate of all Latin American countries: 1.6 in the late 1990s (Roschelle et al., 2004).

The fertility reduction in many other countries, although dramatic, has not taken them below replacement. For example, in the 1970s, Kenya had the highest fertility level in the world: 8 children per woman. By 1998, it had declined to 4.8 per woman (Mburugu & Adams, 2004). In South Africa, women were averaging 6 children in the 1960s, and less than 3 in the 1990s (Ziehl, 2004). The decline in urban India, from 7 to 3 children per woman, does not hold for the masses of rural India (Singh, 2004), however. Bangladesh has seen a drop from a total fertility rate of 7 in the 1970s to 4.5 in 1990 (Nosaka, 2000).

The most frequently discussed causes of reduced fertility worldwide are the increase in women's education and their employment outside the home. Other reasons explain the declines in Bangladesh and China, however. Bangladesh, Nosaka (2000) said,

> is characterized by factors conventionally considered to be unfavorable to declining fertility, such as dominance of a rural environment, low levels of socioeconomic development, and the subjugated status of women. The country's fertility decline is largely the result of the availability of effective, modern contraceptives [even in rural areas]. (p. 485)

This is most interesting, because many family planning programs have not been nearly as effective as that in Bangladesh. China is, of course, a well-known example of fertility decline from the 1980s through the first half of the 1990s. This, according to Zeng Yi (2002), is the result of direct government intervention in the form of the one-child policy (Yi; see also Sheng, 2004).

The second issue regarding fertility is preference, both for the number of children and gender. Chen and Yi (2004) reported that in Taiwan, "the mean preferred number of children for married women was 4 in 1965, while twenty years later this figure had decreased to an average of 2.4. Along with this downward shift...there was a decrease in the preference for sons" (p. 10), though many young newlyweds want only one child, a male, for economic and lifestyle reasons (Chen & Yi). The reduction in number preferred is not surprising, and is consistent with actual fertility. Preference is often lower than fertility, however, an indication—as Azadarmaki (2004) pointed out for Iran—that "many families have more than they would have wished for" (p. 20).

The traditional preference for sons was because they inherited the family property, were responsible for caring for their parents in old age, and were to give them a proper burial (see Modo, 2004). This preference is still found in China, Kenya (Mburugu & Adams, 2004), and elsewhere. In cities worldwide, the economic value of children is not what it was in the rural areas, so the economic basis for male preference is less clear. As Hird and Abshoff (2000) stated, "Given that children are less an economic necessity, and more an economic burden taken on to fulfill adults' desires, the reasons for having children have significantly changed" (p. 361). Koh and Tan (2000), commenting on the Chinese middle class in Singapore, said that children provide companionship and are valued for their emotional ties (p. 527).

The value of children brings us to socialization, or childrearing. The cross-cultural literature makes it obvious that, although the role of parents is central, many people, institutions, and issues are involved in childrearing. Thus, the first question is: Who does it? Chen and Yi (2004) described Taiwanese childrearing thus:

...centers of individual activities have been shifted from familial settings to other social institutions including schools, dormitories, factories, governmental agencies, and mass media. As a result, while the family is still seen as the primary agent of childhood socialization, other family functions such as being provider of information and training for children have declined and been replaced. (p. 12)

Hannele Forsberg (2004), describing the upbringing of children in Finland, stated this point somewhat differently:

> In Finnish society, the upbringing and socialization of children occurs not only in family and close relationships, but also in relation with various other institutions, such as the day-care center, the school, the health care system, the media, the parents' jobs, etc. ...In the moral sense, however, the primary responsibility for upbringing is considered to rest with the child's own parents and family. (p. 9)

One of the key factors in childrearing today is the employment of women outside the home. In some societies, the responsibility for caring for the young falls to other relatives, especially grandparents. In many other societies, small children are cared for in formal day-care facilities. Dumon (2004) explained the situation in Belgium, breaking it down by age: Babies under 3 months old are cared for by the parents (read "mother"). From 3 to 6 months, about one third of Belgian children are in "creches." And when "children reach the age of 6 months, more than half of them are taken into care on a regular basis. The formal care outweighs the informal care" (p. 10).

So care for preschoolers falls to parents (mostly mothers), other kin, and day-care centers, with the major independent variables being rural or urban residence, single parenthood, and the mother's employment.

How are children raised, and what do parents want out of them? In the Middle East, boys are raised to be responsible for kin and property as adults. Azadarmaki (2004) made clear, however, that in Iran, emotional attachments between parents and children are strong throughout life. By emotional relationships, according to Azadarmaki, "we mean sustained and continuous interactions and feelings, which continue between parents and children until their death" (p. 21). The expression of emotions, however, is acceptable for girls, not boys.

Children's obedience and respect have been expected by parents in the Middle East, Africa, Southeast Asia, Latin America, and elsewhere in the world. That this is lessening was stated clearly in the Kenya chapter of the *Handbook* (Mburugu & Adams, 2004):

> ...children *do not respect* or listen to their parents as they once did. This concern again, is not unique to Kenya. A general feeling on the part of parents is that lack of control over children is coupled with a lack of respect from the children. Several respondents noted that, when they were young, they entered a room on their knees when a parent or

grandparent was present. Of course, any of the factors that make children more independent and self reliant—such as education—are also related to a lessening of expressed respect. (p. 19)

Parental permissiveness and child independence are correlated with more education and less respect on the part of children. As Toth and Somlai (2004) stated,

Relations between parents and children in Hungary follow the international trends that can be observed over a longer period of several decades. Among these, special mention must be made of the weakening of the authoritarian approach to child-raising and the strengthening of *a permissive attitude to child-raising in families*. (italics in original, p. 9)

There has been a decline in the value put on good behavior and obedience, with more emphasis on tolerance and a sense of responsibility.

Trost and Levin (2004) referred to the same modern changes as leaning toward liberal and democratic childrearing. Using different terminology, Richter and Kytir (2004) spoke of tolerance and cooperation between children and their parents in Austria: "Parents feel that it is important to make their children responsible, independent, and tolerant persons having good manners. However, only one quarter believe that children's obedience is crucial to child rearing" (p. 7). Again, de Vaus (2004) stated that in Australia,

Independence for both boys and girls is highly valued. Virtually everyone agrees that children should be encouraged to express their opinions, question things, and be curious, and two-thirds agree that a thirteen-year-old should be learning to be independent of his/her parents. (p. 8)

The significance of the emphasis on independence is that the investment in children is in *their* future, not just in the parents' old age. Education, a worldwide phenomenon, when coupled with the reduction in fertility and control of childhood diseases, makes each child a treasure to be nurtured and developed. The link between education and fertility is, of course, not generalizable to the millions of downtrodden and poor of the world.

An extreme outcome of the focus on children's welfare is found in the effect of China's one-child policy on family life. A result is that such Chinese children do not have siblings or cousins, but only parents and grandparents. Sheng (2004) claimed that this has created "a generation of 'little emperors,' children who have not had to share...the attention of their parents and grand-parents" (p. 9).

Despite the emphasis on equal education and equal opportunity for boys and girls in some (particularly Western) societies, as stated earlier, boys and girls are not treated equally in many societies. An extreme example is India, where Singh (2004) described differences in socialization by gender as follows:

As the preference for sons in Indian society is quite strong, girls are often reported as neglected within the family. ...A girl may be so neglected from her childhood that she comes to expect very little from her life. By the time she becomes an adult, she tends to lose all self-worth or respect for herself. (p. 32)

Not only is there a difference in the treatment of boys and girls in many societies, but fathers also may play a minor role as compared with mothers. This is true of intact families, but even more so in cases of single mothering. Roschelle et al. (2004) noted that the difficulties associated with single motherhood are exacerbated by "the fact that many Cuban fathers do not help raise their children, provide child support, or even see their children" (p. 21).

So what have I found out about socialization worldwide? Families, especially mothers, are central to childrearing. Kin, day care, schools, and even the media all play important roles in the lives of children, however. Parents increasingly expect independence from their children, and although the parents might wish for obedience and respect, they recognize that the children's success may leave little room for the filial piety of the past. Finally, in the majority of societies, boys are still valued more than girls, though this is changing with the weakening of lineal inheritance systems.

Gender

It has been impossible to speak of pairing, fertility, or socialization without noting gender differences. In fact, the issue of gender permeates the family literature to the point that it might have been tempting to omit it from the list of topics and simply allow it to arise throughout the discussion. Certain gender-based issues deserve separate attention, however, and will receive it now.

In the beginning comments on what is known, I noted that a set of international universals revolve around gender. The increase in women's education and occupational opportunities, although occurring more rapidly in the more developed parts of the world, can be found virtually everywhere. And whereas women's status in the public sphere may be rising, the result has not been gender equality. For one thing, as women's labor force participation has increased, "positions associated with such experience have not appeared to open up" (Dubeck, 1998, p. 3), nor have the support mechanisms—child care and male support—expanded along with women's opportunities.

Even in societies known for their public policy of equality, such as Sweden and Israel, gender differences continue to exist. Katz and Lavee (2004) stated that, in Israel, the

progress in gender equality is not reflected in the type of occupations, organizational status, or incomes of men and women. Despite some changes in the past two decades, the labor market is still segregated, with women most frequently employed in education, health and welfare services, while occupying only one-fifth of managerial positions. Additionally, many women work part time. (p. 13)

Although the pull factors are important for women, Kathleen Gerson (1998) noted that in the United States and other postindustrial societies, there are also push factors leading to women's employment. "In addition to the pull of job opportunities, factors such as divorce, declining male wages, and the general devaluation of homemaking…have pushed most women to build their lives around paid work" (regardless of spouses and children; p. 12).

Women's opportunities differ from society to society, being greater in the economically developed (or postindustrial) and urban parts of the world. In addition, urban men are more likely to take on domestic responsibilities. For example, Lu, Maume, and Bellas (2000) stated that

> Urban Chinese husbands spend significantly more time on household labor than rural Chinese husbands. Urban husbands who contribute more household labor absolutely and/or relatively are those with employed wives, those with higher education levels, and those whose earnings are closer to their wives'. (p. 210)

Even when men take on more domestic labor, however, the home is still considered the wife's domain (see Roschelle et al., 2004). In fact, this is as universal a fact as increased women's extra-familial opportunities. Amaro (2004) described the wife's domestic domain well:

> Women's traditional tasks, usually related to domestic work, have not disappeared. Women continue to be responsible for the house, the husband, and the children. …It is the same when the man helps with domestic tasks. The traditional pattern still prevails, as the man is usually seen as helping the woman and not as carrying out a male role. (p. 12)

This neotraditional division of labor is best expressed by the male phrase, "I help out around the house." And although the amount of housework done by men has increased along with women's employment, two other changes have also occurred. First, in cities, there is more paid household help, and second, less housework is done.

The increase in men's household labor deserves one more comment. It appears that an egalitarian ideology has taken root in the younger generation, so in countries such as Austria, "young men are more willing to do household chores than older men" (Richter & Kytir, 2004, p. 8). The age factor would, of course, account for many of the changes being discussed in this article.

One further gender-based issue deserves mention. Katz and Lavee (2004) mentioned the small percentage of managerial positions held by women in Israel. Political positions have been male-dominated cross-nationally until recently. This is changing slowly and, in some instances, tokenistically. Uganda, for example, has sought to have a representative

number of women in government at all levels. In the 1980s, Norway's prime minister

> decided that at least 40 percent of her Government had to be women.…However, reality did not follow ideology.…Men are still most common among decision makers in politics as well as in industries and other companies. (Trost & Levin, 2004, pp. 11–12)

Mirsky and Radlett (2000) examined social change and the world's families from the perspective of women. Their title, *No Paradise Yet*, is unmistakable, making it clear that women are still struggling to change the unequal bases for marriage and divorce; that they are seeking the necessary legislation to prevent abuse of all kinds; that they still lack access to land and financial security; that they are trying to end discrimination and harassment in the workplace and in educational settings; and that they are attempting to raise men's awareness of these issues. Thus, worldwide changes in family roles are occurring, but the world's nations are still far from gender equality.

Summary and Conclusions

In this article, I reviewed the unevenness of family scholarship worldwide. I noted why certain societies or societal subgroups are missing from or infrequently represented in sociological family research. In addition, certain family topics are inadequately treated cross-culturally, either because rapid change is occurring (e.g., the lineal kin systems) or because the topic is sensitive (e.g., violence or family intimacy).

Some cross-cultural information on families is generalizable, however. Marriage is increasingly a matter of individual choice. It is still popular, but has given way somewhat to cohabitation, to living apart together, or to divorce and remarriage. Fertility is declining worldwide, and socialization (at least in the growing middle classes) is likely to emphasize independence and achievement. Finally, women's current situation is best labeled "opportunity without equality."

So where are families headed in a globalizing and individualizing world? Gerson (1998) argues that the fact that "these social and economic changes are both international in scope and highly interrelated suggests that they are also irreversible" (p. 14). Although it is tempting to agree, we can at least admit that change is everywhere. This is an exciting time to be studying the world's families. You will find this special issue of the *Journal of Marriage and Family*, edited by Laura Sanchez, adding to your knowledge—and excitement.

References

Adams, B. N. (1974). Doing survey research cross-culturally: Some approaches and problems. *Journal of Marriage and the Family, 36*, 568–573.

Adams, B. N. (1999). Cross-cultural and U.S. kinship. In M. B. Sussman, S. K. Steinmetz, & G. Peterson (Eds.), *Handbook of marriage and the family* (pp. 77–91). New York: Plenum.

Adams, B. N., & Trost, J. (Eds.). (2004). *Handbook of world families*. Thousand Oaks, CA: Sage.

Al-Haj, M. (1995). Kinship and modernization in developing societies: The emergence of instrumentalized kinship. *Journal of Comparative Family Studies, 26*, 311–328.

Al-Naser, F. (2004). Kuwait's families. In B. N. Adams & J. Trost (Eds.), *Handbook of world families* (chap. 23). Thousand Oaks, CA: Sage.

Amaro, F. (2004). Portugal's families: Past and current trends. In B. N. Adams & J. Trost (Eds.), *Handbook of world families* (chap. 15). Thousand Oaks, CA: Sage.

Azadarmaki, T. (2004). Families in Iran: The contemporary situation. In B. N. Adams & J. Trost (Eds.), *Handbook of world families* (chap. 21). Thousand Oaks, CA: Sage.

Blumberg, P. M., & Paul, P. W. (1975). Continuities and discontinuities in upper-class marriages. *Journal of Marriage and the Family, 37*, 75–89.

Chen, Y.-H., & Yi, C.-C. (2004). Taiwan's families. In B. N. Adams & J. Trost (Eds.), *Handbook of world families* (chap. 8). Thousand Oaks, CA: Sage.

Daly, K. J., & Dienhart, A. (1998). Negotiating parental involvement: Finding time for children. In D. Vannoy & P. J. Dubeck (Eds.), *Challenges for work and family in the twenty-first century* (pp. 111–122). New York: Aldine de Gruyter.

de Vaus, D. (2004). Australian families. In B. N. Adams & J. Trost (Eds.), *Handbook of world families* (chap. 4). Thousand Oaks, CA: Sage.

Dubeck, P. J. (1998). The need and challenge to better integrate work and family life in the twenty-first century. In D. Vannoy & P. J. Dubeck (Eds.), *Challenges for work and family in the twenty-first century* (pp. 3–8). New York: Aldine de Gruyter.

Dumon, W. (2004). Belgium's families. In B. N. Adams & J. Trost (Eds.), *Handbook of world families* (chap. 10). Thousand Oaks, CA: Sage.

Forsberg, H. (2004). Finland's families. In B. N. Adams & J. Trost (Eds.), *Handbook of world families* (chap. 12). Thousand Oaks, CA: Sage.

Gerson, K. (1998). Gender and the future of the family: Implications for the postindustrial workplace. In D. Vannoy & P. J. Dubeck (Eds.), *Challenges for work and family in the twenty-first century* (pp. 11–21). New York: Aldine de Gruyter.

Goode, W. J. (1963). *World revolution and family patterns*. New York: Free Press.

Harvey, C. D. H. (2004). Families in Canada. In B. N. Adams & J. Trost (Eds.), *Handbook of world families* (chap. 24). Thousand Oaks, CA: Sage.

Hird, M. J., & Abshoff, K. (2000). Women without children: A contradiction in terms? *Journal of Comparative Family Studies, 31*, 347–366.

Jelin, E. (2004). The family in Argentina: Modernity, economic crisis, and politics. In B. N. Adams & J. Trost (Eds.), *Handbook of world families* (chap. 18). Thousand Oaks, CA: Sage.

Kamerman, S. B., & Kahn, A. J. (1997). *Family change and family policies in Great Britain, Canada, New Zealand, and the United States*. New York: Oxford University Press.

Katz, R., & Lavee, Y. (2004). Families in Israel. In B. N. Adams & J. Trost (Eds.), *Handbook of world families* (chap. 22). Thousand Oaks, CA: Sage.

Koh, E. M. L., & Tan, J. (2000). Favoritism and the changing value of children: A note on the Chinese middle class in Singapore. *Journal of Comparative Family Studies, 31*, 519–528.

Lee, K.-k. (2004). South Korean families. In B. N. Adams & J. Trost (Eds.), *Handbook of world families* (chap. 7). Thousand Oaks, CA: Sage.

Levin, I., & Trost, J. (1999). Living apart together. *Community, Work and Family, 3*, 279–294.

Lu, Z. Z., Maume, D. J., & Bellas, M. L. (2000). Chinese husbands' participation in household labor. *Journal of Comparative Family Studies, 31*, 191–215.

Martin, T. C. (2002). Consensual unions in Latin America: Persistence of a dual nuptiality system. *Journal of Comparative Family Studies, 33*, 35–55.

Mburugu, E. K., & Adams, B. N. (2004). Families in Kenya. In B. N. Adams & J. Trost (Eds.), *Handbook of world families* (chap. 1). Thousand Oaks, CA: Sage.

Miller, R. R., & Browning, S. L. (2000). How construction of ethnicity and gender contribute to shaping non-traditional family patterns. *Journal of Comparative Family Studies, 31*, 301–307.

Mirsky, J., & Radlett, M. (Eds.). (2000). *No paradise yet: The world's women face the new century*. London: Panos Institute and Zed Books.

Modo, I. V. O. (2004). Nigerian families. In B. N. Adams & J. Trost (Eds.), *Handbook of world families* (chap. 2). Thousand Oaks, CA: Sage.

Mozny, I., & Katrnak, T. (2004). The Czech family. In B. N. Adams & J. Trost (Eds.), *Handbook of world families* (chap. 11). Thousand Oaks, CA: Sage.

Nauck, B., & Klaus, D. (2004). Families in Turkey. In B. N. Adams & J. Trost (Eds.), *Handbook of world families* (chap. 17). Thousand Oaks, CA: Sage.

Nosaka, A. (2000). Effect of child gender preference on contraceptive use in rural Bangladesh. *Journal of Comparative Family Studies, 31*, 485–501.

Richter, R., & Kytir, S. (2004). Families in Austria. In B. N. Adams & J. Trost (Eds.), *Handbook of world families* (chap. 9). Thousand Oaks, CA: Sage.

Roschelle, A. R., Toro-Morn, M. I., & Facio, E. (2004). Families in Cuba: From colonialism to revolution. In B. N. Adams & J. Trost (Eds.), *Handbook of world families* (chap. 19). Thousand Oaks, CA: Sage.

Schvanefeldt, P. L., Young, M. H., & Schvanefeldt, J. D. (2001). Dual-resident marriages in Thailand: A comparison of two cultural groups of women. *Journal of Comparative Family Studies, 32*, 347–360.

Sheng, X. (2004). Chinese families. In B. N. Adams & J. Trost (Eds.), *Handbook of world families* *ch*ap. 5). Thousand Oaks, CA: Sage.

Singh, J. P. (2004). The contemporary Indian family. In B. N. Adams & J. Trost (Eds.), *Handbook of world families* (chap. 6). Thousand Oaks, CA: Sage.

Toth, O., & Somlai, P. (2004). Families in Hungary. In B. N. Adams & J. Trost (Eds.), *Handbook of world families* (chap. 14). Thousand Oaks, CA: Sage.

Trost, J., & Levin, I. (2004). Scandinavian families. In B. N. Adams & J. Trost (Eds.), *Handbook of world families* (chap. 16). Thousand Oaks, CA: Sage.

Vincent, S. (2000). Flexible families: Capitalist development and crisis in rural Peru. *Journal of Comparative Family Studies, 31*, 155–170.

Wallace, M. (1998). Downsizing the American dream: Work and family at century's end. In D. Vannoy & P. J. Dubeck (Eds.), *Challenges for work and family in the twenty-first century* (pp. 23–38). New York: Aldine de Gruyter.

Walters, L. H., Warzywoda-Kruszynska, W., & Gurko, T. (2002). Cross-cultural studies of families: Hidden differences. *Journal of Comparative Family Studies, 33*, 433–449.

Yi, Z. (2002). A demographic analysis of family households in China, 1982–1995. *Journal of Comparative Family Studies, 33*, 15–34.

Ziehl, S. (2004). Families in South Africa. In B. N. Adams & J. Trost (Eds.), *Handbook of world families* (chap. 3). Thousand Oaks, CA: Sage.

UNIT 2

Exploring and Establishing Relationships

Unit Selections

Key Points to Consider

- What is your view of the basis for who we are? Is it nature or is it nurture? What is the role of culture in determining appropriate behavior for men and women?

- What do you look for in a mate? Would you be willing to settle for less? Why or why not? Do you think you follow a story line in your relationships? What can be done to change your story line, if you have one?

Student Website

www.mhcls.com/online

Internet References

Further information regarding these websites may be found in this book's preface or online.

Bonobo Sex and Society
  http://songweaver.com/info/bonobos.html

Go Ask Alice!
  http://www.goaskalice.columbia.edu/index.html

The Kinsey Institute for Research in Sex, Gender, and Reproduction
  http://www.indiana.edu/~kinsey/

Mysteries of Odor in Human Sexuality
  http://www.pheromones.com

The Society for the Scientific Study of Sexuality
  http://www.sexscience.org

By and large, humans are social animals, and as such, we seek out meaningful connections with other humans. John Bowlby, Mary Ainsworth, and others have proposed that this drive toward connection is biologically based and is at the core of what it means to be human. However it plays out in childhood and adulthood, the need for connection—to love and be loved—is a powerful force moving us to establish and maintain close relationships. At the same time, our biology influences the way in which we relate to each other and the way in which we create and maintain relationships.

As we explore various possibilities, we engage in the complex business of relationship building. In this business, many processes occur simultaneously: messages are sent and received; differences are negotiated; assumptions and expectations are or are not met. The ultimate goals are closeness and continuity.

How we feel about others and what we see as essential to these relationships play an important role in our establishing and maintaining relationships. In this unit, we look at factors that underlie the establishment of relationships as well as the beginning stages of relationships.

The first subsection explores the role of socialization and biology in the development of who we are and how they affect how we relate to the world. The first article, "Gender Bender" argues that gender identity comes from a complex mix of genetics, prenatal maternal hormones, and social cues. "What Makes You Who You Are" offers general information on the interaction of nature and nurture. This article, by Matt Ridley, explores the joint contributions of genes (nature) as well as the relative influence of the environment (nurture).

The second subsection takes a broad look at factors that influence the building of meaningful connections and at the beginning stages of adult relationships. The first essay, "This Thing Called Love" takes a cross-cultural perspective on the nature of romantic love. Among its interesting and controversial suggestions is that passionate love has a natural life span and shares characteristics with obsessive-compulsive disorder. "Great Expectations" questions the idea that one should search for an ideal mate—a soul mate. Such a quest may put so much pressure on relationships that they are almost guaranteed to fail.

In the third subsection, mate selection is examined. "Go Ahead, Kiss Your Cousin: Heck, Marry Her If You Want To" may surprise some readers. In it, the author discusses one of the more common forms of marriage across the globe–marriage between cousins. "New Technologies and Our Feelings: Romance on the Internet," addresses the promise and pitfalls of trying to find a romantic (and possible life) partner on the Internet.

The next subsection addresses an important aspect of adult relationships: sexuality. Sexuality, especially satisfying long-term passion, is more than correct technique or a biological drive. In "Lust for the Long Haul," the author encourages the reader to engage in soul searching and personal exploration in order to achieve a rewarding sex life. "Reinventing Sex," on the other

hand, looks at the dramatic changes that are taking place in the use of technology and attitudes toward sex and sexual behavior.

The fifth subsection looks at conception and pregnancy. "A New Fertility Factor" discusses the growing controversy over the use of high technology to allow couples to conceive children. Injections of fertility drugs are expensive and have some health risks, as are in vitro fertilization and other clinical manipulations of egg, sperm, and uterine tissue.

Studies suggest that mind-body programs may be just as effective without the high price tags and health risks. "The Abortion Wars" examines the current state of things 30 years after *Roe v. Wade*. Both sides continue to battle, as no middle ground has (or perhaps can be) found. "Brave New Babies" explores new fertility technologies and the ethical question of how these technologies should be used. Is gender an appropriate selection criteria for implantation?

In the final subsection, the articles focus on the idea of the next generation. In "And Now, the Hard Part: That Sweet Little Thing Is About the Commandeer Your Life," Lauren Picker writes that although most couples look forward to the birth of their first child, the reality of the new baby sometimes decimates their lives in unexpected ways. The author implies that parents need patience and time to adjust. The following articles focus on adoption. In "Adopting a New American Family," the evolving nature of adoption in the United States, with increasing use of international adoptions and open adoption, in which birth parents and adoptive parents maintain contact after the adoption, are chronicled. The article, "After the Bliss," describes Post-Adoption Depression Syndrome (PADS), a potentially serious psychological response that occurs during the transition to parenthood among adoptive parents. Similar to the experience of parents following a birth, parents who have newly adopted a child must deal with physical and psychological effects of adding a child to their family.

Gender Bender

New research suggests genes and prenatal hormones could have more sway in gender identity than previously thought.

SADIE F. DINGFELDER
Monitor staff

"It's a boy!" announces the doctor to the exhausted mother, a determination the physician makes instantly. And most of the time, the observed sex of an infant does match the genetic sex—with two X chromosomes producing a girl, and an X plus a Y resulting in a boy.

But in the rare cases where they do not, when prenatal development goes awry and genetic boys are born looking more like girls or vice versa, physicians and parents generally assign the newborn a sex. Most often the child becomes female, because female genitals are easier to construct, says William G. Reiner, MD, a child psychiatrist and urologist at the University of Oklahoma health services center.

The prevailing theory behind this long-standing practice, says Reiner, has been that a person reared as a girl will eventually embrace that category. Now, however, new research by Reiner suggests that perhaps such assumptions ought not to be made. A study by Reiner and John Gearhart, MD, of Johns Hopkins University, finds that biology—in particular the hormonal influences on developing infants' brains—programs children to eventually identify as either male or female, almost regardless of social influences, at least in the case of the children he's studied.

"It's fair to say that some people in the world of psychology have held that [gender] is socially derived, learned behavior," says Reiner. "But our findings do not support that theory."

However, other researchers, such as Sheri Berenbaum, PhD, a psychologist at Pennsylvania State University, maintain that determinates of gender identity may be more complex than that.

"Genetic and hormonal factors are just two of the many influences on gender identity and gender-typical behavior—social influences are certainly very important as well," she says. "And all of these factors seem to interact throughout a child's development."

New Findings

This isn't the view of Reiner and Gearhart though, who point to the findings of their study, published in the Jan. 22 issue of the *New England Journal of Medicine* (Vol. 350, No. 4). The study found that some infants whose brains were exposed to male hormones in utero later identified as male even though they were raised as female and underwent early-childhood operations. Reiner says that indicates that prenatal sex differentiation can at least sometimes trump social influences.

The study followed 16 genetic males with a rare disorder called cloacal exstrophy. Children with this disorder are born without penises, or with very small ones, despite having normal male hormones, normal testes and XY-chromosome pairs. Fourteen of these children underwent early sex-reassignment surgery and were raised as girls by their parents, who were instructed not to inform them of their early medical histories.

The researchers assessed the gender identities and behaviors of these children when they were anywhere from 5 to 16 years old using a battery of measures including the Bates Child Behavior and Attitude Questionnaire and the Child Game Participation Questionnaire. Researchers also asked the children whether they categorized themselves as boys or girls.

> **"Obviously, gender is both a biological and social phenomenon," says Ruble. "Researchers now really need to look carefully at the unfolding of biologically driven processes in interaction with social influences during the first three years of life and beyond."**
>
> *Diane Ruble*
> *New York University*

Of the 14 children raised as females, three spontaneously declared they were male at the initial assessment. At the most recent follow-up, six identified as males, while three reported unclear gender identity or would not talk with researchers. The two participants raised as males from birth continued to identify as male throughout the study.

All of the participants exhibited male-typical behavior, such as rough-and-tumble play and having many male friends.

"If you are looking at the genetic and hormonal male, [sexual identity may be] not plastic at all," says Reiner. "And it appears to be primarily influenced by biology."

Some researchers, such as Kenneth J. Zucker, PhD, a psychologist and the head of the child and adolescent gender identity clinic at Toronto's Centre for Addiction and Mental Health, applaud Reiner's study for renewing interest in the biological determinants of gender and calling into question the notion of some that gender identity is mainly socially constructed and determined by socialization.

That's not to say, however, that socialization isn't still a major or important factor, Zucker emphasizes. "The debate is still up in the air because there are other centers who have studied kids with the same diagnosis, and the rate of changeover from female to male is nowhere near what Reiner is reporting," he explains. "It must be something about their social experience that is accounting for this difference."

Contradictory Evidence

Backing Zucker's belief that socialization still plays a major role—and biology is only part of the story—is research by Sheri Berenbaum, PhD, a psychologist at Pennsylvania State University, and J. Michael Bailey, PhD, a psychologist at Northwestern University.

In a study published in the March 2003 issue of the *Journal of Clinical Endocrinology & Metabolism* (Vol. 88, No. 3), they investigated the gender identity of genetic girls born with congenital adrenal hyperplasia (CAH). Girls with this disorder do not produce enough of the hormone cortisol, which causes their adrenal glands to produce an excess of male sex hormones. As a result, they develop in a hormonal environment that's between that of typical boys and typical girls. These girls tend to have ambiguous genitals, and like the infants with cloacal exstrophy, they generally undergo surgery to remake their bodies in the mold of typical females.

The researchers recruited 43 girls with CAH ages 3 to 18 and assessed their gender-typical behaviors and gender identities using a nine-item questionnaire. One question, for example, asks the child if she would take the opportunity to be magically turned into a boy.

In comparison with a control group of normal girls, those with CAH answered questions in a more masculine way. How-ever, when compared with hormonally normal girls who identified as tomboys, they scored closer to typical girls. And few, says Berenbaum, actually identified as male.

"They behave in some ways more like boys, but they self-identify as girls," she explains.

According to Berenbaum, this shows that prenatal hormones, while important determinates of gendered behavior, aren't the only ones.

"Social influences are also pretty important," she says. "I think the interesting question is how biological predisposition affects our socialization experiences."

Diane Ruble, PhD, a New York University psychologist specializing in early childhood gender identity, agrees.

"In Sheri's work, the hormonal exposure has some masculinizing influence on their play behavior," says Ruble. "That may feed into difficulties that children have even if the hormonal exposure prenatally did not actually directly affect their identities as girls or boys."

For example, she says, a girl who discovers that her behavior is slightly masculine may feel more like a typical boy than girl. She may then primarily socialize with boys, leading to even more male-typical behavior.

"Obviously, gender is both a biological and social phenomenon," says Ruble. "Researchers now really need to look carefully at the unfolding of biologically driven processes in interaction with social influences during the first three years of life and beyond."

Further Reading

Berenbaum, S.A., & Bailey, J.M. (2003). Effects on gender identity of prenatal androgens and genital appearance: Evidence from girls with congenital adrenal hyperplasia. *Journal of Clinical Endocrinology and Metabolism, 88,* 1102–1106.

Martin, C.L., & Ruble, D.N. (in press). Children's search for gender cues: Cognitive perspectives on gender development. *Current Directions in Psychological Science.*

Martin, C.L., Ruble, D.N., & Szkrybalo, J. (2002). Cognitive theories of early gender development. *Psychological Bulletin, 128*(6), 903–933.

Reiner, W.G., & Gearhart, J.P. (2004). Discordant sexual identity in some genetic males with cloacal exstrophy assigned to female sex at birth. *The New England Journal of Medicine, 350*(4), 333–341.

Zucker, K. J. (1999). Intersexuality and gender identity differentiation. *Annual Review of Sex Research, 10,* 1–69.

From *Monitor on Psychology,* April 2004, pages 48–49. Copyright © 2004 by the American Psychological Association. Reprinted with permission.

What Makes You Who You Are

Which is stronger—nature or nurture? The latest science says genes and your experience interact for your whole life

MATT RIDLEY

THE PERENNIAL DEBATE ABOUT NATURE AND NUR-TURE—which is the more potent shaper of the human essence?—is perennially rekindled. It flared up again in the London *Observer* of Feb. 11, 2001. REVEALED: THE SECRET OF HUMAN BEHAVIOR, read the banner headline. ENVIRONMENT, NOT GENES, KEY TO OUR ACTS. The source of the story was Craig Venter, the self-made man of genes who had built a private company to read the full sequence of the human genome in competition with an international consortium funded by taxes and charities. That sequence—a string of 3 billion letters, composed in a four-letter alphabet, containing the complete recipe for building and running a human body—was to be published the very next day (the competition ended in an arranged tie). The first analysis of it had revealed that there were just 30,000 genes in it, not the 100,000 that many had been estimating until a few months before.

Details had already been circulated to journalists under embargo. But Venter, by speaking to a reporter at a biotechnology conference in France on Feb. 9, had effectively broken the embargo. Not for the first time in the increasingly bitter rivalry over the genome project, Venter's version of the story would hit the headlines before his rivals'. "We simply do not have enough genes for this idea of biological determinism to be right," Venter told the *Observer*. "The wonderful diversity of the human species is not hard-wired in our genetic code. Our environments are critical."

In truth, the number of human genes changed nothing. Venter's remarks concealed two whopping nonsequiturs: that fewer genes implied more environmental influences and that 30,000 genes were too few to explain human nature, whereas 100,000 would have been enough. As one scientist put it to me a few weeks later, just 33 genes, each coming in two varieties (on or off), would be enough to make every human being in the world unique. There are more than 10 billion combinations that could come from flipping a coin 33 times, so 30,000 does not seem such a small number after all. Besides, if fewer genes meant more free will, fruit flies would be freer than we are, bacteria freer still and viruses the John Stuart Mill of biology.

Fortunately, there was no need to reassure the population with such sophisticated calculations. People did not weep at the humiliating news that our genome has only about twice as many genes as a worm's. Nothing had been hung on the number 100,000, which was just a bad guess.

But the human genome project—and the decades of research that preceded it—did force a much more nuanced understanding of how genes work. In the early days, scientists detailed how genes encode the various proteins that make up the cells in our bodies. Their more sophisticated and ultimately more satisfying discovery—that gene expression can be modified by experience—has been gradually emerging since the 1980s. Only now is it dawning on scientists what a big and general idea it implies: that learning itself consists of nothing more than switching genes on and off. The more we lift the lid on the genome, the more vulnerable to experience genes appear to be.

This is not some namby-pamby, middle-of-the-road compromise. This is a new understanding of the fundamental building blocks of life based on the discovery that genes are not immutable things handed down from our parents like Moses' stone tablets but are active participants in our lives, designed to take their cues from everything that happens to us from the moment of our conception.

Early Puberty

Girls raised in fatherless households experience puberty earlier. Apparently the change in timing is the reaction of a **STILL MYSTERIOUS** set of genes to their **ENVIRONMENT**. Scientists don't know how many **SETS OF GENES** act this way

For the time being, this new awareness has taken its strongest hold among scientists, changing how they think about everything from the way bodies develop in the womb to how new species emerge to the inevitability of homosexuality in some people. (More on all this later.) But eventually, as the general population becomes more attuned to this interdependent view, changes may well occur in areas as diverse as education, medicine, law and religion. Dieters may learn precisely which combination of fats, carbohydrates and proteins has the greatest effect on their individual waistlines. Theologians may develop a whole new theory of free will based on the observation that learning expands our capacity to choose our own path. As was true of Copernicus's observation 500 years ago that the earth orbits the sun, there is no telling how far the repercussions of this new scientific paradigm may extend.

To appreciate what has happened, you will have to abandon cherished notions and open your mind. You will have to enter a world in which your genes are not puppet masters pulling the strings of your behavior but puppets at the mercy of your behavior, in which instinct is not the opposite of learning, environmental influences are often less reversible than genetic ones, and nature is designed for nurture.

Fear of snakes, for instance, is the most common human phobia, and it makes good evolutionary sense for it to be instinctive. Learning to fear snakes the hard way would be dangerous. Yet experiments with monkeys reveal that their fear of snakes (and probably ours) must still be acquired by watching another individual react with fear to a snake. It turns out that it is easy to teach monkeys to fear snakes but very difficult to teach them to fear flowers. What we inherit is not a fear of snakes but a predisposition to learn a fear of snakes—a nature for a certain kind of nurture.

Before we dive into some of the other scientific discoveries that have so thoroughly transformed the debate, it helps to understand how deeply entrenched in our intellectual history the false dichotomy of nature vs. nurture became. Whether human nature is born or made is an ancient conundrum discussed by Plato and Aristotle. Empiricist philosophers such as John Locke and David Hume argued that the human mind was formed by experience; nativists like Jean-Jacques Rousseau and Immanuel Kant held that there was such a thing as immutable human nature.

Homosexuality
GAY MEN are more likely to have **OLDER BROTHERS** than either gay women or heterosexual men. It may be that a **FIRST MALE FETUS** triggers an immune reaction in the mother, **ALTERING THE EXPRESSION** of key gender genes

It was Charles Darwin's eccentric mathematician cousin Francis Galton who in 1874 ignited the nature-nurture controversy in its present form and coined the very phrase (borrowing the alliteration from Shakespeare, who had lifted it from an Elizabethan schoolmaster named Richard Mulcaster). Galton asserted that human personalities were born, not made by experience. At the same time, the philosopher William James argued that human beings have more instincts than animals, not fewer.

In the first decades of the 20th century, nature held sway over nurture in most fields. In the wake of World War I, however, three men recaptured the social sciences for nurture: John B. Watson, who set out to show how the conditioned reflex, discovered by Ivan Pavlov, could explain human learning; Sigmund Freud, who sought to explain the influence of parents and early experiences on young minds; and Franz Boas, who argued that the origin of ethnic differences lay with history, experience and circumstance, not physiology and psychology.

Galton's insistence on innate explanations of human abilities had led him to espouse eugenics, a term he coined. Eugenics was enthusiastically adopted by the Nazis to justify their campaign of mass murder against the disabled and the Jews. Tainted by this association, the idea of innate behavior was in full retreat for most of the middle years of the century. In 1958, however, two men began the counterattack on behalf of nature. Noam Chomsky, in his review of a book by the behaviorist B.F. Skinner, argued that it was impossible to learn human language by trial and error alone; human beings must come already equipped with an innate grammatical skill. Harry Harlow did a simple experiment that showed that a baby monkey prefers a soft, cloth model of a mother to a hard, wire-frame mother, even if the wire-frame mother provides it with all its milk; some preferences are innate.

Fast-forward to the 1980s and one of the most stunning surprises to greet scientists when they first opened up animal genomes: fly geneticists found a small group of genes called the hox genes that seemed to set out the body plan of the fly during its early development—telling it roughly where to put the head, legs, wings and so on. But then colleagues studying mice found the same hox genes, in the same order, doing the same job in Mickey's world—telling the mouse where to put its various parts. And when scientists looked in our genome, they found hox genes there too.

Hox genes, like all genes, are switched on and off in different parts of the body at different times. In this way, genes can have subtly different effects, depending on where, when and how they are switched on. The switches that control this process—stretches of DNA upstream of genes—are known as promoters.

Small changes in the promoter can have profound effects on the expression of a hox gene. For example, mice have short necks and long bodies; chickens have long necks and short bodies. If you count the vertebrae in the necks and thoraxes of mice and chickens, you will find that a mouse has seven neck and 13 thoracic vertebrae, a chicken 14 and seven, respectively. The source of this difference lies in the promoter attached to HoxC8, a hox gene that helps shape the thorax of the body. The promoter is a 200-letter paragraph of DNA, and in the two species it differs by just a handful of letters. The effect is to alter the expression of the HoxC8 gene in the development of the chicken embryo. This means the chicken makes thoracic vertebrae in a different part of the body than the mouse. In the python, HoxC8 is expressed right from the head and goes on being expressed for most of the body. So pythons are one long thorax; they have ribs all down the body.

To make grand changes in the body plan of animals, there is no need to invent new genes, just as there's no need to invent new words to write an original novel (unless your name is Joyce). All you need do is switch the same ones on and off in different patterns. Suddenly, here is a mechanism for creating large and small evolutionary changes from small genetic differences. Merely by adjusting the sequence of a promoter or adding a new one, you could alter the expression of a gene.

Divorce
If a **FRATERNAL TWIN** gets divorced, there's a **30% CHANCE** that his or her twin will get divorced as well. If the twins are **IDENTICAL**, however, one sibling's divorce **BOOSTS THE ODDS** to 45% that the other will split

In one sense, this is a bit depressing. It means that until scientists know how to find gene promoters in the vast text of the genome, they will not learn how the recipe for a chimpanzee differs from that for a person. But in another sense, it is also uplifting, for it reminds us more forcefully than ever of a simple truth that is all too often forgotten: bodies are not made, they grow. The genome is not a blueprint for constructing a body. It is a recipe for baking a body. You could say the chicken embryo is marinated for a shorter time in the HoxC8 sauce than the mouse embryo is. Likewise, the development of a certain human behavior takes a certain time and occurs in a certain order, just as the cooking of a perfect souffle requires not just the right ingredients but also the right amount of cooking and the right order of events.

How does this new view of genes alter our understanding of human nature? Take a look at four examples.

Language Human beings differ from chimpanzees in having complex, grammatical language. But language does not spring fully formed from the brain; it must be learned from other language-speaking human beings. This capacity to learn is written into the human brain by genes that open and close a critical window during which learning takes place. One of those genes, FoxP2, has recently been discovered on human chromosome 7 by Anthony Monaco and his colleagues at the Wellcome Trust Centre for Human Genetics in Oxford. Just having the FoxP2 gene, though, is not enough. If a child is not exposed to a lot of spoken language during the critical learning period, he or she will always struggle with speech.

Crime Families
GENES may influence the way people respond to a "crimogenic" **ENVIRONMENT**. How else to explain why the **BIOLOGICAL** children of criminal parents are more likely than their **ADOPTED** children to break the law?

Love Some species of rodents, such as the prairie vole, form long pair bonds with their mates, as human beings do. Others, such as the montane vole, have only transitory liaisons, as do chimpanzees. The difference, according to Tom Insel and Larry Young at Emory University in Atlanta, lies in the promoter up-

stream of the oxytocin-and vasopressin-receptor genes. The insertion of an extra chunk of DNA text, usually about 460 letters long, into the promoter makes the animal more likely to bond with its mate. The extra text does not create love, but perhaps it creates the possibility of falling in love after the right experience.

Antisocial Behavior It has often been suggested that childhood maltreatment can create an antisocial adult. New research by Terrie Moffitt of London's Kings College on a group of 442 New Zealand men who have been followed since birth suggests that this is true only for a genetic minority. Again, the difference lies in a promoter that alters the activity of a gene. Those with high-active monoamine oxidase A genes were virtually immune to the effects of mistreatment. Those with low-active genes were much more antisocial if maltreated, yet—if anything—slightly less antisocial if not maltreated. The low-active, mistreated men were responsible for four times their share of rapes, robberies and assaults. In other words, maltreatment is not enough; you must also have the low-active gene. And it is not enough to have the low-active gene; you must also be maltreated.

Homosexuality Ray Blanchard at the University of Toronto has found that gay men are more likely than either lesbians or heterosexual men to have older brothers (but not older sisters). He has since confirmed this observation in 14 samples from many places. Something about occupying a womb that has held other boys occasionally results in reduced birth weight, a larger placenta and a greater probability of homosexuality. That something, Blanchard suspects, is an immune reaction in the mother, primed by the first male fetus, that grows stronger with each male pregnancy. Perhaps the immune response affects the expression of key genes during brain development in a way that boosts a boy's attraction to his own sex. Such an explanation would not hold true for all gay men, but it might provide important clues into the origins of both homosexuality and heterosexuality.

TO BE SURE, EARLIER SCIENTIFIC DISCOVERIES HAD HINTED AT the importance of this kind of interplay between heredity and environment. The most striking example is Pavlovian conditioning. When Pavlov announced his famous experiment a century ago this year, he had apparently discovered how the brain could be changed to acquire new knowledge of the world—in the case of his dogs, knowledge that a bell foretold the arrival of food. But now we know how the brain changes: by the real-time expression of 17 genes, known as the CREB genes. They must be switched on and off to alter connections among nerve cells in the brain and thus lay down a new long-term memory. These genes are at the mercy of our behavior, not the other way around. Memory is in the genes in the sense that it uses genes, not in the sense that you inherit memories.

In this new view, genes allow the human mind to learn, remember, imitate, imprint language, absorb culture and express instincts. Genes are not puppet masters or blueprints, nor are they just the carriers of heredity. They are active during life; they switch one another on and off; they respond to the environment. They may direct the construction of the body and brain in

ANCIENT QUARREL

How much of who we are is learned or innate is an argument with a fruitful but fractious pedigree

Nature We may be destined to be bald, mourn our dead, seek mates, fear the dark

IMMANUEL KANT
His philosophy sought a native morality in the mind

FRANCIS GALTON
Math geek saw mental and physical traits as innate

KONRAD LORENZ
Studied patterns of instinctive behavior in animals

NOAM CHOMSKY
Argued that human beings are born with a capacity for grammar

Nurture But we can also learn to love tea, hate polkas, invent alphabets and tell lies

JOHN LOCKE
Considered the mind of an infant to be a tabula rasa, or blank slate

IVAN PAVLOV
Trained dogs to salivate at the sound of the dinner bell

SIGMUND FREUD
Felt we are formed by mothers, fathers, sex, jokes and dreams

FRANZ BOAS
Believed chance and environs are key to cultural variation

the womb, but then almost at once, in response to experience, they set about dismantling and rebuilding what they have made. They are both the cause and the consequence of our actions.

Will this new vision of genes enable us to leave the nature-nurture argument behind, or are we doomed to reinvent it in every generation? Unlike what happened in previous eras, science is explaining in great detail precisely how genes and their environment—be it the womb, the classroom or pop culture—interact. So perhaps the pendulum swings of a now demonstrably false dichotomy may cease.

It may be in our nature, however, to seek simple, linear, cause-and-effect stories and not think in terms of circular causation, in which effects become their own causes. Perhaps the idea of nature via nurture, like the ideas of quantum mechanics and relativity, is just too counterintuitive for human minds. The urge to see ourselves in terms of nature versus nurture, like our instinctual ability to fear snakes, may be encoded in our genes.

MATT RIDLEY is an Oxford-trained zoologist and science writer whose latest book is *Nature via Nurture* (HarperCollins)

This Thing Called Love

L AUREN S LATER

My husband and I got married at eight in the morning. It was winter, freezing, the trees encased in ice and a few lone blackbirds balancing on telephone wires. We were in our early 30s, considered ourselves hip and cynical, the types who decried the institution of marriage even as we sought its status. During our wedding brunch we put out a big suggestion box and asked people to slip us advice on how to avoid divorce; we thought it was a funny, clear-eyed, grounded sort of thing to do, although the suggestions were mostly foolish: Screw the toothpaste cap on tight. After the guests left, the house got quiet. There were flowers everywhere: puckered red roses and fragile ferns. "What can we do that's really romantic?" I asked my newly wed one. Benjamin suggested we take a bath. I didn't want a bath. He suggested a lunch of chilled white wine and salmon. I was sick of salmon.

What can we do that's really romantic? The wedding was over, the silence seemed suffocating, and I felt the familiar disappointment after a longed-for event has come and gone. We were married. Hip, hip, hooray. I decided to take a walk. I went into the center of town, pressed my nose against a bakery window, watched the man with flour on his hands, the dough as soft as skin, pushed and pulled and shaped at last into stars. I milled about in an antique store. At last I came to our town's tattoo parlor. Now I am not a tattoo type person, but for some reason, on that cold silent Sunday, I decided to walk in. "Can I help you?" a woman asked.

"Is there a kind of tattoo I can get that won't be permanent?" I asked.

"Henna tattoos," she said.

She explained that they lasted for six weeks, were used at Indian weddings, were stark and beautiful and all brown. She showed me pictures of Indian women with jewels in their noses, their arms scrolled and laced with the henna markings. Indeed they were beautiful, sharing none of the gaudy comic strip quality of the tattoos we see in the United States. These henna tattoos spoke of intricacy, of the webwork between two people, of ties that bind and how difficult it is to find their beginnings and their elms. And because I had just gotten married, and because I was feeling a post wedding letdown, and because I wanted something really romantic to sail me through the night, I decided to get one.

"Where?" she asked.

"Here," I said. I laid my hands over my breasts and belly.

She raised her eyebrows. "Sure," she said.

I am a modest person. But I took off my shirt, lay on the table, heard her in the back room mixing powders and paints. She came to me carrying a small black-bellied pot inside of which was a rich red mush, slightly glittering. She adorned me. She gave me vines and flowers. She turned my body into a stake supporting whole new gardens of growth, and then, low around my hips, she painted a delicate chain-linked chastity belt. An hour later, the paint dry, I put my clothes back on, went home to film my newly wed one. This, I knew, was my gift to him, the kind of present you offer only once in your lifetime. I let him undress me.

"Wow," he said, standing back.

I blushed, and we began.

We are no longer beginning, my husband and I. This does not surprise me. Even back then, wearing the decor of desire, the serpentining tattoos, I knew they would fade, their red-clay color bleaching out until they were gone. On my wedding day I didn't care.

I do now. Eight years later, pale as a pillowcase, here I sit, with all the extra pounds and baggage time brings. And the questions have only grown more insistent. Does passion necessarily diminish over time? How reliable is romantic love, really, as a means of choosing one's mate? Can a marriage be good when Eros is replaced with friendship, or even economic partnership, two people bound by bank accounts?

Let me be clear: I still love my husband. There is no man I desire more. But it's hard to sustain romance in the crumb-filled quotidian that has become our lives. The ties that bind have been frayed by money and mortgages and children, those little imps who somehow manage to tighten the knot while weakening its actual fibers. Benjamin and I have no time for chilled white wine and salmon. The baths in our house always include Big Bird.

If this all sounds miserable, it isn't. My marriage is like a piece of comfortable clothing; even the arguments have a feel of fuzziness to them, something so familiar it can only be called home. And yet …

In the Western world we have for centuries concocted poems and stories and plays about the cycles of love, the way it morphs and changes over time, the way passion grabs us by our flung-back throats and then leaves us for something saner. If *Dracula*—

the frail woman, the sensuality of submission—reflects how we understand the passion of early romance, the *Flintstones* reflects our experiences of long-term love: All is gravel and somewhat silly, the song so familiar you can't stop singing it, and when you do, the emptiness is almost unbearable.

We have relied on stories to explain the complexities of love, tales of jealous gods and arrows. Now, however, these stories—so much a part of every civilization—may be changing as science steps in to explain what we have always felt to be myth, to be magic. For the first time, new research has begun to illuminate where love lies in the brain, the particulars of its chemical components.

Anthropologist Helen Fisher may be the closest we've ever come to having a doyenne of desire. At 60 she exudes a sexy confidence, with corn-colored hair, soft as floss, and a willowy build. A professor at Rutgers University, she lives in New York City, her book-lined apartment near Central Park, with its green trees fluffed out in the summer season, its paths crowded with couples holding hands.

Fisher has devoted much of her career to studying the biochemical pathways of love in all its manifestations: lust, romance, attachment, the way they wax and wane. One leg casually crossed over the other, ice clinking in her glass, she speaks with appealing frankness, discussing the ups and downs of love the way most people talk about real estate. "A woman unconsciously uses orgasms as a way of deciding whether or not a man is good for her. If he's impatient and rough, and she doesn't have the orgasm, she may instinctively feel he's less likely to be a good husband and father. Scientists think the fickle female orgasm may have evolved to help women distinguish Mr. Right from Mr. Wrong."

One of Fisher's central pursuits in the past decade has been looking at love, quite literally, with the aid of an MRI machine. Fisher and her colleagues Arthur Aron and Lucy Brown recruited subjects who had been "madly in love" for an average of seven months. Once inside the MRI machine, subjects were shown two photographs, one neutral, the other of their loved one.

What Fisher saw fascinated her. When each subject looked at his or her loved one, the parts of the brain linked to reward and pleasure—the ventral tegmental area and the caudate nucleus—it up. What excited Fisher most was not so much finding a location, an address, for love as tracing its specific chemical pathways. Love lights up the caudate nucleus because it is home to a dense spread of receptors for a neurotransmitter called dopamine, which Fisher came to think of as part of our own endogenous love potion. In the right proportions, dopamine creates intense energy, exhilaration, focused attention, and motivation to win rewards. It is why, when you are newly in love, you can stay up all night, watch the sun rise, run a race, ski fast down a slope ordinarily too steep for your skill. Love makes you bold, makes you bright, makes you run real risks, which you sometimes survive, and sometimes you don't.

I first fell in love when I was only 12, with a teacher. His name was Mr. McArthur, and he wore open-toed sandals and sported a beard. I had never had a male teacher before, and I thought it terribly exotic. Mr. McArthur did things no other teacher dared to do. He explained to us the physics of farting.

He demonstrated how to make an egg explode. He smoked cigarettes at recess, leaning languidly against the side of the school building, the ash growing longer and longer until he casually tapped it off with his finger.

What unique constellation of needs led me to love a man who made an egg explode is interesting, perhaps, but not as interesting, for me, as my memory of love's sheer physical facts. I had never felt anything like it before. I could not get Mr. McArthur out of my mind. I was anxious; I gnawed at the lining of my cheek until I tasted the tang of blood. School became at once terrifying and exhilarating. Would I see him in the hallway? In the cafeteria? I hoped. But when my wishes were granted, and I got a glimpse of my man, it satisfied nothing; it only inflamed me all the more. Had he looked at me? Why had he not looked at me? When would I see him again? At home I looked him up in the phone book; I rang him, this in a time before caller ID. He answered.

"Hello?" Pain in my heart, ripped down the middle. Hang up. Call back. "Hello?" I never said a thing.

Once I called him at night, late, and from the way he answered the phone it was clear, even to a prepubescent like me, that he was with a woman. His voice fuzzy, the tinkle of her laughter in the background. I didn't get out of bed for a whole day.

Sound familiar? Maybe you were 30 when it happened to you, or 8 or 80 or 25. Maybe you lived in Kathmandu or Kentucky; age and geography are irrelevant. Donatella Marazziti is a professor of psychiatry at the University of Pisa in Italy who has studied the biochemistry of lovesickness. Having been in love twice herself and felt its awful power, Marazziti became interested in exploring the similarities between love and obsessive-compulsive disorder.

She and her colleagues measured serotonin levels in the blood of 24 subjects who had fallen in love within the past six months and obsessed about this love object for at least four hours every day. Serotonin is, perhaps, our star neurotransmitter, altered by our star psychiatric medications: Prozac and Zoloft and Paxil, among others. Researchers have long hypothesized that people with obsessive-compulsive disorder (OCD) have a serotonin "imbalance." Drugs like Prozac seem to alleviate OCD by increasing the amount of this neurotransmitter available at the juncture between neurons.

Marazziti compared the lovers' serotonin levels with those of a group of people suffering from OCD and another group who were free from both passion and mental illness. Levels of serotonin in both the obsessives' blood and the lovers' blood were 40 percent lower than those in her normal subjects. Translation: Love and obsessive-compulsive disorder could have a similar chemical profile. Translation: Love and mental illness may be difficult to tell apart. Translation: Don't be a fool. Stay away.

Of course that's a mandate none of us can follow. We do fall in love, sometimes over and over again, subjecting ourselves, each time, to a very sick state of mind. There is hope, however, for those caught in the grip of runaway passion—Prozac. There's nothing like that bicolored bullet for damping down the sex drive and making you feel "blah" about the buffet. Helen Fisher believes that the ingestion of drugs like Prozac jeopardizes one's ability to fall in love—and stay in love. By dulling the keen edge of love and its associated libido, relationships go stale. Says Fisher, "I know of one couple on the edge of divorce.

The wife was on an antidepressant. Then she went off it, started having orgasms once more, felt the renewal of sexual attraction for her husband, and they're now in love all over again."

Psychoanalysts have concocted countless theories about why we fall in love with whom we do. Freud would have said your choice is influenced by the unrequited wish to bed your mother, if you're a boy, or your father, if you're a girl, Jung believed that passion is driven by some kind of collective unconscious. Today psychiatrists such as Thomas Lewis from the University of California at San Francisco's School of Medicine hypothesize that romantic love is rooted in our earliest infantile experiences with intimacy, how we felt at the breast, our mother's face, these things of pure unconflicted comfort that get engraved in our brain and that we ceaselessly try to recapture as adults. According to this theory we love whom we love not so much because of the future we hope to build but because of the past we hope to reclaim. Love is reactive, not proactive, it arches us backward, which may be why a certain person just "feels right." Or "feels familiar." He or she is familiar. He or she has a certain look or smell or sound or touch that activates buried memories.

Love and obsessive-compulsive disorder could have a similar chemical profile. Translation: Love and mental illness may be difficult to tell apart. Translation: Don't be a fool. Stay away.

When I first met my husband, I believed this psychological theory was more or less correct. My husband has red hair and a soft voice. A chemist, he is whimsical and odd. One day before we married he dunked a rose in liquid nitrogen so it froze, whereupon he flung it against the wall, spectacularly shattering it. That's when I fell in love with him. My father, too, has red hair, a soft voice, and many eccentricities. He was prone to bursting into song, prompted by something we never saw.

However, it turns out my theories about why I came to love my husband may be just so much hogwash. Evolutionary psychology has said good riddance to Freud and the Oedipal complex and all that other transcendent stuff and hello to simple survival skills. It hypothesizes that we tend to see as attractive, and thereby choose as mates, people who look healthy. And health, say these evolutionary psychologists, is manifested in a woman with a 70 percent waist-to-hip ratio and men with rugged features that suggest a strong supply of testosterone in their blood. Waist-to-hip ratio is important for the successful birth of a baby, and studies have shown this precise ratio signifies higher fertility. As for the rugged look, well, a man with a good dose of testosterone probably also has a strong immune system and so is more likely to give his partner healthy children.

Perhaps our choice of mates is a simple matter of following our noses. Claus Wedekind of the University of Lausanne in Switzerland did an interesting experiment with sweaty T-shirts. He asked 49 women to smell T-shirts previously worn by unidentified men with a variety of the genotypes that influence both body odor and immune systems. He then asked the women to rate which T-shirts smelled the best, which the worst. What Wedekind found was that women preferred the scent of a T-shirt worn by a man whose genotype was most different from hers, a genotype that, perhaps, is linked to an immune system that possesses something hers does not. In this way she increases the chance that her offspring will be robust.

It all seems too good to be true, that we are so hardwired and yet unconscious of the wiring. Because no one to my knowledge has ever said, "I married him because of his B.O." No. We say, "I married him (or her) because he's intelligent, she's beautiful, he's witty, she's compassionate." But we may just be as deluded about love as we are when we're *in* love. If it all comes down to a sniff test, then dogs definitely have the edge when it comes to choosing mates.

W hy doesn't passionate love last? How is it possible to see a person as beautiful on Monday, and 364 days later, on another Monday, to see that beauty as bland? Surely the object of your affection could not have changed that much. She still has the same shaped eyes. Her voice has always had that husky sound, but now it grates on you—she sounds like she needs an antibiotic. Or maybe you're the one who needs an antibiotic, because the partner you once loved and cherished and saw as though saturated with starlight now feels more like a low-level infection, tiring you, sapping all your strength.

Studies around the world confirm that, indeed, passion usually ends. Its conclusion is as common as its initial flare. No wonder some cultures think selecting a lifelong mate based on something so fleeting is folly. Helen Fisher has suggested that relationships frequently break up after four years because that's about how long it takes to raise a child through infancy. Passion, that wild, prismatic insane feeling, turns out to be practical after all. We not only need to copulate; we also need enough passion to start breeding, and then feelings of attachment take over as the partners bond to raise a helpless human infant. Once a baby is no longer nursing, the child can be left with sister, aunts, friends. Each parent is now free to meet another mate and have more children.

Biologically speaking, the reasons romantic love fades may be found in the way our brains respond to the surge and pulse of dopamine that accompanies passion and makes us fly. Cocaine users describe the phenomenon of tolerance: The brain adapts to the excessive input of the drug. Perhaps the neurons become desensitized and need more and more to produce the high—to put out pixie dust, metaphorically speaking.

Maybe it's a good thing that romance fizzles. Would we have railroads, bridges, planes, faxes, vaccines, and television if we were all always besotted? In place of the ever evolving technology that has marked human culture from its earliest tool use, we would have instead only bonbons, bouquets, and birth control. More seriously, if the chemically altered state induced by romantic love is akin to a mental illness or a drug-induced euphoria, exposing yourself for too long could result in psychological damage. A good sex life can be as strong as Gorilla Glue, but who wants that stuff on your skin?

Once upon a time, in India, a boy and a girl fell in love without their parents' permission. They were from different castes, their relationship radical and unsanctioned. Picture it: the sparkling sari, the boy in white linen, the clandestine meetings on tiled terraces with a fat, white moon floating overhead. Who could deny these lovers their pleasure, or condemn the force of their attraction?

Their parents could. In one recent incident a boy and girl from different castes were hanged at the hands of their parents as hundreds of villagers watched. A couple who eloped were stripped and beaten. Yet another couple committed suicide after their parents forbade them to marry.

Anthropologists used to think that romance was a Western construct, a bourgeois by-product of the Middle Ages. Romance was for the sophisticated, took place in cafés, with coffees and Cabernets, or on silk sheets, or in rooms with a flickering fire. It was assumed that non-Westerners, with their broad familial and social obligations, were spread too thin for particular passions. How could a collectivist culture celebrate or in any way sanction the obsession with one individual that defines new love? Could a lice-ridden peasant really feel passion?

Easily, as it turns out. Scientists now believe that romance is panhuman, embedded in our brains since Pleistocene times. In a study of 166 cultures, anthropologists William Jankowiak and Edward Fischer observed evidence of passionate love in 147 of them. In another study men and women from Europe, Japan, and the Philippines were asked to fill out a survey to measure their experiences of passionate love. All three groups professed feeling passion with the same searing intensity.

But though romantic love may be universal, its cultural expression is not. To the Fulbe tribe of northern Cameroon, poise matters more than passion. Men who spend too much time with their wives are taunted, and those who are weak-kneed are thought to have fallen under a dangerous spell. Love may be inevitable, but for the Fulbe its manifestations are shameful, equated with sickness and social impairment.

In India romantic love has traditionally been seen as dangerous, a threat to a well-crafted caste system in which marriages are arranged as a means of preserving lineage and bloodlines. Thus the gruesome tales, the warnings embedded in fables about what happens when one's wayward impulses take over.

Today love marriages appear to be on the rise in India, often in defiance of parents' wishes. The triumph of romantic love is celebrated in Bollywood films. Yet most Indians still believe arranged marriages are more likely to succeed than love marriages. In one survey of Indian college students, 76 percent said they'd marry someone with all the right qualities even if they weren't in love with the person (compared with only 14 percent of Americans). Marriage is considered too important a step to leave to chance.

Studies around the world confirm that, indeed, passion usually ends. No wonder some cultures think selecting a lifelong mate based on something so fleeting is folly.

Renu Dinakaran is a striking 45-year-old woman who lives in Bangalore, India. When I meet her, she is dressed in Western-style clothes—black leggings and a T-shirt. Renu lives in a well-appointed apartment in this thronging city, where cows sleep on the highways as tiny cars whiz around them, plumes of black smoke rising from their sooty pipes.

Renu was born into a traditional Indian family where an arranged marriage was expected. She was not an arranged kind of person, though, emerging from her earliest days as a fierce tennis player, too sweaty for saris, and smarter than many of the men around her. Nevertheless at the age of 17 she was married off to a first cousin, a man she barely knew, a man she wanted to learn to love, but couldn't. Renu considers many arranged marriages to be acts of "state-sanctioned rape."

Renu hoped to fall in love with her husband, but the more years that passed, the less love she felt, until, at the end, she was shrunken, bitter, hiding behind the curtains of her in-laws' bungalow, looking with longing at the couple on the balcony across from theirs. "It was so obvious to me that couple had married for love, and I envied them. I really did. It hurt me so much to see how they stood together, how they went shopping for bread and eggs."

Exhausted from being forced into confinement, from being swaddled in saris that made it difficult to move, from resisting the pressure to eat off her husband's plate, Renu did what traditional Indian culture forbids one to do. She left. By this time she had had two children. She took them with her. In her mind was an old movie she'd seen on TV, a movie so strange and enticing to her, so utterly confounding and comforting at the same time, that she couldn't get it out of her head. It was 1986. The movie was *Love Story*.

"Before I saw movies like *Love Story*, I didn't realize the power that love can have," she says.

Renu was lucky in the end. In Mumbai she met a man named Anil, and it was then, for the first time, that she felt passion. "When I first met Anil, it was like nothing I'd ever experienced. He was the first man I ever had an orgasm with. I was high, just high, all the time. And I knew it wouldn't last, couldn't last, and so that infused it with a sweet sense of longing, almost as though we were watching the end approach while we were also discovering each other."

When Renu speaks of the end, she does not, to be sure, mean the end of her relationship with Anil; she means the end of a certain stage. The two are still happily married, companionable, loving if not "in love," with a playful black dachshund they bought together. Their relationship, once so full of fire, now seems to simmer along at an even temperature, enough to keep them well fed and warm. They are grateful.

"Would I want all that passion back?" Renu asks. "Sometimes, yes. But to tell you the truth, it was exhausting."

From a physiological point of view, this couple has moved from the dopamine-drenched state of romantic love to the relative quiet of an oxytocin-induced attachment. Oxytocin is a hormone that promotes a feeling of connection, bonding. It is released when we hug our long-term spouses, or our children. It is released when a mother nurses her infant. Prairie voles, animals with high levels of oxytocin, mate for life. When scientists block oxytocin receptors in these rodents, the animals don't form monogamous bonds and tend to roam. Some researchers speculate that autism, a disorder marked by a profound inability to forge and maintain social connections, is linked to an oxytocin deficiency. Scientists have been experimenting by treating autistic people with oxytocin, which in some cases has helped alleviate their symptoms.

In long-term relationships that work—like Renu and Anil's—oxytocin is believed to be abundant in both partners. In long-term relationships that never get off the ground, like Renu and her first husband's, or that crumble once the high is gone, chances are the couple has not found a way to stimulate or sustain oxytocin production.

"But there are things you can do to help it along," says Helen Fisher. "Massage. Make love. These things trigger oxytocin and thus make you feel much closer to your partner."

Well, I suppose that's good advice, but it's based on the assumption that you still want to have sex with that boring windbag of a husband. Should you fake-it-till-you-make-it?

"Yes," says Fisher. "Assuming a fairly healthy relationship, if you have enough orgasms with your partner, you may become attached to him or her. You will stimulate oxytocin."

This may be true. But it sounds unpleasant. It's exactly what your mother always said about vegetables: "Keep eating your peas. They are an acquired taste. Eventually, you will come to like them."

But I have never been a peas person.

I t's 90 degrees on the day my husband and I depart, from Boston for New York City, to attend a kissing school. With two kids, two cats, two dogs, a lopsided house, and a questionable school system, we may know how to kiss, but in the rough and tumble of our harried lives we have indeed forgotten how to *kiss*.

The sky is paved with clouds, the air as sticky as jam in our hands and on our necks. The Kissing School, run by Cherie Byrd, a therapist from Seattle, is being held on the 12th floor of a rundown building in Manhattan. Inside, the room is whitewashed; a tiled table holds bottles of banana and apricot nectar, a pot of green tea, breath mints, and Chapstick. The other Kissing School students—sometimes they come from as far away as Vietnam and Nigeria—are sprawled happily on the bare floor, pillows and blankets beneath them. The class will be seven hours long.

Byrd starts us off with foot rubs. "In order to be a good kisser," she says, "you need to learn how to do the foreplay before the kissing." Foreplay involves rubbing my husband's smelly feet, but that is not as bad as when he has to rub mine. Right before we left the house, I accidentally stepped on a diaper the dog had gotten into, and although I washed, I now wonder how well.

"Inhale," Byrd says, and shows us how to draw in air.

"Exhale," she says, and then she jabs my husband in the back. "Don't focus on the toes so much," she says. "Move on to the calf."

Byrd tells us other things about the art of kissing. She describes the movement of energy through various chakras, the manifestation of emotion in the lips; she describes the importance of embracing all your senses, how to make eye contact as a prelude, how to whisper just the right way. Many hours go by. My cell phone rings. It's our babysitter. Our one-year-old has a high fever. We must cut the long lesson short. We rush out. Later on, at home, I tell my friends what we learned at Kissing School: We don't have time to kiss.

A perfectly typical marriage. Love in the Western world.

Luckily I've learned of other options for restarting love. Arthur Aron, a psychologist at Stony Brook University in New York, conducted an experiment that illuminates some of the mechanisms by which people become and stay attracted. He recruited a group of men and women and put opposite sex pairs in rooms together, instructing each pair to perform a series of tasks, which included telling each other personal details about themselves. He then asked each couple to stare into each other's eyes for two minutes. After this encounter, Aron found most of the couples, previously strangers to each other, reported feelings of attraction. In fact, one couple went on to marry.

Novelty triggers dopamine in the brain, which can stimulate feelings of attraction. So riding a roller coaster on a first date is more likely to lead to second and third dates.

Fisher says this exercise works wonders for some couples. Aron and Fisher also suggest doing novel things together, because novelty triggers dopamine in the brain, which can stimulate feelings of attraction. In other words, if your heart flutters in his presence, you might decide it's not because you're anxious but because you love him. Carrying this a step further, Aron and others have found that even if you just jog in place and then meet someone, you're more likely to think they're attractive. So first dates that involve a nerve-racking activity, like riding a roller coaster, are more likely to lead to second and third dates. That's a strategy worthy of posting on Match.com. Play some squash. And in times of stress—natural disasters, blackouts, predators on the prowl—lock up tight and hold your partner.

In Somerville, Massachusetts, where I live with my husband, our predators are primarily mosquitoes. That needn't stop us from trying to enter the windows of each other's soul. When I propose this to Benjamin, he raises an eyebrow.

"Why don't we just go out for Cambodian food?" he says.

"Because that's not how the experiment happened."

As a scientist, my husband is always up for an experiment. But our lives are so busy that, in order to do this, we have to make a plan. We will meet next Wednesday at lunchtime and try the experiment in our car.

On the Tuesday night before our rendezvous, I have to make an unplanned trip to New York. My husband is more than happy to forget our date. I, however, am not. That night, from my hotel room, I call him.

"We can do it on the phone," I say.

"What am I supposed to stare into?" he asks. "The keypad?"

"There's a picture of me hanging in the hall. Look at that for two minutes. I'll look at a picture I have of you in my wallet."

"Come on," he says.

"Be a sport," I say. "It's better than nothing."

Maybe not. Two minutes seems like a long time to stare at someone's picture with a receiver pressed to your ear. My husband sneezes, and I try to imagine his picture sneezing right along with him, and this makes me laugh.

Another 15 seconds pass, slowly, each second stretched to its limit so I can almost hear time, feel time, its taffy-like texture, the pop it makes when it's done. Pop pop pop. I stare and stare at my husband's picture. It doesn't produce any sense of startling intimacy, and I feel defeated.

Still, I keep on. I can hear him breathing on the other end. The photograph before me was taken a year or so ago, cut to fit my wallet, his strawberry blond hair pulled back in a ponytail. I have never really studied it before. And I realize that in this picture my husband is not looking straight back at me, but his pale blue eyes are cast sideways, off to the left, looking at something I can't see. I touch his eyes. I peer close, and then still closer, at his averted face. Is there something sad in his expression, something sad in the way he gazes off?

I look toward the side of the photo, to find what it is he's looking at, and then I see it: a tiny turtle coming toward him. Now I remember how he caught it after the camera snapped, how he held it gently in his hands, showed it to our kids, stroked its shell, his forefinger moving over the scaly dome, how he held the animal out toward me, a love offering. I took it, and together we sent it back to the sea.

Great Expectations

Summary: Has the quest to find the perfect soul mate done more harm than good? Psychologists provide insight into how the never-ending search for ideal love can keep you from enjoying a marriage or a healthy relationship that you already have.

POLLY SHULMAN

Q: How do you turn a good relationship sour?

A: Pursue your inalienable right to happiness, hot sex, true love and that soul mate who must be out there somewhere.

Marriage is dead! The twin vises of church and law have relaxed their grip on matrimony. We've been liberated from the grim obligation to stay in a poisonous or abusive marriage for the sake of the kids or for appearances. The divorce rate has stayed constant at nearly 50 percent for the last two decades. The ease with which we enter and dissolve unions makes marriage seem like a prime-time spectator sport, whether it's Britney Spears in Vegas or bimbos chasing after the Bachelor.

Long live the new marriage! We once prized the institution for the practical pairing of a cash-producing father and a home-building mother. Now we want it all—a partner who reflects our taste and status, who sees us for who we are, who loves us for all the "right" reasons, who helps us become the person we want to be. We've done away with a rigid social order, adopting instead an even more onerous obligation: the mandate to find a perfect match. Anything short of this ideal prompts us to ask: Is this all there is? Am I as happy as I should be? Could there be somebody out there who's better for me? As often as not, we answer yes to that last question and fall victim to our own great expectations.

Nothing has produced more unhappiness than the concept of the soul mate.

That somebody is, of course, our soul mate, the man or woman who will counter our weaknesses, amplify our strengths and provide the unflagging support and respect that is the essence of a contemporary relationship. The reality is that few marriages or partnerships consistently live up to this ideal. The result is a commitment limbo, in which we care deeply for our partner but keep one stealthy foot out the door of our hearts. In so doing, we subject the relationship to constant review: Would I be happier, smarter, a better person with someone else? It's a painful modern quandary. "Nothing has produced more unhappiness than the concept of the soul mate," says Atlanta psychiatrist Frank Pittman.

Consider Jeremy, a social worker who married a businesswoman in his early twenties. He met another woman, a psychologist, at age 29, and after two agonizing years, left his wife for her. But it didn't work out—after four years of cohabitation, and her escalating pleas to marry, he walked out on her, as well. Jeremy now realizes that the relationship with his wife was solid and workable but thinks he couldn't have seen that 10 years ago, when he left her. "There was always someone better around the corner—and the safety and security of marriage morphed into boredom and stasis. The allure of willing and exciting females was too hard to resist," he admits. Now 42 and still single, Jeremy acknowledges, "I hurt others, and I hurt myself."

Like Jeremy, many of us either dodge the decision to commit or commit without fully relinquishing the right to keep looking—opting for an arrangement psychotherapist Terrence Real terms "stable ambiguity." "You park on the border of the relationship, so you're in it but not of it," he says. There are a million ways to do that: You can be in a relationship but not be sure it's really the right one, have an eye open for a better deal or something on the side, choose someone impossible or far away.

Yet commitment and marriage offer real physical and financial rewards. Touting the benefits of marriage may sound like conservative policy rhetoric, but nonpartisan sociological research backs it up: Committed partners have it all over singles, at least on average. Married people are more financially stable, according to Linda Waite, a sociologist at the University of Chicago and a coauthor of The Case for Marriage: Why Married People are Happier, Healthier and Better Off. Both married men and married women have more assets on average than singles; for women, the differential is huge.

We're in commitment limbo: We care deeply for our partner but keep one stealthy foot out the door of our heart.

The benefits go beyond the piggy bank. Married people, particularly men, tend to live longer than people who aren't married. Couples also live better: When people expect to stay together, says Waite, they pool their resources, increasing their individual standard of living. They also pool their expertise—in cooking, say, or financial management. In general, women improve men's health by putting a stop to stupid bachelor tricks and bugging their husbands to exercise and eat their vegetables. Plus, people who aren't comparing their partners to someone else in bed have less trouble performing and are more emotionally satisfied with sex. The relationship doesn't have to be wonderful for life to get better, says Waite: The statistics hold true for mediocre marriages as well as for passionate ones.

The pragmatic benefits of partnership used to be foremost in our minds. The idea of marriage as a vehicle for self-fulfillment and happiness is relatively new, says Paul Amato, professor of sociology, demography and family studies at Penn State University. Surveys of high school and college students 50 or 60 years ago found that most wanted to get married in order to have children or own a home. Now, most report that they plan to get married for love. This increased emphasis on emotional fulfillment within marriage leaves couples ill-prepared for the realities they will probably face.

Because the early phase of a relationship is marked by excitement and idealization, "many romantic, passionate couples expect to have that excitement forever," says Barry McCarthy, a clinical psychologist and coauthor—with his wife, Emily McCarthy—of Getting It Right the First Time: How to Build a Healthy Marriage. Longing for the charged energy of the early days, people look elsewhere or split up.

Flagging passion is often interpreted as the death knell of a relationship. You begin to wonder whether you're really right for each other after all. You're comfortable together, but you don't really connect the way you used to. Wouldn't it be more honest—and braver—to just admit that it's not working and call it off? "People are made to feel that remaining in a marriage that doesn't make you blissfully happy is an act of existential cowardice," says Joshua Coleman, a San Francisco psychologist.

Coleman says that the constant cultural pressure to have it all—a great sex life, a wonderful family—has made people ashamed of their less-than-perfect relationships and question whether such unions are worth hanging on to. Feelings of dissatisfaction or disappointment are natural, but they can seem intolerable when standards are sky-high. "It's a recent historical event that people expect to get so much from individual partners," says Coleman, author of Imperfect Harmony, in which he advises couples in lackluster marriages to stick it out—especially if they have kids. "There's an enormous amount of pressure on marriages to live up to an unrealistic ideal."

Michaela, 28, was drawn to Bernardo, 30, in part because of their differences: She'd grown up in European boarding schools, he fought his way out of a New York City ghetto. "Our backgrounds made us more interesting to each other," says Michaela. "I was a spoiled brat, and he'd been supporting himself from the age of 14, which I admired." Their first two years of marriage were rewarding, but their fights took a toll. "I felt that because he hadn't grown up in a normal family, he didn't grasp basic issues of courtesy and accountability," says Michaela. They were temperamental opposites: He was a

screamer, and she was a sulker. She recalls, "After we fought, I needed to be drawn out of my corner, but he took that to mean that I was a cold bitch." Michaela reluctantly concluded that the two were incompatible.

In a society hell-bent on individual achievement and autonomy, working on a difficult relationship may get short shrift.

In fact, argue psychologists and marital advocates, there's no such thing as true compatibility.

"Marriage is a disagreement machine," says Diane Sollee, founder of the Coalition for Marriage, Family and Couples Education. "All couples disagree about all the same things. We have a highly romanticized notion that if we were with the right person, we wouldn't fight." Discord springs eternal over money, kids, sex and leisure time, but psychologist John Gottman has shown that long-term, happily married couples disagree about these things just as much as couples who divorce.

"There is a mythology of 'the wrong person,'" agrees Pittman. "All marriages are incompatible. All marriages are between people from different families, people who have a different view of things. The magic is to develop binocular vision, to see life through your partner's eyes as well as through your own."

The realization that we're not going to get everything we want from a partner is not just sobering, it's downright miserable. But it is also a necessary step in building a mature relationship, according to Real, who has written about the subject in How Can I Get Through to You: Closing the Intimacy Gap Between Men and Women. "The paradox of intimacy is that our ability to stay close rests on our ability to tolerate solitude inside a relationship," he says. "A central aspect of grown-up love is grief. All of us long for—and think we deserve—perfection." We can hardly be blamed for striving for bliss and self-fulfillment in our romantic lives—our inalienable right to the pursuit of happiness is guaranteed in the first blueprint of American society.

This same respect for our own needs spurred the divorce-law reforms of the 1960s and 1970s. During that era, "The culture shifted to emphasize individual satisfaction, and marriage was part of that," explains Paul Amato, who has followed more than 2,000 families for 20 years in a long-term study of marriage and divorce. Amato says that this shift did some good by freeing people from abusive and intolerable marriages. But it had an unintended side effect: encouraging people to abandon relationships that may be worth salvaging. In a society hell-bent on individual achievement and autonomy, working on a difficult relationship may get short shrift, says psychiatrist Peter Kramer, author of Should You Leave?

We get the divorce rate that we deserve as a culture, says Peter Kramer.

"So much of what we learn has to do with the self, the ego, rather than giving over the self to things like a relationship," Kramer says. In our competitive world, we're rewarded for our individual achievements rather than for how we help others. We value independence over cooperation, and sacrifices for values like loyalty and continuity seem foolish. "I think we get the divorce rate that we deserve as a culture."

The steadfast focus on our own potential may turn a partner into an accessory in the quest for self-actualization, says Maggie Robbins, a therapist in New York City. "We think that this person should reflect the beauty and perfection that is the inner me—or, more often, that this person should compensate for the yuckiness and mess that is the inner me," says Robbins. "This is what makes you tell your wife, 'Lose some weight—you're making me look bad,' not 'Lose some weight, you're at risk for diabetes.'"

Michaela was consistently embarrassed by Bernardo's behavior when they were among friends. "He'd become sullen and withdrawn—he had a shifty way of looking off to the side when he didn't want to talk. I felt like it reflected badly on me," she admits. Michaela left him and is now dating a wealthy entrepreneur. "I just thought there had to be someone else out there for me."

The urge to find a soul mate is not fueled just by notions of romantic manifest destiny. Trends in the workforce and in the media create a sense of limitless romantic possibility. According to Scott South, a demographer at SUNY-Albany, proximity to potential partners has a powerful effect on relationships. South and his colleagues found higher divorce rates among people living in communities or working in professions where they encounter lots of potential partners—people who match them in age, race and education level. "These results hold true not just for unhappy marriages but also for happy ones," says South.

The temptations aren't always living, breathing people. According to research by psychologists Sara Gutierres and Douglas Kenrick, both of Arizona State University, we find reasonably attractive people less appealing when we've just seen a hunk or a hottie—and we're bombarded daily by images of gorgeous models and actors. When we watch Lord of the Rings, Viggo Mortensen's kingly mien and Liv Tyler's elfin charm can make our husbands and wives look all too schlumpy.

Kramer sees a similar pull in the narratives that surround us. "The number of stories that tell us about other lives we could lead—in magazine articles, television shows, books—has increased enormously. We have an enormous reservoir of possibilities," says Kramer.

And these possibilities can drive us to despair. Too many choices have been shown to stymie consumers, and an array of alternative mates is no exception. In an era when marriages were difficult to dissolve, couples rated their marriages as more satisfying than do today's couples, for whom divorce is a clear option, according to the National Opinion Research Center at the University of Chicago.

While we expect marriage to be "happily ever after," the truth is that for most people, neither marriage nor divorce seem to have a decisive impact on happiness. Although Waite's research shows that married people are happier than their single counterparts, other studies have found that after a couple years of marriage, people are just about as happy (or unhappy) as they were before settling down. And assuming that marriage will automatically provide contentment is itself a surefire recipe for misery.

"Marriage is not supposed to make you happy. It is supposed to make you married," says Pittman. "When you are all the way in your marriage, you are free to do useful things, become a better person." A committed relationship allows you to drop pretenses and seductions, expose your weaknesses, be yourself—and know that you will be loved, warts and all. "A real relationship is the collision of my humanity and yours, in all its joy and limitations," says Real. "How partners handle that collision is what determines the quality of their relationship."

Such a down-to-earth view of marriage is hardly romantic, but that doesn't mean it's not profound: An authentic relationship with another person, says Pittman, is "one of the first steps toward connecting with the human condition—which is necessary if you're going to become fulfilled as a human being." If we accept these humble terms, the quest for a soul mate might just be a noble pursuit after all.

POLLY SHULMAN is a freelance writer in New York City.

From *Psychology Today* Magazine, March/April 2004, pp. 33–34, 37–38, 41–42. Copyright © 2004 by Sussex Publishers, Inc. Reprinted by permission.

Go Ahead, *Kiss* Your Cousin

Heck, Marry Her If You Want To

RICHARD CONNIFF

In Paris in 1876 a 31-year-old banker named Albert took an 18-year-old named Bettina as his wife. Both were Rothschilds, and they were cousins. According to conventional notions about inbreeding, their marriage ought to have been a prescription for infertility and enfeeblement.

In fact, Albert and Bettina went on to produce seven children, and six of them lived to be adults. Moreover, for generations the Rothschild family had been inbreeding almost as intensively as European royalty, without apparent ill effect. Despite his own limited gene pool, Albert, for instance, was an outdoorsman and the seventh person ever to climb the Matterhorn. The American du Ponts practiced the same strategy of cousin marriage for a century. Charles Darwin, the grandchild of first cousins, married a first cousin. So did Albert Einstein.

In our lore, cousin marriages are unnatural, the province of hillbillies and swamp rats, not Rothschilds and Darwins. In the United States they are deemed such a threat to mental health that 31 states have outlawed first-cousin marriages. This phobia is distinctly American, a heritage of early evolutionists with misguided notions about the upward march of human societies. Their fear was that cousin marriages would cause us to breed our way back to frontier savagery—or worse. "You can't marry your first cousin," a character declares in the 1982 play *Brighton Beach Memoirs.* "You get babies with nine heads."

So when a team of scientists led by Robin L. Bennett, a genetic counselor at the University of Washington and the president of the National Society of Genetic Counselors, announced that cousin marriages are not significantly riskier than any other marriage, it made the front page of *The New York Times.* The study, published in the *Journal of Genetic Counseling* last year, determined that children of first cousins face about a 2 to 3 percent higher risk of birth defects than the population at large. To put it another way, first-cousin marriages entail roughly the same increased risk of abnormality that a woman undertakes when she gives birth at 41 rather than at 30. Banning cousin marriages makes about as much sense, critics argue, as trying to ban childbearing by older women.

The marriage of Albert Rothschild and Bettina Rothschild was the result of four generations of inbreeding in the banking dynasty—a practice advocated by the family founder Mayer Amschel Rothschild. His intention was certainly a fruitful one if the Darwinian measure of capitalistic success is the preservation of wealth.

But the nature of cousin marriage is far more surprising than recent publicity has suggested. A closer look reveals that moderate inbreeding has always been the rule, not the exception, for humans. Inbreeding is also commonplace in the natural world, and contrary to our expectations, some biologists argue that this can be a very good thing. It depends in part on the degree of inbreeding.

The idea that inbreeding might sometimes be beneficial is clearly contrarian. So it's important to acknowledge first that inbreeding can sometimes also go horribly wrong—and in ways that, at first glance, make our stereotypes about cousin marriage seem completely correct.

A closer look reveals that moderate inbreeding has always been the rule, not the exception, for humans

In the Yorkshire city of Bradford, in England, for instance, a majority of the large Pakistani community can trace their origins to the village of Mirpur in Kashmir, which was inundated by a new dam in the 1960s. Cousin marriages have been customary in Kashmir for generations, and more than 85 percent of Bradford's Pakistanis marry their cousins. Local doctors are seeing sharp spikes in the number of children with serious genetic disabilities, and each case is its own poignant tragedy. One couple was recently raising two apparently healthy children. Then, when they were 5 and 7, both were diagnosed with neural degenerative disease in the same week. The children are now slowly dying. Neural degenerative diseases are eight times more common in Bradford than in the rest of the United Kingdom.

The great hazard of inbreeding is that it can result in the unmasking of deleterious recessives, to use the clinical language of geneticists. Each of us carries an unknown number of genes—an individual typically has between five and seven—capable of killing our children or grandchildren. These so-called lethal recessives are associated with diseases like cystic fibrosis and sickle-cell anemia.

Most lethal genes never get expressed unless we inherit the recessive form of the gene from both our mother and father. But when both parents come from the same gene pool, their children are more likely to inherit two recessives.

So how do scientists reconcile the experience in Bradford with the relatively moderate level of risk reported in the *Journal of Genetic Counseling?* How did Rothschilds or Darwins manage to marry their cousins with apparent impunity? Above all, how could any such marriages ever possibly be beneficial?

The traditional view of human inbreeding was that we did it, in essence, because we could not get the car on Saturday night. Until the past century, families tended to remain in the same area for generations, and men typically went courting no more than about five miles from home—the distance they could walk out and back on their day off from work. As a result, according to Robin Fox, a professor of anthropology at Rutgers University, it's likely that 80 percent of all marriages in history have been between second cousins or closer.

Factors other than mere proximity can make inbreeding attractive. Pierre-Samuel du Pont, founder of an American dynasty that believed in inbreeding, hinted at these factors when he told his family: "The marriages that I should prefer for our colony would be between the cousins. In that way we should be sure of honesty of soul and purity of blood." He got his wish, with seven cousin marriages in the family during the 19th century. Mayer Amschel Rothschild, founder of the banking family, likewise arranged his affairs so that cousin marriages among his descendants were inevitable. His will barred female descendants from any direct inheritance. Without an inheritance, female Rothschilds had few possible marriage partners of the same religion and suitable economic and social stature—except other Rothschilds. Rothschild brides bound the family together. Four of Mayer's granddaughters married grandsons, and one married her uncle. These were hardly people whose mate choice was limited by the distance they could walk on their day off.

Some families have traditionally chosen inbreeding as the best strategy for success because it offers at least three highly practical benefits. First, such marriages make it likelier that a shared set of cultural values will pass down intact to the children.

Second, cousin marriages make it more likely that spouses will be compatible, particularly in an alien environment. Such marriages may be even more attractive for Pakistanis in Bradford, England, than back home in Kashmir. Intermarriage decreases the divorce rate and enhances the independence of wives, who retain the support of familiar friends and relatives. Among the 19th-century du Ponts, for instance, women had an equal vote with men in family meetings.

Finally, marrying cousins minimizes the need to break up family wealth from one generation to the next. The rich have frequently chosen inbreeding as a means to keep estates intact and consolidate power.

Moderate inbreeding may also produce biological benefits. Contrary to lore, cousin marriages may do even better than ordinary marriages by the standard Darwinian measure of success, which is reproduction. A 1960 study of first-cousin marriages in 19th-century England done by C. D. Darlington, a geneticist at Oxford University, found that inbred couples produced twice as many great-grandchildren as did their outbred counterparts.

Consider, for example, the marriage of Albert and Bettina Rothschild. Their children were descended from a genetic pool of just 24 people (beginning with family founders Mayer Amschel and Gutle Rothschild), and more than three-fifths of them were born Rothschilds. In a family that had not inbred, the same children would have 38 ancestors. Because of inbreeding, they were directly descended no fewer than six times each from Mayer and Gutle Rothschild. If our subconscious Darwinian agenda is to get as much of our genome as possible into future generations, then inbreeding clearly provided a genetic benefit for Mayer and Gutle.

And for their descendants? How could the remarkably untroubled reproductive experience of intermarried Rothschilds differ so strikingly from that of intermarried families in Bradford?

The consequences of inbreeding are unpredictable and depend largely on what biologists call the founder effect: If the founding couple pass on a large number of lethal recessives, as appears to have happened in Bradford, these recessives will spread and double up through intermarriage. If, however, Mayer and Gutle Rothschild handed down a comparatively healthy genone, their descendants could safely intermarry for generations—at least until small deleterious effects inevitably began to pile up and produce inbreeding depression, a long-term decline in the well-being of a family or a species.

A founding couple can also pass on advantageous genes. Among animal populations, generations of inbreeding frequently lead to the development of coadapted gene complexes, suites of genetic traits that tend to be inherited together. These traits may confer special adaptations to a local environment, like resistance to disease.

The evidence for such benefits in humans is slim, perhaps in part because any genetic advantages conferred by inbreeding may be too small or too gradual to detect. Alan Bittles, a professor of human biology at Edith Cowan University in Australia, points out that there's a dearth of data on the subject of genetic disadvantages too. Not until some rare disorder crops up in a place like Bradford do doctors even notice intermarriage.

Something disturbingly eugenic about the idea of better-families-through-inbreeding also causes researchers to look away. Oxford historian Niall Ferguson, author of *The House of Rothschild,* speculates that that there may have been "a Rothschild 'gene for financial acumen,' which intermarriage somehow helped to perpetuate. Perhaps it was that which made the Rothschilds truly exceptional." But he quickly dismisses this as "unlikely."

At the same time, humans are perfectly comfortable with the idea that inbreeding can produce genetic benefits for domesticated animals. When we want a dog with the points to take Best in Show at Madison Square Garden, we often get it by taking individuals displaying the desired traits and "breeding them back" with their close kin.

Researchers have observed that animals in the wild may also attain genetic benefits from inbreeding. Ten mouse colonies may set up housekeeping in a field but remain separate. The dominant male in each colony typically inbreeds with his kin. His genes rapidly spread through the colony—the founder effect again—and each colony thus becomes a little different from the others, with double recessives proliferating for both good and ill effects. When the weather changes or some deadly virus blows through, one colony may end up better adapted to the new circumstances than the other nine, which die out.

Inbreeding may help explain why insects can develop resistance almost overnight to pesticides like DDT: The resistance first shows up as a recessive trait in one obscure family line. Inbreeding, with its cascade of double recessives, causes the trait to be expressed in every generation of this family—and under the intense selective pressure of DDT, this family of resistant insects survives and proliferates.

The obvious problem with this contrarian argument is that so many animals seem to go out of their way to avoid inbreeding. Field biologists have often observed that animals reared together from an early age become imprinted on one another and lack mutual sexual interest as adults; they have an innate aversion to homegrown romance.

But what they are avoiding, according to William Shields, a biologist at the State University of New York College of Environmental Science and Forestry at Syracuse, is merely incest, the most extreme form of inbreeding, not inbreeding itself. He argues that normal patterns of dispersal actually encourage inbreeding. When young birds leave the nest, for instance, they typically move four or five home ranges away, not 10 or 100; that is, they stay within breeding distance of their cousins. Intense loyalty to a home territory helps keep a population healthy, according to Shields, because it encourages "optimal inbreeding." This elusive ideal is the point at which a population gets the benefit of adaptations to local habitat—the co-adapted gene complexes—without the hazardous unmasking of recessive disorders.

Genetic and metabolic tests can now screen for about 100 recessive disorders

In some cases, outbreeding can be the real hazard. A study conducted by E. L. Brannon, an ecologist at the University of Idaho, looked at two separate populations of sockeye salmon, one breeding where a river entered a lake, the other where it exited. Salmon fry at the inlet evolved to swim downstream to the lake. The ones at the outlet evolved to swim upstream. When researchers crossed the populations, they ended up with salmon young too confused to know which way to go. In the wild, such a hybrid population might lose half or more of its fry and soon vanish.

It is, of course, a long way from sockeye salmon and inbred insects to human mating behavior. But Patrick Bateson, a professor of ethology at Cambridge University, argues that outbreeding has at times been hazardous for humans too. For instance, the size and shape of our teeth is a strongly inherited trait. So is jaw size and shape. But the two traits aren't inherited together. If a woman with small jaws and small teeth marries a man with big jaws and big teeth, their grandchildren may end up with a mouthful of gnashers in a Tinkertoy jaw. Before dentistry was commonplace, Bateson adds, "ill-fitting teeth were probably a serious cause of mortality because it increased the likelihood of abscesses in the mouth." Marrying a cousin was one way to avoid a potentially lethal mismatch.

Bateson suggests that while youngsters imprinting on their siblings lose sexual interest in one another they may also gain a search image for a mate—someone who's not a sibling but *like* a sibling. Studies have shown that people overwhelmingly choose spouses similar to themselves, a phenomenon called assortative mating. The similarities are social, psychological, and physical, even down to traits like earlobe length. Cousins, Bateson says, perfectly fit this human preference for "slight novelty."

So where does this leave us? No scientist is advocating intermarriage, but the evidence indicates that we should at least moderate our automatic disdain for it. One unlucky woman, whom Robin Bennett encountered in the course of her research, recalled the reaction when she became pregnant after living with her first cousin for two years. Her gynecologist professed horror, told her the baby "would be sick all the time," and advised her to have an abortion. Her boyfriend's mother, who was also her aunt, "went nuts, saying that our baby would be retarded." The woman had an abortion, which she now calls "the worst mistake of my life."

Science is increasingly able to help such people look at their own choices more objectively. Genetic and metabolic tests can now screen for about 10 recessive disorders. In the past, families in Bradford rarely recognized genetic origins of causes of death or patterns of abnormality. The likelihood of stigma within the community or racism from without also made people reluctant to discuss such problems. But new tests have helped change that. Last year two siblings in Bradford were hoping to intermarry their children despite a family history of thalassemia, a recessive blood disorder that is frequently fatal before the age of 30. After testing determined which of the children carried the thalassemia gene, the families were able to arrange a pair of carrier-to-noncarrier first-cousin marriages.

Such planning may seem complicated. It may even be the sort of thing that causes Americans, with their entrenched dread of inbreeding, to shudder. But the needs of both culture and medicine were satisfied, and an observer could only conclude that the urge to marry cousins must be more powerful, and more deeply rooted, than we yet understand.

Reprinted with permission from *Discover* magazine, August 2003, pp. 60-64. © 2003 by Richard Conniff. Reprinted by permission of the author.

Interracial Intimacy

White-black dating, marriage, and adoption are on the rise. This development, however, is being met with resistance—more vocally by blacks than by whites

RANDALL KENNEDY

Americans are already what racial purists have long feared: a people characterized by a great deal of racial admixture, or what many in the past referred to distastefully as "mongrelization." In pigmentation, width of noses, breadth of lips, texture of hair, and other telltale signs, the faces and bodies of millions of Americans bear witness to interracial sexual encounters. Some were joyful, passionate, loving affairs. Many were rapes. Others contained elements of both choice and coercion. These different kinds of interracial intimacy and sexual depredation all reached their peak in the United States during the age of slavery, and following the Civil War they decreased markedly. Since the end of the civil-rights revolution interracial dating, interracial sex, and interracial marriage have steadily increased, as has the number of children born of interracial unions. This development has prompted commentators to speak of the "creolization" or "browning" or "beiging" of America.

Over the years legions of white-supremacist legislators, judges, prosecutors, police officers, and other officials have attempted to prohibit open romantic interracial attachments, particularly those between black men and white women. From the 1660s to the 1960s, forty-one territories, colonies, or states enacted laws—anti-miscegenation statutes—barring sex or marriage between blacks and whites, and many states ultimately made marriage across the color line a felony. Such laws crystallized attitudes about interracial intimacy that remain influential today, but all were invalidated by the U.S. Supreme Court in 1967, in the most aptly named case in all of American constitutional history: *Loving* v. *Commonwealth of Virginia*. Although white and black Americans are far more likely to date and marry within their own race than outside it, the cultural environment has changed considerably since *Loving*. Recall what happened in the spring of 2000, when George W. Bush, at a crucial moment in his primary campaign, paid a highly publicized visit to Bob Jones University, in South Carolina. During that visit he offered no criticism of the university's then existing prohibition against interracial dating. In the controversy that ensued, no nationally prominent figures defended Bob Jones's policy. Public opinion not only forced Bush to distance himself from Bob Jones but also prompted the notoriously stubborn and reactionary administration of that institution to drop its ban.

The de-stigmatization in this country of interracial intimacy is profoundly encouraging. Against the tragic backdrop of American history, it is a sign that Frederick Douglass may have been right when he prophesied, even before the abolition of slavery, that eventually "the white and colored people of this country [can] be blended into a common nationality, and enjoy together… the inestimable blessings of life, liberty and the pursuit of happiness."

The great but altogether predictable irony is that just as white opposition to white-black intimacy finally lessened, during the last third of the twentieth century, black opposition became vocal and aggressive. In college classrooms today, when discussions about the ethics of interracial dating and marriage arise, black students are frequently the ones most likely to voice disapproval.

Marital Integration

Despite some ongoing resistance (a subject to which I will return), the situation for people involved in interracial intimacy has never been better. For the most part, the law prohibits officials from taking race into account in licensing marriages, making child-custody decisions, and arranging adoptions. Moreover, the American public accepts interracial intimacy as it never has before. This trend will almost certainly continue; polling data and common observation indicate that young people tend to be more liberal on these matters than their elders.

In 1960 there were about 51,000 black-white married couples in the United States; in 1970 there were 65,000, in 1980 there were 121,000, in 1990 there were 213,000, and by 1998 the number had reached 330,000. In other words, in the past four decades black-white marriages increased more than sixfold. And black-white marriages are not only becoming more numerous. Previously, the new couples in mixed marriages tended to be older than other brides and grooms. They were frequently veterans of divorce, embarking on second or third marriages. In recent years, however, couples in mixed marriages seem to be marrying younger than their pioneering predecessors and seem more inclined to have children and to pursue all the other "normal" activities that married life offers.

It should be stressed that black-white marriages remain remarkably rare—fewer than one percent of the total. In 1998, when 330,000 black-white couples were married, 55,305,000 couples were married overall. Moreover, the racial isolation of blacks on the marriage market appears to be greater than that of other people of color: much larger percentages of Native Americans and Asian-Americans marry whites. According to 1990 Census data, in the age cohort twenty-five to thirty-four, 36 percent of U.S.-born Asian-American husbands and 45 percent of U.S.-born Asian-American wives had white spouses; 53 percent of Native American husbands and 54 percent of Native American wives had white spouses. Only eight percent of African-American husbands and only four percent of African-American wives had white spouses. The sociologist Nathan Glazer was correct in stating, in *The Public Interest* (September 1995), that "blacks stand out uniquely among the array of American ethnic and racial groups in the degree to which marriage remains within the group." Of course, the Native American and Asian-American populations are so much smaller than the African-American population that relatively few intermarriages make a big difference in percentage terms. But the disparity is real: it has to do not only with demographics but also with generations' worth of subjective judgments about marriageability, beauty, personality, comfort, compatibility, and prestige. Even now a wide array of social pressures continue to make white-black marriages more difficult and thus less frequent than other inter-ethnic or interracial marriages.

Nevertheless, the trend toward more interracial marriage is clear, as is a growing acceptance of the phenomenon. Successful, high-profile interracial couples include the white William Cohen (a former senator from Maine and the Secretary of Defense under Bill Clinton) and the black Janet Langhart; and the white Wendy Raines and the black Franklin Raines (he is a former director of the Office of Management and Budget and the CEO of Fannie Mae). Some African-Americans whose positions make them directly dependent on black public opinion have nonetheless married whites without losing their footing. A good example is Julian Bond, the chairman of the board of directors of the National Association for the Advancement of Colored People. Though married to a white woman, Bond ascended to the chairmanship of the oldest and most influential black-advancement organization in the country in 1998, and as of this writing continues to enjoy widespread support within the NAACP.

There are other signs that black-white romance has become more widely accepted; indeed, it is quite fashionable in some contexts. One is advertising. When advertisers addressing general audiences use romance to deliver their messages, they most often depict couples of the same race. But now at least occasionally one sees interracial couples deployed as enticements to shop at Diesel or Club Monaco, or to buy furniture from Ikea, jeans from Guess, sweaters from Tommy Hilfiger, cologne from Calvin Klein, or water from Perrier.

Scores of interracial support groups have emerged across the country, among them Kaleidoscope, at the University of Virginia; Students of Mixed Heritage at Amherst College; Interracial Family Club, in Washington, D.C.; Half and Half, at Bryn Mawr; and Mixed Plate, at Grinnell. Although most of these organizations lack deep roots, many display a vigor and resourcefulness that suggest they will survive into the foreseeable future.

They stem from and represent a community in the making. It is a community united by a demand that the larger society respect and be attentive to people who by descent or by choice fall outside conventional racial groupings: interracial couples, parents of children of a different race, and children of parents of a different race. Those within this community want it known that they are not products or agents of an alarming mongrelization, as white racists still believe; nor are they inauthentic and unstable in-betweeners, as some people of color would have it. They want security amid the established communities from which they have migrated. They want to emerge from what the writer Lise Funderburg has identified as the "racial netherworld," and they want to enjoy interaction with others without regret or fear, defensiveness or embarrassment.

"Sleeping White"

African-Americans largely fall into three camps with respect to white-black marriage. One camp, relatively small, openly champions it as a good. Its members argue that increasing rates of interracial marriage will decrease social segregation, encourage racial open-mindedness, enhance blacks' access to enriching social networks, elevate their status, and empower black women in their interactions with black men by subjecting the latter to greater competition in the marketplace for companionship.

A second camp sees interracial marriage merely as a choice that individuals should have the right to make. For example, while noting in *Race Matters* (1993) that "more and more white Americans are willing to interact sexually with black Americans *on an equal basis*," Cornel West maintains that he views this as "neither cause for celebration nor reason for lament." This is probably the predominant view among blacks. It allows a person simultaneously to oppose anti-miscegenation laws and to disclaim any desire to marry across racial lines. Many African-Americans are attracted to this position, because, among other things, it helps to refute a deeply annoying assumption on the part of many whites: that blacks would like nothing more than to be intimate with whites and even, if possible, to become white.

A third camp opposes interracial marriage, on the grounds that it expresses racial disloyalty, suggests disapproval of fellow blacks, undermines black culture, weakens the African-American marriage market, and feeds racist mythologies, particularly the canard that blacks lack pride of race.

Such opposition has always been a powerful undercurrent. When Walter White, the executive secretary of the NAACP, divorced his black wife (the mother of their two children) and married a white woman from South Africa, in 1949, the Norfolk (Virginia) *Journal and Guide* spoke for many blacks when it asserted, "A prompt and official announcement that [White] will not return to his post… is in order." Part of the anger stemmed from apprehension that segregationists would seize upon White's marriage to substantiate the charge that what black male civil-rights activists were really after was sex with white women. Part stemmed from a widespread sense that perhaps White thought no black woman was good enough for him.

By the late 1960s, with the repudiation of anti-miscegenation and Jim Crow laws, increasing numbers of blacks felt emboldened to openly oppose mixed marriages. "We Shall Overcome" was giving way to "Black Power": improving the image of blacks in the minds of whites seemed less important than cultivating a deeper allegiance to racial solidarity. To blacks, interracial intimacy compromised that allegiance. The African-American social reformer George Wiley dedicated himself to struggles for racial justice as a leading figure in the Congress for Racial Equality (CORE) and the founder of the National Welfare Rights Organization. Yet many black activists denounced him for marrying and remaining married to a white woman. When he addressed a rally in Washington, D.C., on African Liberation Day in April of 1972, a group of black women heckled him by chanting, "Where's your white wife? Where's your white wife?" When he attempted to focus his remarks on the situation of black women, the hecklers merely took up a different chant: "Talking black and sleeping white."

Other politically active blacks married to whites—James Farmer, a founder of CORE, and Julius Hobson, a tenacious activist in Washington—faced similar pressure. Julius Lester, a longtime member of the Student Nonviolent Coordinating Committee, wrote a book with one of the most arresting titles of that flamboyant era: *Look Out, Whitey! Black Power's Gon' Get Your Mama!* (1968). But to many black activists, Lester's writings and ideas were decidedly less significant than his choice of a white wife. To them, his selection bespoke hypocrisy. Ridiculing Lester, one black woman wrote a letter to the editor of *Ebony* in which she suggested that it was foolish to regard him as a trustworthy leader. After all, she cautioned, he couldn't even "crawl out of bed" with whites.

The "sleeping white" critique embarrassed a wide variety of people as distinctions between the personal and the political evaporated. At many colleges and universities black students ostracized other blacks who dated (much less married) whites. A black student who wanted to walk around "with a blonde draped on his arm" could certainly do so, a black student leader at the University of Washington told St. Clair Drake, a leading African-American sociologist. "All we say," the student continued, "is don't try to join the black studies association." Drake himself became the target of this critique. When he visited his old high school in 1968, he says, the Black Student Union refused to have anything to do with him, because he was involved in an interracial relationship. Drake's classmate Charles V. Hamilton, a co-author, with Stokely Carmichael, of *Black Power: The Politics of Liberation in America* (1967), was shunned for the same reason.

In some instances black opposition to interracial intimacy played a part in destroying a marriage. A dramatic example is the breakup of Everett LeRoi Jones (now known as Amiri Baraka) and Hettie Jones. LeRoi Jones was born of middle-class black parents in Newark, New Jersey, in 1934. For two years he attended Howard University, which he detested. He served in the Air Force for a short time, and in 1957 he moved to Greenwich Village. He worked for the magazine *Record Changer* and was a co-editor, with Hettie Cohen, of *Yugen*, an avant-garde magazine that published writings by William Burroughs, Gregory Corso, Allen Ginsberg, Jack Kerouac, Charles Olson, and Jones himself. Hettie Cohen was a woman of Jewish parentage who had grown up in suburban New York and attended Mary Washington, the women's college of the University of Virginia.

Jones and Cohen married in 1958. Although his parents accepted the marriage easily, her parents totally opposed it.

For a while LeRoi and Hettie Jones lived together in what she remembers as a loving relationship. But then the pressure of bohemian penury, the demands of two children, and mutual infidelities (including one in which LeRoi fathered a baby by another woman who also happened to be white) caused their marriage to falter. Other forces also emerged to doom the union: LeRoi's deep internal tensions, his ambition to become a black leader, and the growing sense in many black communities that no purported leader could be trusted who "talked black but slept white."

As the black protest movement gathered steam in the early sixties, Jones aimed at becoming an important figure in it. At the same time, his career as a writer blossomed. He wrote well-regarded poetry, social and political essays, and a significant book, *Blues People* (1963), on the history of African-American music. What made LeRoi Jones a celebrity, however, and what ensures him a niche in American literary history, is his two-act play *Dutchman*, which opened in New York City in March of 1964. In *Dutchman* a reticent, bookish middle-class black man named Clay meets a white temptress named Lula in a New York subway car. The play consists mainly of their verbal combat. Angered by Clay's refusal to dance with her, Lula shouts, "Come on, Clay. Let's rub bellies on the train… Forget your social-working mother for a few seconds and let's knock stomachs. Clay, you liver-lipped white man. You would-be Christian. You ain't no nigger, you're just a dirty white man." Clay responds in kind.

> "Tallulah Bankhead!… Don't you tell me anything! If I'm a middle-class fake white man… let me be… Let me be who I feel like being. Uncle Tom. Thomas. Whoever. It's none of your business… I sit here, in this buttoned-up suit, to keep myself from cutting all your throats… You great liberated whore! You fuck some black man, and right away you're an expert on black people. What a lotta shit that is."

But Lula has the last word, so to speak: she suddenly stabs Clay to death. Other passengers throw his body out of the subway car and depart. Alone, Lula re-occupies her seat. When another black man enters the car, she begins her lethal routine anew.

Though living in a predominantly white, bohemian environment when he wrote *Dutchman*, Jones had begun to believe that it was blacks to whom he should be addressing his art. Increasingly successful, he was also becoming increasingly radical in his condemnation of white American society. Asked by a white woman what white people could do to help the race problem, Jones replied, "You can help by dying. You are a cancer. You can help the world's people with your death." An outrageous statement coming from anyone, this comment was even more arresting coming from a man who was married to a white woman. Jones was by no means alone in living within this particular contradiction. He noted in his autobiography that at one point he and some other black intellectuals objected to the presence of white radicals on a committee they were in the process of establishing. "What was so wild," he recalled, "was that some of us were talking about how we didn't want white people on the committee but we were all hooked up to white women… Such were the contradictions of that period of political organization."

The more prominent Jones became, however, the more critics, both black and white, charged him with being hypocritical. The critic Stanley Kauffmann, for example, asserted that Jones constituted an exemplary figure in "the Tradition of the Fake." Stung by such charges, infatuated with black-nationalist rhetoric, inspired by the prospect of re-creating himself, and bored with a disappointing marriage, LeRoi Jones divorced Hettie Jones in 1965.

Throughout the black-power era substantial numbers of African-Americans loudly condemned black participation in interracial relationships (especially with whites), deeming it to be racial betrayal. A reader named Joyce Blake searingly articulated this sentiment in a letter to the editor of the *Village Voice*.

It really hurts and baffles me and many other black sisters to see our black brothers (?) coming down the streets in their African garbs with a white woman on their arms. It is fast becoming a standard joke among the white girls that they can get our men still—African styles and all…

It certainly seems to many black sisters that the Movement is just another subterfuge to aid the Negro male in procuring a white woman. If this be so, then the black sisters don't need it, for surely we have suffered enough humiliation from both white and black men in America.

A Demographic Betrayal?

Although racial solidarity has been the principal reason for black opposition to intermarriage over the years, another reason is the perception that intermarriage by black men weakens black women in the marriage market. A reader named Lula Miles asserted this view in an August 1969 letter to the editor of *Ebony*. Responding to a white woman who had expressed bewilderment at black women's anger, Miles wrote, "Non-sister wonders why the sight of a black man with a white woman is revolting to a black woman… The name of the game is 'competition.' Non-sister, you are trespassing!"

Another letter writer, named Miraonda J. Stevens, reinforced this point: "In the near future there aren't going to be enough nice black men around for us [black women] to marry." This "market" critique of interracial marriage has a long history. In 1929 Palestine Wells, a black columnist for the Baltimore *Afro-American*, wrote,

I have a sneaking suspicion that national intermarriage will make it harder to get husbands. A girl has a hard time enough getting a husband, but methinks 'twill be worse. Think how awful it would be if all the ofay girls with a secret hankering for brown skin men, could openly compete with us.

Forty-five years later an *Ebony* reader named Katrina Williams echoed Wells. "The white man is marrying the white woman," she wrote. "The black man is marrying the white woman. Who's gonna marry me?"

Behind her anxious question resides more than demographics: there is also the perception that large numbers of African-American men believe not only that white women are relatively more desirable but that black women are positively unattractive.

Again the pages of *Ebony* offer vivid testimony. A reader named Mary A. Dowdell wrote in 1969,

Let's just lay all phony excuses aside and get down to the true nitty, nitty, NITTY- GRITTY and tell it like it really is. Black males hate black women just because they are black. The whole so-called Civil Rights Act was really this: "I want a white woman because she's white and I not only hate but don't want a black woman because she's black."… The whole world knows this.

Decades later African-American hostility to interracial intimacy remained widespread and influential. Three examples are revealing. The first is the movie *Jungle Fever* (1991), which portrays an interracial affair set in New York City in the early 1990s. The director, Spike Lee, made sure the relationship was unhappy. Flipper Purify is an ambitious, college-educated black architect who lives in Harlem with his black wife and their young daughter. Angie Tucci, a young white woman, works for Purify as a secretary. Educated only through high school, she lives in Bensonhurst, Brooklyn, with her father and brothers, all of whom are outspoken racists. One evening when Flipper and Angie stay late at his office, work is superseded by erotic longing tinged with racial curiosity. He has never been sexually intimate with a white woman, and she has never been sexually intimate with a black man. They close that gap in their experience, and then stupidly confide in indiscreet friends, who carelessly reveal their secret. Angie's father throws her out of the family home after viciously beating her for "fucking a black nigger." Flipper's wife, Drew, throws him out as well. Flipper and Angie move into an apartment together, but that arrangement falls apart rather quickly under the pressure of their own guilt and uncertainty and the strong disapproval they encounter among blacks and whites alike.

The second example is Lawrence Otis Graham's 1995 essay "I Never Dated a White Girl." Educated at Princeton University and Harvard Law School, Graham sought to explain why "black middle-class kids… [who are] raised in integrated or mostly white neighborhoods, [and] told to befriend white neighbors, socialize and study with white classmates, join white social and professional organizations, and go to work for mostly white employers" are also told by their relatives, "Oh, and by the way, don't ever forget that you are black, and that you should never get so close to whites that you happen to fall in love with them." Graham did more than explain, however; he justified this advice in a candid polemic that might well have been titled "Why I Am *Proud* That I Never Dated a White Girl."

The third example is "Black Men, White Women: A Sister Relinquishes Her Anger," a 1993 essay by the novelist Bebe Moore Campbell. Describing a scene in which she and her girlfriends spied a handsome black celebrity escorting a white woman at a trendy Beverly Hills restaurant, Campbell wrote,

In unison, we moaned, we groaned, we rolled our eyes heavenward. We gnashed our teeth in harmony and made ugly faces. We sang "Umph! Umph! Umph!" a cappella-style, then shook our heads as we lamented for the ten thousandth time the perfidy of black men and cursed trespassing white women who dared to "take our men."… Before lunch was over I had a headache, indigestion, and probably elevated blood pressure.

Only a small percentage of black men marry interracially; one report, published in 1999, estimated that seven percent of married black men have non-black wives. But with poverty, imprisonment, sexual orientation, and other factors limiting the number of marriageable black men, a substantial number of black women feel this loss of potential mates acutely. In 1992 researchers found that for every three unmarried black women in their twenties there was only one unmarried black man with earnings above the poverty level. Given these realities, black women's disparagement of interracial marriage should come as no surprise. "In a drought," Campbell wrote, "even one drop of water is missed."

Compiling a roster of prominent blacks—Clarence Thomas, Henry Louis Gates Jr., Quincy Jones, Franklin A. Thomas, John Edgar Wideman—married to or otherwise romantically involved with whites, Graham voiced disappointment. When a prominent black role model "turns out to be married to a white mate," he wrote, "our children say, 'Well, if it's so good to be black, why do all my role models date and marry whites?'... As a child growing up in the 'black is beautiful' 1970s, I remember asking these questions."

Anticipating the objection that his views amount to "reverse racism," no less an evil than anti-black bigotry, Graham wrote that his aim was neither keeping the races separate nor assigning superiority to one over the other. Rather, he wanted to develop "solutions for the loss of black mentors and role models at a time when the black community is overrun with crime, drug use, a high dropout rate, and a sense that any black who hopes to find... career success must necessarily disassociate himself from his people with the assistance of a white spouse." He maintained,

> It's not the discrete decision of any one of these individuals that makes black America stand up and take notice. It is the cumulative effect of each of these personal decisions that bespeaks a frightening pattern for an increasingly impoverished and wayward black community. The cumulative effect is that the very blacks who are potential mentors and supporters of a financially and psychologically depressed black community are increasingly deserting the black community en masse, both physically and emotionally.

The Case for Amalgamation

Although Graham's view is widespread, there are blacks who not only tolerate but applaud increasing rates of interracial intimacy. The most outspoken and distinguished African-American proponent of free trade in the marital marketplace is the Harvard sociologist Orlando Patterson. Patterson makes three main claims. First, he maintains that interracial marriage typically gives people access to valuable new advice, know-how, and social networks. "When we marry," he writes in *Rituals of Blood: Consequences of Slavery in Two American Centuries*, "we engage in an exchange of social and cultural dowries potentially far more valuable than gold-rimmed china. The cultural capital exchanged in ethnic intermarriage is considerably greater than that within ethnic groups."

Patterson's second claim is that removing the informal racial boundaries within the marriage market would especially benefit black women—because large numbers of white men are and will increasingly become open to marrying black women, if given a chance. He notes that if only one in five nonblack men were to court black women, the pool of potential spouses available to those women would immediately double. According to Patterson, this would be good not only because it would make marriage more accessible to black women but also because larger numbers of white (and other) suitors might well fortify black women in their dealings with black men. As Patterson sees it, by forswearing nonblack suitors, many black women have senselessly put themselves at the mercy of black men, who have declined to be as accommodating as they might be in the face of greater competition.

Patterson's third claim is that widespread intermarriage is necessary to the integration of blacks into American society. He agrees with the writer Calvin Hernton that intermarriage is "the crucial test in determining when a people have completely won their way into the mainstream of any given society." In *Ordeals of Integration* he therefore urges blacks, particularly women, to renounce their objections to interracial intimacy. Higher rates of intermarriage "will complete the process of total integration as [blacks] become to other Americans not only full members of the political and moral community, but also people whom 'we' marry," he counsels. "When that happens, the goal of integration will have been fully achieved."

Some may question whether higher rates of interracial marriage will do as much or signify as much as Patterson contends. The history of racially divided societies elsewhere suggests that it will not. Addressing "the uncertain legacy of miscegenation," Professor Anthony W. Marx, of Columbia University, writes that despite considerable race mixing in Brazil, and that country's formal repudiation of racism, Brazil nonetheless retains "an informal racial order that [discriminates] against 'blacks and browns.'" Contrary to optimistic projections, Brazil's multiracialism did not so much produce upward mobility for dark Brazilians as reinforce a myth of mobility. That myth has undergirded a pigmentocracy that continues to privilege whiteness. A similar outcome is possible in the United States. Various peoples of color—Latinos, Asian-Americans, Native Americans, and light-skinned African-Americans—could well intermarry with whites in increasingly large numbers and join with them in a de facto alliance against darker-skinned blacks, who might remain racial outcasts even in a more racially mixed society.

Historically, though, at least in the United States, openness to interracial marriage has been a good barometer of racial enlightenment in thought and practice. As a general rule, those persons most welcoming of interracial marriage (and other intimate interracial associations) are also those who have most determinedly embraced racial justice, a healthy respect for individualistic pluralism, and a belief in the essential oneness of humanity.

RANDALL KENNEDY is a professor at Harvard Law School. He is the author of *Nigger* (2002) and *Interracial Intimacies: Sex, Marriage, Identity, and Adoption*, published by Pentheon Books, January 7, 2003.

New Technologies and Our Feelings

Romance on the Internet

CHRISTINE ROSEN

When Samuel F. B. Morse sent his first long-distance telegraph message in 1844, he chose words that emphasized both the awe and apprehension he felt about his new device. "What hath God wrought?" read the paper tape message of dots and dashes sent from the U.S. Capitol building to Morse's associates in Baltimore. Morse proved prescient about the potential scope and significance of his technology. In less than a decade, telegraph wires spread throughout all but one state east of the Mississippi River; by 1861, they spanned the continent; and by 1866, a transatlantic telegraph cable connected the United States to Europe.

The telegraph, and later, the telephone, forever changed the way we communicate. But the triumph wrought by these technologies was not merely practical. Subtly and not so subtly, these technologies also altered the range of ways we reveal ourselves. Writing in 1884, James Russell Lowell wondered a bit nervously about the long-term consequences of the "trooping of emotion" that the electric telegraph, with its fragmented messages, encouraged. Lowell and others feared that the sophisticated new media we were devising might alter not just how we communicate, but how we feel.

Rapid improvement in communication technologies and the expansion of their practical uses continue unabated. Today, of course, we are no longer tethered to telegraph or telephone wires for conversation. Cell phones, e-mail, Internet chatrooms, two-way digital cameras—we can talk to anyone, anywhere, including those we do not know and never see. The ethical challenges raised by these new communication technologies are legion, and not new. Within a decade of the invention of the telephone, for example, we had designed a way to wiretap and listen in on the private conversations flourishing there. And with the Internet, we can create new or false identities for ourselves, mixing real life and personal fantasy in unpredictable ways. The "confidence man" of the nineteenth century, with his dandified ruses, is replaced by the well-chosen screen name and false autobiography of the unscrupulous Internet dater. Modern philosophers of technology have studied the ethical quandaries posed by communication technologies—questioning whether our view of new technologies as simply means to generally positive ends is naïve, and

encouraging us to consider whether our many devices have effected subtle transformations on our natures.

But too little consideration has been given to the question of how our use of these technologies influences our emotions. Do certain methods of communication flatten emotional appeals, promote immediacy rather than thoughtful reflection, and encourage accessibility and transparency at the expense of necessary boundaries? Do our technologies change the way we feel, act, and think?

Love and E-Mail

There is perhaps no realm in which this question has more salience than that of romantic love. How do our ubiquitous technologies—cell phones, e-mail, the Internet—impact our ability to find and experience love? Our technical devices are of such extraordinary practical use that we forget they are also increasingly the primary medium for our emotional expression. The technologies we use on a daily basis do not merely change the ways, logistically, we pursue love; they are in some cases transforming the way we think and feel about what, exactly, it is we should be pursuing. They change not simply how we find our beloved, but the kind of beloved we hope to find. In a world where men and women still claim to want to find that one special person—a "soul mate"—to spend their life with, what role can and should we afford technology and, more broadly, science, in their efforts?

Love After Courtship

The pursuit of love in its modern, technological guise has its roots in the decline of courtship and is indelibly marked by that loss. Courtship as it once existed—a practice that assumed adherence to certain social conventions, and recognition of the differences, physical and emotional, between men and women—has had its share of pleased obituarists. The most vigorous have been feminists, the more radical of whom appear to take special delight in quelling notions of romantic love. Recall Andrea Dworkin's infamous equation of marriage and rape, or Germaine Greer's terrifying rant in *The Female Eunuch*: "Love, love, love—all the wretched cant of it, masking egotism, lust, masochism, fantasy under a mythology of sentimental postures, a welter of self-induced miseries and joys, blinding and masking the essential personalities in the frozen gestures of courtship, in the kissing and the dating and the desire, the compliments and the quarrels which vivify its barrenness." Much of this work is merely an unpersuasive attempt to swaddle basic human bitterness in the language of female empowerment. But such sentiments have had their effect on our culture's understanding of courtship.

More thoughtful chroniclers of the institution's demise have noted the cultural and technological forces that challenged courtship in the late nineteenth and early twentieth century, eroding the power of human chaperones, once its most effective guardians. As Leon Kass persuasively argued in an essay in *The Public Interest*, the obstacles to courtship "spring from the very heart of liberal democratic society and of modernity altogether." The automobile did more for unsupervised sexual exploration than many technologies in use today, for example, and by twentieth century's end, the ease and availability of effective contraceptive devices, especially the birth control pill, had freed men and women to pursue sexual experience without the risk of pregnancy. With technical advances came a shift in social mores. As historian Jacques Barzun has noted, strict manners gave way to informality, "for etiquette is a barrier, the casual style an invitation."

Whether one laments or praises courtship's decline, it is clear that we have yet to locate a successful replacement for it—evidently it is not as simple as hustling the aging coquette out the door to make way for the vigorous debutante. On the contrary, our current courting practices—if they can be called that—yield an increasing number of those aging coquettes, as well as scores of unsettled bachelors. On college campuses, young men and women have long since ceased formally dating and instead participate in a "hooking up" culture that favors the sexually promiscuous and emotionally disinterested while punishing those intent on commitment. Adults hardly fare better: as the author of a report released in January by the Chicago Health and Social Life Survey told CNN, "on average, half your life is going to be in this single and dating state, and this is a big change from the 1950s." Many men and women now spend the decades of their twenties and thirties sampling each other's sexual wares and engaging in fits of serial out-of-wedlock domesticity, never finding a marriageable partner.

In the 1990s, books such as *The Rules*, which outlined a rigorous and often self-abnegating plan for modern dating, and observers such as Wendy Shalit, who called for greater modesty and the withholding of sexual favors by women, represented a well-intentioned, if doomed, attempt to revive the old courting boundaries. Cultural observers today, however, claim we are in the midst of a new social revolution that requires looking to the future for solutions, not the past. "We're in a period of dramatic change in our mating practices," Barbara Dafoe Whitehead told a reporter for *U.S. News & World Report* recently. Whitehead, co-director of the National Marriage Project at Rutgers University, is the author of *Why There are No Good Men Left,* one in a booming mini-genre of books that offer road maps for the revolution. Whitehead views technology as one of our best solutions—Isolde can now find her Tristan on the Internet (though presumably with a less tragic finale). "The traditional mating system

where people met someone in their neighborhood or college is pretty much dead," Whitehead told CBS recently. "What we have is a huge population of working singles who have limited opportunities to go through some elaborate courtship."

Although Whitehead is correct in her diagnosis of the problem, neither she nor the mavens of modesty offer a satisfactory answer to this new challenge. A return to the old rules and rituals of courtship—however appealing in theory—is neither practical nor desirable for the majority of men and women. But the uncritical embrace of technological solutions to our romantic malaise—such as Internet dating—is not a long-term solution either. What we need to do is create new boundaries, devise better guideposts, and enforce new mores for our technological age. First, however, we must understand the peculiar challenges to romantic success posed by our technologies.

Full Disclosure

Although not the root cause of our romantic malaise, our communication technologies are at least partly culpable, for they encourage the erosion of the boundaries that are necessary for the growth of successful relationships. Our technologies enable and often promote two detrimental forces in modern relationships: the demand for total transparency and a bias toward the oversharing of personal information.

To Google or Not to Google

With the breakdown of the old hierarchies and boundaries that characterized courtship, there are far fewer opportunities to glean information about the vast world of strangers we encounter daily. We can little rely on town gossips or networks of extended kin for background knowledge; there are far fewer geographic boundaries marking people from "the good part of town"; no longer can we read sartorial signals, such as a well-cut suit or an expensive shoe, to place people as in earlier ages. This is all, for the most part, a good thing. But how, then, do people find out about each other? Few self-possessed people with an Internet connection could resist answering that question with one word: Google. "To google"—now an acceptable if ill-begotten verb—is the practice of typing a person's name into an Internet search engine to find out what the world knows and says about him or her. As one writer confessed in the *New York Observer*, after meeting an attractive man at a midtown bar: "Like many of my twenty-something peers in New York's dating jungle, I have begun to use Google.com, as well as other online search engines, to perform secret background checks on potential mates. It's not perfect, but it's a discreet way of obtaining important, useless and sometimes bizarre information about people in Manhattan—and it's proven to be as reliable as the scurrilous gossip you get from friends."

That is—not reliable at all. What Google and other Internet search engines provide is a quick glimpse—a best and worst list—of a person, not a fully drawn portrait. In fact, the transparency promised by technologies such as Internet search engines is a convenient substitute for something we used to assume would develop over time, but which fewer people today seem willing to cultivate patiently: trust. As the single Manhattanite writing in the *Observer* noted, "You never know. He seemed nice that night, but he could be anyone from a rapist or murderer to a brilliant author or championship swimmer."

In sum, transparency does not guarantee trust. It can, in fact, prove effective at eroding it—especially when the expectation of transparency and the available technological tools nudge the suspicious to engage in more invasive forms of investigation or surveillance. One woman I interviewed, who asked that her name not be revealed, was suspicious that her live-in boyfriend of two years was unfaithful when her own frequent business trips took her away from home. Unwilling to confront him directly with her doubts, she turned to a technological solution. Unbeknownst to him, she installed a popular brand of "spyware" on his computer, which recorded every keystroke he made and took snapshots of his screen every three minutes—information that the program then e-mailed to her for inspection. "My suspicions were founded," she said, although the revelation was hardly good news. "He was spending hours online looking at porn, and going to 'hook-up' chatrooms seeking sex with strangers. I even tracked his ATM withdrawals to locations near his scheduled meetings with other women."

She ended the relationship, but remains unrepentant about deploying surveillance technology against her mate. Considering the amount of information she could find out about her partner by merely surfing the Internet, she rationalized her use of spyware as just one more tool—if a slightly more invasive one—at the disposal of those seeking information about another person. As our technologies give us ever-greater power to uncover more about each other, demand for transparency rises, and our expectations of privacy decline.

The other destructive tendency our technologies encourage is over-sharing—that is, revealing too much, too quickly, in the hope of connecting to another person. The opportunities for instant communication are so ubiquitous—e-mail, instant messaging, chatrooms, cell phones, Palm Pilots, BlackBerrys, and the like—that the notion of making ourselves unavailable to anyone is unheard of, and constant access a near-requirement. As a result, the multitude of outlets for expressing ourselves has allowed the level of idle chatter to reach a depressing din. The inevitable result is a repeal of the reticence necessary for fostering successful relationships in the long term. Information about another person is best revealed a bit at a time, in a give-and-take exchange, not in a rush of overexposed feeling.

The Bachelor

Perhaps the best example of this tendency is reality TV and its spawn. Programs like *The Bachelor* and *The Bachelorette*, as well as pseudo-documentary shows such as *A Dating Story* (and *A Wedding Story* and *A Baby Story*) on The Learning Channel, transform the longings of the human heart into top Nielsen ratings by encouraging the lovelorn to discuss in depth and at length every feeling they have, every moment they have it, as the cameras roll. Romances begin, blossom, and occasionally end in the space of half an hour, and audiences—privy to even the most excruciatingly staged expressions of love and devotion—neverthe-

less gain the illusion of having seen "real" examples of dating, wedding, or marriage.

On the Internet, dating blogs offer a similar sophomoric voyeurism. One dating blogger, who calls himself Quigley, keeps a dreary tally of his many unsuccessful attempts to meet women, peppering his diary with adolescent observations about women he sees on television. Another dating blogger, who describes herself as an "attractive 35-year old," writes "A Day in the Life of Jane," a dating diary about her online dating travails. Reflecting on one of her early experiences, she writes: "But what did I learn from Owen? That online dating isn't so different from regular dating. It has its pros and cons: Pros—you learn a lot more about a person much more quickly, that a person isn't always what they seem or what you believe them to be, that you have to be really honest with yourself and the person you are communicating with; Cons—uh, same as the pros!"

BadXPartners.com

Successful relationships are not immune to the over-sharing impulse, either; a plethora of wedding websites such as SharetheMoments.com and TheKnot.com offer up the intimate details of couples' wedding planning and ceremonies—right down to the brand of tie worn by the groom and the "intimate" vows exchanged by the couple. And, if things go awry, there are an increasing number of revenge websites such as BadXPartners.com, which offers people who've been dumped an opportunity for petty revenge. "Create a comical case file of your BadXPartners for the whole world to see!" the website urges. Like the impulse to Google, the site plays on people's fears of being misled, encouraging people to search the database for stories of bad exes: "Just met someone new? Think they are just the one for you? Well remember, they are probably someone else's X …. Find out about Bill from Birmingham's strange habits or Tracy from Texas' suspect hygiene. Better safe than sorry!"

Like the steady work of the wrecking ball, our culture's nearly-compulsive demand for personal revelation, emotional exposure, and sharing of feelings threatens the fragile edifice of newly-forming relationships. Transparency and complete access are exactly what you want to avoid in the early stages of romance. Successful courtship—even successful flirtation—require the gradual peeling away of layers, some deliberately constructed, others part of a person's character and personality, that make us mysteries to each other.

Among Pascal's minor works is an essay, "Discourse on the Passion of Love," in which he argues for the keen "pleasure of loving without daring to tell it." "In love," Pascal writes, "silence is of more avail than speech…there is an eloquence in silence that penetrates more deeply than language can." Pascal imagined his lovers in each other's physical presence, watchful of unspoken physical gestures, but not speaking. Only gradually would they reveal themselves. Today such a tableau seems as arcane as Kabuki theater; modern couples exchange the most intimate details of their lives on a first date and then return home to blog about it.

"It's difficult," said one woman I talked to who has tried—and ultimately soured on—Internet dating. "You're expected to be both informal and funny in your e-mails, and reveal your likes and dislikes, but you don't want to reveal so much that you appear desperate, or so little so that you seem distant." We can, of course, use these technologies appropriately and effectively in the service of advancing a relationship, but to do so both people must understand the potential dangers. One man I interviewed described a relationship that began promisingly but quickly took a technological turn for the worse. After a few successful dates, he encouraged the woman he was seeing, who lived in another city, to keep in touch. Impervious to notions of technological etiquette, however, she took this to mean the floodgates were officially open. She began telephoning him at all hours, sending overly-wrought e-mails and inundating him with lengthy, faxed letters—all of which had the effect not of bringing them closer together, which was clearly her hope, but of sending him scurrying away as fast as he could. Later, however, he became involved in a relationship in which e-mail in particular helped facilitate the courtship, and where technology—bounded by a respect on the part of both people for its excesses—helped rather than harmed the process of learning about another person. Technology itself is not to blame; it is our ignorance of its potential dangers and our unwillingness to exercise self-restraint in its use that makes mischief.

The Modern-Day Matchmaker

Internet dating offers an interesting case study of these technological risks, for it encourages both transparency and oversharing, as well as another danger: it insists that we reduce and market ourselves as the disembodied sum of our parts. The woman or man you might have met on the subway platform or in a coffee shop—within a richer context that includes immediate impressions based on the other person's physical gestures, attire, tone of voice, and overall demeanor—is instead electronically embalmed for your efficient perusal online.

And it is a booming business. Approximately forty percent of American adults are single, and half of that population claims to have visited an online dating site. Revenue for online dating services exceeded $302 million in 2002. There is, not surprisingly, something for the profusion of tastes: behemoth sites such as Match.com, Flirt.com, Hypermatch.com, and Matchmaker.com traffic in thousands of profiles. Niche sites such as Dateable.org for people with disabilities, as well as sites devoted to finding true love for foot fetishists, animal lovers, and the obese, cater to smaller markets. Single people with religious preferences can visit Jdate.com (for Jewish dates), CatholicSingles.com, and even HappyBuddhist.com to find similarly-minded spiritual singles. As with any product, new features are added constantly to maintain consumer interest; even the more jaded seekers of love might quail at Match.com's recent addition to its menu of online options: a form of "speed dating" that offers a certain brutal efficiency as a lure for the time-challenged modern singleton.

A Case Study

One woman I interviewed, an attractive, successful consultant, tried online dating because her hectic work schedule left her little time to meet new people. She went to Match.com, entered her zip code, and began perusing profiles. She quickly decided to post her own. "When you first put your profile on Match.com," she said, "it's like walking into a kennel with a pork chop around your neck. You're bombarded with e-mails from men." She received well over one hundred solicitations. She responded to a few with a "wink," an electronic gesture that allows another person to know you've seen their profile and are interested—but not interested enough to commit to sending an e-mail message. More alluring profiles garnered an e-mail introduction.

After meeting several different men for coffee, she settled on one in particular and they dated for several months. The vagaries of online dating, however, quickly present new challenges to relationship etiquette. In her case, after several months of successful dating, she and her boyfriend agreed to take their Match.com profiles down from the site. Since they were no longer "single and looking," but single and dating, this seemed to make sense—at least to her. Checking Match.com a week later, however, she found her boyfriend's profile still up and actively advertising himself as available. They are still together, although she confesses to a new wariness about his willingness to commit.

The rapid growth of Internet dating has led to the erosion of the stigma that used to be attached to having "met someone on the Internet" (although none of the people I interviewed for this article would allow their names to be used). And Internet dating itself is becoming increasingly professionalized—with consultants, how-to books, and "expert" analysis crowding out the earlier generation of websites. This February, a "commonsense guide to successful Internet dating" entitled *I Can't Believe I'm Buying This Book* hit bookstores. *Publishers Weekly* describes the author, an "Internet dating consultant," as "a self-proclaimed online serial dater" who "admits he's never sustained a relationship for more than seven months," yet nevertheless "entertainingly reviews how to present one's self on the Web."

Designing the "dating software" that facilitates online romance is a science all its own. *U.S. News & World Report* recently described the efforts of Michael Georgeff, who once designed software to aid the space shuttle program, to devise similar algorithms to assess and predict people's preferences for each other. "Say you score a 3 on the introvert scale, and a 6 on touchy-feely," he told a reporter. "Will you tend to like somebody who's practical?" His weAttract.com software purports to provide the answer. On the company's website, amid close-ups of the faces of a strangely androgynous, snuggling couple, weAttract—whose software is used by Match.com—encourages visitors to "Find someone who considers your quirks adorable." Fair enough. But the motto of weAttract—"Discover your instinctual preferences"—is itself a contradiction. If preferences are instinctual, why do you need the aid of experts like weAttract to discover them?

We need them because we have come to mistrust our own sensibilities. What is emerging on the Internet is a glorification of scientific and technological solutions to the challenge of finding love. The expectation of romantic happiness is so great that extraordinary, scientific means for achieving it are required—or so these companies would have you believe. For example, Emode, whose pop-up ads are now so common that they are the Internet equivalent of a swarm of pesky gnats, promotes "Tickle Matchmaking," a service promising "accurate, Ph.D. certified compatibility scores with every member!"

EHarmony.com

The apotheosis of this way of thinking is a site called eHarmony.com, whose motto, "Fall in love for the right reasons," soothes prospective swains with the comforting rhetoric of professional science. "Who knew science and love were so compatible?" asks the site, which is rife with the language of the laboratory: "scientifically-proven set of compatibility principles," "based on 35 years of empirical and clinical research," "patent-pending matching technology," "exhaustively researched" methods, and "the most powerful system available." As the founder of eHarmony told *U.S. News & World Report* recently, we are all too eager—desperate, even—to hustle down the aisle. "In this culture," he said, "if we like the person's looks, if they have an ability to chatter at a cocktail party, and a little bit of status, we're halfway to marriage. We're such suckers." EHarmony's answer to such unscientific mating practices is a trademarked "Compatibility Matching System" that promises to "connect you with singles who are compatible with you in 29 of the most important areas of life." As the literature constantly reminds the dreamy romantics among us, "Surprisingly, a good match is more science than art."

EHarmony's insistence that the search for true love is no realm for amateurs is, of course, absurdly self-justifying. "You should realize," their website admonishes, after outlining the "29 dimensions" of personality their compatibility software examines, "that it is still next to impossible to correctly evaluate them on your own with each person you think may be right for you." Instead you must pay eHarmony to do it for you. As you read the "scientific" proof, the reassuring sales pitch washes over you: "Let eHarmony make sure that the next time you fall in love, it's with the right person."

In other words, don't trust your instincts, trust science. With a tasteful touch of contempt, eHarmony notes that its purpose is not merely dating, as it is for megasites such as Match.com. "Our goal is to help you find your soul mate." Four pages of testimonials on the website encourage the surrender to eHarmony's expertise, with promises of imminent collision with "your" soul mate: "From the minute we began e-mailing and talking on the phone, we knew we had found our soul mate," say Lisa and Darryl from Dover, Pennsylvania. "It took some time," confessed Annie of Kansas City, Missouri, "but once I met John, I knew that they had made good on their promise to help me find my soul mate."

Some observers see in these new "scientific" mating rituals a return to an earlier time of courtship and chaperoned dating. *Newsweek* eagerly described eHarmony as a form of "arranged marriage for the digital age, without the all-powerful parents," and Barbara Dafoe Whitehead argues that the activities of the Internet love seeker "reflect a desire for more structured dating." Promoters of these services see them as an improvement on the mere cruising of glossy photos encouraged by most dating sites, or the unrealistic expectations of "finding true love" promoted by popular culture. Rather, they say, they are like the chaperones of courtship past—vetting appropriate candidates and matching them to your specifications.

Not Real Matchmakers

As appealing as this might sound, it is unrealistic. Since these sites rely on technological solutions and mathematical algorithms, they are a far cry from the broader and richer knowledge of the old-fashioned matchmaker. A personality quiz cannot possibly reveal the full range of a person's quirks or liabilities. More importantly, the role of the old-fashioned matchmaker was a social one (and still is in certain communities). The matchmaker was embedded within a community that observed certain rituals and whose members shared certain assumptions. But technological matchmaking allows courtship to be conducted entirely in private, devoid of the social norms (and often the physical signals) of romantic success and failure.

Finally, most Internet dating enthusiasts do not contend with a far more alarming challenge: the impact such services have on our idea of what, exactly, it is we should be seeking in another person. Younger men and women, weaned on the Internet and e-mail, are beginning to express a preference for potential dates to break down their vital stats for pre-date perusal, like an Internet dating advertisement. One 25-year old man, a regular on Match.com, confessed to *U.S. News & World Report* that he wished he could have a digital dossier for all of his potential dates: "It's, 'OK, here's where I'm from, here's what I do, here's what I'm looking for. How about you?'" One woman I spoke to, who has been Internet dating for several years, matter-of-factly noted that even a perfunctory glance at a potential date's résumé saves valuable time and energy. "Why trust a glance exchanged across a crowded bar when you can read a person's biography in miniature before deciding to strike up a conversation?" she said. This intolerance for gradual revelation increases the pace of modern courtship and erodes our patience for many things (not the least of which is commencement of sexual relations). The challenge remains the same—to find another person to share your life with—but we have allowed the technologies at our disposal to alter dramatically, even unrecognizably, the way we go about achieving it.

The Science of Feeling

This impulse is part of a much broader phenomenon—the encroachment of science and technology into areas once thought the province of the uniquely intuitive and even the ineffable. Today we program computers to trounce human chess champions, produce poetry, or analyze works of art, watching eagerly as they break things down to a tedious catalog of techniques: the bishop advances, the meter scans, the paintbrush strokes across the canvas. But by enlisting machines to do what once was the creative province of human beings alone, we deliberately narrow our conceptions of genius, creativity, and art. The *New York Times* recently featured the work of Franco Moretti, a comparative literature professor at Stanford, who promotes "a more rational literary history" that jettisons the old-fashioned reading of texts in favor of statistical models of literary output. His dream, he told reporter Emily Eakin, "is of a literary class that would look more like a lab than a Platonic academy."

Yet this "scientific" approach to artistic work yields chillingly antiseptic results: "Tennyson's mind is to be treated like his intestines after a barium meal," historian Jacques Barzun noted with some exasperation of the trend's earlier incarnations. Critic Lionel Trilling parodied the tendency in 1950 in his book, *The Liberal Imagination*. By this way of thinking, Trilling said, the story of Romeo and Juliet is no longer the tragic tale of a young man and woman falling in love, but becomes instead a chronicle of how, "their libidinal impulses being reciprocal, they activated their individual erotic drives and integrated them within the same frame of reference."

What Barzun and Trilling were expressing was a distaste for viewing art as merely an abstraction of measurable, improvable impulses. The same is true for love. We can study the physiological functions of the human heart with echocardiograms, stress tests, blood pressure readings, and the like. We can examine, analyze, and investigate ad nauseum the physical act of sex. But we cannot so easily measure the desires of the heart. How do you prove that love exists? How do we know that love is "real"? What makes the love of two lovers last?

There is a danger in relying wholly or even largely on science and technology to answer these questions, for it risks eroding our appreciation of the ineffable things—intuition and physical attraction, passion and sensibility—by reducing these feelings to scientifically explained physiological facts. Today we catalog the influence of hormones, pheromones, dopamine, and serotonin in human attraction, and map our own brains to discover which synapses trigger laughter, lying, or orgasm. Evolutionary psychology explains our desire for symmetrical faces and fertile-looking forms, even as it has little to tell us about the extremes to which we are taking its directives with plastic surgery. Scientific study of our communication patterns and techniques explains why it is we talk the way we do. Even the activities of the bedroom are thoroughly analyzed and professionalized, as women today take instruction from a class of professionals whose arts used to be less esteemed. Prostitutes now run sex seminars, for example, and a recent episode of Oprah featured exotic pole dancers who teach suburban housewives how to titillate their husbands by turning the basement rec room into a simulacrum of a Vegas showgirl venue.

Science continues to turn sex (and, by association, love and romance) into something quantifiable and open to manipulation and solution. Science and technology offer us pharmaceuticals to enhance libido and erectile function, and popular culture responds by rigorously ranking and discussing all matters sexual—from the disturbingly frank talk of female characters on Sex and the City to the proliferation of "blind date" shows which subject hapless love-seekers to the withering gaze of a sarcastic host and his viewing audience. "What a loser!" cackled the host of the reality television program Blind Date, after

one ignominious bachelor botched his chance for a good night kiss. "The march of science," Barzun wrote, "produces the feeling that nobody in the past has ever done things right. Whether it's teaching or copulation, it has 'problems' that 'research' should solve by telling us just how, the best way."

Test-Driving Your Soul Mate

Why is the steady march of science and technology in these areas a problem? Shouldn't we be proud of our expanding knowledge and the tools that knowledge gives us? Not necessarily. Writing recently in the journal Techné, Hector Jose Huyke noted the broader dangers posed by the proliferation of our technologies, particularly the tendency to "devalue the near." "When a technology is introduced it, presumably, simply adds options to already existing options," he writes. But this is not how technology's influence plays out in practice. In fact, as Huyke argues, "as what is difficult to obtain becomes repeatedly and easily accessible, other practices and experiences are left out—they do not remain unchanged." The man who sends an e-mail to his brother is not merely choosing to write an e-mail and thus adding to his range of communication options; he is choosing not to make a phone call or write a letter. A woman who e-mails a stranger on the Internet is choosing not to go to a local art exhibit and perhaps meet someone in person. "Communications technologies indeed multiply options," says Huyke. "An increase in options, however, does not imply or even serve an advance in communications." Technologies, in other words, often make possible "what would otherwise be difficult to obtain." But they do so by eliminating other paths.

Personal Ads

Love and genuine commitment have always been difficult to attain, and they are perhaps more so today since it is the individual bonds of affection—not family alliance, property transfer, social class, or religious orthodoxy—that form the cornerstone of most modern marriages. Yet there remains a certain grim efficiency to the vast realm of love technologies at our disposal. After a while, perusing Internet personal ads is like being besieged by an aggressive real estate agent hoping to unload that tired brick colonial. Each person points out his or her supposedly unique features with the same banal descriptions ("adventurous," "sexy," "trustworthy") never conveying a genuine sense of the whole. Machine metaphors, tellingly, crop up often, with women and men willingly categorizing themselves as "high maintenance" or "low maintenance," much as one might describe a car or small kitchen appliance. As an executive of one online dating service told a reporter recently, "If you want to buy a car, you get a lot of information before you even test-drive. There hasn't been a way to do that with relationships."

But we have been "test driving" something: a new, technological method of courtship. And although it is too soon to deliver a final verdict, it is clear that it is a method prone to serious problems. The efficiency of our new techniques and their tendency to focus on people as products leaves us at risk of understanding ourselves this way, too—like products with certain malfunctioning parts and particular assets. But products must be constantly improved upon and marketed. In the pursuit of love, and in a world where multiple partners are sampled before one is selected, this fuels a hectic culture of self-improvement—honing the witty summary of one's most desirable traits for placement in personal advertisements is only the beginning. Today, men and women convene focus groups of former lovers to gain critical insights into their behavior so as to avoid future failure; and the perfection of appearance through surgical and non-surgical means occupies an increasing amount of people's time and energy.

Our new technological methods of courtship also elevate efficient communication over personal communication. Ironically, the Internet, which offers many opportunities to meet and communicate with new people, robs us of the ability to deploy one of our greatest charms—nonverbal communication. The emoticon is a weak substitute for a coy gesture or a lusty wink. More fundamentally, our technologies encourage a misunderstanding of what courtship should be. Real courtship is about persuasion, not marketing, and the techniques of the laboratory cannot help us translate the motivations of the heart.

The response is not to retreat into Luddism, of course. In a world where technology allows us to meet, date, marry, and even divorce online, there is no returning to the innocence of an earlier time. What we need is a better understanding of the risks of these new technologies and a willingness to exercise restraint in using them. For better or worse, we are now a society of sexually liberated individuals seeking "soul mates"—yet the privacy, gradualism, and boundaries that are necessary for separating the romantic wheat from the chaff still elude us.

Alchemy

Perhaps, in our technologically saturated age, we would do better to rediscover an earlier science: alchemy. Not alchemy in its original meaning—a branch of speculative philosophy whose devotees attempted to create gold from base metals and hence cure disease and prolong life—but alchemy in its secondary definition: "a power or process of transforming something common into something precious." From our daily, common interactions with other people might spring something precious—but only if we have the patience to let it flourish. Technology and science often conspire against such patience. Goethe wrote, "We should do our utmost to encourage the Beautiful, for the Useful encourages itself." There is an eminent usefulness to many of our technologies—e-mail and cell phones allow us to span great distances to communicate with family, friends, and lovers, and the Internet connects us to worlds unknown. But they are less successful at encouraging the flourishing of the lasting and beautiful. Like the Beautiful, love occurs in unexpected places, often not where it is being sought. It can flourish only if we accept that our technologies and our science can never fully explain it.

CHRISTINE ROSEN is a senior editor of *The New Atlantis* and resident fellow at the Ethics and Public Policy Center. Her book *Preaching Eugenics: Religious Leaders and the American Eugenics Movement* was just published by Oxford University Press.

Lust for the Long Haul

The road to long-term passion starts with a surprise: intimacy requires soul-searching, not romancing. Love is an existential challenge, and the reward is a sex life that grows richer (and raunchier) with time.

ELIZABETH DEVITA-RAEBURN

When my husband and I started dating, we quickly became one of those obnoxious couples who couldn't keep their hands off each other. We kissed every time we stopped at a crosswalk—in New York, that's a lot. At Starbucks we were so grotesque—staring into each other's eyes, stroking each other's arms—that when the branch removed its tables and converted to carryout, we wondered if we were the reason. Once, during a protracted public goodbye, a group of teenagers actually screeched at us to get a room.

We did more than that. We got married. Like most couples in the throes of passion, we were smug, convinced that all the clichés about things slowing down described partners who weren't meant to be together in the first place. But slowly, things did cool off. We still loved one another, still held hands. But the crosswalk kissing and the subway platform clinches faded away. Instead of long weekend mornings in bed, we started getting up early and going to the gym.

I couldn't help (a) noticing, and (b) torturing myself about what it meant. You'd have to be hiding under a rock for the last decade not to know that half of all marriages now end in divorce, and that sexual difficulties are one of the leading complaints of unhappy couples. Was this how it begins?

It's some consolation that many other Americans face the same question. In the benchmark survey of desire, roughly one-third of all adults reported having some kind of sexual problem during the previous year. Some pundits blame gender politics, job stress and cultural changes. Others, more cynical, point to the monotony of marriage. But these plausible (and socially acceptable) explanations obscure a more disquieting truth. Sex, and more importantly, intimacy, are grown-up skills, and most of us, metaphorically speaking, are still in junior high. We're still clinging to the idea of romance, when real intimacy requires something a lot more difficult: pushing past your own limits to become a more fully developed human being.

Conventional wisdom holds that an intimate couple thinks pretty much the same way about most things. You connect seamlessly—especially in bed. But according to the radical ideas of the marital and sex therapist David Schnarch, we've got it all backward. "Sex is inherently based on intimacy. The problem is that most people have a very misguided idea of what intimacy means," he says. "There's this idea that your partner is going to make you feel good and validate you." It's our cultural template for "true" love. Think Tom Cruise in *Jerry McGuire* declaring his love for Renée Zellweger: "You complete me," he says, with trembling lip.

Except that no one has a marriage like that. What's more, says Schnarch, no one should. Sure, the you-complete-me stuff works fine in the beginning. It's even fun. Like two people cinched together for a three-legged race, there is satisfaction in getting the groove of operating side-by-side with perfect fluidity. But when you try to keep those tethers on indefinitely, reality intrudes. Two people aren't going to agree on every move. And they'll get tired of always accommodating the other—by keeping quiet, by moving the same way, by propping the other one up.

Sooner or later, a lot of these three-legged marriages wind up in gridlock: Each partner is increasingly frustrated by the other's apparent unwillingness to get on the same page—and each becomes increasingly annoyed and worried about it. It's in this juncture, where the conflict between real intimacy and wishful thinking rears its head, that many of us notice the sex ain't what it used to be. But while we fear that this is the beginning of the end, Schnarch says it's often when things finally start to go right. It means marriage is beginning the relentless process of doing what it's supposed to do, nudging us away from the Renée-Tom model of partnership and forcing us to figure out who we are as individuals.

Real intimacy is frightening. It requires a kind of openness, honesty and self-respect that most of us aren't used to. But Schnarch's 30 years of counseling couples has convinced him that it's worth it. A truly intimate connection between adults is less volatile, because couples aren't ticked off about what their partner is or isn't doing to prop them up. It's more solid, because it's based on reality. "Ultimately, you get through gridlock and get to a place of more honest self-disclosure, where the focus is on being known, rather than being validated," he says. Best of all, the sex often becomes more relaxed, creative and connected. Literally and figuratively, no one's hiding in the dark anymore.

Sex Shockers

Everything you know about sex is only a first step. Most advice for couples doesn't go far enough—as a result, basic truths about long-term passion are surprising.

WE CAN ALL RECITE the mantras of modern sex advice: Tell your partner what you want; focus on how your body feels; relax. Since it's only natural, goes this idea, great sex is a matter of getting over your hang-ups, loving your partner and "letting go."

Yet something doesn't add up, as the huge market for self-help books and advice columnists proves. As a nation, we're not getting any. We crave sexual bliss—but all our relaxing and getting-in-touch isn't helping most of us. When the standard advice doesn't work, you feel like a failure: Too uptight. Not "in your body." Worse, maybe you're not really in love.

While the "relax and connect" advice isn't wrong, it's just a first step, addressing mechanics rather than the deeper dynamics at the heart of sexuality.

1. **MANY PEOPLE DON'T REALLY WANT GREAT SEX.** Good sexual experiences can be emotionally overpowering—mind-blowing, rather than warm and comforting. Lusty sex requires you to confront all kinds of worries—getting so close to your partner that he or she overwhelms you, or being rejected at an intensely vulnerable moment. It may even put you in touch with your own mortality, reminding you that your partner won't always be around. Great sex requires inner reserves to tolerate the angst.

2. **IT GETS BETTER WITH AGE.** Even though young people get aroused more quickly, amazing sex is a specialty of people in their 50s and 60s, contends Schnarch. In youth, women struggle to be sexual but not "cheap"; men are easily threatened. Midway through life, you have a stronger sense of self and are less self-conscious and insecure.

3. **COMPROMISE MAY NOT WORK.** Trade-offs (I'll do this if you'll do that) may seem egalitarian, but in practice, each partner rules out anything that makes him or her uptight. The couple is left with a limited repertoire that guarantees boredom, not to mention scorekeeping and resentment when one partner is less enthusiastic than the other. Better to take the initiative and challenge yourself to try something new.

4. **WOMEN LIKE HOT SEX.** Women are often much more interested than men in talking about "fucking"—horny, lusty, intense sex—Schnarch reports. But in bed, they often hold back out of shame or fear of making their partner feel inadequate. A lot of couples think that married sex is supposed to be gentle, affectionate "making love"—and feel guilty if they want to get nasty.

5. **SEX ISN'T A SKILL.** The hoopla about techniques is a red herring. If you think of sex as a set of talents, you're going to wind up focused on doing it right, rather than on who you're doing it with. Likewise, giving your partner a technical playbook (there but not here, this way and not that way) leads to mechanically proficient, predictable and emotionally dead sex. You may also not know exactly what you want—it changes! Pushing your own limits by organically exploring new sexual styles fosters more sizzle.

6. **CANCEL THE ORGASM DERBY.** More orgasms don't equal better sex. Lots of people can perform in bed—all the parts work just fine—but are never really satisfied, because they're too emotionally disconnected. That's usually said about men rather than women, but both sexes are capable of being physically aroused without getting any erotic charge, and both can have orgasms without really enjoying the sex. Instead of focusing on orgasms, pay more attention to the emotional and physical connection: Can you become intensely aware of your partner during sex? Can you make contact?

7. **TUNE IN—DON'T SPACE OUT.** Shutting down your brain, focusing on your sensations and going into a trance state, or fantasizing about others, all of which sex therapists often recommend, may help you have decent sex, since it can jumpstart your engine. But by zeroing in on your body or your thoughts alone, you've tuned out your partner. You're also vulnerable to distractions: The mood can easily be shattered by a car alarm. Shifting your focus to include your partner can make the experience much more intense.

—Kathleen McGowan

Learning The Language of Sex

WHEN COUPLES DO try to address their sexual problems, they often focus on mechanics: Viagra, lingerie, trying out new positions. But sex—even terrible sex—isn't engineering, says Schnarch. It's a language, and its content is everything else happening in the marriage. The woman who doesn't say a word but barely opens her knees for her husband is actually speaking volumes. Ditto the man who is so intent upon pleasing his unpleasable wife that he frequently loses his erection. "Even the way couples avoid having sex is a window into who they are together," he says.

Often, sexual disconnect has a similar refrain: I can't show you who I really am. People's mistaken ideas about intimacy have made them overly reliant on a partner for their own sense of self. You demand that your partner approve of you, and you begin to count on him or her to reassure you that you're normal and that your feelings are valid. This makes it difficult to be completely open or honest with each other anymore. One or both of you begins to feel suffocated, and the intense vulnerability of sexual passion that was so easy in the early days becomes impossible.

Tammy, 36, and her husband, Jack, 34, struggled for years with mismatched sexual desire. Jack wanted to have sex all the time. Tammy avoided it. "I pretty much didn't care if I never had sex again," she says now. For her marriage's sake, she'd tried supplements and testosterone cream to increase her desire. They hadn't worked. Nor had a therapist who'd advised Tammy to try a little novelty—like running a hairbrush all over her husband's body. "I already didn't want to have sex," says Tammy, still irritated, "and I definitely didn't want to do that." By the time they wound up at Schnarch's office, they were inches away from divorce.

Through three intensive days in therapy, it became obvious that Tammy's problem wasn't biological. Jack was needy, emotionally, and looked to Tammy to make him feel better, in and out of bed. Tammy, like many women, played the caregiver role to the hilt. She was a teacher, she had two small children, and she was even contemplating a new career as a nurse.

They began to realize, with Schnarch's guidance, that although they felt estranged from each other, they were in fact completely interdependent. Jack didn't know how to soothe himself when he was feeling anxious. He looked to Tammy, and to sex, for that. For her part, Tammy had no idea how to take care of her own feelings, or even what they were. Nor did she have the energy, because so much went to propping up Jack. In some unconscious way, by avoiding sex with him, she was saying *no more*.

With time, one of you begins to feel suffocated, and the vulnerability of sexual passion becomes impossible.

For their relationship to survive, each needed to take a step back and change how they individually dealt with their own emotions, rather than leaning on—and resenting—the other. Jack had to learn to deal with his neediness on his own, and recognize that he couldn't expect his wife to do it for him. Tammy had to figure out who she was and what she wanted, or live her life without really ever knowing herself—much less getting to be known by anyone else. And she had to speak up when she disagreed, rather than keep quiet in order to not rock the boat.

A year later, Tammy and Jack are utterly honest with each other. No hiding. "Before we would just not talk about any of our problems because we didn't want to get each other upset," Tammy says. Now, she says, they always say what they are thinking or feeling, regardless of the reaction they anticipate. "It can be very uncomfortable," she admits. "And I'm still working on tact." But in their case, she says, it changed everything. Over the course of several months spent learning to be themselves together, Tammy's sex drive returned. They're happier than they've ever been, she says: "We just renewed our vows in Vegas."

How Sex Makes Grown-ups

Schnarch's way of thinking about the interdependence of sex and intimacy is a big shift from the traditional focus on anxiety as a primary cause of sexual difficulty. Problems in the bedroom are too often seen as distinct from the emotional struggles of marriage and partnership. But Schnarch—and a few other therapists—have developed an alternative view, one that puts partnership at the heart of sexuality and puts both sexuality and intimacy at the center of human development. Sexual difficulties are a kind of emotional Rorschach test that offers a glimpse into not just the dynamics of the relationship, but the continuing agenda of growing into a fully autonomous human being.

Sex isn't engineering. It's a language, and its content is everything else happening in the marriage.

Schnarch says that what happens with many troubled couples is analogous to what happens in children as they mature emotionally. A key developmental task of adolescence is to form separate and unique identities from our parents. (That's what the dismissive remarks and the skin piercings are all about.) We assume that by the time we're married, we're past all that. Not true, says Schnarch. We've merely switched our focus from our parents to our spouses. Temporarily, some of us adopt joined-at-the-hip intimacy as an archetype of marriage. But the rebelliousness, the need to separate ourselves, kicks in again. You know it, Schnarch says, when you begin to find yourself more at odds with your partner and less sexually attracted to each other than you used to be.

Or you know it when you engage in something he calls arguing about reality. That is, you both experience an event—a movie, or a remembered moment from your past together. But you see it in entirely different ways, and you can't stop arguing until one of you caves in. Schnarch describes one couple's memories of the birth of their first child. The wife thought it was the closest moment they'd ever shared—but her husband remembered being nauseated by the blood. Their contradictory views of this event became part of a bitter argument that surfaced again and again. Because neither of them would accept the other's point of view, they felt that they were drifting apart. In Schnarch's view, this difference of opinion was normal, not an indication that their relationship was falling apart. They are, after all, two different people.

Schnarch's treatment usually involves intense four-day sessions, and doesn't lend itself to quick tips. All the same, there are basic behavioral shifts that he finds can benefit many unhappy couples. They all involve the same process: Each partner takes responsibility for his or her own emotions and learns to tolerate the idea that his or her partner is not a spiritual twin. That means no longer expecting a partner to validate you—so that he or she can admit that sometimes your ideas are half-baked, rather than always reassuring you that you're right. You examine your own behavior and see what you expect others to do for you that you could be doing on your own—for example, learning to feel good about yourself without requiring someone else's praise and compliments.

Staying Cool When Things Get Tense

True love can be tough going: Owning up to your feelings, tolerating disagreements with your partner, and running the risk of feeling inadequate in bed takes gumption—and the ability to withstand a lot of anxiety. One key is learning how to soothe yourself.

"It can be as simple as regulating your body: deep breathing, sitting in a less tense position, or taking a moment to reflect," says psychologist Ruth Morehouse, Schnarch's wife and office partner. Once you've let some of your physical anxiety dissipate, you can address the mental aspects of your emotional tension: telling yourself you've been through this before and survived, reminding yourself that your partner isn't *trying* to drive you insane. Essentially, you give yourself an extra beat between stimulus and reaction so that you think before you act or blurt. You acknowledge the feelings, but don't let them threaten your sense of self or determine how you respond.

In the longer term, anxiety-reducing habits such as Pilates, listening to classical music, meditation, running or cooking also help increase your threshold. Most people already have a number of self-soothing tools they use in their life, says Morehouse—it's often a matter of recognizing what you already do and learning to apply it to situations that make you particularly uncomfortable. If you're doing it right, you'll feel calmer and more in control, says Morehouse. And it'll give you greater freedom to be authentic around your partner—come what may.

—EDR

Marriage Isn't the Only Struggle

STAKING OUT YOUR OWN identity is a particular challenge in marriage, but it crops up in other relationships, too. The basic struggle is the same: Figuring out where "I" ends and "we" begin.

- **ON THE JOB:** Ideally, you want to be part of a harmonious team, but also respected for speaking your mind. Negotiating your level of autonomy is a new task in each workplace, says Morehouse, and some employers are more amenable to exploration than others. Tread carefully.
- **WITH FRIENDS:** When a friend says something hurtful, should you assert yourself, or let it slide? Many women back away rather than try to address and resolve the conflict, often out of a misguided desire to be "nice." Deep, meaningful friendships—which can last longer than many marriages—often have something in common, says Morehouse: "At some point, someone was willing to take a risk and speak up."
- **WITH KIDS:** Think of the mother whose e-mail address starts with "juliesmom." Parents, particularly mothers, get lost in this demanding role, to the point that everything the kids do (or don't do) feels like a reflection of them. The urge to control their kids' lives becomes overwhelming and unhealthy. "Parents who have no sense of self can be very destructive to the people they love," says Schnarch.

Child rearing is an excellent opportunity to develop your boundaries, says Horehouse. Host likely, you'll be watching your kids struggle with the same issues. At some point, for instance, your kids will probably have to decide whether to go along with the crowd, dress differently or stick up for a less popular friend. Most likely, you'll feel compelled to tell them that standing up for themselves is important. The question to ask yourself: Do you practice what you preach?

—EDR

But don't expect your partner to applaud when you tell the truth about yourself. Learn to lick your own wounds—it's not your partner's job to soothe you, it's yours. Try to tell the truth for the right reason. Being honest doesn't mean being vindictive. "The idea is that you are telling each other the truth, even when it is difficult, out of caring and commitment, not because you're pissed off and want to carve each other up," he says. The irony, says Schnarch, is that rather than increasing conflict between couples—as you would think might happen—emotional honesty has the opposite effect. The issue is no longer about what your partner does or doesn't do: You can accept that they, like all people, have their own limitations and failings. Instead, the focus shifts to you, and whether you're being a grown-up—or not.

The Joys of Adulthood

Schnarch is still something of a maverick in the field of sex therapy. Talk to 10 sex therapists (I did), and you'll get 10 strong opinions. Some think he's done the sex and marital therapy version of cracking the code of DNA. Others find his ideas interesting, but don't believe that they apply to all couples. Many say they incorporate a little of what he preaches into their practice—"like a spice in a tomato sauce." The Atlanta-based marital therapist Frank Pittman, author of a self-help book

Happy Adult, is one whose approach resembles Schnarch's. "What he's doing is teaching people the joys of adulthood," he says, "of the wonderful things that can happen in a relationship when you take responsibility for yourself, whether you've got your pants on at the moment or not."

The reward for all of this hard work, say Schnarch, Pittman and others, is a kind of intimacy that helps you be more of the person you want to be and supports an intense lifelong bond. In return you are seen, known and understood—truly—for who you are. And loved and desired, to boot. It's a rare thing, perhaps the most powerful connection we can hope for.

With this outing of yourself, so to speak, goes a greater freedom in bed. You're no longer pretending. Schnarch considers the ability, for example, to look into your partner's eyes while engaged in a sexual act or in the midst of orgasm to be the height of intimacy. It's an act of mutual self-revelation that cannot be matched almost anywhere else in life. "Once people try it, they totally get what real intimacy is about," he says.

Eye-to-eye sex is not for the faint of heart. Even Schnarch's wife, psychologist Ruth Morehouse, who now works with him as a marital and sex therapist and uses his techniques, confesses to having had her doubts. At the time that her husband was developing his ideas in the 1980s, she says, she wasn't crazy about them. She describes herself at that time as fairly reliant on others to give her great feedback about herself, personally and professionally. She wasn't too keen to grow up, in the way her husband advocated. And the eyes-open thing, well. "At first, I was mad at him for even suggesting that this is something that people were supposed to do," says Morehouse. "It was a stretch for me. At first, I literally couldn't keep my eyes open. After a couple of times, I was able to do it, and it made sex more emotional and meaningful. It's now a routine part of my sex life."

Don't expect your partner to applaud when you tell the truth about yourself. Learn to nurse your own wounds.

Does this mean that all sexual issues can be solved this way? Probably not. Growing up won't do a lot for a faulty blood vessel that's contributing to an erection problem. Or for the couple who are genuinely exhausted from chasing small children around all day. But it maps out some promising new territory, where personal growth and existential concerns become as much a part of sexual therapy as do anxiety and pathology. Schnarch is creating a new way of thinking built on growth and possibilities. Making relationships, and sex, better. How could anyone not be fascinated by the potential?

As for me, I suspect I still have a lot of growing up to do. (Arguing about reality? Guilty.) And I haven't dared bring up the idea of eyes-open sex with my husband yet, for fear he'll take me up on it. I have a feeling I'd have to keep my eyes open with pliers. But I am intrigued. And now, as I stand on subway platforms or street corners, watching couples who really ought to get a room groping one another without shame, I don't feel as if I've been banished to the land of slippers and ratty bathrobes. Because according to Schnarch's model, in which sex only gets better as you get older and wiser, I'm ahead of the game. Or at least those couples. And that makes me feel smug all over again.

ELIZABETH DEVITA-RAEBURN is the author of the *Empty Room: Surviving the Loss of a Brother or Sister at Any Age.*

From *Psychology Today*, January/February 2006, pp. 41–42, 44, 47–48. Copyright © 2006 by Sussex Publishers, Inc. Reprinted by permission.

Reinventing Sex

New Technologies and Changing Attitudes

New technologies will promote pleasure, simulate reality, improve performance, and thwart disease.

Eric Garland

Tends in family, religion, health, education, and technology are changing how we view and discuss sexual matters — including marriage, courtship, and the act itself—and what they mean in our lives. Though new confusions will arise from increasing freedoms, sex in 2025 will be healthier and safer than ever before. There will be less shame, more tolerance, and less violence. Sexual activity will even become widely accepted as an important aspect of healthy aging and a regular component of geriatric life.

While a great deal of published research on sex today covers pregnancy, disease, and violence, comparatively little expert literature available deals with how sex will change in coming decades, according to a 2003 white paper by the Planned Parenthood Federation of America. This makes sense, because these topics pose the greatest risks to health and society. Very little research shows positive trends in human interaction. Not enough understanding exists to show how the basic human function of sexual behavior will shift along with trends in society and technology.

The mainstream media cover changes in divorce and dating, but the ways in which sexuality and attitudes toward sex will change in coming decades are topics that require more investigation. Indeed, the media will cover many of these shifts, leaving fewer people to feel isolated about their natural inclinations. Unfortunately, few sexuality topics are deemed appropriate to discuss forthrightly, despite the fact that so much regarding sex is changing under our noses.

For example, it has become acceptable and even commonplace for macho sports heroes, NFL coaches, and NASCAR drivers to talk about erectile dysfunction and hawk products like Viagra and Levitra during football broadcasts. DirecTV allows satellite television viewers to download adult movies at home instead of facing the embarrassment of renting them from 16-year-old video store clerks. Even blockbuster fiction is not exempt from profound changes in sexual attitudes and open discussion of sexual variation: Characters in the murder mystery *The DaVinci Code* believe in

communion with God though the holy act of sex instead of through a formal church structure. Despite condemning this idea as inflammatory and heretical, religious leaders offered only a tepid response to author Dan Brown and coordinated few if any boycotts.

It is not always easy to uncover trends in sexuality; there is little to show the subtle ways sex has an impact on society. The following trends are changing the way we practice and think about sex and sexuality. To explore how sex will change, I will discuss social trends and technological trends separately.

Waning Church Influence

Without church structures to lay down rules, individuals have more choices than ever before on morality issues such as sex, and they will have even more choices in the future. Formal church structures have been telling people what they can do sexually and how they should feel about it. It is natural that sexual activity will be judged by society, as this behavior fundamentally affects the health and prosperity of social groups from the tribe to the nationstate. Historically, formal churches have dictated these rules, but their authority in modern society seems to be slipping, along with church attendance.

Generation X and the millennial generation have not experienced organized churches having so much sway on any subject, even trivial ones, as previous generations have. A 1996 study by the American Society of Newspaper Editors found that 34% of Gen X believes that religion is important, compared with 44% of baby boomers. Furthermore, only 27% of Gen X considers themselves religious, compared with 35% of boomers. Churches, especially the ones that claim premarital and extramarital sex are sins, have been powerless against the sexual revolution. Technologies such as hormone-based birth control and good old vulcanized rubber cut people free from the real consequences of sex—birth out of wedlock and disease, for example. Without the influence of the church, individuals must decide for themselves the moral and ethical consequences of their actions.

Future generations will see even less dogma from church figures over sexual issues in 2025, and will associate less guilt about sex as coming directly from recommendations of the church.

This lack of religious structure is resulting in an increase in individual spiritual structures. While church attendance is down, more people identify themselves as simply "spiritual." The desire to be close to God has not waned, but traditional structures may not fit every person. As there are more individual spiritual structures, so will there be more people deciding what in their behavior is right and wrong—especially as it pertains to sex.

One implication of this freedom is more confusion. There will be more choice, but less of the comforting feeling that we are living our personal lives the "right way." We can also expect further backlash from cultural conservatives who prefer to follow the sexual values of the nineteenth and twentieth centuries. As more individual spiritual structures and new sexual mores pop up, we can expect fundamentalists to have plenty of reason to stay in business.

Swinging Seniors

The impact of the aging of the baby-boom generation is staggering. In 2000, 35 million people were 65 years of age or older. By 2020, that number will increase to 70 million people. The United States will be remade in the image of its aging citizens.

If you only paid attention to the media, you would think that sex is only the dominion of the young—unless you count superstars like Jack Nicholson and Michael Douglas, who always seem to fall in love with younger actresses both onscreen and off. The media give the impression that young people have most of the sex out there. In reality, most of the sex in the coming decades will be enjoyed by people older than 50.

Studies show that an active sex life is a normal and essential part of healthy aging. In 1989, Judy Breitschneider and Norma McCoy conducted a study of 200 nursing-home residents with a median age of 86 to study their sexual habits. The vast majority of these seniors, both men and women, were thinking about sex regularly. A majority engaged in some sort of physical intimacy, and 66% of the men claimed to be engaged in regular intercourse.

The results of the study showed that people tend to keep having sex into advanced age if the human body is not stunted by obesity or illness, which precludes sexual activity at any age. Furthermore, the test group of the Breitschneider-McCoy study was raised in an era that was not nearly as sexually positive, having come of age just after the First World War. Future generations of elderly will have been raised with a more open attitude toward healthy sex.

People will enjoy more sex for more of their lives than anytime in history. If medical technologies extend the normal life span into the 90s or 100s, then the average person will be sexually active for 80 years. That's a lot of time to explore sex, and many decades to explore and enjoy after the kids are out of the house.

With high rates of divorce and increasing life span, the biggest group of singles could be senior citizens. When we think of a singles bar today, an image of drunken revelers between the ages of 21 and 40 springs to mind. But when divorcees and retirees become the largest number of freewheeling swingers, there could be whole new neighborhoods devoted to the Silver Singles Scene.

Single men will be in demand. Women will outnumber men 2.5 to 1 past the age of 80. Futurist Joseph Coates has been forecasting a possible increase in geriatric lesbianism for years based on the idea that all people need intimacy, and if men are not around to provide this basic human need, then women may provide it for each other. For future generations reared in the belief that homosexual behavior is natural, this may not be implausible.

Television and the Internet

Though individuals today are significantly freer to discuss sex compared to 100 years ago, openness toward erotic media is not new. Egyptian, Greek, Roman, and other ancient artifacts show the prevalence of erotica on scrolls, pottery, frescos, and other media. But never in history has there been so much communication on all types of sexual subjects. Now, all kinds of information about sex is available instantly from any Internet device. Sources range from U.S. Centers for Disease Control and Prevention statistics on sexually transmitted disease to full-streaming video of fringe hard-core pornography.

One arbiter of loosening public attitudes toward sex is that censors are relaxing on television. Television has come a long way from the days when married characters shocked viewers by sleeping in the same double bed. Clearly, television censors now allow much more frank discussion of sexual behavior. On television these days, once-taboo topics such as homosexuality barely count as risqué: *Will & Grace* and *Queer Eye for the Straight Guy* camp up gay culture, while on cable, *Queer As Folk* shows gays in explicit situations. While these shows may push current boundaries, 15 years ago they simply would not have been possible.

Other sexual variations also see the light on readily available, popular programming. On MTV, the pioneering reality show *The Real World* shows bisexual group sex. On an episode of CBS's popular detective show *CSI: Crime Scene Investigation*, a murder victim is shown to be in a community of "plushies," a group of people who enjoy sex while dressed up like stuffed animals. Never before has there been such open discussion on the fetishes, proclivities, and preferences that are part of all human diversity.

Where television leaves off, the Internet picks up. People have quickly adopted the Internet as a place to connect for sex, courtship, and marriage, and as social networks grow through online communities and relaxing morality, more people will feel comfortable exploring the more-unusual aspects of their sexual selves. Indeed, the Internet has connected fetishists in ways mainstream society never could, and there is growing consciousness that these specialist facets of human behavior are far from statistically unusual or weird. Since the workplace is usually a sensitive place to advance an interest in sadomasochism, cross-dressing, or other sexual tastes, but the Internet is well suited for this type of conversation due to the anonymity it makes possible. The Internet is able to connect those with sexual interests shared by few while serving as a way to anonymously introduce one's proclivities to an appreciative audience. As a result, fetish communities are thriving online.

Who would have thought that Adam Smith's vision of a perfect capitalist market—many suppliers meeting customers' demands, free and perfect information, and limited government intervention—would apply to the world of dating? On the Internet, Web sites such as Match.com and Nerve.com provide a virtual online marketplace for sex partners and potential mates. Such sites consist of databases with electronic search engines that can make it easy to find a partner. Site members and visitors can define searches by broad categories like age and locale, or more-specific predilections. The result of such ease-of-use and availability —and anonymity—is that online dating services are surging in popularity among young people comfortable with online technologies, as well as with older singles who may not benefit from social networks of single friends, local singles bars, or convenient geography.

In the future, these communities will allow people with very specific sexual preferences to find exactly what they are looking for.

Pornography and Voyeurism

Ubiquitous broadband Internet, inexpensive displays, computing, and video cameras will definitely have their effect on sex. Specifically, there will be more pornography everywhere. For the first time, everyone will be only a click away from explicit hard-core pornography, potentially from inexpensive handheld devices that most, if not all, consumers can afford.

As wireless communication devices shrink in size and price and increase in power, young people will have access to wireless Internet through inexpensive devices by 2025, according to columnist Rupert Goodwins of ZDNet UK, an online business-technology site. Future generations will reach sexual maturity with full access to as much erotic material as they want.

Ever-tinier technology brings with it other issues. Inexpensive video cameras built into cell phones spell a bright future for voyeurism. One result of this will be that it may become harder to get away with infidelity and other types of indiscretions in a world where it is practically free to record video and audio. Motorola ran an advertisement in 2003 showing a novel use for its embedded camera phones: A young woman at a bar spies a friend's boyfriend cheating with another woman, and she videotapes and immediately sends the evidence to the girlfriend. We can expect similar occurrences in the future as such devices proliferate.

Voyeurism is a popular theme on television today, especially since the advent of reality television shows. Consider ABC's *The Bachelor,* where a man chooses among potential mates in front of millions of viewers, or Fox's *Temptation Island*, where viewers peep in on the ability of couples to be monogamous in the face of sexual advances by paid models and actors. Perhaps television viewers are getting used to airing their sexual behaviors before their neighbors, and maybe this could result in more understanding of human behavior. Whatever the case, spying on other people's sexual habits is becoming the norm and will continue as a popular activity in the future.

Disease Prevention

The future of sexually transmitted diseases (STDs) is key to the future of sex, as so much anxiety about sex stems from fear of disease, unwanted pregnancy, and violence. Two factors—that many people spread STDs without knowing it and that doctors and patients remain embarrassed about discussing sexual health—continue to contribute to the steady increase in the occurrence of STDs among sexually active adults. The challenge is to let more people know they have an STD without their having to make a special, embarrassing trip to the doctor and to do so inexpensively. Today, patients must go to a clinic to determine their sexual health by giving a blood, urine, or swab sample, and the sample must be sent to a lab to be centrifuged and tested. This takes days and can cost patients or insurance companies more than $100.

Telemedicine could help reduce costs and mitigate embarrassment caused by special trips to the doctor. Research is under way in the field of *biomarkers*—chemical entities that would identify the presence of a disease easily. The National Institutes of Health are funding a multidisciplinary effort to identify biomarkers that will allow early intervention and treatment of diseases from cancer to Alzheimer's to STDs. The University of North Carolina has picked up on this initiative to advance its goal of improving women's health care, and early prevention of STDs and identification of biomarkers are among its top priorities.

This research into biomarkers could dovetail with falling costs of microfluidic assays, MEMS (microelectromechanical systems) devices, and telemedicine. Many of these technologies promise to make it possible to analyze fluid samples at home and without expensive lab equipment, and if processing cannot happen in the home, samples could be analyzed and sent to a lab via a more-powerful home network.

The goal will be for lovers to become more certain about the health of their partners. One day, perhaps sex will no longer be a potential health hazard. In the far future, STDs could be eradicated, but in the meantime, the best we can do is to prevent their spread.

As pharmaceutical therapies become key to solving many health issues, sex and sexual dysfunction will see more-effective and interesting new drugs. Due to direct-to-consumer advertising of such drugs as Viagra, anyone who watches football games or nightly newscasts becomes aware that sexual dysfunction is not uncommon. Instead of being ashamed about physical shortcomings, viewers are encouraged to talk to partners and physicians about their sex lives. Pharmaceutical companies have positioned this not as weakness, but as something that strong, successful men do to solve a problem. These kinds of attitudes will lead to less shame about sex as we teach younger generations not to fear their bodies and to challenge some of the frailties of aging as well.

Erectile dysfunction medications are helping medicalize sexual problems, much in the same way we are coming to destigmatize depression and other mental illnesses. This leads me to consider the future of another myth: "Love Potion #9." With billions of dollars every year going into research into the central nervous system, we are getting closer to understanding the neurological behavior of love and lust. We may eventually find ways to influence these emotions.

We have only begun to understand the role of neurotransmitters such as dopamine and serotonin in how we perceive the world. In the last few decades, we have made major strides in understanding how these neurotransmitters affect sadness, happiness, clinical depression, or even our ability to experience paranoid schizophrenic hallucinations. Theresa L. Crenshaw's book *The Alchemy of Love and Lust: How Our Sex Hormones Influence Our Relationships* (Pocket Books, 1997) details how neurotransmitters fluctuate in the course of relationships to add to feelings of love and lust that other people inspire in us. As this research continues in the next 20 years, we will have greater insight into the biological roots of these feelings. Pharmaceutical companies might even advance drugs to help ailing relationships. A pill that gives lovers the rush of serotonin they felt when first in love might help them through rough spots in a marriage. As life spans increase and marriages last 50, 70, or even more years, a little help may be welcome.

> **"A wild card to consider is if scientists finally discover a cure for AIDS, [which] might result in greater sexual abandon."**

A wild card to consider is if scientists finally discover a cure for AIDS. Reducing the threat of incapacitation and death from AIDS might result in greater sexual abandon—and an increase in pregnancy, herpes, or syphilis.

Sex Toys

Researchers are working hard to realize Woody Allen's "orgasmatron" as visualized in his futuristic film *Sleeper* (1973). One U.S. surgeon has already patented a pacemakersized device implanted under the skin that triggers an orgasm, and begun a clinical trial approved by the U.S. Food and Drug Administration. As of November 2003, only one woman had completed the trial, which requires implantation of electrodes directly into the spine. The married woman claimed not to have had an orgasm in four years, but reported multiple orgasms the first day of using the new device. A full implant of the device would cost about $22,000, but imagine the market if the device's size and price shrank due to nanoelectronics and given FDA approval.

Physical toys could improve with materials science producing substances that feel more like skin and with greater viscosity. Pornographic movies, the most popular form of sexual entertainment, will see technological improvements on two fronts: *computer graphic displays* and *haptics* or "telefeel" technology that stimulates the body to create a sensation offered by the software. Both of these approaches intend to create more-realistic simulations.

Computer graphics and animation have gone from abstract to very lifelike in the past 30 years—consider, for example, the difference between computer graphics in 1980 and

recent movies like *Shrek* or *Toy Story*. Animators have been using the increasing availability of computer processing to increase the resolution with which they can create images and effectively simulate the appearance of straight lines, curves, colors, and shadows—all the same things we see in nature. The more processing we provide, the more animators can create smooth, flowing images that fool the eye. Such developments, when applied to adult material, will result in more-realistic and consequently more-erotic images.

Haptics, or the telecommunication of sensations using a computer interface, is another frontier in simulation. Haptic technologies allow a computer to feed sensations such as pressure, vibration, texture, and heat back to a person to simulate the physical sensations of real objects. A crude example is the joystick controller of the Sony Playstation that vibrates during certain video games when the player is struck on screen. An example of an advanced version of haptics was demonstrated at Rutgers University, where engineers designed a haptic glove to translate the experience of squeezing a ball. The glove enabled the user to perceive the texture and pressure of the virtual object as if it really existed.

Once eye-fooling graphics are combined with haptics that simulate virtual physical worlds, technicians will create software to better simulate people's sexual fantasies, approaching the limit of fooling us into believing they are really happening. The social implications of such simulations raise some interesting questions. For instance, pornography involving children and featuring violence is illegal principally on the notion that it harms those who make the films. But if virtual reality could recreate those films without involving real people, is there harm? Will we still ban such content based on the idea that even thinking about it is bad because you may do it in real life?

Like all things pertaining to sex, this maelstrom of trends will mean different things to different people, but on the positive side, I foresee:

- Less guilt, less shame, more communication, and more sense of freedom to explore.
- Greater acceptability of sex as a regular part of healthy aging.
- Plenty of room to explore one's desires through simulation.
- Less risk of disease.
- More communication in the mainstream media and between people, resulting in fewer hang-ups.

A healthier, more-open sex life awaits us, stretching on for decades. That is a future to want to stick around for.

ERIC GARLAND is a principal with Agos Dynamics Group, 145 Lakeview Terrace, Burlington, Vermont 05401. E-mail egarland@agosdynamics.com. His last article for THE FUTURIST, "Online Music: The Sound of Success," appeared in the November-December 2003 issue.

A New Fertility Factor

Stress is just one of many obstacles to pregnancy, but it's one you can control

ALICE D. DOMAR, PH.D.

Melissa was 33 when I met her, and she'd been trying to get pregnant for more than two years. Fertility tests had found nothing wrong with her or her husband. Yet all she had gained from two cycles of injected fertility medication was some extra weight. And though she was running 20 miles a week to reduce stress, the experience had left her feeling overwhelmed and isolated. Melissa was crying almost every day when she joined the 10-week mind-body program I oversee in Boston, but she soon realized that she was neither helpless nor alone. Supported by peers and counselors, she dialed back on her running regimen (excessive exercise can hamper fertility), gave up caffeine and alcohol, and started practicing relaxation techniques. After five weeks she resumed fertility-drug injections and conceived on her next cycle. Her daughter arrived nine happy months later.

There are many myths about becoming pregnant. In truth, deciding to adopt a child doesn't boost the odds of conception. Nor does taking a vacation, having a glass of wine before sex or trying an unusual new position. But frustrated couples shouldn't assume that mind-body medicine is irrelevant to their quest for pregnancy. Studies are now confirming what Melissa's experience implies. Distress can hamper fertility—and relieving distress can help improve your chances of conceiving. Though practices like meditation and yoga certainly can't guarantee pregnancy, they have now established their place along with high-tech medicines and procedures.

What do we really know about fertility and the mind? For starters, we know that infertility is stressful. Women who have difficulty conceiving suffer as much anxiety and depression as women with heart disease or cancer. A recent study found that 40 percent of them were anxious or depressed. This shouldn't be surprising. Procreation is one of the strongest instincts in the animal kingdom. Males will die fighting for a chance to mate, and females will die to protect their young. Moreover, most people assume they are fertile. When you've spent your adult life taking precautions to *avoid* pregnancy, it's a shock to discover that you can't make it happen at will. Treatment can add to the anguish. You get poked, prodded, injected, inspected and operated on, and you have mechanical sex on schedule.

No one has proved that feelings of distress actually cause infertility, but there are good reasons to think so. Women with a his-

Going Beyond Inspections and Injections

High-tech fertility treatments may work better when patients receive emotional support as well.

- Psychotherapy: Helps turn negative thoughts ("I'll never get pregnant") into positive ones ("I'm doing everything I can").
- Relaxation: Healthy approaches such as yoga and meditation can help prevent dependence on caffeine and alcohol, which decrease fertility.
- Group support: Shifts patients' focus from getting pregnant to getting on with life. Opens other paths to parenthood.

tory of depression are twice as likely to suffer from the problem—and research has shown that distressed women are less responsive to treatment. In one recent trial, high-tech fertility procedures were 93 percent less effective in highly distressed women than in those reporting less emotional upset.

Can mind-body medicine counter these effects? The first mind-body fertility program started in 1987 at Boston's Deaconess Hospital. Thousands of patients have since participated, and the results have been encouraging. Approximately 45 to 50 percent become pregnant within six months (success rates are closer to 20 percent when patients lack psychological support), and most participants experience a significant reduction in both physical and psychological symptoms. My own research supports these observations. With funding from the National Institute of Mental Health, I conducted a controlled clinical trial comparing women in mind-body programs with those receiving only routine medical care. Pregnancy and delivery rates were nearly three times higher among the women who got the additional support. In yet another study, Turkish researchers found that couples attempting in vitro fertilization achieved a 43 percent pregnancy rate when their treatment included psychological help, but only a 17 percent success rate when it didn't.

Women with fertility problems suffer as much distress as women with heart disease or cancer

Mind-body fertility programs vary, but the ones I have led share several key features. Besides practicing relaxation techniques, participants learn to cut back on caffeine and alcohol, and they use cognitive behavioral therapy to transform negative thoughts ("I will never have a baby") into positive ones ("I am doing everything I can to try to get pregnant"). Indeed, our pro-grams focus less on getting pregnant than on getting your life back—and thinking about all the possible paths to parenthood, including adoption and egg or sperm donation. Similar programs are taking shape in many parts of the world, and their patients are enjoying similar benefits: less distress, higher pregnancy rates and a better quality of life.

Adapted from "6 Steps to Increased Fertility" by Robert L. Barbieri, M.D.; Alice D. Domar, Ph.D., and Kevin R. Loughlin, M.D. (*Fireside*, 2001). For more information about mind-body techniques and fertility go to health.harvard.edu/Newsweek.

The Abortion Wars

30 years after Roe v. Wade

LINDA FELDMANN

Staff writer of The Christian Science Monitor

WASHINGTON

Audrey Diehl will never forget the time her mother took her to an abortion-rights rally in downtown San Antonio. Ms. Diehl was 9 years old, and antiabortion protesters shoved posters of aborted fetuses in her face. But it wasn't the images that upset the girl. It was "the act," she says, "all that yelling."

"That crystallized for me the zealotry of the antichoice movement," says Diehl, now a 25-year-old living in Los Angeles. "It made me more understanding of why people need to continue to voice prochoice ideas."

Yet until recently, Diehl says, she took the right to abortion for granted. Like many women who have no memory of life before the Supreme Court legalized abortion in its historic Roe v. Wade ruling—30 years ago today—she wasn't active in the abortion-rights movement.

Now, since the election of the second President Bush, who is pursuing antiabortion policies on many fronts, and has the potential to name enough Supreme Court justices to overturn Roe, Diehl is scared. And she's just started volunteering at her local Planned Parenthood.

Across the country, at the American Life League in Stafford, Va., Sara McKalips is hard at work at the Rock for Life project, trying to get young people to join the fight against abortion. She says she has always opposed abortion, but didn't become active until she was 18 and saw pictures of aborted fetuses on the Internet. She knows, she says, that "from the moment of fertilization, a unique human being exists who deserves to be protected."

While at Messiah College in Grantham, Pa., she supposed most of her fellow students were also against abortion. "But most students didn't really do anything with their prolife beliefs," says Ms. McKalips, who graduated last May. "The prolife movement needs people to take more of a stand on the issue and be less compromising."

These two young women, members of a generation who have lived their entire lives under Roe, are in a way atypical for their activism. Since 1973, nearly 38 million abortions have been performed in the US—yet a majority of Americans are conflicted on the issue, and avoid it.

But those with firmly held beliefs, like Diehl and McKalips, still number in the millions. And they reflect what author Lawrence Tribe has called an enduring "clash of absolutes" that's made Roe v. Wade one of the most contentious Supreme Court rulings ever handed down—one that has had a profound impact on American culture and politics, and, in the eyes of some scholars and activists, could one day be overturned.

Jan. 22, 1973

Frances Kissling was the director of an abortion clinic in New York City on the day that Roe v. Wade was handed down. She remembers arriving at work at 8 a.m. and "having kids in their dirty cars sitting in the parking lot, having driven from Kentucky and Connecticut and wherever, being afraid, dealing with the fact that they've just come from someplace where abortion was illegal to a place where it was legal."

Then the legal and cultural earthquake struck. In two 7–2 decisions—Roe v. Wade and Doe v. Bolton—abortion was declared a constitutionally protected right, under a right to privacy not explicitly stated in the Constitution, but developed through Supreme Court precedent. Though the justices ruled that states could regulate and ultimately ban abortion as pregnancies progressed, there was no mistaking the fundamental shift.

"It was a shock," says Ms. Kissling, now president of Catholics for Free Choice. "No one expected it."

In his dissent, Justice Byron White castigated the majority for holding that "the Constitution of the United States values the convenience, whim or caprice of the putative mother more than the life or potential life of the fetus."

Justice William Rehnquist decried the trimester system laid out by the majority as "judicial legislation."

At the time, abortion was legal in only four states—New York, Hawaii, Alaska, and Washington. Suddenly, it was legal everywhere. But for abortion-rights forces, the celebration didn't last long. The antiabortion movement, centered at first in the Catholic Church, galvanized and fought abortion on many levels—at the clinics, in state legislatures and courts, in the US Congress, and back in the Supreme Court itself. Abortion-rights forces have played defense ever since.

Regional abortion rates – and availability

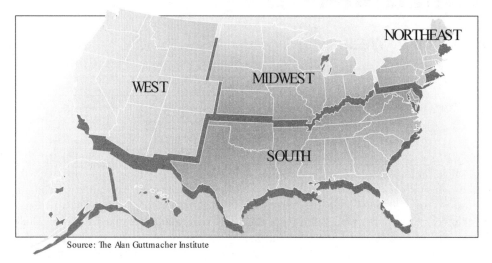

	NORTHEAST	WEST	SOUTH	MIDWEST
Abortions per 1,000 women aged 15-44 in 2000	28.0	24.9	19.0	15.9
Counties without abortion clinics in 2000	50%	78%	91%	94%

Source: The Alan Guttmacher Institute

Since 1973, attitudes toward abortion, as charted by Gallup and the General Social Survey, have held remarkably stable even as the public has become more liberal on other social issues, such as gay rights and women's equality.

"There has been some movement in a prolife direction, but you'd have to get out a magnifying glass" to see it, says Ted Jelen, a political scientist at the University of Nevada at Las Vegas and an author on the subject. "Fifteen percent are prolife, about a quarter to a third are prochoice, and the balance, it depends."

Opinion experts suggest that the effectiveness of the antiabortion movement has bumped up against other trends—such as higher education levels and less affiliation with organized religion—that might otherwise have liberalized opinion toward abortion. When framed around the question of whose choice an abortion decision should be, the public clearly favors the woman. Two-thirds of the public also consistently oppose overturning Roe.

Still, the way abortion is perceived has evolved since 1973. At the time of Roe, discussion centered on the woman's rights. But the rise of technology has altered that.

"All the remarkable developments in fetology and the images we now have of an embryo—how quickly you start to get all those characteristics that we call human, measurable brain activity, and so on—have made it impossible for anyone to make a coherent argument that it's just a blob that isn't human yet," says Jean Bethke Elshtain, a professor at the University of Chicago divinity school. "Clearly, it's a nascent human being. It's not going to be a giraffe."

What makes America's abortion wars so remarkable is how public and political they've been. Part of that speaks to the larger US cultural mosaic—the conflicts of a country that is both deeply religious and committed to secularism, a nation that invented mod-

ern feminism but remains ambivalent about women's roles. America's highly legalistic culture has also made it inevitable that a matter as private as reproduction would wind up in the courts.

Has 30 years of legalized abortion made Americans more cavalier on issues of human life, as some antiabortion advocates had warned?

Not necessarily: On physician-assisted suicide and euthanasia, Americans remain queasy, ethicists say. Public discomfort over the use of embryonic stem cells and human cloning has also shown that "there is still a moral seriousness in the American people that is quite uplifting," says Professor Elshtain.

Looked at another way, it's not necessarily true that banning abortion would enhance respect for life. Consider Romania under former President Nicolae Ceaucescu, says Ms. Kissling of Catholics for Free Choice: Abortion was strictly illegal—and unwanted children packed orphanages.

But abortion critics also say that, in fact, women facing unwanted pregnancies in this country don't have as much "choice" as the abortion-rights side claims.

"As a woman, my concern with 30 years of Roe is that it has created an abortion mentality," says Carrie Gordon Earll, a bioethics analyst at Focus on the Family, a conservative organization based in Colorado Springs.

"Even though most Americans don't like abortion," she says, "it has become the cultural default—almost an automatic assumption that a woman in a less-than-ideal pregnancy will at least consider it."

Since Roe, support systems that existed to help women with unwanted pregnancies—such as homes for unwed mothers—have shrunk. A classic cry among abortion-rights forces has been that abortion critics care more about the unborn than the born.

US abortion rate*

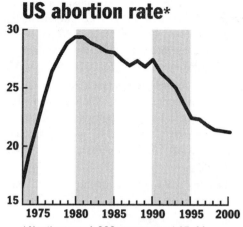

*Abortions per 1,000 women aged 15-44

US abortion clinics*

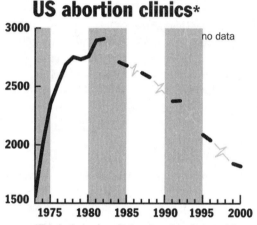

no data

*This includes hospital and nonhospital providers

Source for above: The Alan Guttmacher Institute

By the numbers...

Worldwide, about 46 million abortions occur each year. Twenty million are illegally obtained.

Among American women, almost half of pregnancies are unintended. About half of those end in abortion—1.3 million annually.

Between 1994 and 2000, the US abortion rate fell more than 10 percent, in part because of the growing availability of emergency contraception.

Abortion rates are at their lowest levels since 1974. They peaked in 1980–1981.

Of American women obtaining abortions, 52 percent are under 25. Women aged 20 to 24 account for 33 percent of abortions, and women under 20 obtain 19 percent of abortions.

In 2000, 87 percent of US counties had no abortion clinic, and 34 percent of women of childbearing age lived in those counties. In addition, 31 percent of US metropolitan areas had no abortion facilities.

Between 1996 and 2000, the number of abortion providers declined 11 percent. It's been dropping since 1982.

In 1997, 57 percent of obstetrician/gynecologists performing abortions were aged 50 or older.

Eighty-two percent of large, nonhospital abortion facilities were harassed in 2000; most clinics are picketed at least 20 times a year. From 1985 to 2000, the proportion of large providers reporting bomb threats dropped from 48 percent to 15 percent.

The 1996–2000 abortion rate was highest in Washington, D.C.—68.1 abortions per 1,000 women—and lowest in Wyoming, where 1 in 1,000 women had an abortion.

Source: The Alan Guttmacher Institute

But in recent years, the antiabortion movement has built up a network of crisis-pregnancy centers—clinics where pregnant women can go for help with prenatal and postnatal care. Care Net, an umbrella organization for these centers in Sterling, Va., estimates that there are now about 2,500 in the US; in 1980, there were less than 500.

A Declining Abortion Rate

Amid all the fierce debate and violence surrounding abortion clinics and doctors, the number and rate of abortions in America has steadily declined. The reasons are hotly debated. Prochoice advocates credit the growth of emergency contraception, a high-dose birth-control pill a woman can take after unprotected sex to prevent pregnancy. In general, a wider range of contraceptive choices means women are doing a better job of using contraception, they say.

Both abstinence and the use of contraceptives are on the rise among teenagers, in particular, so fewer are getting pregnant to begin with. Among girls aged 15 to 19, the abortion rate has

been dropping since the late 1980s—and fell another 27 percent between 1994 and 2000.

Another factor that may be contributing to the overall decline in abortions is the availability of ultrasound technology, showing the earliest fetal development—which, some observers suggest, leads some women to think twice about ending pregnancies.

But the bottom line is that the US still has one of the highest abortion rates in the industrialized West. And the abortion war is only intensifying.

Now that Republicans control both the White House and Congress, abortion opponents are readying a major push for new restrictions, starting with a ban on so-called "partial birth abortions." Another bill would ban transporting a minor across state lines for an abortion so that she can avoid parental-notification laws; a third would criminalize harming a fetus during an attack on a pregnant woman.

Laws protecting clinic entrances have helped reduce clinic violence, and litigants have successfully used racketeering laws to thwart some of the most extreme antiabortion activists. Since 2000, US government approval of medical abortion through the use of mifepristone (RU486) has given women an alternative to surgical abortion.

Yet abortion-rights leaders still feel they are losing ground, and acknowledge that their opponents have gotten savvier about shaping public opinion and "chipping away" at abortion rights. Since 1982, the number of abortion providers has been declining.

But there are still young people eager to join the shrinking ranks, inspired by stories of risky, sometimes deadly, abortions before legalization.

Angel Foster, a medical student at Harvard University, is training for a career in women's reproductive health—including providing abortions. As a young adolescent, she learned of her mother's illegal, pre-Roe abortion.

"That experience was extremely traumatic for her—not the abortion itself, but what she had to do to get it," says Ms. Foster, who, as president-elect of Medical Students for Choice, is working to beef up medical-school curricula on abortion and other issues of women's reproductive health.

Foster has also worked in countries where abortion is illegal, such as Egypt, and seen firsthand what she calls the "psychological and physical consequences of a shortage of reproductive services." But is she really willing to risk her life, working in a clinic in this country? "Even when I have kids, I can imagine doing this," she says. "My husband and I have discussed this."

Could Roe Be Overturned?

To some abortion-rights advocates, the Supreme Court is only one vote away from undoing 30 years of nationwide legalized abortion. But more likely, say legal scholars, there would need to be a larger shift in the court's composition for such an earthshaking ruling. And even if the court eventually had a solid majority of justices who believed Roe v. Wade was improperly decided, it's unclear that it would undo what many analysts, including antiabortion conservatives, call "settled law."

"What's hard for people who lack an acquaintance with the Supreme Court to understand is what a tremendously negative institutional, historical impact there would be on the stature of the court if they were to overturn it," says David Garrow, a historian at Emory Law School in Atlanta. "That's why I think it could never happen."

But if that day were to come, the legality of abortion would once again vary state by state. According to NARAL Pro-Choice America, 17 states currently have greater protection for reproductive choice than the federal Constitution; 17 other states "could face sweeping criminal bans on abortion" if Roe were reversed.

Conservative writer Marvin Olasky prefers to look at the movement through a cultural lens. The culture that accepts abortion is changing, he says, and the current view that Roe is acceptable will eventually seem untenable. That, he suggests, could eventually lead to a legal shift. "How long did it take the court to overturn Plessy v. Ferguson?" he asks, referring to the 1896 case that endorsed racial segregation. "That took 60 years. We're halfway there."

Brave New Babies

Parents now have the power to choose the sex of their children. But as technology answers prayers, it also raises some troubling questions.

CLAUDIA KALB

SHARLA MILLER OF GILLETTE, WYO., ALWAYS wanted a baby girl, but the odds seemed stacked against her. Her husband, Shane, is one of three brothers, and Sharla and her five siblings (four girls, two boys) have produced twice as many males as females. After the Millers' first son, Anthony, was born in 1991, along came Ashton, now 8, and Alec, 4. Each one was a gift, says Sharla, but the desire for a girl never waned. "I'm best friends with my mother;' she says. "I couldn't get it out of my mind that I wanted a daughter." Two years ago Sharla, who had her fallopian tubes tied after Alec's birth, began looking into adopting a baby girl. In the course of her Internet research, she stumbled upon a Web site for the Fertility Institutes in Los Angeles, headed by Dr. Jeffrey Steinberg, where she learned about an in vitro fertilization technique called preimplantation genetic diagnosis. By creating embryos outside the womb, then testing them for gender, PGD could guarantee with almost 100 percent certainty—the sex of her baby. Price tag: $18,480, plus travel. Last November Sharla's eggs and Shane's sperm were mixed in a lab dish, producing 14 healthy embryos, seven male and seven female. Steinberg transferred three of the females into Sharla's uterus, where two implanted successfully. If all goes well, the run of Miller boys will end in July with the arrival of twin baby girls. "I have three wonderful boys," says Sharla, "but since there was a chance I could have a daughter, why not?"

The brave new world is definitely here. After 25 years of staggering advances in reproductive medicine—first test-tube babies, then donor eggs and surrogate mothers—technology is changing babymaking in a whole new way. No longer can science simply help couples have babies, it can help them have the kind of babies they want. Choosing gender may obliterate one of the fundamental mysteries of procreation, but for people who have grown accustomed to taking 3-D ultrasounds of fetuses, learning a baby's sex within weeks of conception and scheduling convenient delivery dates, it's simply the next logical step. That gleeful exclamation, "It's a boy!" or "It's a girl!" may soon just be a quaint reminder of how random births used to be.

Throughout history, humans have wished for a child of one sex or the other and have been willing to do just about anything to get it. Now that gender selection is scientifically feasible, in-

terest in the controversial practice (banned, except for medical reasons, in the United Kingdom) is exploding. Despite considerable moral murkiness, Americans are talking to their doctors and visiting catchy Web sites like www.choosethesexofyourbaby.com and myboyorgirl.com—many of them offering money-back guarantees. In just the last six months, Steinberg's site has had 85,000 hits. At the Genetics and IVF Institute (GIVF) in Fairfax, Va., an FDA clinical trial of a sophisticated sperm-sorting technology called MicroSort is more than halfway to completion. Through radio, newspaper and magazine ads ("Do you want to choose the gender of your next baby?"), the clinic has recruited hundreds of eager couples, and more than 400 babies out of 750 needed for the trial have been born. Other couples continue to flock to older, more low-tech and questionable sperm-sorting techniques like the Ericsson method, which is offered at about two dozen clinics nationwide. By far, the most provocative gender-selection technique is PGD. Some clinics offer the procedure as a bonus for couples already going through fertility treatments, but a small number are beginning to provide the option for otherwise healthy couples. Once Steinberg decided to offer PGD gender selection to all comers, he says, "word spread like wildfire."

The ability to create baby Jack or baby Jill opens a high-tech can of worms. While the advances have received kudos from grateful families, they also raise loaded ethical questions about whether science is finally crossing a line that shouldn't be crossed. Even fertility specialists are divided over whether choosing a male or female embryo is acceptable. If couples can request a baby boy or girl, what's next on the slippery slope of modern reproductive medicine? Eye color? Height? Intelligence? Could picking one gender over the other become the 21st century's form of sex discrimination? Or, as in China, upset the ratio of males to females? Many European countries already forbid sex selection; should there be similar regulations in the United States? These explosive issues are being debated in medical journals, on university ethics boards and at the highest levels in Washington. Just last week the President's Council on Bioethics discussed proposals for possible legislation that would ban the buying and selling of human embryos and far-out reproductive experimentation, like creating human-animal hybrids. While the recommendations—part of a report due out this spring—do not suggest limiting IVF or gender selection, the goals are clear: the government should clamp down before technology goes too far. "Even though people have strong differences of opinion on some issues," says council chair and leading bioethieist Leon Kass, "all of us have a stake in keeping human reproduction human."

After their first son, Jesse, was born in 1988, Mary and Sam Toedtman tried all sorts of folksy remedies to boost their chances of having a girl. When Jesse was followed by Jacob, now 10, and Lucas, 7, it seemed clear that boys would be boys in the Toedtman family. Sam has two brothers and comes from a line of boys 70 years long. So, after a lot of serious thinking, the Toedtmans decided to enroll in GIVF's clinical trial of MicroSort for "family balancing." That's the popular new term for gender selection by couples who already have at least one child and want to control their family mix. Since MicroSort's family balance trial began in 1995, more than 1,300 couples have signed on—almost 10 times more than joined a companion trial aimed at avoiding genetic illnesses that strike boys. GIVF is actively recruiting new candidates for both trials. In 2003 a second MicroSort clinic was opened near Los Angeles, and a third is planned for Florida this year. GIVF hopes MicroSort will become the first sperm-sorting device to receive the FDA's stamp of approval for safety and effectiveness. "This will completely change reproductive choices for women, and that's very exciting," says MicroSort's medical director, Dr. Keith Blauer. "We hope to make it available to as many couples as possible."

The MicroSort technology—created originally by the Department of Agriculture to sort livestock sperm—works by mixing sperm with a DNA-specific dye that helps separate X's from Y's.The majority of couples who use MicroSort for gender selection have no fertility problems and use standard artificial insemination to conceive. The technique is far from perfect: most participants have to make more than one attempt, each costing at least $2,500, to get pregnant. And not all end up with the gender of choice. At last count, 91 percent of couples who requested an "X sort" gave birth to a baby girl and 76 percent who chose a "Y sort" produced a boy. It worked for the Stock family. Six-month-old Amberlyn was spared the debilitating neuromuscular disorder that plagues her brother, Chancellor, 7. The Toedtmans were lucky, too. Though it took three tries to get pregnant, Mary finally delivered a girl, Natalie, last April. "She's a total joy," she says.

Determined as she was, Toedtman says she would not have felt comfortable creating embryos to ensure that Natalie was Natalie and not Nathaniel. But a small number of others, knowing that their chance of success with PGD is exponentially better, are becoming pioneers in the newest form of family planning. Available at a limited number of clinics nationwide, PGD was designed and originally intended to diagnose serious genetic diseases in embryos, like Tay-Sachs and cystic fibrosis, before implantation. Over the last decade the technology has allowed hundreds of couples, many of whom have endured the death of sick children, to have healthy babies. Today, some doctors are using PGD to increase the odds of successful IVF pregnancies by screening out chromosomally abnormal embryos.

Some of those patients are asking about gender—and it's their right to do so, many doctors say. After an embryo screening, "I tell them it's normal and I tell them it's male or female," says PGD expert Yury Verlinsky of the Reproductive Genetics Institute in Chicago. "It's their embryo. I can't tell them which one to transfer."

It's one thing to allow infertile couples to choose gender after PGD. Creating embryos solely to sort boys from girls sets off ethical and moral alarm bells. In the last year or so, several clinics have begun to offer the procedure for gender balance without restrictions. Steinberg, of Fertility Institutes, says his team methodically debated the pros and cons before doing so. The logic, he says, is simple: "We've been offering sperm sorting for 20 years without any stipulations. Now, in 2004, I can offer almost 100 percent success with PGD. Why would I make it less available?" Steinberg's clinic, which also has offices in Las Vegas and Mexico, will soon perform its 100th PGD sex-selection procedure. So far, about 40 babies have been born, every one of them the desired sex. It's unclear how many couples will actually want to endure the hefty cost, time commitment and physical burden of fertility drugs and IVF just to ensure gender. But the idea is intriguing for a lot of couples. "I've had friends and neighbors discreetly inquire," says Dr. David Hill, head of ART Reproductive Center in Beverly Hills, Calif., where about 5 to 10 percent of patients are requesting PGD solely for sex selection. Hill has no problem offering it, but he respects colleagues who say no. "This is a really new area," he says. "It's pretty divided right now as to those who think it's acceptable and those who don't."

Dr. Mark Hughes, a leading PGD authority at Wayne State University School of Medicine in Detroit, is one of the latter. "The last time I checked, your gender wasn't a disease," he says. "There is no illness, no suffering and no reason for a physician to be involved. Besides, we're too busy helping desperate couples with serious disease build healthy families." At Columbia University, Dr. Mark Sauer balks at the idea of family balance. "What are you balancing? It discredits the value of an individual life." For those few patients who ask for it, "I look them straight in the face and say, 'We're not going to do that'." And at Northwestern, Dr. Ralph Kazer says bluntly: " 'Gattaca' was a wonderful movie. That's not what I want to do for a living."

One of the most vexing concerns is what some consider gender selection's implicit sexism. When you choose one sex, the argument goes, you reject the other. In Asia girls have been aborted or killed, and populations skewed, because of favoritism toward boys. Could the same thing happen here? GIVF's Blauer says the vast majority of MicroSort couples want girls, not boys, though that could change if Y-sort statistics improve. At Hill's clinic, about 65 percent request boys; at Steinberg's, 55 percent. "It's not going to tip the balance one way or the other," he says. But what if a couple doesn't get the boy or girl they desire? PGD comes as close as it gets to guaranteeing outcome, but there remains the thorny question of what to do with "wrong sex" embryos. Opponents worry that they'll be destroyed simply because they're male or female, but the options are identical for everyone going through IVF: discard the extras, freeze them for later use, donate them or offer them up for scientific research. As for MicroSort, of the more than 500 pregnancies achieved so far, four have been terminated at other facilities (GIVF won't perform abortions) because of "non-desired gender," says Blauer. "It's important to realize that couples have reproductive choice in this country," he says, but "the vast majority of patients want another healthy child and are happy with either gender."

Just beyond these clinical worries lies a vast swamp of ethical quandaries and inherent contradictions. People who support a woman's right to choose find themselves cringing at the idea of terminating a fetus based on sex. Those who believe that embryos deserve the status of personhood decry their destruction, but gender selection could result in fewer abortions. Choosing sex can skew male-female ratios, but it might also reduce overpopulation. Requesting a girl could mean she will be more desired by her parents, but it's also possible she'll grow up and decide she'd rather have been a boy. "Children are going to hold their parents responsible for having made them this way," says bioethicist Kass, "and that may not be as innocent as it sounds."

And then there is the most fundamental conflict of all: science versus religion. One Korean-American couple, with two daughters has been on both sides. Feeling an intense cultural pressure to produce a son, the woman, 31, attended a MicroSort information session, where Blauer reviewed the technique. Intrigued, she went back for a second session and convinced her husband to come along. When it was time to move forward, though, a greater power took over. "I don't think God intended us to do that," she says. "We decided we should just pray about it and leave it up to God."

There are no laws against performing gender selection in the United States. Many people believe that the safety and effectiveness of reproductive technologies like PGD should be regulated, says Kathy Hudson, of the Genetics and Public Policy Center at Johns Hopkins, which recently polled 1,200 Americans on the topic. But, she says, many Americans "are uncomfortable with the government being the arbiter of how to use these technologies." Meanwhile, fertility doctors look to the American Society for Reproductive Medicine for professional standards. John Robertson, head of ASRM's ethics committee, says preconception techniques like MicroSort "would be fine once safety is established." So far, MicroSort reports, 2.4 percent of its babies have been born with major malformations, like Down syndrome, compared with 3 to 4 percent in the general population. But until the trial is completed, there are no definitive data. As for PGD, the ASRM currently discourages its use for sex selection, but Robertson says he wouldn't rule out the possibility that it might become acceptable in the future.

So what, in the end, should we make of gender selection? Will programming of human DNA before birth become inevitable? "I learned a long time ago never to say never," says Rick Myers, chief of Stanford's genetics department. Still, he says, traits we're all worried about, like height, personality and intelligence, aren't the products of single genes. They're cooked in a complex stew of DNA and environment—a stew that boggles scientists, even those with IQs so high you'd swear they were bioengineered. And even if we could create designer Uma Thurmans, would we want to? Sharla Miller and Mary Toedtman say absolutely not. "That's taking it too far," says Miller.

We wouldn't be human if we didn't fantasize about the sci-fi universe around the corner. Steinberg, who has worked in IVF since its conception in the 1970s, remembers finding notes on his windshield in the early days that said, TEST-TUBE BABIES HAVE NO SOUL. The very idea of creating life outside the womb "was unthinkable," he says. And yet, some 1 million test-tube babies later, the practice has become routine. The same will likely be true of gender selection, says Robin Marantz Henig, author of the new book "Pandora's Baby," a history of IVF "The more it's done," she says, "the less you're going to see concerns."

Lizette Frielingsdorf doesn't have any. She and her husband have three boys—Jordan, 8, Justin, 6, and Jake, 5—and one MicroSort girl, Jessica, who just turned 2. "I call her my $15,000 baby. We felt like we won the lottery," says Frielingsdorf "Probably once a week someone will say, 'You got your girl. How did you do that?' and I'll say, 'Here's the number.' I want others to experience the same joy we have." No doubt, many will.

Barren

Coming to Terms with a Lost Dream

DEBORAH DERRICKSON KOSSMANN

WHEN I WAS 5, I listed several things I wanted to be when I grew up: teacher, archaeologist (my mother had wanted to be that and had explained what it was), author, and mother. I have always thought of myself as an archaeologist of sorts, dusting off bones from my clients' emotional digs, figuring out how they fit together to make an understandable history. I teach graduate students. I write. But I have not become a mother. What does it mean to be barren, unable to grow anything in the land that is the body?

Infertility is about the body. One's identity becomes defined by what the body does or does not do. During my first miscarriage, I experienced slow, aching cramps and the punch of the uterus as if it were saying, "No, not now, not time." There was no happy announcement of pregnancy, only the feeling of sadness when the bleeding came. By the time we learned I was pregnant, it was already over.

The second pregnancy began with more Clomid, a medication we were using to stimulate ovulation, and a new set of medical procedures, including a test called a hysterosalpingogram. No one understands why some women unexpectedly get pregnant after having this test. Perhaps a slight blockage exists, perhaps the dye they use is like Liquid-Plumr. Envision pipes opening up as the gunky stuff drains away. During the test, I lay on the table with the sheet covering my bottom half, the nurse and the doctor directing me: "Here you relax.... Here you breathe.... We'll see your uterus above on that screen." I had to turn my head from the hard table to see it. But first I focused on an image: blue dye being threaded into me, the shock of its entry almost like sexual intrusion. Not rape; I wanted this, didn't I? The goal was to find the blocked places, to make my body a host that could grow things. The dye entered and my body fought back. Above me, my uterus floated, distinct, not looking like those pictures in biology books. Mine is elongated, a shapely part of me, like a pink heart. Tubes stretched out from it. Momentarily fascinated, I ignored the physical discomfort as I looked inside myself.

The test took place two weeks before my nephew, Michael (my sister's third child), was born. My husband and I visited the hospital, bringing my sister Chinese food—greasy egg rolls, noodles in sauce. She was tired, but happy. She tried not to be too happy, mindful of our struggles with infertility, as she gave Michael to me to hold. Looking back, I wonder if my uterus at that moment opened and if somehow that muscle inside me relaxed, allowing my egg to roll downward and inside. I picture the egg, cartoonlike, smiling.

The night after Michael's birth, we conceived. My husband dreamed that night of a blond boy in a bucket. He told me the next morning we were pregnant, but I didn't believe him. And then, suddenly, we were. It was Christmastime and I was tired, green, and hungry. I told people early: I couldn't contain our news. For a long time after the first miscarriage, we'd waited to try and get pregnant, and we'd waited through more cycles on the medication. Now, I read things about babies. I imagined ourselves dividing over and over inside me. We had a nickname for it. We called it "Pea." I stayed green and tired and full of indigestion. My temperature stayed up. My breasts began to hurt all the time and grow larger. My husband noted this outward sign. He began to buy books about finances, investments. He was worrying about building our nest with enough twigs and sticks to weave securely for the egg—the blond boy in the bucket.

On Super Bowl Sunday, we returned from brunch with friends and some part of me felt different. Several days earlier, I'd finally stopped taking my temperature, believing at last my hormone levels would remain high. Then it appeared: a rusty red spot as I wiped myself. I started to panic. I went to the bathroom every hour. Each time, it was still there, another drop. It was a stop sign, red light, a flashing siren light on the top of a police car telling us to pull over, stop driving. I called the doctor—not *my* doctor, but the doctor on call. He sounded irritated. He was probably watching the game, eating snack foods, and drinking beer. I told him what was happening. "Call tomorrow for an ultrasound appointment," he said. "There's nothing to do today."

Should I rest, lie down?

"You can do that if you want," he said. "It probably won't matter."

In the hours that followed, I thought about my wedding day when my sister was several months pregnant with my second niece, Maddie. Right after the reception, she began bleeding. Her doctor put her on bed-rest for more than a month. We still shiver to think of Maddie's not being; we were so close to losing her. After the phone call to the doctor, I lay in bed and cried because I knew what was happening. My uterus was clenching, not to hold on, but to let go. It was like a star falling. You don't exactly see the trajectory, only the brief light and the memory that once it was reality, if only for the briefest breath. I lay flat and very still. Sometimes, when I was a child with a fever, I'd look at the corners of my bedroom ceiling and imagine walking on it like it was the floor. What a strange possibility if the whole world could be upside-down! In the suspended shadows, I'd hang in the wrong direction and try to experience that fevered moment before the world swung back.

The next morning, when I called for the ultrasound appointment, they told me to drink fluids. I drank, ten, twenty, thirty ounces. I was still drinking on the way to the hospital. I was still bleeding. "Many women spot early in their pregnancies. I've read this and it could be true," I told my husband. "My sister bled and it was bright red and Maddie is here now. It could be true, couldn't it?" My husband nodded a little distractedly and held my hand. It was as if he'd already begun dissembling the nest, knocking twigs everywhere.

I stripped off all my clothes and put on my blue gown and bracelet. My husband sat with me. It was a funeral of waiting.

At the hospital, the technician ran the probe over my abdomen. "You didn't drink enough. Go drink more," she said accusingly. I was sitting in a room with pamphlets about sexually transmitted diseases and bladder infections, and I was drowning myself with water. I felt myself float like a balloon, and still the technician said it was not enough water. She said with annoyance now, "We can't read it this way. We'll do a transvaginal. Now go urinate." I peed and peed and peed. Then she brought out the condom-covered probe, which I helped her put inside me. It reminded me of a stick shift on one of those driving video games. She stared at the incomprehensible screen that was turned slightly away from me. My husband seemed not to notice the weirdly pornographic quality to the whole interaction. "I can't see," the technician said, "I'll be right back." But I knew already what I knew—that something had happened. The radiologist came in and said, "I'm sorry. It stopped growing a week or so ago." She compared the size of the yolk with the technicians' developmental chart and moved the probe around again inside me. I began to cry then, just wanted to get up and go somewhere like those animals that howl and howl, deep in the forest.

But first we had to walk back to the obstetrician's office. My doctor was almost tearful at the news. The nurse-practitioner was actually crying. She asked me, "Do you want to wait? Or we can do a dilation and evacuation (D&E) and see if we can get a tissue sample. Then we can maybe figure out what happened. You don't have to wait and then bleed. You can know it's finished." I could barely think because I was that animal howling, but I made the D&E appointment for the next day. I knew that was better: I couldn't stand to wait.

The next day, we checked into the hospital. I told the admissions person the reason for our visit and cried. I told the doctor doing the surgery what had happened when she asked, and I cried again. I stripped off all my clothes and put on the blue gown and bracelet. My husband sat with me. He held my rings because I was not allowed to wear them into surgery. It was a funeral of waiting.

After they came to take me into surgery, he waited in the other room like those old movies where they show the father pacing the waiting area during the baby's delivery. I was still sobbing when they wheeled me into the operating room. The surgical team put my feet up into high stirrups. The anesthesiologist said something that I didn't hear because it was suddenly dark. My obstetrician had cautioned, "Don't worry about whatever you say or do during the procedure." Afterward, when I woke up after the surgery, a nurse was hovering over me, my face was wet, and my hands held a ball of damp tissues. I knew I'd said and done things I couldn't remember as they carefully cleaned out that beautiful elongated space inside me that must have clenched its muscled will against the intrusion, the loss, and the flowing out.

After the second miscarriage, we both took the nest apart. A friend once told me about some misguided birds that had built a nest by her front door inside a large flowerpot. One of the eggs—a finch egg, she thinks—was accidentally knocked out and broken. Thinking about that story, I wondered if the bird missed the shattered egg. After the D&E, I stayed home for a few days in the dark house in stunned silence. I read two murder mysteries in 24 hours. I slept. But mostly, I just sat quietly and took painkillers for the cramps. It was raining outside, a winter rain, the hard, cold kind. I sat in my living room for almost three hours before I noticed that it was raining *inside* the house, a steady drip in the entranceway. I put a pot under it and sat some more. My husband didn't know what to do. He held me, but as is the way with wild animals, I'd found a cave and remained in it.

We visited a high-risk specialist who told us nothing we hadn't figured out already. She offered us a different medication, the possibility of a study. We both underwent full panels of genetic testing and filled vials of blood in the lab. The results of the D&E testing came back. The obstetrician showed us the numbers and pronounced them "normal." He told me they couldn't be sure if they'd obtained the right tissue. It was so early in the pregnancy that the tissue they used may have been from the embryo or my own body. He was gentle and encouraging about trying again. He said, "If you want to, and whenever you feel ready." There seemed to be no answers for what was termed "secondary infertility." After all, I'd finally been able to get pregnant when on medication, hadn't I?

When I visited my sister during this time, I didn't hold my nephew. He was exactly nine months ahead of the child I was missing. My husband and I decided to try again and spent more months on drugs and off drugs with no conception. The anniversary of the first miscarriage passed. Then the anniversary of the due date of the second miscarriage approached. I tried to speak to my husband from the cave. "It's a harder time than I expected," I said, "The 28th will be difficult." He said he understood. The 28th passed, and he said nothing. On the 29th, I climbed out of my cave and tried to beat some conversation out of him. Where had he gone? He no longer guarded the cave, no longer grieved as I did. "I want our old life back," he said. He said he didn't really want children, maybe never did. Men and women grieve differently, the literature claims. I wanted to rip at his seeming indifference with unforgiving claws.

We talked to resolve our differences. But in order to have children, we needed to agree to proceed with the medical process we'd been going through. And then we needed to decide at what level we'd stop treatment. Imagine two posturing like a bull and a matador. After several conversations like this, our battle became scripted. One wave of the cape and we were off. We began to avoid the ring. We began to avoid sex. Once when we were scheduled to have sex—neither of us called these times making love at this point—my husband turned to me and said in a businesslike voice, "Okay, let's pretend we're in a lab and they're forcing us." We took turns elaborating this scenario so much that our laughter rang over the bed and bounced back to us until we could make love.

How can I explain what the infertility journey does to a sex life? First, there's fun, the joy of trying to make something. Then, there's the fear of making something you will lose. Then, there's the stress of having to make something on a schedule and the fact that hoping at all becomes so painful. The pain is like a small, deep cut that won't heal.

When the third miscarriage happened, we barely talked. I knew the pregnancy was over three days before the bleeding started. I was now so attuned to my body that I almost swore I could feel when the egg released. I tried to control what I could. I kept my butt elevated for 20 minutes after sex, even though it was futile. But I told myself maybe it would matter and at least I could do something. When the bleeding for the miscarriage began, I cried in the bathroom at the community mental health center where I worked, big heaving sobs that I tried to stifle, since I told myself the patients used the same bathroom, and I didn't want to upset or have to comfort them. I was glad I'd had the D&E last time, since each change of pads and tampons now made me wonder, Was this life? Was *this*?

In the infertility specialist's office, the new doctor, a reproductive endocrinologist, sat across from me. He said, "You seem stressed by your situation," and asked if I wanted to see their psychologist. This would have been funny at any other time, since I'm a psychologist married to a psychologist, and had already been seeing a psychologist on and off during the whole ordeal. This new doctor seemed to believe that, because I was starting anew with him, the past three years and three miscarriages didn't count. "Here are new vitamins and new blood work and more medication," he said. I wasn't very hopeful, but I took the medication and felt myself ovulate days before I was supposed to. I took the ovulation test at work between patients and brought it home to my husband, because I didn't even trust myself to read its results right any more. He thought I'd ovulated, too. He said this carefully, since I was wild with hormones. When I called the doctor panicked and afraid we'd missed another opportunity to get pregnant, the doctor said I couldn't have ovulated. We scheduled time to have sex as soon

as the doctor's office called back because we knew it was the "right" time. We lay on the yellow, sun-warmed afternoon bed and tried to make a baby. We didn't.

Time to Stop

At the next doctor's visit, when he told us we could try stronger drugs or in vitro fertilization (though there were still no known reasons for the miscarriages) and when he said the words "let's take another blood test," I knew. I knew, just as I knew when it was time to break up with somebody or change jobs, that it was time to stop. I told my husband on the way home. I didn't say it directly, however. I told him (half in the cave) that I was getting rid of all the oversized clothes and borrowed maternity outfits I'd been keeping. Once home, I angrily cleaned out closets and drawers. I was getting rid of the clothes that no longer fit me or were no longer about who I was or wanted to be.

That night and for the whole week following, as my husband and I climbed into bed, we listened to a confused mockingbird singing in the dark, just outside our window. He was looking for a mate, looking to make a bird family. He was singing at the wrong time, but what a song of trills and warbles and fakery! He sang as if his life depended upon finding his mate. The week after his glorious midnight performances brought only silence. In all that darkness, could he have found something?

I began working out every day at the gym and lost all the weight I'd gained, reclaiming my body. I began writing poetry again, stories and words about grief. I quit my 30-hour-a-week administrative job at the community mental heath center. I remembered that I once liked my husband as a friend and that, while neither of us was perfect dealing with our infertility or each other, as a couple, we'd survived.

I suddenly felt tears push at the back of my eyelids as the thought welled up that I would never make a cake like this for my daughter.

Bodily scars linger. I have bigger breasts from the pregnancies and, possibly, some other physical effects from the medications I took. I struggle with my feelings about what it means to be female and not give birth. I recently walked into a hair salon where four pregnant women and one woman with an infant sat. It reminded me in an instant that I'm different from other women: I won't hold a child that looks like my husband and me.

But there are also moments of solace. My husband jokingly holds our favorite cat up next to his cheek and grins. "See the resemblance?" he asks. A few months ago, I attended the opening of an art exhibit held by a young woman who'd been one of my first long-term psychotherapy clients. She made textured and original ceramic pieces symbolizing parts of her personality, and she'd wanted me to see them. (They were too big to bring to my office.) She stood next to me with shining eyes and excitement at the fulfillment of making something, and I recognized that I'd helped in this. The years we'd worked together had created something in her that, in turn, created something else, healthy and full of her life energy.

I'm an aunt. In some cultures this is an important and respected position—someone who doesn't have her own children, but loves others' children as if they were her own. My first niece, Sarah, is 8 years old, as old as my relationship with my husband. We attended her birthday party and watched as she blew out the candles on the orange, pumpkin-shaped cake that my sister had crafted. My family sang "Happy Birthday" in all different keys to her happy face. I suddenly felt tears push at the back of my eyelids as the thought welled up that I'd never make a cake like this for my daughter.

My 5-year-old niece, Maddie, was pleased that I hung her artwork on my kitchen door. "Aunt Debbie," she asked holding a small fistful of tiny yellow flowers she'd bunched up with tape borrowed from my drawer, "Can you hang these up? These are for you." I looked at the small wilted weeds, the same yellow as her hair and her ruffled dress. She was smiling at me and I was acutely aware of the ache her gifts sometimes caused. She was not my own child, yet my love for her touched the emptiness inside me.

My nephew Michael was talking. He said, "Aunt Bebbie." When I visited my sister, he played a new game with me, jumping off the coffee table into my arms over and over, sure that I'd catch him. And I did, every time, though each time he flew into the air and I held him, I remembered what had slipped from my grasp.

How long does it take to give birth to oneself as a childless woman? A year after we'd stopped all the procedures and the medications, given up the idea of trying, and continued along our changed life path, I suddenly became pregnant. On a television show, a surprise situation like ours should have turned out fine. It didn't. I had another early miscarriage. For a while after this, I halfheartedly entertained thoughts about adoption. This was fantasy, a way to imagine a life that ran parallel to this one, in some other universe. That alternative life included a little boy or girl running through our backyard, playing pretend under the peach tree. I began to realize that I'd always be barren if I continued to hold onto the idea that a child should be in me and pro-

duced by me. If I believed this idea, planted in me when I was a child myself, I'd always have only a weed-filled field, scrub trees, and emptiness. Here, in this infertile place, I kept the grief about "Pea" and the other lost embryos, along with the fantasies about what might have been.

A second-floor room in our house had been painted bright yellow before we'd moved in, six years ago. I said it would make a great baby's room. Each morning, it filled with sunshine, and several contented cats stretched out in its warm spots. A few weeks ago, my husband suggested moving my home office from the corner of the basement into the yellow room. To take my creativity upstairs meant reorganizing the whole house—moving heavy furniture to different rooms, carrying what seemed like endless numbers of books from bookshelf to bookshelf, opening boxes, tossing files I hadn't looked at in a wile, cleaning out old pictures, and deciding what I should take with me. In the middle of the chaos, my husband leaned over my shoulder as I ordered office furniture online. He joked in a low inviting voice, "Come upstairs, out of the cave, write happy things in the yellow room."

Once I moved into the yellow room, I could see from my windows the neighbors' houses and their children running between the fenced backyards. In our own yard, the peach tree, planted from a dried pit, is now mature enough to begin bearing juicy fruit itself. Inside my new room, I see lots of photographs of my husband and me with our nieces and nephew, snapshots of our friends and family, and pictures of the places the two of us have visited together. High on a bookshelf, almost out of reach, sits a small, closed box, a gift from my husband's aunt, from the days before the second miscarriage. Inside, protected in white tissue paper, nestles a pair of green, hand-knit baby booties.

DEBORAH DERRICKSON KOSSMANN, PSY.D., is a clinical psychologist in private practice and also works in a multidisciplinary medical oncology practice. She is a journalist, essayist, and poet. Address: 1709 Langhorne-Newton Rd., Suite 2, Langhorne, PA 19047. E-mails to the author may be sent to drskoss@aol.com.

A form of this article originally appeared in "Families, Systems & Health", 18, No. 4, Winter 2000, pp. 479-484. From *Psychotherapy Networker*, July/August 2002, pp. 40-45, 58. © 2002 by Deborah Derrickson Kossmann. All rights reserved.

Who's Raising Baby?

Challenges to Modern-Day Parenting

Anne R. Pierce

Drive through the empty streets of our neighborhoods and ask yourself not merely where the children have gone but where childhood has gone. It is most unlikely you will see such once-familiar scenes as these: a child sitting under a tree with a book, toddlers engaged in collecting leaves and sticks, friends riding bikes or playing tag, parents and their offspring working together in the yard, families (in no hurry to get anywhere) strolling casually along. Today's children are too busy with other things to enjoy the simple pleasures children used to take for granted. Preoccupied with endless "activities" and diversions, they have little time for simply going outside.

Where are the children and what are they doing? They are in day-care centers, now dubbed "learning centers." They are in "early childhood programs" and all-day kindergarten. They are acquiring new skills, attending extracurricular classes, and participating in organized sports. They are sitting in front of the computer, the TV, and the Play Station. They are not experiencing the comfortable ease of unconditional love, nor the pleasant feeling of familiarity. They are not enjoying a casual conversation, nor are they playing. They are working—at improving their talents, at competing with their peers, at "beating the enemy" in a video game, at just getting by, at adapting to the new baby-sitter or coach, at not missing Mom or Dad. They, like their computers, are "on." Being, for them, is doing, adjusting, coping. Parenting, for us, is providing them with things to do.

Young children expend their energy on long days in group situations, in preschool and after-school programs, in music and athletic lessons. For much-needed relaxation, they collapse in front of the TV or computer, the now-defining features of "homelife." Relaxation no longer signifies quiet or repose. The hyperactive pace of children's television shows and video games, always accompanied by driving music, exacerbates and surpasses the fast pace of modern life. Children stare at the screen, though the inanity, violence, and doomsday sociopolitical messages of the programming are anything but reassuring.

From doing to staring, from staring to doing. There is little room in this scenario for idle contentment, playful creativity, and the passionate pursuit of interests. Alternatives to this framework for living are provided neither in thought nor in deed by busy parents who, themselves, end their rushed days with television and escapism.

Before nursery school starts, most children who can afford it have attended "classes," from gymnastics to ballet, piano, or swimming. Infant "swim lessons," in which an instructor in diving gear repeatedly forces screaming babies underwater so that they are forced to swim, are now commonplace. Day-care centers claim to give toddlers a head start in academic advancement and socialization. Increasing numbers of bright young children spend time with tutors or at the learning center to attain that ever-elusive "edge."

Children in elementary school now "train" and lift weights in preparation for their sports. Football and track are new options for first-graders. A recent trend in elementary athletic programs is to recruit professional coaches, due to the supposed competitive disadvantage of amateur coaching done by parents. It is more common for young children to "double up," participating in two team sports at a time. A constantly increasing selection of stimulating activities lures modern families, making downtime more elusive.

What used to be "time for dinner" (together) is, more often than not, time for family members to rush and scatter in different directions. A typical first-grade soccer team practices two evenings a week, from 6:00 to 7:30. The stress involved in getting six-year-olds fed and in gear by practice time and, after practice, bathed and in bed at an appropriate hour is obvious. And yet, if you attend a first-grade soccer game, you'll likely find parents eager to discover the activities of other people's children and anxious to sign their children up for—whatever it might be. Some parents appear to be jealous of the activities others have discovered.

The New Conformism—Afraid of Missing Out

In asking scores of parents about the purpose of all this activity, I have never received a clear or, to my mind, satisfactory answer. The end, apparently, is unclear apart from the idea, often expressed, that if one's child starts activities later than other children, he (or she) will be "left behind." Some of the more cohesive explanations I have received are these: A mother described herself as being "swept along by the inevitable"; she didn't want her young daughter to be "the only one missing out." A couple explained their determination to expose their toddler to a wide variety of opportunities so that he would know which sports he excelled in "by the time things get competitive." A father said, simply, that he saw his role in terms of making sure his children were "the best at something," and with all the other kids starting activities at such an early age, this meant that his kids "had to start even earlier."

In effect, this is the "do what everyone else does, only sooner and more intensely" theory of child rearing. This theory creates a constant downward pressure upon children of a younger and younger age. This was evident to me when my youngest son entered kindergarten and I discovered he was within a small minority of boys who had not *already* participated in team sports. Only five years earlier, my oldest son was within the sizable majority of kindergartners whose parents had decided kindergarten was a little too early for such endeavors. (First grade was then the preferred starting point.)

The more families subscribe to this "lifestyle," the more there is another reason for pushing kids off to the races: If no children are around to play with, then, especially for only children, organized activities become their only opportunity to "play" with other kids. Playing is thus thoroughly redefined.

The philosophy of child rearing as a race and of homelife as oppressive for women compels families toward incessant action. Love, nurture, and, concomitantly, innocence have been demoted as compared to experience and exposure. The family is viewed as a closedness to experience, the nurturing role within the family as the most confining of all. Indeed, busyness supplants togetherness in many modern families.

One legacy of Freud, Piaget, Pavlov, and the behaviorists, neodevelopmentalists, and social scientists who followed them has been the decreasing respect for the child's being and the increasing emphasis upon his "becoming." The child is seen as "socializable" and is studied as a clinical object whose observable response to this or that "environmental stimulus" becomes more important than his deeper, more complicated features. With the clinical interpretation of childhood, social engineering projects and "activities" that make the child's world more stimulating gain momentum.

Conformism, convenience, and new interpretations of childhood are, then, contributing factors in the hectic existence and the premature introduction to academics that parents prescribe for their children.

In addition to the advantage that all this activity supposedly gives children, there is also the element of convenience. If parents are too busy to supervise their children, it behooves them to keep the kids so busy and under the auspices of so many (other) adults that they are likely to "stay out of trouble." Such is the basis of many modern choices. Children

spend much of their time exhausted by activities, the purposes of which are ill construed.

Conformism, convenience, and new interpretations of childhood are, then, contributing factors in the hectic existence and the premature introduction to academics that parents prescribe for their children. For example, before the 1960s, it was generally believed that placing young children in out-of-home learning programs was harmful. The concern for the harmfulness of such experiences was abandoned when these learning programs became convenient and popular.

Education As 'Socialization'

In *Miseducation: Preschoolers at Risk*, David Elkind expressed dismay at the fact that age-inappropriate approaches to early education have gained such momentum despite the undeniable evidence that pushing children into formal academics and organized activities before they are ready does more harm than good. He lamented, "In a society that prides itself on its preference for facts over hearsay, on its openness to research, and on its respect for 'expert' opinion, parents, educators, administrators, and legislators are ignoring the facts, the research and the expert opinion about how young children learn and how best to teach them.... When we instruct children in academic subjects, or in swimming, gymnastics, or ballet, at too early an age, we miseducate them; we put them at risk for short-term stress and long-term personality damage for no useful purpose."

Elkind pointed to the consistent result of reputable studies (such as that conducted by Benjamin Bloom) that a love of learning, not the inculcation of skills, is the key to the kind of early childhood development that can lead to great things. These findings, warned Elkind, point to the fallacy of early instruction as a way of producing children who will attain eminence. He noted that with gifted and talented individuals, as with children in general, the most important thing is an excitement about learning: "Miseducation, by focusing on skills to the detriment of motivation, pays an enormous price for teaching infants and young children what amounts to a few tricks."

He further observed that those advocating early instruction in skills and early out-of-home education rely upon youngsters who are very disadvantaged to tout early education's advantages. "Accordingly, the image of the competent child introduced to remedy the understimulation of low-income children now serves as the rationale for the overstimulation of middle-class children."

Dr. Jack Westman of the Rockford Institute, renowned child psychiatrist Dr. Stanley Greenspan, and brain researcher Jane Healy are among the many unheeded others who warn of the implications of forcing the "childhood as a race" approach upon young children. Laments Westman, "The result is what is now referred to as the 'hothousing movement' for infants and toddlers devoted to expediting their development. This is occurring in spite of the evidence that the long-term outcomes of early didactic, authoritarian approaches with younger children relate negatively to intellectual development."

In an interview for Parent and Child magazine, Dr. Greenspan insisted that young children suffer greatly if there is inadequate "emotional learning" in their daily lives.

In an interview for "*Parent and Child*" magazine, Dr. Greenspan insisted that young children suffer greatly if there is inadequate "emotional learning" in their daily lives. Such learning, he explained, is both a requisite for their ability to relate well with others and the foundation of cognitive learning. "Emotional development and interactions form the foundation for all children's learning— especially in the first five years of life. During these years, children abstract from their emotional experiences constantly to learn even the most basic concepts. Take, for example, something like saying hello or learning when you can be aggressive and when you have to be nice—and all of these are cues by emotions."

In *Endangered Minds: Why Children Don't Think and What We Can Do About It*, Healy states the case for allowing young children to play with those who love them before requiring them to learn academic skills. She intones, "Driving the cold spikes of inappropriate pressure into the malleable heart of a child's learning may seriously distort the unfolding of both intellect and motivation. This self-serving intellectual assault, increasingly condemned by teachers who see its warped products, reflects a more general ignorance of the growing brain.... Explaining things to children won't do the job; they must have the chance to experience, wonder, experiment, and act it out for themselves. It is this process, throughout life, that enables the growth of intelligence."

Healy goes so far as to describe the damaging effect on the "functional organization of the plastic brain" in pushing too hard too soon: "Before brain regions are myelinated, they do not operate efficiently. For this reason, trying to 'make' children master academic skills for which they do not have the requisite maturation may result in mixed-up patterns of learning.... It is possible to force skills by intensive instruction, but this may cause a child to use immature, inappropriate neural networks and distort the natural growth process."

Play is a way for children to relish childhood, prepare for adulthood, and discover their inner passions.

Play is important for intellectual growth, the exploration of individuality, and the growth of a conscience. Play is a way for children to relish childhood, prepare for adulthood, and discover their inner passions. Legendary psychoanalyst D.W. Winnicott warned us not to underestimate the importance of play. In *The Work and Play of Winnicott*, Simon A. Grolnick elucidates Winnicott's concept of play.

Play in childhood and throughout the life cycle helps to relieve the tension of living, helps to prepare for the serious, and sometimes for the deadly (e.g., war games), helps define and redefine the boundaries between ourselves and others, helps give us a fuller sense of our own personal and bodily being. Playing provides a trying-out ground for proceeding onward, and it enhances drive satisfaction.... Winnicott repeatedly stressed that when playing becomes too drive-infested and excited, it loses its creative growth-building capability and begins to move toward loss of control or a fetishistic rigidity.... Civilization's demands for controlled, socialized behavior gradually, and sometimes insidiously, supersedes the psychosomatic and aesthetic pleasures of open system play.

When we discard playtime, we jeopardize the child's fresh, creative approach to the world. The minuscule amount of peace that children are permitted means that thinking and introspection are demoted as well. Thought requires being, not always doing. Children who are not allowed to retreat once in a while into themselves are not allowed to find out what is there. Our busy lives become ways of hiding from the recesses of the mind. Teaching children to be tough and prepared for the world, making them into achieving doers instead of capable thinkers, has its consequences. Children's innate curiosity is intense. When that natural curiosity has no room to fulfill itself, it burns out like a smothered flame.

In an age when "socialization" into society's ideals and mores is accepted even for babies and toddlers, we should remember that institutionalized schooling even for older children is a relatively new phenomenon. Mass education was a post-Industrial Revolution invention, one that served the dual purposes of preparing children for work and freeing parents to contribute fully to the industrial structure. No longer was work something that families did together, as a unit.

The separation of children from the family's work paved the way for schools and social reformers to assume the task of preparing children for life. This is a lofty role. As parents, we need to inform ourselves as to what our children are being prepared *for* and *how* they are being prepared.

Although our children's days are filled with instruction, allowing them little time of their own, we seem frequently inattentive as to just what they are learning. As William Bennett, Allan Bloom, and others have pointed out, recent years have been characterized by the reformulation of our schools, universities, and information sources according to a relativist, left-leaning ideology saturated with cynicism. This ideology leaves students with little moral-intellectual ground to stand on, as they are taught disrespect not only for past ideas and literary works but for the American political system and Judeo-Christian ethics. Such works as *The Five Little Peppers and How They Grew* and *Little Women* are windows into the soul of a much less cynical (and much less hectic) time.

Teaching children about the great thinkers, writers, and statesmen of the past is neglected as the very idea of greatness and heroism is disputed. Thus, the respect for greatness that might have caused children to glance upward from their TV show or activity and the stories about their country's early history that might have given them respect for a time when computer games didn't exist are not a factor in their lives. The word *preoccupied* acquires new significance, for children's minds are stuffed with the here and now.

The Devaluation Of Homelife

The busyness of modern child rearing and the myopia of the modern outlook reinforce each other. The very ideas that education is a race and that preschool-age children's participation in beneficial experience is more important than playing or being with the family are modern ones that continually reinforce themselves for lack of alternatives. Our busy lives leave insufficient time to question whether all this busyness is necessary and whether the content of our childrens' education is good.

The possibility that children might regard their activities less than fondly when they are older because these activities were forced upon them is not addressed. The possibility that they may never find their own passionate interests is not considered. (I came across an interesting television show that discussed the problem middle-school coaches are having with burned-out and unenthusiastic participants in a wide range of sports. The coaches attributed this to the fact that children had already been doing these sports for years and were tired of the pressure.)

One needs time to be a thinker, freedom to be creative, and some level of choice to be enthusiastic. Families can bestow upon children opportunities for autonomy while at the same time giving them a stable base to fall back upon and moral and behavioral guidelines. Having a competitive edge is neither as important nor as lasting as the ability to lead a genuine, intelligently thought-out, and considerate life.

Some of the best learning experiences happen not in an institution, not with a teacher, but in a child's independent "research" of the world at hand.

Some of the best learning experiences happen not in an institution, not with a teacher, but in a child's independent "research" of the world at hand. As the child interprets the world around her, creates new things with the materials available to her, and extracts new ideas from the recesses of her mind, she is learning to be an active, contributing participant in the world. She occupies her physical, temporal, and intellectual space in a positive, resourceful way. Conversely, if she is constantly stuffed with edifying "opportunities," resentment and lack of autonomy are the likely results.

In *The Erosion of Childhood*, Valerie Polakow insists upon the child's ability to "make history" as opposed to simply receiving it. Lamenting the overinstitutionalization of children in day care and school, she warns, "Children as young as a year old now enter childhood institutions to be formally schooled in the ways

of the social system and emerge eighteen years later to enter the world of adulthood having been deprived of their own history-making power, their ability to act upon the world in significant and meaningful ways." She adds, "The world in which children live—the institutional world that babies, toddlers and the very young have increasingly come to inhabit and confront—is a world in which they become the objects, not the subjects of history, a world in which history is being made of them."

Day care provides both too much stimulation of the chaotic, disorganized kind, which comes inevitably from the cohabitation of large numbers of babies and toddlers, and too much of the organized kind that comes, of necessity, from group-centered living. It provides too little calm, quiet, space, or comfort and too little opportunity to converse and relate to a loving other.

Imagine, for example, a parent sitting down with her child for a "tea party." As she pours real tea into her own cup and milk into her child's, the "how to do things" is taken seriously. The child is encouraged to say "thank you" and to offer cookies to his mother, and their chat begins. Although they are pretending to be two adults, the ritual is real; it occurs in a real home setting; it provides the child with real food and a real opportunity for "mature" conversation. The mother says, "I'm so glad to be here for tea. How have you been?" The child, enjoying the chance to play the part of his mother's host, answers, "Fine! Would you like another cookie?" "Oh yes, thank you," answers his mother. "These cookies are delicious!" The child is learning about civilized behavior.

Children living in the new millennium need a refuge from the impersonal, the mechanical, and the programmed. We must provide them with more than opportunities for skill learning, socialization, and competition.

Then, picture the toy tea set at the learning center. Two children decide "to have tea." They fight over who has asked whom over. When one child asks, "How have you been?" the other loses interest and walks away. Too much of this peer-centered learning and not enough of adult-based learning clearly has negative implications for social development. The child simply cannot learn right from wrong, proper from improper, from other children who themselves have trouble making these distinctions.

Homelife that provides a break from group action has innumerable advantages for older children as well. Think of the different learning experiences a child receives from sitting down at the dinner table with his family and from gulping down a hamburger on the way to a nighttime game. In one case, the child has the opportunity to learn about manners and conversation. In the other, he is given another opportunity to compete with peers. (This is not to deny the benefits of being part of a team but simply to state that homelife itself is beneficial.) I hear many parents of high-school students complain about the competitive, selfish manner of today's students. And, yet, most of these students have not a moment in their day that is not competitive.

How can we expect children to value kindness and cooperation when their free time has been totally usurped by activities wherein winning is everything? At home, winning is not everything (unless the child expends all his time trying to "beat the enemy" in a video game). At home, a child is much more likely to be reprimanded for not compromising with his siblings than for not "defeating" them. If homelife provides children with time to define their individuality and interact with family members (and all the give-and-take implied), then it is certainly an invaluable aspect of a child's advancement.

Children living in the new millennium need a refuge from the impersonal, the mechanical, and the programmed. We must provide them with more than opportunities for skill learning, socialization, and competition. Otherwise, something will be missing in their humanness. For to be human is to have the ca-

pacity for intimate attachments based upon love (which can grow more intimate because of the closeness that family life provides); it is to reason and to have a moral sense of things; it is to be capable of a spontaneity that stems from original thought or from some passion within.

We must set our children free from our frenetic, goal-oriented pace. We must create for them a private realm wherein no child-rearing "professional" can tread. Within this secure space, the possibilities are endless. With this stable base to fall back upon, children will dare to dream, think, and explore. They will compete, learn, and socialize as the blossoming individuals that they are, not as automatons engineered for results.

ANNE R. PIERCE is an author and political philosopher who lives in Cincinnati with her husband and three children. As a writer, she finds that bringing up children in the modern world gives her much food for thought.

And Now, the Hard Part

That sweet little thing is about to commandeer your life. Be prepared.

LAUREN PICKER

Amber Krystallis isn't getting out much these days. She spends every waking moment at someone else's beck and call, performing a dizzying blur of tasks that never seem to satisfy her commander, much less elicit a thank-you. "He's fussy most of the time," allows the Bronxville, New York, fashion-industry assistant who often toils away in the middle of the night, logging only about four or five hours of sleep. Preparing to unveil a designer's latest collection? Hardly. Krystallis is on maternity leave, caring for her infant son, Jackson, and realizing that new parenthood is a kind of endless episode of "Survivor"—without the sweeping views.

Whoever came up with the Peace Corps motto "The toughest job you'll ever love" probably wasn't a parent. Most expectant couples are braced for sleep deprivation and dirty diapers. But the reality is much, much harder in ways that even the most informed new parents may find surprising. Research shows that marriage takes a hit when baby makes three. Gen-X parents, in particular, are reeling. According to a 2003 analysis of 90 studies involving 31,000 married people, the drop in marital satisfaction after the first baby's birth is a staggering 42 percent larger among the current generation of parents than their predecessors. "The finding is particularly strong for women with infants," adds Jean Twenge, an assistant professor of psychology at San Diego State University and a coauthor of the review. Satisfaction dips even lower (though only slightly) with each successive child. Studies also suggest that one third to one half of new-parent couples experience as much marital distress as couples already in therapy for marital difficulties. No wonder the National Marriage Project at Rutgers University concluded in its 2004 annual report, "Children seem to be a growing impediment for the happiness of marriages."

Part of the problem is simply the bone-grinding demands of child care, which can push a couple's relationship not just to the back burner but clear off the stovetop. "I'm so burned out at the end of the day that I have nothing left for my husband. All I want to do is get in my bed, read my book and escape," confesses Amelia Gerlin, a Shelburne, Vermont, at-home mother of two children.

Tensions like these have probably been around since Neanderthal parents grunted at each other. But for the current generation of new parents—who tend to be older and already juggling

careers—the hurdles are higher because the expectations are, too. It's not enough to raise a nice kid; she's got to be ahead of the developmental curve and involved in arts and athletic activities (while fueled only by nutritious, organic snacks, of course). The couples' individual roles change as well. She becomes a diaper-changing lactation machine; he feels pressured to earn big money. "A new baby often trips couples back into stereotypical roles and gender expectations of each other. It's a very hard thing to resist," says Barbara Risman, co-chair of the Council on Contemporary Families in New York. While the expectation is for fathers to be more involved than ever (and many are), it is still Mom who does most of the work. "I'm definitely taking the June Cleaver role," allows Mara Barth, a mom from Wilmette, Illinois, who left her job as a travel consultant six weeks before the birth of her son, Sam, in October. Though her husband knows his way around a Pamper, she tends to change most of the diapers; she also makes sure the pantry is stocked and dinner is on the table (even if it means ordering in). Barth has no complaints. But a University of California, Berkeley, study that tracked 100 couples from first pregnancy through the child's transition to kindergarten found that the No. 1 source of conflict in the first three years of parenthood is the division of labor. The couples had expected a more 50-50 arrangement than they ended up with, explains psychologist Carolyn Pape Cowan, who, with her husband, documented these findings in "When Partners Become Parents: The Big Life Change for Couples." The Cowans also found that when Dad doesn't step up, Mom is more likely to report symptoms of depression. "That's not a good recipe for parenting or for the couple's relationship," says Cowan.

What's a parent to do? Drawing on data from a 13-year study, Seattle-based psychologist and marriage expert John Gottman found that couples who are most likely to remain happy after becoming parents are those in which the husband admires his wife, keeps romance alive and understands his wife's inner life. (It helps if the woman reciprocates, but, according to Gottman, it's Hubby's behavior that makes the difference.) Gottman also encourages couples to communicate with kindness. Instead of screaming, "You lazy s.o.b.! Do I have to do everything?" take a deep breath, lose the edge in your tone and say, "I know you're sleep-deprived, too. But will you please put the dishes away?" And to preserve intimacy, Gottman urges parents to go out on regular dates—without the wee ones.

Of course, parents aren't the only ones who struggle with the arrival of a new baby. Many older siblings don't exactly feel the love. "It's very hard to share someone you love," explains Nancy Samalin, author of "Loving Each One Best," a book about raising siblings. James Srebnick would surely agree. His parents tried to prepare the toddler for the arrival of his little brother last fall; they talked about what it would be like and read books about becoming a big brother. James was onboard, happily kissing his mommy's belly as the pregnancy progressed. Then Andrew arrived. "He freaked," recalls Jessica Goldman Srebnick, a hospitality-industry executive in Miami Beach, Florida. Sometimes James would even try to hit the baby. With plenty of one-on-one time with both of his parents, James rallied. "Now, when he wakes up in the morning he says, 'Where's A.J.?' He'll go see the baby and say, Good morning, buddy,' which makes my heart sing," notes Srebnick.

Some family members' hearts are singing from the get-go. You can pretty much count on Grandma and Grandpa to be smitten with the new generation. And unless grandparents weigh in a little too often with unsolicited advice or direction, the arrival of grandchildren can draw a couple closer to their own families of origin, as well as to in-laws with whom they now share a history and a future. "It's been really great for my relationship with my parents. I struggled with them in days gone by, but now, with the kids, they adore them and they help me quite a bit," says Amelia Gerlin, who lives near her parents.

Grandparents can make great pinch-sitters—a lifeline to stressed-out parents. Pity those who don't have it. "It would be easy if we had parents or family in town," says Toby Page, an airline-industry buyer in Frisco, Texas. He and his wife ultimately decided that it made sense for Kimberly to quit her job to stay home with baby Austin.

Like Kimberly Page, about one third of American women leave the work force after starting a family; another third dial back to part-time hours. It's a decision with which many struggle, and either choice brings its own stresses. Working parents must juggle their professional demands with their family's needs; couples who give up one income often grapple with financial worries. After all, those little bundles of joy cost a bundle of green. According to Baby Bargains, a popular, money-saving guide for new and expectant parents, providing a baby with the basics comes in at $6,200. The U.S. Department of Agriculture estimates that it costs middle-class Americans $178,590 to raise a child to the age of 18, a staggering amount that doesn't even include college.

But you can't put a price tag on the incalculable joys of parenthood. While a baby will upend your life as you know it, the new arrival can also enrich your existence in ways you couldn't imagine, in the process transforming a marriage into a family. "Both [my husband] and I keep saying it's just amazing how much you can love this little person," marvels Amber Krystallis. "When he wakes me up in the middle of the night, I'm still happy to see him." How many people in your life can you say that about?

Adopting A New American Family

Adoption plays a key role in our nation's diversity, experts say, and merits more attention from psychology.

JAMIE CHAMBERLIN
Monitor staff

Adoption is redefining the American family: International and transracial adoptions are speeding up the nation's diversity by creating more multicultural families and communities. And as more same-sex couples and single parents adopt, and more grandparents adopt their grandchildren following parental abuse or neglect, the 21st century American family has many looks and meanings, notes journalist Adam Pertman in his best seller "Adoption Nation: How The Adoption Revolution is Transforming America" (Basic Books, 2001).

In addition, adoption itself has changed over the last 20 years, experts say. Due to policy changes in many states, adoptions tend to be much more open than in years past, when adoption records were sealed and adopted children couldn't access their personal histories. Many adopted children have contact with their biological parents—or "birth-parents." In the case of many kinship or foster-care adoptions, they may also see members of their own extended family.

The increasingly diverse adoption population, and these changes in adoption policy and practice, are spurring the need for more research, say psychologists who study adoption. For starters, says longtime adoption researcher Harold Grotevant, PhD, of the department of family social science at the University of Minnesota (UM), researchers should be studying how to help children navigate their membership in multiple families and cultures. Research is also lacking on such issues as how adults adopted as children cope with issues of identity and loss, or with emotions that emerge when they start a family.

What's more, few practitioners specialize or receive graduate training in helping clients navigate these and related issues, such as the emotions that can accompany the decision to search out a biological mother. Those who do specialize in adoption or in disorders that may accompany international adoptions, such as attachment disorders, are likely to live in metropolitan areas and may be inaccessible to families in rural areas.

"More and more, people in small towns are adopting," says Cheryl Rampage, PhD, of the Family Institute at Northwestern University. "The factors that lead to adoption happen across the spectrum and geography of the country."

Research Strides

Among those striving to fill the adoption research gaps is UM associate professor of psychology Richard Lee, PhD, who participates in the university's multidisciplinary International Adoption Project, a large-scale survey of Minnesota parents who adopted internationally between 1990 and 1998. In the project, led by developmental psychologist Megan Gunnar, PhD, UM researchers surveyed more than 2,500 parents about their children's health, development and adjustment. They also asked participants whether their employers offered leave for the adoption, how their kids have fared academically and how they managed adoption costs, among other topics.

Lee, a second-generation Korean American, says his personal friendships with many in the Korean-American adoption community spurred his interest in this overlooked segment of the Asian American population. He's using the data to explore cultural socialization practices in families who have adopted internationally. Some adoptive parents expose their children to their birth culture by sending them to language classes and culture camps or setting up playdates with other internationally adopted children. They may also make a conscious effort to talk with their child about racism and discrimination. But what's not known, Lee maintains, is how these efforts affect their children's well-being or cultural or ethnic identity, or provide a buffer against racism or discrimination as they grow older.

"We presume that if parents socialize kids in a certain way, those outcomes will be protective factors," says Lee. "But there is actually very little research on that."

Grotevant, also of UM, heads a separate longitudinal study, the Minnesota Texas Adoption Research Project, on how openness in adoption affects the adopted child and members of the "adoptive kinship network," which includes the child, the extended adoptive family and the extended birth family. Among the salient findings of the first two waves of his study—conducted when the children were between 4 and 12 years old and 12 and 20 years old—is that, within the group of families having some birth-parent contact, higher degrees of collaboration and communication between the child's adoptive parents and birth-mothers were linked to better adjustment in the children during middle childhood. Grotevant is now gathering a third wave of data as the children—now in their 20s—become adults. He's looking at how they transition from school to work, how they have fared academically, their identity and interpersonal relationships, and if they are searching for or have contact with their birth-mother.

"We know from the research literature that many adopted children are in their 20s and 30s when they begin to seek information about their birth-relatives," says Grotevant. He's also asking the young adults what advice they have for people considering adoption, which he hopes—along with the rest of his findings—can be used to inform adoption practice and policy.

Like Grotevant, Rutgers University psychologist David Brodzinsky, PhD, is hoping his findings from a national survey of adoption agency opportunities for gay and lesbian adoptive parents can guide future policy on adoption. The study, conducted in 2003 through the Evan B. Donaldson Adoption Institute, showed that 60 percent of the agencies he surveyed were willing to accept applications from gay men and lesbians, but less then 39 percent had made such placements. Only 18 to 19 percent actively recruited adoptive parents in the gay and lesbian community, he notes.

"The trend has been for supporting gay and lesbian adoption—most states do, but a few ban it or have barriers that make it difficult," says Brodzinsky, a senior fellow at the institute.

Serving Families

The majority of adoptive parents turn to adoption agencies—or social work or adoption support groups—for postadoption counseling or services, but a handful of psychologists are also serving the adoption community. Take, for example, Martha Henry, PhD, of the Center for Adoption Research at the University of Massachusetts Medical School. As director of education and training there, Henry teaches an eight-week adoption course to medical students each semester that covers such topics as how to work with adoptive and foster-care families and to discuss adoption with couples facing infertility.

When she's not teaching medical students, Henry educates elementary school teachers on ways to keep their classrooms comfortable for children who were adopted or are in the foster-care system.

"Lots of classroom assignments are based on that perfect family model with two parents, a child, a dog and a picket fence," she says, such as asking children to bring in baby pictures to teach about change. That kind of activity is inappropriate if a class includes an adopted child, adds Henry.

"There are other ways to do the same lesson with something that doesn't put a child in a situation of having to say, 'I don't have a picture from when I was a baby,'" says Henry.

Likewise, psychologist Amanda Baden, PhD, a Chinese-American who was adopted from Hong Kong, teaches a course on adoption issues—which she believes is unique in any psychology training program—as part of a master's-level counseling program at Montclair State University in New Jersey. In it, she covers many of the issues she sees in her part-time practice working with families and individuals who are part of transracial adoptions. Many of her clients struggle with such issues as whether to search for their birth-mothers and how to manage conflicts between their birth culture and race and their adopted culture and race.

Cheryl Rampage sees many of these same issues in the Northwestern University Family Institute's Adoptive Families Program, which offers counseling and psychotherapy to adoptive families and school outreach programs that train teachers on adoption sensitivity. The program also hosts the Adoption Club, a biweekly support group for local adopted 7 to 11 year olds. The club is geared to preteens because in these years, "for the first time, loss becomes a real issue," she says. Preschool-age adopted children tend to talk about their being adopted matter-of-factly, but at 7 or 8 these same children start to feel scared and sad when they think of this other family they lost, says Rampage.

Through the club, children draw family pictures, play games and write stories or perform plays about adoption.

According to Baden, the adoption community could benefit if more psychologists specialized in adoption issues like Henry and Rampage do.

"Psychologists often think adoption is social work's domain," she says. "Psychologists have a tremendous amount to offer.... Adoption and the issues associated with it have moved beyond the domains of case management and adoption placements. It's time for psychologists to use their skills to develop treatment protocols and counseling process research."

The 4th Biennial Conference on Adoption will be held at St. John's University in New York City, Oct. 13–14, 2006. The meeting will include workshops, speakers and programs on adoption that are geared to teachers, mental health professionals and families. For more information, contact conference organizers Amanda Baden, PhD, and Rafael Javier, PhD, at **baden@transracialadoption.net**.

In addition, the Second International Conference on Adoption Research will be held July 17–21, 2006 at the University of East Anglia in Norwich, England. For more information, visit the conference Web site at **www.icar2.org.uk**.

After the Bliss

For many adoptive moms, post-baby depression is a real and painful ordeal. Shelley Page reports why it happens and how to feel better.

SHELLEY PAGE

The women in the new mothers' circle eyed me warily. I'd sat politely listening as they discussed their C-section scars, cracked nipples, and nighttime feedings, and now, apparently, it was my turn. I had suffered insomnia, jet lag, and a radical life change, but I didn't feel I had a right to complain. After all, I'd been reminded so often, "You're lucky, you did it the easy way."

A thin, sparrow-like woman asked with a big grin: "Why did you adopt?" before adding with a sweet smile, "Infertility problems, I guess?"

Of course, my reasons for adopting were none of their business, yet I felt the need to explain. I mumbled something about health problems, and then I was on my feet, fumbling my way out of there. Trudging home through the snow, I reprimanded myself: Stay indoors, don't go near biological mothers. What were you thinking?

As an adoptive mother, I sometimes seemed to have little in common with other new moms. My baby was months old, not weeks. And I had different issues—insensitive comments, for example, or worries about a shorter parental leave. There was only one thing that I was certain I shared with some biological mothers: I was depressed.

Not What I Expected

From the heights of euphoria two months earlier, when my daughter was placed in my arms for the first time, I had slid into despair. Despite a few attempts to get out and socialize, I mostly lay on the couch watching bad movies, ordering take-out, occasionally shaking a rattle in front of my daughter's face, and praying my husband would come home to rescue me.

"The cows, let's go see the cows," he said one afternoon, before hanging up the phone to rush home. I remember that day as the lowest point of my depression. It was the middle of winter. The sky was gray, like the unwashed blankets piling up in the laundry basket. He thought a visit to the Ottawa Experimental Farm would cheer me up, so within an hour of my pleading phone call, he was pushing us around the heated barn, from Jersey to Holstein.

Far from feeling better, I ached for the poor cows, trapped in pens with nowhere to go. "This is so bleak," I moaned. At a restaurant later, I wept and could only choke down half a veggie burger.

It wasn't supposed to be this way. My lovely daughter, Cleo, was deeply content, had a sharp sense of humor even as an infant, and pretty much slept through the night. I knew how blessed we were, yet, some days I could manage little more than popping in a Teletubbies video. Or I'd get a head of steam to make organic baby food, then leave the ingredients on the counter all day as I slumped in front of the TV.

Isolation just added to my despair. To mention my depression to my extended family, or the biological moms at a play group, seemed like heresy. I tried it a few times and got remarks like: "Don't be silly, you had it easy, you didn't have to give birth or breastfeed." Besides, women get depressed after birth because of their hormones. Don't they?

When we went through the adoption process, our adoption agency prepared us for the unexpected: a sick child, a difficult journey, developmental delays. But no one mentioned that some adoptive mothers, and even dads, wrestle mightily with depression—perhaps because it's only recently that depression among adoptive parents has become an area for study, and many psychologists bluntly say they've never heard of such a condition.

What Does This Mean?

Post-Adoption Depression Syndrome (PADS) is a term coined by June Bond, an adoption advocate from North Carolina who wrote about it in 1995. Bond had encountered panicked, depressed, and overwrought parents. One woman said she could not reconcile the birthmother's feelings of loss and grief with her own sense of satisfaction.

Another North Carolina mother, Harriet McCarthy, suffered profoundly from depression after adopting the first of her three sons, who was then six. "I'd wake up in the middle of the night panicking," she recalls. "He kept throwing temper tantrums, I didn't know why. He didn't want to be hugged. I was angry constantly." She got better only after she was prescribed antidepressants.

Warning Signs

Having just one of the symptoms listed below may not indicate a larger problem. But if you find yourself struggling regularly with a few of these, seek help from a professional.

- Loss of interest in being around other people
- Always on the verge of tears
- Difficulty concentrating or making decisions
- General fatigue of loss of energy
- Difficulty sleeping or increased need for sleep
- Significant weight gain or loss
- Excessive or inappropriate guilt
- Feelings of worthlessness or powerlessness
- A sense of hopelessness
- Loss of enjoyment in things
- Irritability
- Recurring thoughts about death or suicide

When Depression Strikes

Harriet McCarthy, an adoptive mother who has researched and written on post-adoption depression, suggests a few steps to help new adoptive parents cope better.

- **You may want to keep family and friends at bay in the early days**, except for one person who is designated to help with the domestic duties. This gives the nuclear family time to bond and recover.
- **Get exercise.** Go for walks.
- **Set aside special time** for your spouse or partner, if you have one.
- **Schedule time away** from the baby to clear your head.
- **Remember that bonding takes time**, as does "falling in love with your baby," McCarthy warns. "In some cases, we're adopting children with fully formed personalities that may or may not blend with the family. Be patient and realistic."

Curious to see if other adoptive parents shared her experience, last year McCarthy surveyed 3,100 members of an adoption Web site she moderated. Of the 145 parents who answered, over 65 percent said they'd experienced depression after adopting their children. Nearly half of those with symptoms said that they suffered for at least six months, and almost all said depression had affected their health. After she published her survey, McCarthy received e-mails and calls from parents, psychologists, and doctors thanking her for exposing the problem.

For McCarthy, there is no mystery as to why some adoptive mothers are stricken with the blues. First, many have spent years struggling to reach the point of having a child. "Their protracted and unfulfilled hopes, dreams, and longing may cause unrealistic expectations about what it will be like to be a parent," she wrote. "They are unprepared for the grief they feel when reality confronts the child of their imaginations."

Dee Paddock, a psychotherapist based in Denver, points to one culprit: the disconnect between outsiders' assumptions about adoptive parents and the real stresses that any new parent experiences. "The world sees you as this holy, besainted mother because they think you have rescued a child. So it's difficult to be part of the club that says, 'This is so hard,'" says Paddock, herself a mother of three. "The world also says you did it the easy way, which is really dismissive." Paddock believes women with chronic, low-lying depression due to health or infertility issues are at greater risk for post-adoption depression.

Reaching Out

Instead of seeking help, adoptive moms typically try to tough it out because they worry that an admission to their social worker or adoption agency could get them branded as unfit or incompetent parents. Meanwhile, even close friends and relatives don't always understand. If a couple has struggled for a decade to become parents, why aren't they blissed out when a child finally arrives?

That was the experience of a friend of mine, who confided in me that no one took her depression seriously. "They all say I was desperate for a baby, and I asked for this." My friend, who adopted her daughter internationally, didn't want me to use her name in this story for fear that admitting to depression might jeopardize a second adoption. She was prone to depression, but had no idea adoption was a risk factor. If she'd been warned, she might have been better prepared, she thinks. As it was, "I couldn't even make decisions about what to have for dinner."

Adoption is not something you spend your life preparing for. As a girl, I used to act out the ritual of becoming a mom. We'd tuck our baby dolls under our smocks and pretend we were pregnant. When my doll, Betsy, popped out, I would rock her gently. I never imagined Betsy coming from the other side of the world. Neither adoption nor the messy realities of life are child's play. And as adults, many of us are unprepared for the emotional journey that adoption demands.

Some adoptive mothers report being very sad on what is supposed to be the happiest day of their lives: "This isn't my baby, it's someone else's." I, however, was euphoric when we received our eight-month-old daughter. The photographs from our trip to adopt her show a radiant and elated mother. My husband said I entered some state of grace where little bothered me. Then we returned to Ottawa and real life.

While I did my best to keep my chin up, I didn't suffer in silence. I remember sitting slumped in my doctor's office. Not once in our several conversations did either of us consider that it was motherhood making me blue. Instead, we settled on Ottawa's winter weather, and I was prescribed a light box to combat Seasonal Affective Disorder.

Looking back, I wonder why it took me so long to understand what now seem like obvious reasons for my emotional nosedive. Anytime we achieve a major life goal, whether it's graduating from university, landing a dream job, getting married, or having a baby, there is some sort of letdown afterward. For those of us who adopt children of a different race, the health concerns or infertility that led us to choose adoption are suddenly in the forefront, thrust there by the questions that strangers ask when they see us with our children. We also face many of the same problems any new parents do—stress, financial troubles, sleep deprivation, marital strife.

Harriet McCarthy encourages parents to ask for help. The adoption agency we used recently held a session called Shifting Gears, to prepare parents for the emotional pitfalls they might encounter before and after adoption. The agency now gives a resource binder to all adopting families, which includes material on PADS.

One of the most important steps I took was joining a weekly play group for adoptive parents and their children. One early spring day, after four months at home with my daughter, I forced myself to attend. The mothers there asked all the right questions: "Where did you adopt?" "When did you get back?"

"How did you manage adjusting her sleep to Ottawa time?" They got it. That day, as I pushed my daughter home in the stroller, there was a spring in my step. I was on the road back.

When we adopt a second time later this year, I have no fears I will become depressed again. Maybe I'm being unrealistic, but I think I've learned a lot from the first time around. And if I feel isolated, I have a large group of adoptive parents to turn to for support. In fact, I'm unbelievably excited to become a mom again because I know I'm more emotionally prepared.

SHELLEY PAGE lives in Ottawa, Canada, with her husband and two daughters. This article originally appeared in *Today's Parent*.

UNIT 3

Finding a Balance: Maintaining Relationships

Unit Selections

Key Points to Consider

- Is marriage necessary for a happy, fulfilling life? Why is or is not that so? When you think of a marriage, what do you picture? What are your expectations of your (future) spouse? What are your expectations of yourself?

- What are your views on spanking? Why is it seen as an ineffective parenting tool? What are other alternatives? What do you think of them? Why?

- What is the role of fathers in rearing children? How are fathers altered by their involvement in raising children?

- Who do you include in your family? Is everyone legally tied to you?

Student Website

www.mhcls.com/online

Internet References

Further information regarding these websites may be found in this book's preface or online.

Child Welfare League of America
   http://www.cwla.org

Coalition for Marriage, Family, and Couples Education
   http://www.smartmarriages.com

The National Academy for Child Development
   http://www.nacd.org

National Council on Family Relations
   http://www.ncfr.com

Positive Parenting
   http://www.positiveparenting.com

SocioSite
   http://www.pscw.uva.nl/sociosite/TOPICS/Women.html

*A*nd they lived happily ever after... The romantic image conjured up by this well-known final line from fairy tales is not reflective of the reality of family life and relationship maintenance. The belief that somehow love alone should carry us through is pervasive. In reality, maintaining a relationship takes dedication, hard work, and commitment.

We come into relationships, regardless of their nature, with fantasies about how things ought to be. Partners, spouses, parents, children, siblings, and others—all family members have at least some unrealistic expectations about each other. It is through the negotiation of their lives together that they come to work through these expectations and replace them with other, it is hoped, more realistic ones. By recognizing and acting on their own contribution to the family, members can set and attain realistic family goals. Tolerance and acceptance of differences can facilitate this process as can competent communication skills. Along the way, family members need to learn new skills and develop new habits of relating to each other. This will not be easy, and, try as they may, not everything will be controllable. Factors both inside and outside the family may impede their progress.

Even before one enters a marriage or other committed relationship, attitudes, standards and beliefs influence one's choices. Increasingly, choices include whether or not we should commit to such a relationship. From the start of a committed relationship, the expectations both partners have of their relationship have an impact, and the need to negotiate differences is a constant factor. Adding a child to the family affects the lives of parents in ways that they could previously only imagine. Feeling under siege, many parents struggle to know the right way to rear their children. These factors can all combine to make child rearing more difficult than it might otherwise have been. Other family relationships also evolve, and in our nuclear family-focused culture, it is possible to forget that family relationships extend beyond those between spouses, parents, and children.

The initial subsection presents a number of aspects regarding marital and other committed relationships, decisions about even entering such a relationship, and ways of balancing multiple and often competing roles played by today's couples, who hope to fulfill individual as well as couple needs. It is a difficult balancing act to cope with the expectations and pressures of work, home, children, and relational intimacy. In "Contextual Influences on Marriage: Implications for Policy and Intervention," Benjamin Karney and Thomas Bradbury address the importance of understanding the values of different cultural groups as programs to strengthen marriage are proposed. Programs based on the dominant culture are potentially unlikely to fit the needs of members of minority cultures that potentially differ quite significantly from the white, middle class population on which these programs are based. As various cultural groups come to the United States, unwilling to give up the cultural activities and beliefs of their home country, changes have begun to take place in what is expected when we marry. "Marriage at First Sight," the story of arranged marriages in the U.S. Indian community, may be a sample of what to expect.

The next subsection examines the parent/child relationship. In the first article, "Kaleidoscope of Parenting Cultures," author Vidya Thirumurthy provides a look at how culture influences children. She writes about different cultures, for example, collective vs. individualistic ones, and how parenting styles differ so as to affect consequent child development. The next article, "Spanking Children: Evidence and Issues," explores the research on spanking and other forms of corporal punishment. Although harsh punishment is always problematic, results on mild spanking are mixed and somewhat ambiguous. The next reading, "Stress and the Superdad," documents the fact that fathers, as well as mothers, now face conflicting pressures and pulls from work and home and must struggle to find a balance between the two. In "The Kids Are All Right," Sadie Dingfelder reports on research on families headed by gay and lesbian parents. This research shows that children raised in these households are not significantly different from those raised in heterosexual households. "Are Married Parents Really Better for Children?" is an overview of the research on the parent-child relationship and confronts the assumption that there is a single "best" way to raise children. The final article in this section, "The Perma Parent Trap," depicts a growing trend in the United States—that of adult children moving back in with their parents, with the full approval of the parents.

The third and final subsection looks at other family relationships. Sibling relationships can be one of the most important in one's life. They can also be one of the most challenging, especially if one's siblings have special needs. "Being a Sibling" addresses this relationship from the perspective of children. An expanded view of who we include as family members is presented by John Tyler Connoley in "Aunties and Uncles." The final articles in this section address issues of concern among aged family members. "Roles of American Indian Grandparents in Times of Cultural Crises" depicts a significant enculturative role for grandparents, in which they teach about and reinforce their grandchildren's ties to their cultural past. "Aging Japanese Pen Messages to Posterity" depicts elderly family members serving a similar role, but in a more intimate and relationship centered way.

Contextual Influences on Marriage

Implications for Policy and Intervention

ABSTRACT—Current proposals to promote and strengthen marriage among low-income populations focus on values and behavioral skills as primary targets of intervention. Marital research that examines contextual influences on marriage calls these emphases into question. Ethnographic and survey research reveal no evidence that populations experiencing higher rates of divorce value healthy marriages any less than other populations do. Longitudinal and observational research reveals two mechanisms through which the environment of a marriage may enhance or constrain effective relationship maintenance. First, some environments contain fewer sources of support and pose more severe challenges than others, presenting marriages in those environments with greater burdens than marriages in more supportive environments are faced with. Second, when demands external to the marriage are relatively high, even couples with adequate coping skills may have difficulty exercising those skills effectively. Together, such findings suggest that successful policies and interventions to strengthen marriages need to acknowledge the environments within which marriages take place.

BENJAMIN R. KARNEY[1] AND THOMAS N. BRADBURY[2]

To improve the well-being of low-income populations, federal policymakers have begun to emphasize the role of healthy marriages in shaping adult and child outcomes. The justification for this emphasis on marriage has been correlational research demonstrating that stable, fulfilling marriages are associated with improved physical and mental health and higher educational and economic achievement for parents and children and that the absence of such relationships is associated with poorer health and economic outcomes (e.g., Amato, 2001; Kiecolt-Glaser & Newton, 2001). Assuming that the parents' relationship plays a causal role in these associations, policymakers have proposed allocating over 1.5 billion dollars over the next 5 years to fund activities that support couples in forming and maintaining healthy marriages. Legislation currently being debated in the House and Senate specifies eight allowable activities for this funding, all of which involve some form of relationship education—e.g., teaching the value of stable marriages or teaching relationship and communication skills. Federal policy seems to be guided by two perspectives: one emphasizing values and another focusing on skills as primary determinants of marital outcome.

One challenge to applying educational interventions to low-income families stems from the fact that, although the target populations for these initiatives have been selected exclusively on the basis of their environment (i.e., low socioeconomic status), the models guiding educational interventions generally do not address the role of the environment in determining marital outcomes. Behaviorally oriented relationship education, for example, places the responsibility for marital success or failure squarely on the couple, without regard for how their relationship may be affected by the context within which their marriage takes place. Recent marital research that has directly examined the effects of context on couples' relationships calls this emphasis into question. Cross-sectional surveys and longitudinal studies of newlywed couples have begun to identify paths through which communication, problem solving, and other relationship processes may be constrained or enhanced by supports or demands present in a marriage's context. The emerging picture suggests that even skilled and relatively satisfied couples may have difficulty interacting effectively under conditions of stress or diminished resources. Thus, current research on contextual influences on marriage suggests broadening the focus of interventions and policies designed to support healthy families among low-income populations.

Family Values: Who Has Them? Who Needs Them?

Marriages are unquestionably less frequent and less stable in low-income populations. Survey data reveal that, compared to those in high-income populations, women in low-income populations

---

[1]RAND Corporation and [2]University of California, Los Angeles

are half as likely to be married, twice as likely to divorce if married, and several times more likely to bear children outside of marriage (Bramlett & Mosher, 2002; Singh, Matthews, Clarke, Yannicos, & Smith, 1995). The case for offering values education to these individuals rests on the assumption that people in low-income populations do not appreciate the benefits of stable, healthy marriages as much as do people in high-income populations, in which marriage is more common and divorce less common.

In fact, there has been little research on attitudes toward family issues in low-income populations, but what research does exist indicates that members of these populations may value marriage more, not less, than members of middle- or high-income groups do. For example, Edin (2000) conducted lengthy interviews with unmarried mothers receiving welfare, asking them to describe their attitudes and intentions toward marriage. Far from minimizing the importance of marriage, these mothers reported strongly positive feelings about the institution and expressed their own intentions to marry. They described their decisions to postpone marriage as having little to do with their values and more to do with their belief that their current economic circumstances and available partners would be unlikely to lead to an enduring marriage over time. Thus, members of low-income populations may postpone marriage not because they value it too little but rather because they value it so much that they are unwilling to enter into a marriage that has a high risk of ending in divorce.

It is important to note that Edin's data exclude low-income men, who are notoriously underrepresented in family research. However, quantitative survey data from low-income men and women paint a similar picture. A recent survey commissioned by the state of Florida examined family structures and attitudes in a representative sample (Karney, Garvan, & Thomas, 2003). Over 6,000 residents of Florida, Texas, California, and New York were asked in telephone interviews about their own experiences of marriage and families and about their opinions regarding marriage and family issues. Confirming the pattern in the broader census data, low-income respondents were far more likely than high-income respondents to be unmarried, to be divorced, and to be raising children outside of marriage. At the same time, however, compared to middle- or high-income respondents, members of low-income populations on average expressed the same or more positive attitudes toward traditional family structures (see Fig. 1). For example, when asked to rate their agreement with the statement "A happy, healthy marriage is one of the most important things in life," low-income respondents indicated that they agreed or strongly agreed at the same rate as did middle- and high-income respondents. When unmarried respondents were asked if they would like to be married someday, members of low-income households were substantially more likely than members of middle- or high-income households to say yes.

Existing research offers little justification for allocating limited resources toward values education for low-income populations. At least among women in this population, pro-

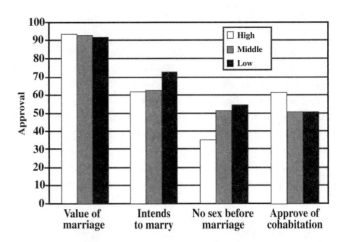

Figure 1 Attitudes toward family issues by household income (high, middle, low). The low-income groups that report the highest rates of divorce, premarital sex, and cohabitation also express the lowest approval of them.

marriage values appear to be in place already, and in any case such values may not be sufficient to bring about stable, fulfilling relationships.

Contextual Influences on Marriage

Whereas there is little evidence that values are associated with decisions to enter into or postpone marriage, there is growing evidence to suggest that the quality of a couple's communication and problem solving is associated with marital outcomes over time (Heyman, 2001; Johnson et al., 2005). Furthermore, several studies provide evidence that premarital education programs focusing on communication can affect problem solving and that such programs may have long-term benefits for marriages (e.g., Halford, Sanders, & Behrens, 2001).

Despite this evidence, the existing research has been limited in two main ways. First, research on marital interaction and premarital education programs has addressed primarily white, college-educated, middle-class samples. In terms of their risk of experiencing marital dysfunction, the support available to them, and the demands they face outside of the marriage, such samples differ greatly from the low-income populations of interest to policymakers. It remains an open question whether programs developed within middle-class populations can be effective for improving the marriages of low-income couples. Second, when assessing relationship processes like problem solving and support, researchers have assumed that such processes are generally stable in the absence of intervention. Research on marital interactions in particular has treated the quality of a couple's communication as a stable, trait-like condition of the relationship that accounts for later marital outcomes. Far less frequent has been research on how marital interactions and relationship processes themselves may vary and develop over time. As a result, the conditions that encourage or discourage effective interactions in marriage remain poorly understood.

Current research on the effects of context and environmental stress on marital processes is beginning to illuminate both of these issues. Drawing from cross-sectional survey research, researchers have begun to examine relationship processes across a wide range of contexts and cultures, to understand how the predictors of marital success may differ depending on the context within which particular marriages form and develop. Using intensive longitudinal designs, researchers have begun to identify the correlates of variability in relationship processes within couples over time, in order to understand the forces that support or constrain couples in their efforts to maintain their relationships. Although it has long been known that marriages under stress report lower marital quality and are at increased risk of dissolution (e.g., Hill, 1949), research adopting these approaches has now elaborated on the mechanisms through which context affects marriage.

Context Shapes the Content of Marital Interactions

An emphasis on relationship skills reflects the assumption that the way couples communicate is more important than the specific issues they discuss. One reason that this assumption has gone unchallenged may be that studies have examined couples in a relatively narrow and privileged segment of the population whose problems are, on average, relatively mild. Surveying a broader range of the population, however, confirms that the couples in different contexts may face different sorts of marital problems. For example, when respondents rated the severity of potential relationship problems in the survey cited earlier (Karney et al., 2003), communication was rated as a relatively severe problem regardless of household income, although it was rated most severe in high-income households (see Fig. 2). Drugs and infidelity, in contrast, were rated as more severe problems by low-income households. Research on middle-class newlyweds indicates that spouses tend to report more severe relationship problems during periods of relatively high stress than they do during periods of relatively low stress (Neff & Karney, 2004). Not surprisingly, the more severe the problems discussed by a couple, the more negatively their communication is rated by objective observers (Vogel & Karney, 2002). Thus, independent of spouses' relationship skills, marriages taking place in more stressful contexts may be more challenging simply due to the increased severity of the obstacles that couples must face inside and outside of their marriages. Interventions that acknowledge those obstacles may prove more effective than interventions addressing communication skills alone.

Context Affects Spouses' Ability to Interact Effectively

When the context of a marriage contains many demands and few sources of support, spouses not only have more severe problems to cope with but may also have diminished ability to exercise the coping skills they possess. A 4-year study of 172 middle-class new-

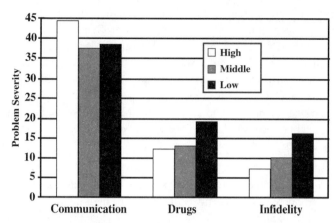

Figure 2 Severity of specific relationship problems by household income (high, middle, and low). Although couples at all income levels report problems with communication, low-income couples are more likely to report problems with drugs or infidelity.

lywed couples (Karney, Story, & Bradbury, 2005) revealed that couples experiencing relatively high levels of chronic stress (e.g., financial difficulties, lack of social support, inadequate employment) not only reported lower marital satisfaction overall but also seemed to have more difficulty maintaining their satisfaction over time. Relative to couples reporting better conditions, those reporting high levels of chronic stress experienced a steeper decline in marital satisfaction over the early years of marriage, a finding that held even after these couples' initially lower levels of satisfaction was controlled for. Moreover, for wives experiencing chronic stress, marital satisfaction was especially reactive to increases in acute stress, such that the same negative life events were associated with steeper declines in satisfaction for stressed wives than they were for less stressed wives.

Why would marital satisfaction be more difficult to maintain when conditions outside of the marriage are more adverse? The activities that maintain relationships take time and energy, so those activities should be harder to undertake under adverse conditions. Supporting this view is an independent study of 82 middle-class newlyweds that examined how spouses' willingness to forgive their partners' negative behaviors was associated with changes in their levels of stress over time (Neff & Karney, 2004). Within-couple analyses revealed that individuals who could excuse their partners' negative behaviors during intervals of relatively low stress were more likely to blame their partners for those same behaviors during periods of relatively high stress. In other words, spouses who are capable of making adaptive responses appear to be less likely to do so when facing challenges outside of their marriages.

It is worth noting that both of these studies sampled from a population experiencing a relatively narrow range of stress. In samples that included severely disadvantaged families, Conger and colleagues (e.g., Conger, Rueter, & Elder, 1999) also showed that economic strain inhibits effective relationship maintenance. Together, such studies begin to suggest how stressful environments come to be associated with negative marital outcomes. Stressful environments not only present couples with more challenges, but they diminish those couples' ability to deal with their challenges effectively.

Implications for Marital Interventions and Policies

Given what is currently known about the effects of context on marriage and marital processes, there are two reasons to expect that, by themselves, interventions developed for middle-class couples may not be adequate to support marriages among the low-income couples of interest to policymakers. First, the skills relevant to solving the problems faced by middle- and upper-income couples may not be relevant to the types of problems (e.g., substance abuse, domestic violence, infidelity) that low-income couples are more likely than other populations to face. Second, even if a set of valuable relationship skills could be identified and taught, those skills may be difficult or impossible to practice in the context of low-income marriage. Effective problem solving will matter little, for example, to couples who have few opportunities to interact together due to demands outside the marriage. Providing such couples with relationship skills training without also addressing the external forces that impede couples' ability to practice those skills may be akin to offering piano lessons to people with no access to a piano.

Providing a solid empirical foundation for interventions to promote and support low-income marriage requires basic research on marriage in this population, not only to identify the processes that make for successful relationships among low-income couples, but also to describe the circumstances that make those processes more or less likely. The unfortunate irony is that, just as this research is needed to inform policy, funding for research on marital outcomes has been explicitly removed from consideration at the National Institute of Mental Health, formerly the major source of support for marital research.

The drive to provide services that improve the lives of low-income families thus presents marital research with a challenge and an opportunity. The challenge is to find ways to specify the minimum conditions that must be met before behavioral skills training can have a positive impact on low-income marriages. The opportunity is the chance to reexamine what is known about the significant predictors of marital outcome in this new context, and thereby to establish which of those predictors are not only significant, but substantial.

Recommended Reading

Bradbury, T.N. & Karney, B.R. (2004). Understanding and altering the longitudinal course of marriage. *Journal of Marriage and Family, 66*, 862–879.

Edin, K., & Kefalas, M. (2005). *Promises I can keep: Why poor women put motherhood before marriage.* Berkeley: University of California Press.

Cherlin, A.J. (2004). The deinstitutionalization of American marriage. *Journal of Marriage and Family, 66*, 848–861.

Acknowledgments—Preparation of this article was supported by Grant R0lMH59712 from the National Institute of Mental Health awarded to the first author, and Grant R01MH48764 from the National Institute of Mental Health awarded to the second author.

References

Amato, P.R. (2001). Children of divorce in the 1990s: An update of the Amato and Keith (1991) meta-analysis. *Journal of Family Psychology, 15*, 355–370.

Bramlett, M.D., & Mosher, W.D. (2002). *Cohabitation, marriage, divorce, and remarriage in the United States* (Vital and Health Statistics Series 23, No. 22). Hyattsville, Maryland: National Center for Health Statistics.

Conger, R.D., Rueter, M.A., & Elder, G.H. (1999). Couple resilience to economic pressure. *Journal of Personality and Social Psychology, 76*, 54–71.

Edin, K. (2000). What do low-income single mothers say about marriage? *Social Problems, 47*, 112–133.

Halford, W.K., Sanders, M.R., & Behrens, B.C. (2001). Can skills training prevent relationship problems in at-risk couples? Four-year effects of a behavioral relationship education program. *Journal of Family Psychology, 15*, 750–768.

Heyman, R.E. (2001). Observation of couple conflicts: Clinical assessment applications, stubborn truths, and shaky foundations. *Psychological Assessment, 13*, 5–35.

Hill, R. (1949). *Families under stress.* New York: Harper & Row.

Johnson, M.D., Cohan, C.L., Davila, J., Lawrence, E., Rogge, R.D., Karney, B.R., Sullivan, K.T., & Bradbury, T.N. (2005). Problem-solving skills and affective expressions as predictors of change in marital satisfaction. *Journal of Consulting and Clinical psychology, 73*, 15–27.

Karney, B.R., Garvan, C.W., & Thomas, M.S. (2003). *Family formation in Florida: 2003 baseline survey of attitudes, beliefs, and demographics relating to marriage and family formation.* Gainesville, FL: University of Florida.

Karney, B.R., Story, L.B., & Bradbury, T.N. (2005). Marriages in context: Interactions between chronic and acute stress among newlyweds. In T.A. Revenson, K. Kayser, & G. Bodenmann (Eds.), *Emerging perspectives on couples' coping with stress* (pp. 13–32). Washington, DC: American Psychological Association.

Kiecolt-Glaser, J.K., & Newton, T.L. (2001). Marriage and health: His and hers. *Psychological Bulletin, 127*, 472–503.

Neff, L.A., & Karney, B.R. (2004). How does context affect intimate relationships? Linking external stress and cognitive processes within marriage. *Personality and Social Psychology Bulletin, 30*, 134–148.

Singh, G.K., Matthews, T.J., Clarke, S.C., Yannicos, T., & Smith, B.L. (1995). *Annual summary of births, marriages, divorces, and deaths: United States, 1994* (Monthly Vital Statistics Report, Vol. 43, No. 13). Atlanta, GA: National Center for Health Statistics.

Vogel, D.L., & Karney, B.R. (2002). Demands and withdrawal in newlyweds: Elaborating on the social structure hypothesis. *Journal of Social and Personal Relationships, 19*, 685–702.

Address correspondence to Benjamin R. Karney, RAND Corporation, 1776 Main Street, P.O. Box 2138, Santa Monica, CA 90407-2138; e-mail: bkarney@rand.org.

Marriage at First Sight

They date, go to U2 concerts, hit bars with pals. But for the sake of tradition and family, even some highly Americanized Indian immigrants agree to wed strangers

PAULA SPAN

On the evening before her engagement, Vibha Jasani found herself on the rooftop terrace of her uncle's house in India, feeling a breeze begin as the sun lowered, gazing out at the city of Rajkot and the mountains beyond, trying to be calm, and failing. She was about to cry, and not with joy.

When her father asked what was wrong, she just shrugged; she could hardly manage a reply. But he knew anyway.

Marrying a pleasant young man she'd just met was not the romance Vibha envisioned when she was a teenager playing volleyball at Annandale High; it was not the kind of courtship she yakked about with her friends at Virginia Tech or her co-workers in Arlington. This felt like—and was—a custom held over from a previous century. But because she was 25 and not-getting-any-younger, her parents had prevailed on her to do something she'd repeatedly vowed she wouldn't: fly to India to find a husband.

She'd spent the past three weeks meeting men—at least one each day—carefully prescreened by her uncle for their suitability. She'd poured them tea and passed platters of sweets and nuts, enduring awkward half-hour conversations that seemed more like interviews. She chose the one she could talk most comfortably with; they went out together three or four times; she met his family. All parties approved, and suddenly 300 people were about to stream into a rented hall the next day to celebrate their engagement, which everyone seemed delighted about, except the prospective bride.

"Everything's so out of control," Vibha worried. "Things just sort of happened." She'd gone along with the flurry of events, sometimes resentfully and sometimes obligingly, but she wasn't sure she could bring herself to take the next step. Her almost-fiancé, Haresh, appeared to be a nice guy—mature, considerate. But was he the man she wanted to spend the next 50 years with? How could she possibly know after such a brief time? What if, once she returned home to Northern Virginia, she was miserable with someone who'd grown up in such a different culture? Or he was? Divorce was not an acceptable option among Indians, in their home country or their new one.

"It's a shot in the dark," she thought, fearful of making a mistake. Maybe she should put a stop to it. Her eyes started to brim.

Her father, not a demonstrative man by nature, gave her a hug. "We only want you to do this if you're 100 percent sure," he told her in their native Gujarati. "If you're not, you don't have to... We just want you to be happy."

She looked at him—his eyes were reddening, too—and felt her opposition ebb away. "Screw it," she decided. "Okay. I can do it."

So the engagement proceeded last March, Vibha wearing a beautiful turquoise ensemble called a lengha and a blank expression. Guests were laughing and celebrating afterward, and she was thinking, with mingled panic and resignation, "Omigod, I'm engaged. I'm *done*." She packed up that night, flew home the following day and began planning a late-November wedding to a man she barely knew.

Now, with the big event just weeks away, Vibha (pronounced VEE-bah) flits around the Beltway, booking a deejay, making last-minute menu decisions, choosing the elaborate henna designs that will be applied to her hands and feet for the ceremony.

Yet even as she checks off the chores in a notebook she's labeled "wedding journal," uncertainty continues to eat at her. Should she really go through with this? Is she doing the right thing?

Arranged Happiness

Vinay Sandhir used to voice a lot of the same doubts about getting married the traditional way. He'd find his own spouse, he insisted. He didn't want a lot of familial meddling. He wanted to fall in love; in fact, "I wanted to be blown off my feet." But he was still single at 33, so one evening, his parents sat him down at their dining room table and had that same you're-not-getting-any-younger talk. So here he is in his home office in Annandale—he's an MBA and a management consultant in health care—printing out the latest batch of e-mailed responses to a matrimonial ad his parents placed in the weekly newspaper India Abroad. It read:

Punjabi parents desire beautiful, professional, never married, US raised girl for handsome son, 34, 5'10"/150, fair, slim, athletic, engineer/MBA, consultant in DC area. Enjoys travel, sports, music. Please reply…

Some of these criteria come from his parents. Vinay (pronounced Vin-NEIGH) thinks it's pointless to talk about appearances—though he himself actually *is* good-looking, rangy and dark-eyed, with an easy grin—since "everyone thinks their kids are beautiful." Nor does he particularly care which Indian state someone's forebears come from. But on this issue, he's yielded to the elder Sandhirs, who will be visiting this evening and will review the new candidates. They think someone from their home region would prove more "compatible."

Education is something they all agree on. The Sandhir family tree is heavy with doctors, including Vinay's father and two elder brothers and their wives. Vinay's intended need not be a physician, but he wants her to be ambitious and successful, "talented at what she does."

The "US raised" stipulation, on the other hand, comes from Vinay, who was 4 when his family settled in Western Maryland. He plays basketball a couple of times a week, lives to scale mountains (that's Mount Rainier—he's climbed it three times—on his screen saver) and ski and raft, caught five U2 concerts during last year's tour. He can't see himself with a woman raised in India, regardless of her graduate degrees. He wants a partner as Americanized as he is, "someone who's shared my experiences, someone I can laugh about things with, someone I don't have to explain everything to."

If such a prospect should surface in this batch, his parents will e-mail her parents, attaching his photo and "biodata," a document providing particulars and describing him as "intelligent, independent, dynamic… also deeply family-oriented and compassionate." If he passes muster, her parents will provide a phone number or e-mail address. Meanwhile, each family will conduct discreet background checks, making inquiries through friends and acquaintances to ensure the other is cultured, respectable, acceptable.

This week's possibilities, Vinay notices, include a health analyst in Toronto; an MBA from NYU; a Maryland social worker. "She'll probably get nixed just because she's older than me," he predicts. Oops, here's a woman he went out with a few times last year, until she stopped answering his e-mails. Chuck that one.

Which leaves 18 new responses to add to the 30 or so they've already received. "I didn't see anything totally, totally great," Vinay says. But he's loosened his requirements, having learned over the past months that this whole arranged marriage thing is more complicated than he'd foreseen.

The Lure of a Love Marriage

Love and marriage, in that order. The ethos so dominates mainstream Western culture, from Billboard charts to Hallmark racks, that other matrimonial approaches barely register. But in much of the Muslim world, in many Asian societies, among Hasidic Jews, and certainly in India—which has sent roughly three-quarters of a million immigrants to the United States since 1980—it's still common for people to pair up the other way around: marriage first, set up by one's elders and wisers, and then, with time, love. It's the historic norm, anthropologists say, not only the way kings and queens cemented strategic alliances, but the way ordinary folks—colonial Americans included—got hitched until comparatively recently.

It's how Vinay's parents married in 1959. Though his mother had never seen his father (he'd glimpsed her), she agreed to the engagement because she trusted her eldest sister, who'd set up the match. Vibha's parents had actually met—she silently served him tea—but hadn't exchanged a word. The album they keep to remember their 1975 wedding looks wonderfully romantic, with black-and-white photos of the groom arriving on horseback and the bride garlanded with marigolds, but they were strangers.

The process is so different now that young Indian Americans, who tend to shudder at the term "arranged marriage," cast about for more palatable phrases. "Semi-arranged marriage," for instance, or "arranged introduction." The updated version is no longer coercive (both the bride and groom have veto power), and traditional dowry transactions have largely been replaced, at least among the urban elite, by mutual exchanges of jewelry and clothing.

Some see these matches as a last resort, but since a single person who's reached the mid-twenties (for a woman) or late twenties (for a man) is probably causing an Indian family some anxiety, the need for a last resort can crop up fairly early in life. So if people haven't met spouses through school or work, or at networking events intended to bring marriageable Indians together, or via Web sites like *Indianmatchmaker.com*, or through newer permutations like the speed-dating sessions staged by a District firm called Mera Pyar ("My Love"), their parents may take up the traditional role.

They run ads, canvass Web sites, put the word out on the community grapevine: Dad's aunt knows a nice Bengali family in Atlanta whose nephew is an electrical engineer. Mom's medical school classmate in Detroit has a cousin with a single daughter working with computers in Bangalore.

After their parents perform due diligence—Hindu marriages are considered a union of two families, not merely two individuals, so bloodlines and reputations matter—the children meet and spend time together and decide whether their relationship has a future. A voluntary process, no different from having your friends fix you up, the fixed-up like to say.

But it *is* different. Families—many of whom disapprove of or forbid dating—don't want to introduce their kids to someone to hang out with or move in with; they want a wedding, and soon. Vinay's relatives think that after he's spent three or four evenings with a woman, he ought to know: She's his future bride or she's history. ("Not how it's going to work," he tells them.) And while both generations talk about having choices, most parents hope kids will choose to marry people of the same religious and ethnic background, the proper socioeconomic and educational level, acceptable lineage. Those are the factors that determine compatibility, not whether both parties treasure walking in the rain.

"It's a little like a debutante ball—'You can select freely, from among this preselected group of people,'" says anthropologist Johanna Lessinger, author of *From the Ganges to the Hudson*.

The so-called Second Generation of Indian immigrants (born here) and the 1.5 Generation (born there, raised here) are growing increasingly restive at these restrictions. They go off to college, where many date and have sex while their parents maintain a don't ask/don't tell policy. After that, though there are no reliable statistics, a growing number appear to opt for the do-it-yourself model known as a "love marriage." It's what Vibha and Vinay expected for themselves.

A preliminary analysis of Indian intermarriage rates in the United States by sociologist Maitrayee Bhattacharyya, a Princeton doctoral candidate, documents this trend. The 1990 Census showed that more than 13 percent of Indian men in this country, and 6 percent of women, were married to non-Indians—clearly love marriages, since Indian families might accept but wouldn't actively arrange such matches. But the rates for those born in the United States were dramatically higher, and among U.S.-born Indians under 35, about half had "married out." Those numbers may decline in the 2000 Census (that data is not yet available) because continuing immigration has broadened the pool, making it easier to meet an Indian spouse. Even so, for many immigrant families the love marriage remains a worrisome phenomenon.

So for all the change, the consensus is that most Indian American parents continue to exert significant influence over their children's courtships, and arranged marriages are common in Fairfax County as well as in Gujarat, the northwest Indian state Vibha's family started emigrating from more than 30 years ago.

Elders are better at this, the theory goes. "At least you know a bit about the boy, who he is and what he does, rather than just being emotional, being attracted to physical appearances, 'Oh, he's so cute,'" explains Vibha's aunt Induben Jasani. "Does he come from a good family? Does he have good morals and values? Character is something we can see a little better than youngsters do."

Besides, arranged marriages help keep traditions alive, stem the tendency toward out-marriage. "There's a sense of ethnic identity tied up in it," Lessinger says. "This is a way of holding on to their Indian-ness."

But a bubbly culture-straddler like Vibha—who's lived here since she was 5 and grew up watching "Xena: Warrior Princess," who speaks Gujarati at home but elsewhere uses 80-mph unaccented English punctuated with *like* and *y'know* and *kinda deal*, who loves Bollywood movies but relaxes from pre-wedding stress by seeing the Eminem flick "8 Mile"—isn't always sure how much Indian-ness to keep and how much Americanness to embrace. She calls herself "pretty much a mix," and in trying to negotiate the milestone of marriage, she sometimes finds herself pretty much mixed up.

Giving It a Shot

"Very hard work, a wedding," says Vibha's father, Ramesh Patel, on a Saturday afternoon with the event bearing down on them. On the living room rug, relatives are helping with the task of the day: dozens of small silver cows, favors for wedding guests, must be enfolded in red or gold foil, then inserted into matching silk bags. Vibha, padding around in bare feet and rumpled clothes, hair in a ponytail, is steeling herself for an afternoon of errands. "Work-run-work-run"—that's her life these days.

This Colonial-style home is what families have in mind when they call themselves, in matrimonial ads, "well settled in U.S.," with a deck overlooking the yard and a Mercedes in the driveway. It looks like any of the other houses along the winding street, except for the rack near the front door where people place their shoes when they enter, and the carved wooden shrine in the dining room where her mother, Shanta, prays daily to Hindu deities. The Patels (Vibha's parents have taken the name of their caste as a surname; Vibha uses the family name Jasani) bought this place in North Springfield 15 years ago, when Ramesh was working 90 hours a week in two different restaurants, saving obsessively to buy a Dunkin' Donuts franchise. He now owns three, in Maryland, while Shanta works at the Postal Service facility at Dulles.

Vibha, who moved home after graduating from Virginia Tech in psychology and management, is in human resources at NCS Pearson, a half-hour drive away in Arlington. She's the eldest of the Patels' three daughters, and by the time she'd been out of school for two years, well, "you have no idea how much the pressure is on for an Indian woman."

"We were worrying," her mother concurs, keeping one eye on the cow-wrapping. "Time was passing." They would have accepted a son-in-law Vibha found on her own, she says. "She had freedom. We didn't tell her no." But "she didn't like anybody. She couldn't find anybody."

To Vibha, this constitutes considerable revisionism. Her own account—mostly related in a series of cell-phone conversations as she drives home from work in her slightly scuffed Honda—reflects the tensions between Indian customs and American expectations.

She had a couple of fairly serious relationships with men in high school and college, for instance, but never dared to tell her parents about them. "It's a no-no; you don't date," she explains one night, steering past the multicultural neon strip malls of Columbia Pike and then along Braddock Road—practically the only time in the day she's alone and free to talk. Anyway, those guys were a "didn't-work-out kinda deal." After graduation, she and her friends went to bars and clubs in the District, drinking and dancing, playing pool with friends, flirting. A smiley extrovert with vast dark eyes, she had no trouble meeting men. It was fun, but "the person you want to marry, you're probably not going to meet in a club," she decided.

Which was starting to matter. Apart from the pointed questions about marriage from family and friends (the Jasani/Patel clan in Northern Virginia, expanding as more relatives immigrate, now numbers about 80), Vibha herself felt increasingly ready to settle down, as virtually all her South Asian friends already had. "I was tired of all these casual relationships," she says. "I wanted something serious."

Her family's first matchmaking effort, an ad in India Abroad, led to a few desultory dates with men who met their ethnic, religious, linguistic, dietetic (the family is vegetarian) and socioeconomic standards. "Didn't click," Vibha found. So her parents returned to a favorite theme. "They'd bring it up, then drop it, then bring it up a month later: 'What do you think of going to India to look for a guy?'"

She resisted for months; she'd spent time in India and feared a "culture gap" with Indian men. "I'm being stereotypical when I say this, but I thought they'd want a wife at home, cooking and cleaning and taking care of them." Vibha had seen her mother play this role daily. "I'm traditional, but I'm not *that* traditional. I wanted someone who'd be fifty-fifty with everything, someone to share the responsibilities." She didn't think she'd find him in Gujarat.

But the Patels didn't drop the idea, and Indian daughters hesitate to defy their parents. Many times her mother had prepared vegetarian meals for Vibha while she was away at college, and her father had driven nearly five hours to Blacksburg to deliver them, then turned around and headed home—how could she now dismiss their wishes? Her father's eldest brother, dying in a nearby hospice with the whole family gathered around, yearned to see her engaged—shouldn't she give him this final pleasure?

"I was just like, okay, I'll give it a shot." She'd get her parents off her case, she told girlfriends from work, assuring them that she expected to return unattached. She and her mother left on their mission a year ago Valentine's Day, with a return flight booked in three weeks.

Thirty Men in Three Weeks

At her uncle's stucco house in Rajkot, Vibha donned a salwar kameez, a tunic over pants with a long scarf. Her uncle had culled 30 suitors from the hundred who'd responded to local newspaper ads, and day after day, as each came to call, the encounters unfolded the same way. First, her mother and uncle chatted briefly with the potential bridegroom as Vibha served refreshments ("I hate that!"). Then the young people could retreat to another room for a brief stab at getting to know each other.

The first man to call was a physician, "fairly intelligent, attractive kinda guy," accompanied by his parents. Their dialogue consisted of a series of standard questions: Hi, how are you? When did you arrive? How was your trip? Tell me about your family: Do you have brothers and sisters? What are your interests? She ran through the responses—fine, thanks; yesterday; uneventful; two sisters; movies and music and computers—that would soon come to feel routine. Meanwhile, she was muttering to herself, "I don't want to do this. Why do I have to do this?" This guy, she concluded, "wasn't that interested, and I wasn't that interested." Next.

There were engineers and pharmacists and dentists. Some, she could tell in the first two minutes, were ruling her out be-

cause her complexion was coppery (there's a cultural preference for light skin) or because she was "normal-sized," not super-slim. That was fine, because anyone who couldn't see beyond looks, who didn't notice that she had a brain and a personality, "I'm like, forget you."

Some seemed a bit intimidated; she wasn't deferential, she was fluent in both Gujarati and English. A few seemed more attracted to her U.S. citizenship, marriage being a legal and comparatively quick route to a green card, than to her. After each session, her family wanted to know how she liked the latest candidate, whether she wanted to get engaged, "like I was going to decide on the spot."

Take the "doctor guy," for whom her family had high hopes. He prattled on about how prestigious his university was and how well he was doing there; he had the self-awareness of a coconut. Her family was disappointed by Vibha's blase response. A doctor! From one of the best schools! "But I didn't believe anything my parents said. They just wanted me to get married." Next.

Though the encounters got easier as the days passed, and she tried to keep an open mind as her uncle had advised, she couldn't really embrace the process. "I'm like, 'No.' 'No.' 'No.'"

The exception was Haresh Umaretiya, slotted in at the last minute when someone canceled. He came by before Vibha had time to dress up or tense up—a tallish engineer her own age, friendly eyes, high cheekbones, "the first one I had a decent conversation with." He was interested in what she had to say. When she asked what he enjoyed doing, "He said, 'I like observing people.' I'm in psychology; we had things in common… He was honest, which was nice… I thought, 'Okay, this could work.'"

He also enjoyed their meeting, it turned out. He thought Vibha was beautiful, but more important, "if you meet local Indian girls, they are shy, they can't reply," he'd found. "She is educated. And she is forward, she can talk." Though frankly, when he called a few days later to see if she'd like to go out, it was her fever to flee the house and the marriage marathon, as much as a desire to see him again, that prompted her to agree.

They went to a local park, bought ice cream cones, sat on the grass and talked. "Totally general, nothing serious. I loved that," Vibha says. "It was like meeting a friend. I felt at ease with him. I had a nice time." A few days later they went to a movie and had dinner together. Three meetings—two more than most local women would've had, an allowance made for Vibha's Western ways—and then it was time to meet his family. "Omigod, a good 20 people came, his father, his brother, his brother's wife, his mom, his aunt, his other aunt… They're all staring at me. Normally, you're supposed to bow your head, not look people in the eye; I'm just sitting there smiling. They're shocked, but they think, 'Well, she's American, she doesn't know.'" They approved anyway.

In Western conceptions of romance, lovers supposedly get carried away by passion. In Indian culture, the wedding process itself sweeps people along, a dizzying round of planning and shopping and crowds and gifts and excitement. Yet even as she agreed to proceed and preparations were underway, Vibha agonized.

From her earlier relationships, she'd learned to be a bit wary of American casualness, people's willingness to dump a girlfriend or boyfriend and then start dating someone new two weeks later. But she had also discovered what it was to fall in love. "This wasn't the same feeling, and I knew the difference so well. I was like, 'Do I really want to be with someone I don't know, and don't know if I'll ever love? Whoa.'"

She swallowed her doubts after her father flew over for the engagement, and they had that teary last-minute talk on the rooftop. After the engagement party, though, when she and Haresh were finally alone in a room, he wanted to kiss her. "And I'm just like, no."

The Sandhir Scale

Vinay Sandhir managed to stave off such dilemmas for years. He had a grand time in a coed dorm at West Virginia University and still skis, hikes and tailgates with his friends from the honors program there. Afterward, he had an "American" girlfriend for six years, a fact he never shared with his parents and they seemed not to notice, even though she was virtually living with him, retreating to her own apartment when they came to visit.

His family is "really conservative" and wouldn't have accepted it, Vinay believes, "unless I was sure I wanted to marry her and fight for her." But he wasn't sure.

When that relationship ended, he dated a business school classmate and a military administrator. Then came the dining room table confrontation. Like most traditional Indians, his parents don't consider their parental duty done until all their children have married. Vinay protested. "I'd say, 'It *is* done! I'm educated! I'm successful!'" He usually turned their inquiries aside with a vague, "We'll see."

But this time he said, "Okay, try it your way." Since childhood, he had felt more American than Indian, but "some soul-searching" after his breakup had led to a realization: "I don't want to be the person who ends the relationship with India and the culture of Indian-ness."

That meant marrying an Indian American, though on his own terms and timetable. So he's been good-naturedly working with his parents to write his 35-word ad and pass along the responses; he's had long phone conversations with prospects he hasn't met; he's launched the series of dinners and brunches that will reveal if any of them "knock my socks off."

If only he could use that decision software a grad school professor gave him. "It would be absolutely perfect! It takes qualitative criteria and gives them a quantitative score." As it happens, though, Vinay has a nondigital means to the same end—his father has developed numeric rankings for the women whose parents respond to their ad. Call it the Sandhir Scale.

"We're not prejudiced against anybody," says Sikander Lal Sandhir, after he and his wife, Prabhat, an elegant couple, have arrived at their son's townhouse and greeted him with affectionate banter. "We're trying to find common factors, language, ancestral background, ethnicity, education… We might be able to guide Vinay."

Everyone settles in Vinay's living room, the stack of new printouts on the coffee table; his father takes out a pen. Some applicants don't even merit a score. The social worker, as Vinay predicted, gets an inked N for Not Rated. "This girl, unfortunately, is almost two years older than Vinay," his father murmurs in his formal English. "We'd prefer a girl who is younger; that's the norm in our culture. And it makes more sense. To start a family at 36—as a physician, I know there could be problems." On to the MBA from NYU.

His scale awards points for education and professional accomplishment: three for an MD or MBA, two for a CPA, one for a bachelor's degree. A woman gets a point if she's a Punjabi Hindu (half a point if she's northern Indian from another state), a point if she's born or raised in this country (deduct half a point if she's been here less than 10 years), a point for a desirable family background. Various physical attributes—slimness, height, fair skin, general attractiveness—can add up to four points. No one's ever received a perfect 10, but anyone with a 6.5 or higher is worth pursuing.

The MBA from NYU, for instance, "has been here for a while, and her family background is similar to ours; the father is a physician," Vinay's father muses, jotting notes. With an Ivy League undergraduate degree, "she gets good marks for her education." He's unimpressed with her photo ("I think she is so-so"), but overall she gets a 6.5. He passes the pages to his wife, who approves, and to Vinay, who shrugs but will forward his standard biodata package.

Sadly, the Sandhir Scale has proved more useful in theory than in reality. Take the dentist from Upstate New York whom his father had rated a 9. After several promising phone chats, Vinay flew up to visit and discovered "a very proper girl" who hadn't left India until she was 18. They seemed culturally out of synch. "No sparks or anything," he decided. Not wanting to make snap judgments, he invited her to Virginia and planned a lively weekend: an Orioles game, hiking in the Shenandoah Valley, brunch on Capitol Hill. Still no sparks. Trying to be gentlemanly, he called afterward to say he'd enjoyed meeting her but didn't think the relationship would "progress."

Sometimes an intriguing woman never replies to *his* e-mail. He's learned, too, that his initial disinclination to juggle several prospects simultaneously, which struck him as callous, was unwise: By the time he'd decided against Candidate A and was ready to move down his list, Candidate B might already be off the market.

At the moment, he's talking with a gynecologist from Alabama and a Houston computer trainer. The Alabaman was in Washington visiting her brother recently, so he took her to Jaleo for tapas and to a Georgetown piano bar.

"A very smart, talented girl," he reports. "Was a connection made, one way or the other?… I didn't feel like I got any closer to making a decision." The Houston woman will be in town in a few weeks; they've made dinner plans. Tonight's review adds two more possibilities to his roster.

He's getting frustrated with the ups and downs and delays. "It's a lot more give and take than people make it out to be," he's discovered. Maybe all those parental warnings were on target, maybe he's waited too long. Certainly, the long-distance process of phoning and meeting all these people is growing unwieldy.

In fact, he's mislaid the number of that pediatrician in New Jersey who got a ringing 8.0 on the Sandhir Scale. But he'll dig it out and call her, he promises his dad. She grew up on Long Island; she likes music and travel, Vinay's own passions. She sounds interesting.

A Tradition in Transition

It has worked this way for thousands of years, immigrant parents tell their acculturated and uneasy offspring. It works better than Americans' impulsive love marriages, which so often split apart. "We have less divorce," Vibha's mother points out. "That's what results tell us."

In fact, the advantages and drawbacks of arranged marriages can't be so easily appraised. The incidence of divorce among Indian-born Americans *is* dramatically lower than among Americans generally, but that partly reflects the continuing stigma of divorce. Even as the divorce rate among Indian Americans appears to be increasing, the topic is rarely discussed. Vibha knows people, including several in her own family, who have divorced, but she doesn't want to talk about them. Divorce reflects poorly on an Indian family, and some proportion of arranged marriages endure not because they are successful or rewarding, but because leaving them would bring such shame.

And many endure because the definition of success differs from Western ideas. Traditional Indians don't expect a partner to be that improbable combination of soul mate/confidante/redhot lover/best friend. "The husband-wife bond is one of reliability and dependability and complementary family roles—raising children, caring for elders," explains Karen Leonard, author of *The South Asian Americans* and a University of California-Irvine anthropologist. "They may communicate very little in intimate ways, and it's still a good marriage."

When marriages do go seriously awry, people like Anuradha Sharma see the fallout. Dozens of support groups have formed across the country for South Asian women victimized by domestic violence. Sharma until recently was executive director of Washington's ASHA (which means "hope" and stands for Asian Women's Self-Help Association). Operating from a secret downtown address, its volunteers accompany clients (primarily Indian, Pakistani and Bangladeshi) to area hospitals and courts and immigration offices, help them find shelter and, sometimes, obtain restraining orders. "I've seen the system of arranged marriage work really well," says Sharma, whose own parents' marriage was arranged. "But the system has a lot of trust built into it, and, in my work, I've also seen men very purposely take advantage of that."

Her vantage point—she's spent a decade with organizations concerned with violence against women—acquaints her particularly well with the most painful stories. Men who live in the United States sometimes visit remote villages in their ancestral countries, accept large dowries and consummate arranged marriages, then leave and don't return. They bring brides here from abroad, exploit and isolate and batter them, then threaten them with deportation or loss of their children if they report the abuse.

"I've had teenagers call, or social workers on behalf of teenagers, to see what we could do for women under 18 who were being whisked off to India or Pakistan and forced into marriage," Sharma says. "I met a couple who tried to have a love marriage, and family members from abroad were stalking and threatening them."

Even without such coercion, some members of the Second Generation find their elders' matchmaking efforts oppressive. "People on the outside think arranged marriage is exotic, it's romantic, it's cute—like that show 'Meet My Folks,'" says Devika Koppikar, a congressional aide weary of fending off attempts to get her married. "It's not."

For years, she laments, her parents have told her she's not accomplished or beautiful enough to land a husband herself, circulated her photo and e-mail address without her permission, enlisted friends and relatives to badger her into accepting men she has no interest in. There is no model, in Indian tradition, of a satisfying life as a single person. Feeling angry and estranged from her family at 31, she's "kind of tempted to just meet someone and head for Vegas."

Koppikar has formed "a two-woman support group" with a friend, a 30-year-old optometrist who broke off one arranged engagement, then nearly cracked under her parents' relentless pressure—"shouts, arguments, tears"—to enter another. She found a South Asian therapist who urged her to move out of her volatile family home, and after one particularly ugly altercation, she did. "I didn't even pack a bag," she says. "I felt I wasn't safe, emotionally."

Even Vibha—whose parents treated her much more respectfully, whose decision to marry Haresh, however difficult, was her own—hopes her youngest sister, just 13, takes a different route. She'd be pleased if Shetal, born here and less tradition-bound than Vibha, could skip "the big ordeal": parental pressures and cross-cultural tensions, a compressed courtship, language difficulties and hassles at the INS office. "I want her to find someone here, on her own, fall in love, get married, be happy," Vibha says.

If young Indian Americans raise their children differently—and people like Vibha and Vinay vow that their kids will be free to date, to be open about their romances, to marry whom they please—then the arranged marriage may not survive more than another generation or two in this country. In India, too, love marriages have grown more common among urban sophisticates.

In matters of courtship and marriage, in fact, young, well-educated Indians often have more social freedom than their American cousins, whose parents' values were fixed when they emigrated decades ago. "They still think of the norms they grew up with as the only acceptable ones. They haven't been able to change, seeing that as a betrayal of Indian-ness," says Padma Rangaswamy, author of *Namaste America* and a Chicago historian. "But Indians in India are happy to change and don't have those hangups. My friends' children in India are all finding their own spouses."

That Vibha didn't shocked her "American" girlfriends. A couple of them met for lunch a few weeks after her Indian sojourn, and she stunned them with her news and her engagement photos. "I looked at her like, 'You're kidding me,'" says Tiffany Obenhein. "Serve somebody tea, have a conversation—and bang, you're getting married? It seemed awfully fast for Vibha, who's so American." It took her friends a moment to recover and offer hugs and congratulations.

But then, the whole venture felt pretty fast to Vibha, too. Back home and back at work, arranging for a priest and a florist and a hall at Martin's Crosswinds in Greenbelt, "everything was so rushed," she says. "I didn't have time to think, and nothing was stopping it."

Can This Be Love?

Haresh arrived in September, after six months of exchanging e-mail and instant messages with his intended, and moved in with her and her family. They got to kiss, finally, slipping off to the basement rec room for privacy, and Vibha was reassured: "He was a great kisser."

And yet… In mid-October, they'd planned to get their license at the county courthouse and be legally married, in order to speed up the immigration paperwork. Vibha canceled the appointment. "I'm like, no, I'm not going to do it. I wasn't sure. Plus, I was sick."

A week later, however, they went ahead and were married in a quick civil ceremony in a lawyer's office, and afterward Haresh made her a promise: He'd never lie to her. She thought that was sweet, she was "definitely moved," yet she didn't feel married. Or even, she acknowledged, in love. Haresh, the more amorous of this pair, sent her doting e-mail messages and a mushy birthday card, and she kept them all and waited for reciprocal feelings to smite her after the big Hindu wedding still to come. "I can't say I love him, but I'm pretty close," was her assessment. "And I know it's going to happen."

Because the thing was, he'd been growing on her week by week, with his quiet thoughtfulness, his steady support. "He puts up with my dad, who's hard to put up with," she reported from her car one night. "I run around doing all this wedding stuff, and he runs around with me. There's always family around—we haven't really spent much time together—but he hasn't complained once."

To Vibha's amazement, he pitched in with dish-washing and vacuuming and garbage-toting; it turned out he'd lived for a time with his grandparents, and helped with household chores when his grandmother was ill. This was major.

"Indian men don't tend to value the role women play, but he understands what they go through and respects it. He's like, why shouldn't women do what they want to do?" He didn't even care if she changed her last name or not, and since he didn't care, she decided she would.

On the Hindu New Year, Haresh was out doing errands with her dad instead of celebrating with the rest of the family at her aunt's house, and Vibha was ticked. "And then I went home and I was in my room and I'm waiting for him to come tell me 'Happy New Year,' and I'm *fuming*!" she recounts. "And I'm still mad about it the next day—and it hits me. Whoa. I missed him."

So the wedding, a four-day extravaganza for nearly 400 guests, is on.

'Body, Mind and Soul'

On Thursday night, a mehndiwalli from Gaithersburg came to the house and painstakingly applied paisley henna patterns to Vibha's hands and feet while her female relatives warbled traditional songs. The darker the mehndi, the more your husband will love you, goes the old saying, by which standard Vibha will have a deeply devoted mate.

Friday night, a few hundred people gathered at the Durga Temple in Lorton for garbas and dandia raas, the traditional Gujarati dances Vibha has loved since childhood, and she and her sisters and Haresh went flying across the floor until they were sweaty and exhausted, and her hair was coming unpinned.

Saturday, the family gathered for prenuptial ceremonies at the house ("Omigod, that was looong").

On Sunday, her wedding day, Vibha surprises even herself with her serenity. The photographer is urging her to smile; the decorator is setting up a glorious gold-embroidered white canopy (called a mandap); there's nothing left to prepare or decide. She might as well relax.

Wearing a ravishing embroidered lengha and extravagant amounts of gold jewelry, her face flecked with traditional bindya dots and her neck encircled by orchids, she's ready to be escorted to the ceremony on her uncle's arm. "Have you seen the mandap?" says Chetan Desai, one of her closest Virginia Tech buddies. "It kicks ass."

Under the canopy, with the bride and groom seated on silvery thrones, the songs and prayers continue for several hours in a mix of Sanskrit and Gujarati with a touch of English. The priest lights the sacred fire in a ziggurat-shaped brazier and Vibha and Haresh slowly circle it four times, symbolizing the stages of life and religious duty. They ask for prosperity and redemption from sin and future calamities. "Let us be like the earth and the sky," which are never separated, the priest intones on behalf of the groom. "Let us join our forces, let us have offspring, let us live a life of 200 years."

"I accept you as my husband and I offer my body, mind and soul to you," is the bride's response.

Vibha's Tech friends, most of whom have love marriages, are keeping a watchful eye on her. They've been a little worried, knowing Vibha's "adventurous spirit," about an arranged marriage to a guy from India. "How's this going to work?" Desai had wondered. "What if he's expecting some old-fashioned, stand-behind-your-man Indian woman?"

But seeing her calm gaze during the ceremony, noticing how glowy she looks at the reception afterward, they feel reassured. "We know her fake smile, her 'everything's all right' mode, but this was real," Desai says afterward, when Vibha and Haresh have left for a week's honeymoon—by a wide margin, the longest time they will ever have spent alone—in Hawaii. "He was happy, she was happy, she was at peace with herself. She was a *bride*."

The Date From Hell

That pediatrician from New Jersey? "We had a really good conversation" on the phone, Vinay says. "We had the same perspective on this whole India Abroad/meeting people stuff... She's very smart, she has passion for her work." She would shortly head overseas, and he wanted to meet her before she left, so they agreed to rendezvous in Philadelphia on a Friday night. Vinay bought tickets to a Sixers game, feeling upbeat.

Alas. "It was raining. It was miserable," he reports. "She was in a bad mood from the get-go." Arriving 45 minutes late, she stepped into a puddle en route to his car, complained about the long walk across the parking lot to the arena, barely initiated a conversation the entire evening. "I don't know if it was me, I don't know if it was the weather, I don't know if it was her day," Vinay says, nursing his disappointment and a glass of pink guava juice while relating the sorry saga to his visiting parents. Her pager went off, he adds, but she didn't have to leave, although he began to wish she did: "How bad is it that you're hoping some kid is sick enough that she has to go in to the hospital?"

En route to a restaurant in a neighborhood neither knew well, "she proceeds to bitch for 15 minutes in the car about how she couldn't read the map." An awkward dinner, a quick drop-off at the train station, "and I don't anticipate ever having to talk to or hear from her again. Because it was the worst, most miserable date of my life. Number one."

He's starting to wonder about this whole arrangement business. "Deep down, I don't think assessing someone from pictures and biodata tells you anything," he says. "There's probably lots of decent people we overlooked. There really isn't a foolproof way of doing it."

But he's still in touch with the Alabama doctor. He sees the Houston woman when she's in town visiting her brother. And there was an interesting ad in India Abroad his parents recently responded to:

Invitation for handsome, caring, outgoing, broad-minded, well-settled professionals, 31-plus; for beautiful, v. fair, slim, educated U.S. raised daughter...

'My Man'

Back from her honeymoon, Vibha Umaretiya seems liberated from frenzy and pressure—and from doubt. When she's with Haresh, she's giggly and charmed; she finds reasons to touch his shoulder, and he squeezes her hand. When she's not with him, when she's finally able to put away her cell phone and actually talk over lunch at the pizza place across from her office, she's expansive, buoyant.

"Now that we're married, I'm okay," she announces. "No more ifs or ands or buts."

Perhaps it's wise that Indian wedding rituals have expanded to incorporate such Western ideas as honeymoons. On Maui there was time to just lie on a beach and listen to the waves, time to get to know the man she'd wed.

"He's really very romantic, more than I am," she confides. On the plane, he kept his arm around her practically the whole flight. At their hotel, he catered to her, fed her morsels from his plate. "So much care, it was just incredible. I'm like, 'Stop the madness.'"

Not that she really wanted him to stop. "He made coffee for me in the morning! I'm like, omigod... He was so sweet; he makes it really easy for me to like him." But what about—that annoying Western question—love? A pause.

"How do you know if you love someone? Does a light come on over your head?" Haresh wants to get his master's degree in engineering; he thinks he could finish in a year and a half. Vibha may decide to start a business one day. They want to buy a condo or a townhouse as soon as they can, have some time as a twosome before the children arrive—at least five years away—and possibly his family arrives, too, if they choose. And because Haresh is soft-spoken and understanding and fair-minded about women's roles, and because she also wants him to do what fulfills him, they will have a good life together.

"He's my man, and he will be my man up until the day I die, or whatever," she muses, launching into a monologue. "The way you feel about a person is constantly changing, y'know?... Maybe there are days when you don't want to deal with him, maybe there'll be days when you don't want to miss a second with him. Do I look forward to spending time with him? Yes. Do I look forward to getting to know him? Yes. Do I like him for what he is? Do I have a deeper understanding of him? Yes."

So how their meeting and their future were arranged, with all the attendant anxieties, is starting to seem beside the point. "For me, it was the right thing," Vibha says. And she laughs. "I never thought I'd do it this way. It's really weird how life works, y'know? But I'm happy with the way it ended up. Seriously happy."

PAULA SPAN (pspan@bellatlantic.net) is a *Post* staff writer.

Kaleidoscope of Parenting Cultures

Vidya Thirumurthy

Educator: Immigrant parents from Asia in my class have a dogmatic parenting style and I don't know how to make them change their parenting style. They show little interest in the class when we discuss parenting issues. Should they not be expected to adapt to this culture? After all, it was their choice to move here.

Vidya: Should we expect them to change?

An uneasy silence pervaded the room full of experienced educators, who are grappling with similar situations. They are clueless as to how to approach it.

I will share here some observations I made of parents and children from over 27 countries who participated in a university preschool program. The emotionally enmeshed relationship between a Jewish parent and child, the teacher-taught behavior of an Indian father, the nonverbal relationship of a Brazilian couple with their child, the filial piety approach of a Chinese father, the friendly and playful demeanor of an African American mother, and the negotiation-oriented and self-explaining conduct of an Euro-American mother are descriptors of only a few characteristics observed among the preschool parents. I rely on a few examples to illustrate some cultural variations in parenting.

What is proper or improper behavior is based on cultural expectations and contexts (Brooks, 1999). Western cultures focus on the empowerment of individualism and autonomy in the child (Rudy, Grusec, & Wolfe, 1999). Freedom and individuality are the core values and parents do not view a child's defiance when asked to comply with a request as a threat. They may disagree with their child; nonetheless, they may still perceive the child's behavior as his/her way of asserting him/herself.

As a contrast, parents in most non-Western cultures believe in imposing absolute standards on their children. They value obedience and expect their children to respect authority. Their goal is to promote interdependency and cooperation. "Interdependence is promoted by fostering intense emotional bonds with children at an early age … children are motivated to cooperate and meet the needs of others, since [their activities] promote a sense of self-worth and emotional security"(Rudy et al., p. 302).

Defiance is the opposite of cooperation and a non-cooperative behavior is perceived as a threat to maintaining their family unity. Asian and Hispanic cultures typically value individualism less and collaboration and cooperation more. They exercise more control over the child to achieve these goals. But most Westerners perceive this approach as being demanding. They fear such parenting styles would result in "poor school achievement among Euro-Americans"(Chao, 1994, p. 1111). Yet, obedience is a virtue for the non-Western parents and they have implicit faith in punishment.

Similarly, Chinese and Asian parents equate parenting to teaching (Rudy et al., 1999). For example, an Indian father expected forceful cooperation rather than cooperation through negotiation when he instructed his son several times each morning to greet his teachers. "Beta (Son), say good morning to all your teachers and friends,"was a mantra he chanted. As a contrast to this, the Brazilian couple would enter very quietly and slip out of the classroom as though they would disturb the serenity of the class. They rarely exchanged greetings with the teacher or with other parents. Smith (1997) explains that Brazilians often use silence as a way to greet others. They seldom greeted or interacted with other parents when they entered the classroom in the morning.

When a child controls the behaviors of his parents, Baumrind (1991) calls it a permissive parenting style. The daily routine of a Jewish couple and their son lasted for about an hour. This little boy had a difficult time letting go of his parents. The observer noticed the emotional entanglement in their relationship—yet another characteristic of the permissive style. "Parents promote the child's assertion of his or her will: Israeli mothers, for example, are more likely than those in Japan to value disobedience when it is a reflection of the child's assertion of individuality"(Osterweil & Nagano, 1991, as cited by Rudy, Grusec, & Wolfe, 1999, p. 302). But what we must realize is that emotionally enmeshed behaviors are considered healthy in many cultures and it is believed to strengthen the bond between parents and children. It cannot be labeled as inappropriate parenting.

The communication patterns of most Euro-American parents were different from the rest. They got down to the eye-level of the children when talking with them. They spoke softly to their children and were non-intrusive. A few of them held their children on their laps or hugged them while they talked. Western culture promotes looking the speaker straight in the eye to show "interest and attention"(Smith, 1997, p. 349). Therefore, making eye contact is considered very important when communicating with others. This; is in stark contrast to many other cultures that teach their children not to establish such eye contact with elders and persons of authority because it is considered disrespectful.

The patterns of parental attitudes and behaviors exhibited in the preschool differed greatly across cultures. The cultural contexts in which parents grew up, the experiences they have had with their own parents, and the experiences they have with their own children affect parent cognition and behavior. Parents hold a mental representation of relationships, which they develop based on their own childhood experiences (Grusec, Hastings, & Mammone, 1994). It does not mean that parents passively accept and mirror the parenting styles of their parents. They filter through the behaviors and absorb only those that are in accordance with their individual beliefs. Thus, variations in approaches illustrate both cultural and individual differences in parenting styles.

Immigrants leave their lands, families, and cultural settings behind. Even though it was their choice to move here, they face an overwhelming challenge in adapting to new situations, land, and culture. Educators can state their expectations clearly and let the parents do it in their own way. As long as there is no abuse, we must strive to help parents maintain their cultural identities and be successful. As one of my students put it, our goal should be to support them in their parenting and help them gain a deeper understanding of our parenting styles.

References

Baumrind, D. (1991). Parenting styles and adolescent development. In R. M. Lerner, A. C. Petersen, & J. Brooks-Gunn (Ed.), Encyclopedia of adolescence (pp. 746–758). New York: Garland.

Brooks, J. (1999). The process of parenting (5th ed). Mountain View, CA: Mayfield.

Chao, R. K. (2004). Beyond parental control and authoritarian parenting style: Understanding Chinese parenting through the cultural notion of training. Child Development, 65, 1111–1119.

Grusec, J., Hastings, P., & Mammone, N. (1994). Parenting cognitions and relationships schemas. In J. Smetana (Ed.), Beliefs about parenting: Origins and developmental implications (pp. 5–19). San Francisco: Jossey-Bass.

Rudy, D., Grusec, J., & Wolfe, J. (1999). Implication of cross-cultural findings for family socialization. Journal of Moral Education, 28, 299–310.

Smith, T. J. (1997). Early childhood development. Upper Saddle River, NJ: Merrill.

—Vidya Thirumurthy,
International/Intercultural Committee

Spanking Children: Evidence and Issues

Abstract

Whether or not to spank children as a discipline practice is controversial among lay and professional audiences alike. This article highlights different views of spanking, key conclusions about its effects, and methodological limitations of the research and the resulting ambiguities that fuel the current debate and plague interpretation. We propose an expanded research agenda to address questions about the goals of parental discipline; the role, if any, that punishment plays in achieving these goals; the effects and side effects of alternative discipline practices; and the impact of punishment on underlying developmental processes.

ALAN E. KAZDIN[1] AND CORINA BENJET

Child Study Center, Yale University School of Medicine, New Haven,
Connecticut (A.E.K.), and National Institute of Psychiatry,
Mexico City, Mexico (C.B.)

Spanking as a way of disciplining children is a topic of broad interest to people involved in the care and education of children (e.g., parents, teachers), as well as to the many professions involved with children, parents, and families (e.g., pediatrics, psychiatry, psychology, and social work). Hitting children is intertwined with religious beliefs, culturalviews, government, law, and social policy and has enormous implications for mental and physical health throughout the world (Krug, Dahlberg, Mercy, Zwi, & Lozano, 2002). Corporal punishment as a means of child discipline at home and at school has been banned by many countries, including Austria, Croatia, Cyprus, Denmark, Finland, Germany, Israel, Italy, Latvia, Norway, and Sweden (Gershoff, 2002). The United Nations (Article 19 of the UN Convention on the Rights of Children) argues against all forms of physical violence in relation to children.

Within the United States, several organizations (e.g., Project No Spank—**http://www.nospank.net/toc.htm**) lobby for an end to hitting children and for according children the same legal protections accorded adults (i.e., laws against being hit by others). Despite the lobbying, spanking is still a "hit" with parents—it is quite prevalent. For example, in the United States, 74% of parents of children 17 years of age or younger use spanking as a discipline technique (Gallup, 1995); 94% of parents of 3- and 4-year-olds use corporal punishment (Straus & Stewart, 1999).

After decades of research, debate continues. In this article, we review key findings about the effects of spanking, issues that limit progress in understanding the effects of spanking, and avenues to move research forward. By discussing the topic, we are not in any way endorsing or advocating the use of spanking. Indeed, integral to the research agenda we propose are questions regarding why so many parents believe hitting is an appropriate and effective form of parental discipline and whether hitting is actually needed to accomplish the goals underlying its use in child rearing.

Spanking Defined

Perhaps the most critical issue that underlies this debate is the definition of spanking. The definition determines who participates in a research study, what studies are included in literature reviews, and, hence, what conclusions are reached. A commonly adopted definition specifies spanking as hitting a child with an open hand on the buttocks or extremities with the intent to discipline without leaving a bruise or causing physical harm. This definition helps separate occasional spanking from more severe corporal punishment (Baumrind, Larzelere, & Cowan, 2002; Consensus Statements, 1996).

Physical abuse usually is defined to encompass corporal punishment that is harsh and excessive, involves the use of objects (e.g., belts, paddles), is directed to parts of the body other than the extremities, and causes or has the potential to cause physical harm. Because many parents report using objects during punishment, behaviors that many professionals might consider as clearly abusive are fairly common and included in some definitions of spanking (Gershoff, 2002). Research on hitting (spanking, corporal punishment) varies widely on whether the definition includes practices that frankly are or blend into abuse.

Three Views of Spanking

Three positions about spanking as a form of discipline capture public and professional views rather well. The *pro-corporal punishment* view is infrequently advocated in research and academic writings, but is alive and well in everyday life. This view is represented by the familiar, cryptic, incomplete, and probably misconstrued biblical quotation, "spare the rod and spoil the child" (Proverbs 13:24). The view underscores the beliefs that desirable consequences (e.g., respect for authority, good behavior, socialization) follow from the use of spanking, untoward consequences result from not spanking, and responsible parenting includes such punishment.

The *anti-corporal punishment* view is that corporal punishment is likely to have short- and long-term deleterious consequences. "Violence begets violence" captures much of this view, which focuses on modeling and social learning as the means by which violence is transmitted from one generation to the next (Straus, 1994). The morality of inflicting pain is also key to this view, so the untoward consequences of hitting are not the only basis for the objection to spanking.

The *conditional corporal punishment* view notes that the effects of spanking are not necessarily negative or positive but may be either depending on other conditions. Spanking can vary along multiple dimensions (e.g., frequency and intensity) and be delivered in many different contexts that may moderate its impact. This view does not advocate spanking, but rather notes that a "blanket injunction" against spanking cannot be supported scientifically (Baumrind, 1996).

Overview of Research Findings

The empirical literature on spanking has been reviewed extensively. The most recent and comprehensive review, completed by Gershoff (2002), consists of a meta-analysis[2] of 88 studies. Gershoff examined the relationship between corporal punishment and compliance of the child, moral internalization, aggression, criminal and antisocial behavior, quality of the parent-child relationship, mental health, and abuse. Spanking tended to be associated with immediate compliance of the child (i.e., desisting the behavior targeted by the punishment), which Gershoff considered to be the only positive outcome evident in her review. On the negative side, spanking was associated with decreased internalization of morals, diminished quality of parent-child relations, poorer child and adult mental health, increased delinquency and antisocial behavior for children, and increased criminal and antisocial behavior for adults; spanking also was associated with an increased risk of being a victim of abuse or of abusing one's own child or spouse.

Reanalyses of studies have underscored the importance of how spanking is defined. Several studies in Gershoff's review included rather harsh punishment that would qualify as physical abuse (e.g., slapping in the face, hitting with an object). Reanalyses indicated the outcomes were more negative in those studies than in studies of less severe punishment (Baumrind et al., 2002). Similarly, other reviews have suggested that very mild spanking used as a backup for mild disciplinary effects may not be detrimental and indeed can reduce noncompliance and fighting (Larzelere, 2000).

It would be difficult to identify a consensus among researchers beyond a few key points. First, the deleterious effects of corporal punishment are likely to be a function of severity and frequency. Harsh punishment is associated with many untoward consequences, including increased morbidity and mortality for major adult forms of illness (e.g., heart disease, cancer, lung disease; Krug et al., 2002). Second, the effects of mild spanking

(an oxymoron to some people) that is occasional, is a backup to other disciplinary procedures such as time out from reinforcement or reasoning, is physically noninjurious, involves an open hand to hit the extremities or buttocks, and inflicts temporary pain are not so clear (Baumrind et al., 2002). Again, there is no advocacy of corporal punishment in this latter view, but merely an acknowledgment that the research does not speak to the consequence of occasional spanking.

Key Issues for Research

Fundamental conceptual and methodological issues plague the literature on spanking. First, the varied definitions of spanking can dictate the conclusions investigators and reviewers reach, as we have noted. Second, assessments of spanking and children's characteristics (e.g., aggression, deviance) often are retrospective and completed by the same rater (the parent). These influences alone can affect the magnitude of correlations of punishment, child characteristics, and outcomes. Third, the time line is rarely established to show that in fact spanking antedated an untoward outcome and that the "outcome" (e.g., child deviance, poor parent-child relations) was not present in advance of or at the same time as spanking. Fourth, spanking could well be a proxy for a host of other variables that in fact relate to untoward child outcomes. For example, compared with parents who spank less, those who spank more read to, play with, and hug their children less; experience higher levels of stress, more major life events, and more difficult, discordant, and abusive marital relations; and have higher rates of mental illness or substance abuse. These other variables, alone or in combination, might explain the effects attributed to spanking. However, redressing these pivotal methodological issues alone would still leave unanswered many critical questions that could inform the use of spanking (see Benjet & Kazdin, 2003).

Goals of Parent Discipline

Presumably, the goals of disciplining children are to decrease some behaviors (e.g., tantrums, talking back), to develop others (e.g., problem solving, playing cooperatively, completing homework), and to promote socialization more generally. It is not at all clear from animal laboratory studies and human applied studies that punishment is among the better strategies for accomplishing these behavior-change goals. For example, decreasing and eliminating inappropriate child behavior in the home can be achieved through positive reinforcement techniques (e.g., from many arrangements that focus on rewarding alternative behaviors) without the use of any punishment (Kazdin, 2001). In addition, noncorporal punishment techniques that are less aversive than spanking (e.g., brief periods of time out from reinforcement, small fines on a point chart) can be effective. The use of spanking raises questions regarding the goals of discipline, whether any punishment is needed to attain them, and, if in fact punishment is needed, whether hitting has any benefit over noncorporal punishment. Comparisons of punishment with nonaversive procedures, even in laboratory analogues, would add pertinent information that could inform debates about spanking. Additionally, the underlying processes motivating parents to spank or to continue to use spanking could be investigated to determine whether they are concordant with the stated goals of spanking.

Concomitant Effects of Punishment

Concomitant effects include any effects outside the direct focus of spanking and encompass the development of prosocial behaviors, misbehavior other than the one to which spanking was directed, and emotional reactions (e.g., crying, anger). Gershoff (2002) found that children who were spanked were more angry, aggressive, and stressed than children who were not disciplined in this way. This finding is in keeping with other applied as well as animal laboratory research showing that punishment can have untoward side effects, including emotional reactions, aggression, and escape from and avoidance of people, settings, and situations associated with punishment (Hutchinson, 1977; Kazdin, 2001). These effects are particularly likely with corporal punishment, but they can occur with low levels of noncorporal punishment as well. Few studies have examined side effects of spanking and how these compare with the side effects that may result from equally effective (or more effective) strategies that do not rely on punishment.

Impact of Corporal Punishment on Development

Child abuse, a more extreme form of corporal punishment than is the focus of this article, can exert biochemical, functional, and structural changes in the brain (e.g., changes in cerebral volume and increased or decreased reactivity to various neurotransmitters; Glaser, 2000). Some of these changes have psychological concomitants (e.g., changes in reactivity to stress and in working memory). We do not wish to imply that spanking necessarily has any similar consequences or effects, but at the same time, it is not clear whether, how, or at what threshold the brain makes the distinction between child abuse and spanking. As a result, the circumstances under which spanking might also have such deleterious effects is uncertain.

Other psychological areas critical to development (e.g., attachment, emotional regulation, stress of the child, parent-child relations) reflect critical brain-behavior-environment interactions that warrant attention. Although we do not challenge reviews claiming that very mild corporal punishment has not been shown to have either beneficial or deleterious effects, we argue that there is a need to look at how spanking might influence psychological processes critical to development. Research has already demonstrated that many developmental processes can be adversely influenced by harsh punishment.

Main Effects and Moderators

It is likely that any effects of parenting discipline practice are moderated by scores of variables related to the child, parent, family, and broader context (e.g., culture). The range of candidate variables to investigate is daunting, but there are exciting possibilities. Advances in molecular genetics will no doubt lead to breakthroughs that move researchers closer to understanding mechanisms and to identifying subgroups of youths who might be especially vulnerable to various discipline practices. For example, boys who are maltreated are likely to develop antisocial behavior if they have a particular gene characteristic related to one of the brain's neurotransmitter systems (Caspi et al., 2002). There are not many models that have been proposed and tested to explain influences that moderate the effects of spanking. This is a difficult topic in part because a study might implicitly endorse spanking as a good, or at least neutral, practice for some children and families and as a detrimental practice for others, or even unwittingly "blame" the child for extreme reactions to corporal punishment. The study of moderators of the effects of spanking is a charged topic because it could be unwittingly construed as advocating hitting some children but not others. We have already raised the question of whether spanking is needed at all in child rearing.

Closing Comments

Objections to spanking are made on moral, humane, and legal grounds (e.g., the immorality of inflicting pain, unequal treatment of children and adults under the law). These objections are critical insofar as they apply to all hitting of children and are independent of the evidence on the effects of spanking. The evidence suggests that spanking that is frequent and harsh is often associated with undesirable mental and physical health outcomes.

The effects of very mild, occasional spanking are not well studied or sufficiently clear from available studies. In one sense, it may be correct to say that current evidence does not establish the deleterious or beneficial effects of very mild spanking. Even so, it may be prudent to caution against the use of spanking because there are nonaversive alternatives for accomplishing the same disciplinary goals, and because it has not been empirically established where the demarcation is between mild spanking that may be safe to use and severe corporal punishment that is known to be dangerous. Moreover, mild spanking can escalate and apparently does mix in with more severe hitting (Gershoff, 2002). Thus, the many health, psychological, and neurological consequences of harsh punishment cannot be dismissed as irrelevant to mild spanking. One of the reasons that there is a debate about the effects of spanking is that investigators who study spanking and the parents and teachers who interact with children cannot adhere consistently to a delimited and crisp definition of spanking or hitting that is "mild and occasional."

From a parenting and policy perspective, the basic question is, why use corporal punishment at all? Mild noncorporal punishments such as brief time out from reinforcement or short-term loss of privileges in the context of praise and rewards can accomplish the goals for which spanking is usually employed. After years of research, critical questions about mild forms of corporal punishment remain. We have suggested some lines of work to inform discussions about the practice of spanking and its effects. More longitudinal studies are needed to help establish time lines between spanking and desirable and undesirable outcomes, competing constructs that may explain the effects attributed to spanking need to be ruled out more persuasively, and animal laboratory studies could be brought to bear more forcefully on the topic. Human and animal laboratory studies evaluating transient and enduring biological and behavioral reactions to punishment will be critical for illuminating the developmental processes that are influenced by corporal punishment and whether distinctions in the severity and frequency of punishment are relevant to these processes.

Recommended Reading

Benjet, C., & Kazdin, A.E. (2003). (See References)
Gershoff, E.T. (2002). (See References) (Multiple commentaries follow this article)
Larzelere, R.E. (2000). (See References)
Straus, M.A., & Stewart, J.H. (1999). (See References)

Acknowledgments—The authors are very grateful for very thoughtful comments provided by Celia B. Fisher and Kimberly Hoagwood. Completion of this article was facilitated by support from the Leon Lowenstein Foundation, the William T. Grant Foundation (98-1872-98), and the National Institute of Mental Health (MH59029).

Notes

1. Address correspondence to Alan E. Kazdin, Child Study Center, Yale University School of Medicine, 230 S. Frontage Rd., New Haven, CT 06520-7900.
2. Meta-analysis combines the effects of several studies using a common unit of analysis. For each study, groups are compared (e.g., children who have been spanked vs. those who have not), and their difference is placed into a common metric that permits studies to be compared and combined.

References

Baumrind, D. (1996). A blanket injunction against disciplinary use of spanking is not warranted by the data. *Pediatrics, 98,* 828–831.

Baumrind, D., Larzelere, R.E., & Cowan, P.A. (2002). Ordinary physical punishment: Is it harmful? Comment on Gershoff (2002). *Psychological Bulletin, 128,* 580–589.

Benjet, C., & Kazdin, A.E. (2003). Spanking children: The controversies, findings, and new directions. *Clinical Psychology Review, 23,* 197–224.

Caspi, A., McClay, J., Moffitt, T.E., Mill, J., Martin, J., Craig, I.W., Taylor, A., & Poulton, R. (2002). Role of genotype in the cycle of violence in maltreated children. *Science, 297,* 851–854.

Consensus Statements. (1996). *Pediatrics, 98,* 853.

Gallup Organization. (1995). *Disciplining children in America: A Gallup poll report.* Princeton, NJ: Author.

Gershoff, E.T. (2002). Parental corporal punishment and associated child behaviors and experiences: A meta-analytic and theoretical review. *Psychological Bulletin, 128,* 539–579.

Glaser, D. (2000). Child abuse and neglect and the brain: A review. *Journal of Child Psychology and Psychiatry and Allied Disciplines, 41,* 97–116.

Hutchinson, R.R. (1977). By-products of aversive control. In W.K. Honig & J.E.R. Staddon (Eds.), *Handbook of operant behavior* (pp. 415–431). Englewood Cliffs, NJ: Prentice-Hall.

Kazdin, A.E. (2001). *Behavior modification in applied settings* (6th ed.). Belmont, CA: Wadsworth.

Krug, E.G., Dahlberg, L.L., Mercy, J.A., Zwi, A.B., & Lozano, R. (2002). *World report on violence and health.* Geneva, Switzerland: World Health Organization.

Larzelere, R.E. (2000). Child outcomes of nonabusive and customary physical punishment by parents: An updated literature review. *Clinical Child and Family Psychology Review, 3,* 199–221.

Straus, M.A. (1994). Should the use of corporal punishment by parents be considered child abuse? Yes. In: M.A. Mason & E. Gambrill (Eds.), *Debating children's lives* (pp. 195–203, 219–222). Thousand Oaks, CA: Sage.

Straus, M.A., & Stewart, J.H. (1999). Corporal punishment by American parents: National data on prevalence, chronicity, severity, and duration, in relation to child and family characteristics. *Clinical Child and Family Psychology Review, 2,* 55–70.

Stress and the Superdad

Like the supermoms before them, today's fathers are struggling to balance work and home

MICHELE ORECKLIN

THE PAST 30 YEARS HAVE SEEN THE emergence of the working mom, the single mom, the supermom, the soccer mom and—because full-time motherhood is often considered a choice rather than a given—the stay-at-home mom. Yet aside from the recent categorization of NASCAR dads (which more pointedly concerns the significance of NASCAR than parenting), the title of dad has rarely been linked to a modifier. It would be wrong, however, to conclude that the role of fathers has remained unaltered; the majority of men today are vastly more involved in the rearing of their children and maintenance of their households than their fathers ever were. That no phrases have been coined to describe such behavior can probably be attributed to the fact that unlike women, men have not particularly organized, united or even been pro-active to effect these reforms but, in essence, adapted to the changes the women in their lives demanded for themselves.

That is not to say men resent the transformation. Data from focus groups, conversations with men around the country and a poll conducted by the men's cable network Spike TV and shared exclusively with TIME suggest that men, most interestingly those in their early 20s through early 40s—the first generation to come of age in the postfeminist era—are adjusting to their evolving roles, and they seem to be doing so across racial and class lines. But in straining to manage their responsibilities at work and home, many men say they don't feel an adequate sense of control in either realm. "There's a push-pull," says Kevin Lee, 40, a photographer in Salt Lake City, Utah, with two small children and a wife who works part time. "I feel like when I'm with the kids, it's great, and I enjoy that time. But in the back of my mind, I'm always thinking that I've got all these other things to do, like work around the house or job-related work."

As pioneer superdads, these men have few role models. Not terribly long ago, a man went out into the world and worked alongside other men, and when he came home, the rest of the family busied itself with making him comfortable. Now, as with women of a generation ago, men are experiencing the notion of a second shift, and they are doing so at a time when downsizing, outsourcing and other vagaries of the economy have made that first shift feel disquietingly unstable. Says Dr. Scott Haltzman, 44, a psychiatrist in Barrington, R.I., with many male clients under 45: "Historically, men felt that if they applied themselves and worked hard, they would continue to rise within an organization." Now they must contend with a shaky economy, buyouts, layoffs and mergers, not to mention rapidly evolving technological advances. Of the 1,302 men polled, 75% said they were concerned about keeping up with changing job skills, and even among those 25 to 34, a presumably more tech-savvy cohort, 79% admitted to such concerns.

There are things men do that women don't see as contributing

There is also uncertainty in men's roles at home. Says Bob Silverstein, an employment consultant and personal life coach in New York City: "Home has become one more place where men feel they cannot succeed." For as much as women desire and demand their husbands' assistance in floor waxing and infant swaddling, many men complain that their wives refuse to surrender control of the domestic domain and are all too adept at critiquing the way their husbands choose to help out. Haltzman, who gathers research on husbands through his SecretsOfMarriedMen.com website, points out that "there are a lot of things men do that women don't define as contributing to the household. If a man is in the yard and notices that the basketball is flat and he pumps it up, he gets no credit because it's not something that needed to get done in the wife's eyes. But from the man's perspective, it's just as important as picking up an article of clothing or doing the wash."

But even while men chafe at not being appreciated around the house, few of them express a desire to return to the roles defined by previous generations. "I would love a reprieve from all the domestic chores," says Steve McElroy, 35, of Barrington, R.I., a father of two whose wife is a full-time professor. "But I wouldn't want it at the expense of my family and what I have with them." Asked by Spike TV to choose how they measure success, only 3% of men said through their work, while 31% said they did so through their faith in God, 26% through being the best person possible, 22% through their network of family and friends, and 17% through maintaining a balance between home and work.

In calibrating an acceptable balance between the two, men came down decisively on the side of family life, with 72%—including those who are single—saying they would sacrifice advancements at work to spend more time at home and 66% saying they would risk being perceived poorly by a superior to ask for a month's paternity leave. In 2002, Mark Carlton, 33, left his job in mechanical design and moved with his wife and two children from Evansville, Ind., to Minneapolis, Minn., when his wife got a better-paying position. While interviewing for a new job, Carlton told potential employers that he expected a "give and take. I give it my all at work, and in return if I have a family issue, I should be able to have the time."

Despite their best intentions, however, men are not necessarily curtailing their work hours. Nearly 68% of men work more than 40 hours a week, and 62% are working on weekends. And men with children are putting in more hours than those without: 60% of them work 41 to 59 hours a week, whereas only 49% of men without kids rack up that many hours.

Even though men say they spend too much time on the job, they don't seem to care about the gender or race of those they work alongside or below. This would appear to be progress over 10 years ago, when many downsized men channeled their frustration toward minorities and women whom they perceived as threats to their professional advancement. Today, the Spike poll shows that 55% of men profess to have no preference for a male or female boss, while 9% actually prefer a woman. Proof that men may now recognize the advantages of having women in the workplace is evident in another poll number: 55% say they have no problem dating someone who earns significantly more than they do.   **—With reporting by Sonja Steptoe/Los Angeles and Sarah Sturmon Dale/Minneapolis**

The Kids Are All Right

Research shows that families headed by gay and lesbian parents are as healthy as traditional families, but misperceptions linger.

SADIE F. DINGFELDER
Monitor staff

Most of the parenting challenges Steven James, PhD, faces are pretty ordinary. For one, James's usually studious son Greg, 9, has recently been refusing to do his geography homework. "He's just not that interested in memorizing states and capitals," says James, who chairs the psychology and counseling program at Vermont's Goddard College.

However, as gay parents, James and his partner, Todd Herrmann, PhD, have some fears that don't keep most other parents up at night. The biggest one, says James, is that their sons, Greg and Max, 4, might be taken away from them if they travel to a hostile place. James and Herrmann's adoption of the two boys is not legally recognized in 11 states and many countries, and as a result they can't safely visit one set of grandparents.

"My dad and his wife were here to visit a few months ago and they asked: 'Why not bring the boys to Oklahoma?' I had to explain: 'Your laws don't respect our adoption. Your state could put the boys into foster homes without any say from me or you,'" says James.

Families such as the James-Hermanns and the challenges they face are becoming increasingly common in the United States. The 2000 U.S. census estimated that 163,879 households with children were headed by same-sex couples. That number is likely to be much larger today, says Charlotte Patterson, PhD, a psychology professor at the University of Virginia.

"More people are choosing to start families in the context of a gay or lesbian identity," she says.

Additionally, the census fails to count the perhaps millions of families where a single gay parent heads the household, says Judith E. Snow, a Michigan-based therapist and author of the book "How It Feels to Have a Gay or Lesbian Parent" (Harrington Park Press, 2004).

But while gay- and lesbian-headed families face a slate of challenges that more traditional families avoid—from legal hassles and homophobia to everyday tasks, such as figuring out how to fill out school forms—research shows that the children with gay or lesbian parents do as well as children with heterosexual parents. Having a gay or lesbian parent doesn't affect a child's social adjustment, school success or sexual orientation, say researchers.

"Sexual orientation has nothing to do with good parenting," notes Armand Cerbone, PhD, who reviewed research on gay and lesbian parenting as chair of APA's Working Group on Same-Sex Families and Relationships.

Challenging Assumptions

Unfortunately, many people are not aware of the three decades of research showing that children of gay or lesbian parents are just as mentally healthy as children with heterosexual parents, notes Cerbone. One such study, published in *Child Development* (Vol. 75, No. 6, pages 1,886–1,898) in 2004, compares a group of 44 teenagers with same-sex couples as parents with an equal number of teenagers with opposite-sex couples as parents. All participants were part of a national, randomly selected sample of teenagers from the National Longitudinal Study of Adolescent Health.

"There were very few group differences between the kids who had been brought up by same- or opposite-sex parents," says Patterson, who conducted the research with students Jennifer Wainright and Stephen Russell, PhD, now an associate professor of sociology at the University of Arizona. One group difference that Patterson was surprised to find: Children of gay and lesbian parents reported closer ties with their schools and classmates. However, says Patterson, the difference was small and needs to be studied further.

Patterson's study debunks the myth that children of gay or lesbian parents have trouble developing romantic relationships due to a missing father- or mother-figure—a concern that judges making custody rulings have cited. Equal numbers of teenagers from each group reported that they had been in a romantic relationship in the previous 18 months. Participants from the two groups did not differ in grade point average, symptoms of depression or self-esteem.

While the sexual orientation of the parents in Patterson's study did not predict the adolescents' social adjustment, the quality of the parent-child relationship did. Children who reported warm relationships with their parents tended to be the most mentally healthy and have the fewest problems in school.

Navigating Same-Sex Parenting: Psychologists' Roles

As gay- and lesbian-headed families become more common, psychologists may see increasing numbers of them in their practices. Most problems such families bring to therapy are typical of any family, says Jane Ariel, PhD, a Wright Institute psychology professor and clinician with many lesbian and gay clients.

"How to keep kids under control, how to manage the load of working and being a parent, how to find time for your partner are common issues," says Ariel.

But there are a few challenges lesbian and gay parents may bring to the session that practitioners might be unfamiliar with, including:

- **Worry about fitness to parent**. Some lesbian parents, for example, come to a therapist concerned that a lack of a male role model might harm their son. Gay dads might similarly worry that their children might suffer from lack of female role models. These concerns might stem from internalized homophobia that therapists can help their clients address, Ariel notes. In such cases, she suggests therapists share with their clients research that shows children of lesbian or gay parents are just as mentally healthy as kids with heterosexual parents (see main story).
- **Concern about homophobia.** Many parents worry that their children will be taunted or even assaulted by their peers as a result of their unusual family structure, says Judith E. Snow, a Michigan-based therapist. Such teasing is likely to happen, but parents can help their kids prepare to respond constructively by role-playing

and by modeling appropriate responses in their day-to-day lives, she says. For example, parents who stand up for themselves without escalating a situation help their children learn to do the same, says Snow.

- **Legal problems.** Same-sex parents have to work through a variety of questions when deciding to start a family—for example, determining which mother will carry the child, and who the sperm donor will be. Custody and adoption arrangements also require thoughtful deliberation on the part of gay and lesbian would-be parents. Depending on the state, it may be impossible to get legal recognition for both parents. Therapists can help clients manage their frustration and cope with any power imbalance that could happen if only one person is considered a parent on paper, says Ariel.
- **Negotiating roles and chores.** Because there isn't a cultural script for lesbian and gay families, these families may especially benefit from open discussions about dividing up responsibility for child-rearing, finances and other household chores, notes Ariel. Therapists who are completely open to unusual family configurations will fare best when facilitating such discussions, she says.

"It's crucial for these couples to feel totally accepted by a therapist," says Ariel. "Any subtle homophobia will show through."

—S. Dingfelder

Patterson's and others' findings that good parenting, not a parent's sexual orientation, leads to mentally healthy children may not surprise many psychologists. What may be more surprising is the finding that children of same-sex couples seem to be thriving, though they live in a world that is often unaccepting of their parents.

In fact, an as-yet-unpublished study by Nanette Gartrell, MD, found that by age 10, about half of children with lesbian mothers have been targeted for homophobic teasing by their peers. Those children tended to report more psychological distress than those untouched by homophobia.

But as a group, the children of lesbian moms are just as well-adjusted as children from more traditional families, according to the data from Gartrell's National Longitudinal Lesbian Family Study. The resilience of the children may, in part, come from their parents' efforts to protect them and prepare them for facing homophobia, says Gartrell, a University of California, San Francisco, psychiatry professor.

"In order to create a homophobia-free space for these children, the moms have had to educate their pediatricians, their child-care workers," says Gartrell. "They are active in the school system and make sure there are training modules in the schools that support diversity including LGBT [lesbian, gay, bisexual and transgendered] families. All this is on top of the usual 24-7 commitment to parenting."

> **"The kids I've interviewed are enormously thoughtful—they are not only sensitive to discrimination to their groups but other groups as well. This is something LGBT families have to offer the world."**
>
> **Nanette Gartrell**
> **University of California, San Francisco**

Sources of Support

Many gay and lesbian parents pull off this feat by plugging into informal support networks, notes Jane Ariel, PhD, a clinician with many gay and lesbian clients, and also a psychology professor at the Wright Institute in Berkeley. Lesbian and gay parents may also look to therapists for help navigating the typical demands of parenthood and the special demands of being a gay parent, she notes.

Psychologists can be particularly helpful if they tune into what some of that extra work entails, says Ariel. Researchers, too, can ameliorate the challenges such families face by continuing to dispel myths about lesbian and gay parents and by educating the public about their findings, notes Cerbone.

Support can also come in the form of gay parents' groups that meet regularly to socialize, trade parenting tips and share information about gay-friendly schools and doctors, says Ariel.

"There is often a very strong, intimate connection with an extended of group of people who become like family and serve some of the same purposes," says Ariel.

The James-Hermanns plugged into such a group through their local Unitarian Universalist church.

"Surrounding ourselves with other gay-dad families has been enormously helpful," says James.

National groups, such as Children of Lesbians and Gays Everywhere (COLAGE) and Parents, Families and Friends of Lesbians and Gays (PFLAG) can also help children with gay or lesbian parents learn how to handle homophobia from their peers, notes Judith Snow. In fact, in her work as a therapist, Snow encourages gay and lesbian parents and their children to tap into COLAGE or similar support networks.

"What these groups do is normalize the whole thing by showing kids they aren't alone and helping them learn the skills to cope with having gay or lesbian parents in a homophobic world," says Snow.

From nagging his kids about homework to teaching them how to confront homophobia, being a gay dad is a lot of work, says James. However, it's also a lot of fun, he says.

"Watching the boys grow and develop into these amazing little people—it has been an incredible experience," he says.

Children of gay and lesbian parents may enrich more than just their parents' lives, says Gartrell.

"The kids I've interviewed are enormously thoughtful—they are not only sensitive to discrimination to their groups but other groups as well," she says. "This is something LGBT families have to offer the world."

Further Reading

- American Psychological Association. (1995). *Lesbian and gay parenting: A resource for psychologists.* Washington, DC: Author.
- Ariel, J., & McPherson, D. (2000). Therapy with lesbian and gay families and their children. *Journal of Marital and Family Therapy, 26,* 421–432.
- Chan, R.W., Brooks, R.C., Raboy, B., & Patterson, C.J. (1998). Division of labor among lesbian and heterosexual parents: Associations with children's adjustment. *Journal of Family Psychology, 12,* 402–419.
- Fulcher, M., Sutfin, E.L., Chan, R.W., Scheib, J.E., & Patterson, C.J. (in press). Lesbian mothers and their children: Findings from the Contemporary Families Study. In A. Omoto & H. Kurtzman (Eds.), *Recent Research on Sexual Orientation, Mental Health, and Substance Abuse.* Washington, DC: American Psychological Association.
- Gartrell, N.G., Deck, A., Rodas, C., Peyser, H., & Banks, A. (in press). The national lesbian family study: Interviews with the 10-year-old children. *Feminism & Psychology.*
- Snow, J.E. (2004). *How it feels to have a gay or lesbian parent.* New York: Harrington Park Press.
- Wainright, J.L., Russell, S.T., & Patterson, C.J. (2004). Psychosocial adjustment, school outcomes, and romantic relationships of adolescents with same-sex parents. *Child Development, 75,* 1886–1898.

For a summary of research on lesbian and gay parenting, visit **http://www.apa.org/pi/lgbc/publications/parent.html**.

What about Black Fathers?

By placing so much emphasis on marriage, public policy could set back efforts to bring unmarried fathers into more constructive contact with their children.

BY RONALD B. MINCY

EMBOLDENED BY THE REDUCTION IN THE WELFARE ROLLS, conservatives have renewed their demands that our welfare system reflect traditional family values, specifically marriage. But if marriage becomes the heavily favored family strategy of welfare policy, family-service providers and other supporters of responsible fatherhood will find it harder to help families as they actually exist—families that are not always headed by married couples.

President Bush, an outspoken supporter of strong marriages, has responded to this conservative social agenda with several policy initiatives. First, the administration's new welfare-reform proposal adds a few key words to the fourth goal of the 1996 welfare-reform act: "to encourage the formation and maintenance of healthy two-parent *married* families and responsible fatherhood [emphasis added]." Next, it dedicates $300 million in federal funds to support marriage-promotion efforts. Then, the plan encourages states to provide (pared-down) child support and commits the federal government to share in the costs.

This proposal may soften the opposition from some women's groups to the marriage emphasis. However, the plan only pays lip service to responsible fatherhood and provides no dedicated federal funds to support such efforts. Thus, responsible-fatherhood groups will have to rely exclusively upon Temporary Assistance for Needy Families or other state funds, for which there are many competing priorities.

Anticipating this new political and policy climate, several fatherhood groups that work in predominantly black communities are preparing to expand services to include marriage. The most important and innovative groups include the Center for Fathers, Families and Workforce Development (CFWD), the National Center for Strategic Nonprofit Planning and Community Lead-

ership (NPCL), and the Institute for Responsible Fatherhood and Family Revitalization (IRFFR).

CFWD is a community-based responsible-fatherhood program that also provides job placement and wage- and career-growth services to disadvantaged fathers in Baltimore. The goal is to encourage fathers, whether married or not, to become more involved in their children's lives, both emotionally and financially, and to develop a better relationship with the child's mother. NPCL is a national intermediary organization that has trained more than 2,500 community-based practitioners and agencies that sponsor them. It works, through federally funded demonstration projects, to combine child-support enforcement and workforce-development efforts in support of fragile families, so that fathers have both the means and the commitment to contribute to the support of their children. The organization's recent international conference brought together more than 1,200 responsible fatherhood practitioners from the United States and around the globe. Both organizations are now developing marriage curricula. IRFFR, founded in the 1980s, is perhaps the oldest community-based responsible-fatherhood program in the country. These groups, and others with roots in the black community, did not need to be persuaded by the current political climate that marriage was vital to rebuilding strong black families.

Some observers may accuse them of opportunism or of selling out to the conservative agenda. However, few of these groups opposed marriage in principle, though they did object when the early rhetoric made marriage seem like a panacea—and when proposals began to surface to make marriage a condition of services or bonus payments. The rhetoric has now become more reasonable. The Bush administration intends to promote "healthy, stable, and happy marriages" and will target its marriage-promotion efforts at couples who choose to receive such services. Like most Americans, black fatherhood groups support this and wish that all the unwed parents who come to them for help were in a position to benefit from such services. As Andrew Billingsley points out in his book *Climbing Jacob's Ladder*, blacks generally have strong family values; however, they often struggle under difficult conditions that make it tough to act on those values. For this reason, Billingsley argues, black communities have had more diverse and complex family systems than whites for as long as blacks have been in this country.

UNMARRIED BUT NOT UNINVOLVED

Fatherhood groups who work in low-income black communities see this diversity and complexity every day. They also know that many young unwed parents, especially fathers, simply are unprepared to assume the responsibilities that would produce the kind of marriages that increase child well-being. For this reason, these groups have expanded their services to help fathers make positive contributions to their children, even while unmarried, and to position themselves to assume the responsibilities that would make it possible for them to one day sustain happy marriages. The new services focus on job retention, wage and career growth, and job placement. Besides employment services, groups are providing legal, educational, team-parenting, substance-abuse, child-support, health, mental-health, spouse-abuse, and other services to meet the needs of clients and their families. They are also improving their capacity to measure program outcomes and diversifying their staff or strengthening existing staff, in hopes that welfare reauthorization would provide additional resources to improve their work with fathers and families. These efforts are consistent with the 1996 goal of encouraging the formation and maintenance of two-parent families.

B UT NOW THE BUSH ADMINISTRATION HAS RAISED THE standard to emphasize marriage per se. And responsible-fatherhood groups that seek to promote marriage in predominantly black communities will find it hard to achieve this higher standard for several reasons. First, there are demographic realities. The percentage of black women of childbearing age (say, 15 to 44 years old) who have never married (41 percent) is just about double the percentage of comparable white women. Second, although cohabitation and unwed births have been rising while marriage has been declining among all race and ethnic groups, these trends are far from convergent for whites, blacks, and other groups.

For example, unwed births are more common among cohabiting Puerto Rican women than among black or non-Hispanic white women. However, an unwed first birth hastens the transition to marriage among non-Hispanic white cohabiting women, has no effect on the transition to marriage among black cohabiting women, and reduces the prospects of marriage among Puerto Rican cohabiting women.

Given these apparent differences in family formation by race and ethnicity, our research team at Columbia University and Princeton University has been using data from a new birth cohort survey to study the likely effects of the administration's approach on black and nonblack children and families. We assume that marriage is the best option even for the children of unwed parents, if only because marriages tend to last longer than cohabiting relationships. However, we also acknowledge the diversity of family systems. In particular, we acknowledge that in black communities (both here and abroad), father-child contact often occurs through nonresidential, visiting relationships between unwed parents, which are less stable than cohabiting relationships. This means that, unlike traditional models of family formation, unwed parents have four options to choose from: no father-child contact, some father-child contact, cohabitation, and marriage. Moreover, it turns out that Billingsley's metaphor powerfully predicts what could happen if the Bush administration's marriage initiatives could be used flexibly to strengthen families, because these options resemble a ladder leading to more intense and enduring forms of father-child contact.

That is, policies often have unintended effects. Thus, the responses of some unwed parents to policies that promote marriage may fall short of the administration's ideal but still result in more intense and enduring forms of father-child contact than would have occurred otherwise. For example, throughout the past two decades, the fraction of low-skilled men who are either working or looking for work has shrunk, despite strong economic growth interrupted by brief recessions. If welfare programs were able to help these men find jobs, some fathers who are not now in regular contact with their children might begin to be. Other fathers who now visit their children might live with them. And still other fathers who are living with their children (and their children's mother) would be married. Moreover, such a policy might have large effects on family formation and father-child contact for black unwed parents and, to a lesser extent, for nonblack unwed parents. Other policies might have the same effects on family formation and father-child contact for black and nonblack unwed parents.

STRENGTHENING FAMILIES AS THEY EXIST

Our study shows that fathers' employment benefits black and nonblack children, no matter where their parents begin on the ladder to more intense and enduring forms of father-child contact. Compared with children whose fathers did not work, children with working fathers were more likely to have some contact with their fathers, more likely to live with their fathers (and mothers in cohabiting relationships), and more likely to live with their fathers in a traditional married family. Having children with one partner rather than multiple partners also increases the odds of maintaining relationships with children, all the way up the ladder, in black and nonblack families alike. However, a mother's work history prior to giving birth increases the odds of cohabitation and marriage among black unwed parents but has no statistically significant effect on the odds of moving up the ladder for nonblacks. Thus, by providing employment services (for men as well as women) and an emphasis on preventing out-of-wedlock births, welfare policy could increase marriage and other forms of father-child contact for blacks and increase (or leave unchanged) the same outcomes for nonblacks.

Other policies would affect these groups or outcomes differently. Higher cash benefits increase the odds that black and nonblack fragile families have some father-child contact and the odds that they cohabit, but have no effect on the odds that they marry. By contrast, more effective child-support enforcement increases the odds of marriage among nonblacks but reduces the odds of father-child contact, without affecting the odds of marriage among blacks.

UNFORTUNATELY, THESE PROMISING POLICY INSTRUMENTS have been sidelined in the current debate. Instead, the administration is placing its entire emphasis on promoting marriage. Our research suggests such efforts would produce mixed results. They might encourage some unwed mothers to marry. We find, for example, that nonblack unwed mothers with some religious affiliation are more likely to marry the fathers of their children than those without a religious affiliation. Black unwed mothers affiliated with faith communities that hold conservative views on family issues are more likely to marry the fathers of their children than are black unwed mothers with no religious affiliation.

However, great caution is required before black communities would embrace such approaches—because the approaches are likely to celebrate the virtues of marriage while stigmatizing unwed births, something blacks traditionally have not done because of historical experience. Although rates have risen in recent decades, single motherhood has been much more common among black families for more than 100 years. The reasons for this are complex. Some black women became single mothers because they (and the fathers of their children) violated social and religious prohibitions against nonmarital sex. Others be-came single mothers because they were raped or their husbands were lynched. Still others became single mothers because their husbands migrated north in search of employment but never returned after job discrimination dashed their hopes.

Often in the painful history of race relations in this country, desertion and victimization were as likely the causes of single motherhood as was moral failure. In any individual case, who could know? Who would ask? In response, the black community developed a tradition of embracing all of its children, even the fair-skinned ones. Under these circumstances, stigmatizing unwed births was impossible. Fortunately, in many respects the circumstances have changed.

THERE IS MOUNTING EVIDENCE THAT CHILDREN ARE BETTER off if they grow up in healthy, married-couple families. This poses a unique challenge for the black community, because the substantial retreat from marriage in the black community has created extraordinarily high rates of childbearing and child rearing among unwed blacks. Marriage proponents would be wise to let this evidence prick the conscience of the nation with this question: How did we allow childbirth and child rearing to divorce themselves from marriage? The diverse race and ethnic groups that now constitute America will have different answers—and different strategies for creating or re-creating the most supportive family arrangements for children.

As they wrestle with this question, each group will be forced to reflect on its past and its future and to develop responses. If the issue is forced by heavily subsidizing marriage, the response that is easiest for whites but hardest for blacks will only provide a common threat against which blacks will rally. This will only distract them from the kind of private, searching dialogue the black community needs to reach into its own soul and find what is best for all its children, those whose parents marry and those whose parents do not.

RONALD B. MINCY *is the Maurice V. Russell Professor of Social Policy and Social Work Practice at Columbia University.*

Adoption by Lesbian Couples

Is it in the best interests of the child?

The report of the American Academy of Pediatrics in February[1] supporting the introduction of legislation to allow the adoption by co-parents of children born to lesbian couples sparked enormous controversy not only within the medical profession but among the public as well. Almost without exception, only the mother who gives birth to or adopts the child may currently be the legal parent, even in cases where a couple plan a family together and raise their child in a stable family unit. The academy has taken the view that children in this situation deserve the security of two legally recognised parents in order to promote psychological wellbeing and to enable the child's relationship with the co-mother to continue should the other mother die, become incapacitated, or the couple separate. This position is based on evidence derived from the research literature on this issue.[2] The *Washington Times* described the stance of the academy as "an unfortunate surrender to political expediency" and accused the academy's Committee on Psychosociological Aspects of Child and Family Health of sacrificing scientific integrity in order to advance an activist agenda.[3] Is it the case that children born to lesbian couples "can have the same advantages and the same expectations for health, adjustment, and development as can parents who are heterosexual," as stated by the academy? Alternatively, is the academy simply pandering to a politically correct agenda?

Two main concerns have been expressed in relation to lesbian mother families: firstly, that the children would be bullied and ostracised by peers and would consequently develop psychological problems, and, secondly, that they would show atypical gender development such that boys would be less masculine in their identity and behaviour, and girls less feminine, than boys and girls from heterosexual families. Lack of knowledge about these children and their parents in the light of a growing number of child custody cases involving a lesbian mother prompted the first wave of studies in the 1970s. This early body of research focused on families where the child had been born into a heterosexual family and then moved with the mother into a lesbian family after the parents' separation or divorce. Regardless of the geographical or demographic characteristics of the families studied, the findings of these early investigations were strikingly consistent. Children from lesbian mother families did not show a higher rate of psychological disorder or difficulties in peer relationships than their counterparts from heterosexual homes. With respect to gender development, there was no evidence of confusion about gender identity among these children, and no difference in sex role behaviour between children in lesbian and heterosexual families for either boys or girls.[4][5]

A limitation of the early investigations was that only school age children were studied. It was argued that sleeper effects may exist such that children raised in lesbian mother families may experience difficulties in emotional wellbeing and in intimate relationships when they grow up. Further, they may be more likely than other children to themselves adopt a lesbian or gay sexual orientation in adulthood, an outcome that has been considered undesirable by courts of law. To address this question, a group of children raised in lesbian mother families in the United Kingdom was followed up to adulthood.[6][7] These young adults did not differ from their counterparts from heterosexual families in terms of quality of family relationships, psychological adjustment, or quality of peer relationships. With respect to their sexual orientation, the large majority of children from lesbian families identified as heterosexual in adulthood.

In recent years, attention has moved from the issue of child custody to whether lesbian women should have access to assisted reproduction procedures, particularly donor insemination, to enable them to have children without the involvement of a male partner. The findings from studies of these families, where the children grow up without a father right from the start, indicate that the children do not differ from their peers in two parent, heterosexual families in terms of either emotional wellbeing or gender development.[8-11] The only clear difference to emerge is that co-mothers in two parent lesbian families are more involved in parenting than are fathers from two parent homes.

A limitation of the existing body of research is that only small volunteer or convenience samples have been studied, and thus mothers whose children are experiencing difficulties may be under-represented. Nevertheless, a substantial body of evidence indicates that children raised by lesbian mothers do not differ from other children in key aspects of psychological development. On the basis of this evidence it seems that the American Academy of Pediatrics acted not out of political correctness but with the intention of protecting children who are likely to benefit from the legal recognition of their second parent. At present in the United Kingdom, lesbian women are individually eligible to adopt children, whether living with a partner or not. However, members of parliament have recently voted to allow unmarried couples, whatever their sexual orientation, to adopt children jointly.

References

1. Committee on Psychosocial Aspects of Child and Family Health. Co-parent or second-parent adoption by same-sex parents. *Pediatrics* 2002;109:339–40.

2. Perrin EC. Technical report: coparent or second-parent adoption by same-sex parents. *Pediatrics* 2002; 109:341–4.

3. Dobson JC. Pediatricians vs children. *Washington Times* 2002 Feb 12.

4. Patterson CJ. Children of lesbian and gay parents. *Child Dev* 1992;63:1025–42.

5. Golombok S. Lesbian mother families. In: Bainham A, Day Sclater S, Richards M, eds. *What is a parent? A socio-legal analysis*. Oxford: Hart Publishing, 1999.

6. Golombok S, Tasker F. Do parents influence the sexual orientation of their children? Findings from a longitudinal study of lesbian families. *Dev Psychol* 1996;32:3–11.

7. Tasker F, Golombok S. *Growing up in a lesbian family*. New York: Guilford Press, 1997.

8. Flaks DK, Ficher I, Masterpasqua F, Joseph G. Lesbian choosing motherhood: a comparative study of lesbian and heterosexual parents and their children. *Developmental Psychology* 1995;31:105–14.

9. Golombok S, Tasker F, Murray C. Children raised in fatherless families from infancy: family relationships and the socioemotional development of children of lesbian and single heterosexual mothers. *J Child Psychol Psychiatry* 1997;38:783–91.

10. Brewaeys A, Ponjaert I, Van Hall E, Golombok S. Donor insemination: child development and family functioning in lesbian mother families. *Hum Reprod* 1997;12:1349–59.

11. Chan RW, Raboy B, Patterson CJ. Psychosocial adjustment among children conceived via donor insemination by lesbian and heterosexual mothers. *Child Dev* 1998;69:443–57.

Susan Golombok, *professor*, Family and Child Psychology Research Centre, City University, London EC1V 0HB (S.E.Golombok@city.ac.uk)

Are Married Parents Really Better for Children?

MARY PARKE

Policy Analyst, Center for Law and Social Policy

Over the past four decades, the patterns of family structure have changed dramatically in the United States. An increase in the numbers and proportion of children born outside of marriage and a rise in divorce rates have contributed to a three-fold increase in the proportion of children growing up in single-parent families since 1960. These changes have generated considerable public concern and controversy, particularly about the effects of these changes on the well-being of children. Over the past 20 years, a body of research has developed on how changes in patterns of family structure affect children. Most researchers now agree that together these studies support the notion that, on average, children do best when raised by their two married, biological parents who have low-conflict relationships.

On average, children do best when raised by their two married, biological parents who have low-conflict relationships.

This research has been cited as justification for recent public policy initiatives to promote and strengthen marriages. However, findings from the research are often oversimplified, leading to exaggeration by proponents of marriage initiatives and to skepticism from critics. While the increased risks faced by children raised without both parents are certainly reason for concern, the majority of children in single-parent families grow up without serious problems. In addition, there continues to be debate about how much of the disadvantages to children are attributable to poverty versus family structure, as well as about whether it is marriage itself that makes a difference or the type of people who get married.

How Has Family Structure Changed?

Single-parent families are much more common today than they were 40 years ago. Rates have increased across race and income groups, but single parenthood is more prevalent among African Americans and Hispanics.

In 1996, 71.5 million children under the age of 18 lived in the U.S. The large majority of these children were living with two parents, one-quarter lived with a single parent, and less than 4 percent lived with another relative or in foster care. Two-thirds of children were living with two married, biological parents, and less than 2 percent with two cohabiting, biological parents. Less than 7 percent lived within a step-family. Twenty percent of children lived with a single mother, 2 percent with a single father, and almost 3 percent lived in an informal step-family—that is, with a single parent and his or her partner.

The majority of children in single-parent families grow up without serious problems.

Many children live in more than one type of family during the course of their childhoods. For instance, the majority of children in step-families have also lived in a single-parent family at some point.

Are Children Better Off If They Grow Up with Their Married, Biological Parents?

In 1994, Sara McLanahan and Gary Sandefur, using evidence from four nationally representative data sets, compared the outcomes of children growing up with both biological parents, with single parents, and with step-parents. McLanahan and Sandefur found that children who did not live with both biological parents were roughly twice as likely to be poor, to have a birth outside of marriage, to have behavioral and psychological problems, and to not graduate from high school. Other studies have reported associations between family structure and child health outcomes. For example, one study found children living in single-parent homes were more likely to experience health problems, such as accidents, injuries, and poisonings.

Utah Has Highest Proportion of Married-Couple Households

Sixty-three percent of all households in Utah in 2000 were maintained by married couples, the highest in the country. Idaho (59 percent) and Iowa (55 percent) were the second and third highest. The states with less than one-half of their households maintained by married couples were geographically dispersed: Massachusetts, Rhode Island, New York, Louisiana, Mississippi, and Nevada. Only 23 percent of households in the District of Columbia were maintained by married couples.

—*U.S. Census Bureau*

Of course, most children in single-parent families will not experience these negative outcomes. But what is the level and degree of risk for the average child? The answer depends on the outcome being assessed as well as other factors. For example, McLanahan and Sandefur reported that single-parent families had a much higher poverty rate (26 percent) than either two-parent biological families (5 percent) or step-families (9 percent). They also found that the risk of dropping out of high school for the average white child was substantially lower in a two-parent biological family (11 percent) than in a single-parent family or step-family (28 percent). For the average African American child, the risk of dropping out of high school was 17 percent in a two-parent family versus 30 percent in a single- or step-parent family. And for the average Hispanic child, the risk of dropping out of school was 25 percent in a two-parent family and 49 percent in a single- or step-parent family.

Up to half of the higher risk for negative educational outcomes for children in single-parent families is due to living with a significantly reduced household income. Other major factors are related to disruptions in family structure, including turmoil a child experiences when parents separate and/or re-couple with a step-parent (including residential instability), weaker connections between the child and his or her non-custodial parent (usually the father), and weakened connections to resources outside of the immediate family—that is, other adults and institutions in the community that the non-custodial parent may have provided access to.

How Do Child Outcomes Vary Among Types of Families?

Comparing two-parent families with all single-parent families often masks important subtleties. Subsequent research has added to our understanding of the range of family structures by examining separately the data for divorced, widowed, never-married, and cohabiting parents, married stepparents, and same-sex couples. While this research has revealed important nuances about the effects of these different family types on children, many questions remain unanswered.

Divorced families. Before they reach adulthood, nearly four out of 10 children will experience the divorce of their parents, and roughly one million children experience their parents' divorce every year. Research shows that, on average, children of divorced parents are disadvantaged compared to children of married parents in the area of educational achievement. Children of divorce are more than twice as likely to have serious social, emotional, or psychological problems as children of intact families—25 percent versus 10 percent.

Most divorced families with children experience enormous drops in income, which lessen somewhat over time but remain significant for years—unless there is a subsequent parental cohabitation or remarriage. Declines in income following divorce account for up to half the risk for children dropping out of high school, regardless of income prior to the divorce. The effects of divorce on children often last through adulthood. For instance, adult children of divorce are more likely to experience depression and their own divorces—as well as earn less income and achieve lower levels of education—compared with adults whose parents remained married.

Never-married mothers. Among children living with single mothers, the proportion living with never-married mothers increased from 7 percent to 36 percent between 1970 and 1996. In 1996, 7.1 million children lived with a never-married parent. Children of never-married mothers are at risk of experiencing negative outcomes and are among those most likely to live in poverty. Roughly 69 percent of children of never-married mothers are poor, compared to 45 percent of children brought up by divorced single mothers. Never-married mothers are significantly younger, have lower incomes, have fewer years of education, and are twice as likely to be unemployed as divorced mothers. A child born to an unmarried mother is less likely to complete high school than a child whose mother is married. While we know the number of children born to never-married mothers, we don't really know how many spend their entire childhoods living with a mother who never marries or cohabits. Part of the increase in children living with never-married mothers is attributable to the increase in children born to cohabiting couples, which are often reported as single-mother families.

Cohabiting-parent families. In 1970, there were 523,000 unmarried-couple households, while in 2000 4.9 million opposite-sex couples cohabited. About 40 percent of cohabiting households in 2000 included children. While this equates to a small proportion of the total children in the U.S., the proportion of children who will live in a cohabiting household at some point during their childhoods is estimated to be four in 10.

Six out of 10 children in cohabiting-parent families live with an informal step-parent, while four out of 10 live with both biological parents. (In comparison, nine out of 10 children in married-couple households live with both biological parents.)

Research suggests that children in cohabiting families are at higher risk of poor outcomes compared to children of married parents partly because cohabiting families have fewer socioeconomic resources and partly because of unstable living situations.

Research also suggests the importance of distinguishing between cohabiting families with two biological parents and those with a biological parent and another partner. Some evidence indicates that school achievement and behavioral problems are similar among children living with both biological parents—regardless of marital status—and that children in both formal and informal step-families also fare similarly in these areas.

Step-families. In 1996, about 7 percent of children, or five million children, lived with a step-parent, and estimates indicate that about one-third of all children today may live with step-parents before reaching adult-hood. More than 90 percent of step-children live with their mother and a step-father. Step-families are at greater risk of dissolution than other marriages; about 60 percent of step-families are disrupted by divorce.

In spite of their better economic circumstances on average, children in step-families face many of the same risks as children of never-married or divorced parents. They are more likely to have negative behavioral, health, and educational outcomes, and they tend to leave home earlier than children who live with both married biological parents. However, the effect sizes are small for many of these differences, and risk levels may vary according to race and level of socioeconomic disadvantage.

Same-sex couple families. The 2000 Census revealed that out of 5.5 million cohabiting couples, about 11 percent were same-sex couples—with slightly more male couples than female. About 163,000 same-sex households in total, lived with children under 18 years old. (This compares with about 25 million married-couple households with children under 18.)

Although the research on these families has limitations, the findings are consistent: children raised by same-sex parents are no more likely to exhibit poor outcomes than children raised by divorced heterosexual parents.

Does Family Structure or Reduced Income Make the Difference?

If the negative effects of single parenthood on child well-being were primarily due to a lack or loss of income, one would expect children living with two adults to do as well as those living with their married, biological parents. But this is not the case. The research shows that children living with cohabiting parents or in a step-family do not do as well as children living with married, biological parents on a number of variables.

Is It Marriage Itself or the Kind of People Who Marry That Makes the Difference?

It is often suggested that the positive effects of marriage on child well-being are likely derived not from marriage itself but from the distinctive characteristics of the individuals who marry and stay married.

Marriage may have certain benefits, such as access to health insurance and tax advantages, that contribute to the increased likelihood of child well-being. It is also possible that those who marry also have attributes unmeasured in existing surveys—such as commitment, loyalty, and future orientation—that dis-

tinguish them from those who don't marry and stay married. It is also possible that marriage itself—the actual act of getting married—changes the attitudes and behaviors of couples in positive ways, as well as those of others towards them.

Doesn't the Quality of the Relationship Matter More Than the Piece of Paper?

The quality of the relationship between parents matters to child well-being. Children who grow up in married families with high conflict experience lower emotional well-being than children who live in low-conflict families, and they may experience as many problems as children of divorced or never-married parents. Research indicates that marital conflict interferes with the quality of parenting. Furthermore, experiencing chronic conflict between married parents is inherently stressful for children, and children learn poor relationship skills from parents who aren't able to solve problems amicably.

What Is the Relationship Between Marriage and Poverty?

Children living with single mothers are five times as likely to be poor as those in two-parent families. Some economists have attributed virtually all of the 25 percent increase in child poverty between 1970 and 1997 to the growth of single-parent families. But are single parents poor because they are not married, or would they have remained poor even if they married available partners? While it is difficult to disentangle the effects of income and family structure, clearly the relationship operates in both directions: poverty is both cause and effect of single parenthood. For example, research evidence indicates that in low-income, African American communities, the high rate of male unemployment is one of the factors that explains why low-income mothers do not marry.

But recent economic simulation studies have found that if two poor unmarried parents marry they are less likely to be poor. Economist Robert Lerman found that married parents suffered less economic hardship than cohabiting parents with the same low income and education. Among the apparent explanations were that married parents are more likely to pool their earnings, husbands work longer hours and earn more, and married families receive more assistance from family, friends, and the community. While marriage itself will not lift a family out of poverty, it may reduce material hardship.

What More Do We Need to Know?

Much remains to be learned about how living in different family structures affects child well-being, including:

- How does moving into and out of different family situations affect children? At what ages are children most vulnerable to these changes? How much of the risk to children is caused by living arrangement instability itself?

- What are the long-term effects of some of these family structure patterns—for example, for children who live in long-term cohabiting families or in long-term, single-parent, never-married families?
- How are children in families from different minority and cultural backgrounds affected by family structure?
- From a child well-being perspective, what are the relevant measures of a "healthy" or "good enough" marriage?

This article was excerpted and reprinted with permission from a policy brief published by the Center for Law and Social Policy (CLASP). The entire brief, including notes and charts, can be downloaded in PDF form from **www.clasp.org/Pubs/Pubs_Couples**. For more information, contact mparke@clasp.org or call (202) 906-8014.

The Perma Parent Trap

PAMELA PAUL

There's always an explanation: A 22-year-old college grad wants to hold out for the right job rather than jump into an underpaid makeshift position. Rents are so inflated, a 25-year-old moving out of her boyfriend's apartment couldn't possibly afford a place of her own. With two bedrooms to spare, parents can rehouse the kids and everyone will benefit.

Whatever the reason, young adults are returning home in increasing numbers—following graduation, the dissolution of a relationship or the loss of a job. They often live rent-free and subsidized, with no scheduled date for departure. But while much attention has been paid to live-at-home "adultescents," little has been said about their parents, many of whom are Baby Boomers who greet their boomerang kids with open arms. For a variety of emotional and demographic reasons—their desire to be close with their kids, a yearning for youth—many of today's parents (the original Peter Pan generation) just don't want their adult children to grow up.

"Parents used to let go when their children reached age 18," says David Anderegg, professor of psychology at Bennington College in Vermont and author of *Worried All the Time: Overparenting in the Age of Anxiety.* "The idea was, if you can go to jail, I'm no longer responsible for you." But that changed during the 1990s, when Baby Boomers' children turned 18 and devoted parents realized that they had poured their emotional and financial resources into their children from the get-go. "Hyper-investment," says Anderegg, "is hard to turn off."

Some argue that permaparenting stems from the indulgence of an immature and spoiled generation. Others blame the phenomenon on the heavy hand of social and economic forces, especially the current recession. And our very definition of adulthood is in flux—with a homestead no longer a key component of adult identity.

But a rising chorus of psychologists and sociologists says parents simply aren't letting go when they ought to—not only impeding their children's adult independence but also hampering their own post-parenting lives. In the absence of an acute crisis or devastating financial setback, the consensus is that parents should look twice at the reasons they continue to shelter their grown offspring. "If parents can get over the idea that they're not being 'parent enough' or that their kids still 'need' them, then they can get on with their new lives," says Roberta Maisel, author of *All Grown Up: Living Happily Ever After with Your Adult Children.*

The combination of high rents and an unstable job market, increased college attendance and delayed marriage and parenting conspire to inch the age of perceived adulthood upward. Bianca Mlotok, an unemployed college graduate who lives with her parents in New Jersey, admits that even at age 27, she doesn't feel like a grown-up. "I'm a mature person, but I think I'm probably not capable of being on my own," she says. "I feel like an adult sometimes, but in other ways I still feel like a child. I guess I see being an adult as more about a certain level of maturity than about some kind of outward sign. Though probably when I start my own family, I'll finally have my own adult identity."

Living on one's own is considered a lesser signpost of adulthood than completing an education or supporting a family.

Bianca isn't the only twentysomething grappling with delayed adulthood. According to a 2003 study by the National Opinion Research Center, most Americans today don't consider a person an adult until age 26, or until she or he has finished school, landed a full-time job, and begun to raise a family. Living independently from one's parents is expected by an average age of 21, yet living on one's own is considered less of a determining factor in reaching adulthood (only 29 percent say it's an "extremely important" step) than completing an education (73 percent) and supporting a family (60 percent).

Shifting parental attitudes toward boomerang kids have much to do with generational differences, the result of each generation correcting and overcorrecting the excesses of the previous one. The wave that preceded the Boomers, the Swing, or Silent, generation (born during the Depression and World War II, 1930-1945) and their children, Generation X (born 1965-1978), were brought up during eras of economic recession, reduced birthrates and familial instability, when raising kids was not a societal focal point. Parents of Boomers "were eager for their kids to grow up and leave the household so that they could be free to pursue their own lives," says generational historian William Strauss. "Boomeranging home was a mark of failure for both children and parents."

In contrast, the Baby Boomers themselves (born between 1946 and 1964) and their Echo Boomer offspring (1979 and 1994) have had the happy fortune to be born during periods of prosperity and family growth that place an emphasis on parenthood. From the 1980s hit *The Cosby Show* to kidcentric TV like Nickelodeon, Boomers were awash in media celebrating the rewards of childrearing and the joys of childhood. Five times more parenting books are published today than in 1970. Ann Hulbert, author of *Raising America: Experts, Parents and a Century of Advice About Children,* says the resultant professionalization of parenting marked a shift from "what was once considered an intuitive, instinctive endeavor into a systematic, intellectualized enterprise."

Keeping the Lines of Communication Open

All this attention, it turns out, has been directed toward raising well-adjusted and well-rounded kids, and guiding those self-same kids into fulfilled adulthood, creating patterns along the way. According to Jane Adams, a social psychologist and author of *When Our Grown Kids Disappoint Us,* previous generations emphasized education and financial independence over all else for their children. In contrast, "Boomers are the first generation for whom their children's emotional fulfillment is a primary goal. Their parental mantra has been, 'Be happy or I'll kill you.'" In an effort to gratify their kids, Boomers have become unusually invested in their lives—determined to have an authentic, intimate relationship with their children.

The Boomer parental mantra: "Be happy or I'll kill you."

To achieve this level of chumminess, parents have often acted less like stern grown ups and more like their kids' peers, joining the youth culture wholeheartedly at the mall, even purchasing the same teen-oriented clothes for themselves. This closeness continues and strengthens as Echo Boomers reach early adulthood. "The generation gap used to be a significant barrier between parents and adult kids," says Roberta Maisel. "But today's fiftysomething parent and twentysomething child have a lot of the same values and desires."

Therese Christophe, a 54-year-old long-separated woman who lives with her 25-year-old son, Alexandre, says the arrangement works well precisely because her son and his friends don't view her as very different from themselves. "They see me as an adult, but they know I'm cool enough to be their friend," she explains. "I don't try to play this mother role. There's always been an equal relationship, and we're very tight. I'm not judgmental of him and he isn't judgmental of me." The result: "Living with my kid is like having a roommate, only a lot better."

Today's twentysomethings and their parents communicate better and are closer, finds family therapist Betty Frain. Indeed, in a recent survey of 1,003 high school students, a whopping 78 percent said that "having close family relationships" ranked highest (above money and fame, among other things) in defining success. But closeness also creates problems. "It becomes hard for these parents to say, 'I'm the leader in this family and it's time for you to go,'" says Frain. "We've gotten too friendly with our kids."

Studies suggest that grown kids' well-being is a major determinant of well-being for midlife parents. But over-identification

with adult children means parents can lose perspective on what's best for one or both parties. "You see your kids' successes and failures as your own and thus try to immunize your child against failure." says Frank Furedi, professor of sociology at the University of Kent in the United Kingdom. With such a high level of emotional and financial investment, many parents see the status of their adult children as a final parental exam. And parents don't want a bad grade either for themselves or for their kids.

Not surprisingly, parental involvement in kids' lives has pushed its way onto campuses, where "helicopter parents" hover, trying to help their kids through college financially, emotionally and even academically. Parents have been known to intervene in roommate disputes following an emotional e-mail plea from a child, or call a professor to question a grade. In response, universities are scheduling special parent orientation events, hiring parental "liaisons" to handle questions and demands, and firing off terse-but-diplomatic guidelines.

The days when parents simply dropped their kids off and waved goodbye are as antiquated as the college mixer. Today, *The Harvard College Handbook for Parents* is rife with messages to back off: "Parents are often tempted to call advisers or administrators or even rush back to Cambridge to 'make sure' that problems are quickly resolved," the 2000-2001 booklet warns. "In fact, these well-intentioned efforts invariably slow the process by which freshmen learn to take responsibility for their dealings with individuals and institutions."

No Help Like Home

The most blatant manifestation of permaparenting is the phenomenon of boomerang kids. According to the 2000 census, 4 million people between the ages of 25 and 34 live with their folks. In a 2003 Monster/JobTrak.com poll of college seniors, 61 percent say they expect to move back home after graduation. Buzzword maven Faith Popcorn has coined a new term, "B2B" or Back-to-Bedroom, which she describes as "the phenomenon of jobless Gen Xers and Gen Ys returning to their parents' homes." NBC's fall lineup includes *Happy Family,* a sitcom about a middle-aged couple who can't get rid of their adult children.

Yet many Boomers don't seem to be trying all that hard to empty the nest. "Boomerang kids are staying at home so they can save money to rent or buy a place of their own instead of living with roommates," says Jane Adams. "Often, they're spending lots of money on clothes and cars and vacations in the process. Unless we put our foot down, why should they move out?"

Parents of college kids intervene in roommate disputes and question grades with professors.

Whereas pre-Boomer parents—the GI and Depression/War Generations—reminded their children constantly of their sacrifices and taught them to be grateful for opportunities (what some might call "guilt-tripping"), Baby Boomers didn't want to do that to their kids. According to Adams, having grown up in an era of relative stability, Boomers inadvertently raised the next generation to feel entitled.

But it's not just privileged white kids hanging out at home. Working-class twentysomethings have long boomeranged following high school or vocational training because entry-level wages make independent living a financial challenge. Still, lower income Americans today are even less able to be independent than just a decade ago, according to Frank Furstenberg Jr., professor of sociology at the University of Pennsylvania and head of the Network on the Transition to Adulthood study. Furthermore, America's growing diversity means more adult children at home come from immigrant and ethnic communities in which living at home during one's twenties is normative and even favorable. A 2002 national survey of Latinos found that 78 percent agreed "it is better for children to live in their parents' home until they get married."

Leaving home is getting tougher across social classes and ethnic backgrounds. In the absence of a stable labor market, and with a lack of federal support (such as the GI Bill for education), "we're throwing a lot of things back on the family that the government was doing before, in terms of job training and housing subsidies," says Stephanie Coontz, professor of history and family studies at Evergreen State College in Washington state. Kids today aren't necessarily slackers, she argues; they're just coming of age when economic and federal forces thwart independence. Parents are stepping in, Coontz says, because they don't really have a choice.

Perhaps expectations are higher as well. Many experts say today's twentysomethings don't want to downscale by sharing a walk-up with three roommates when their middle class parents have a house where they can crash. Boomers don't want their kids to rough it either. "Emotional and financial dependence is a two-way street," says Adams, a Baby Boomer herself. "Our generation has taken it upon ourselves to make our grown kids happy. We've abrogated our responsibility to insist they make a life for themselves. Instead we're providing it for them." Often, if parents don't house their grown kids, those with extra cash will help an adult child purchase a home.

Keith and Virginia Edwards, both 59, have allowed all three of their twenty- and thirtysomething kids to live at home, with spouses and grandchildren in tow, for periods of up to three years. The Edwards's latest boomeranger, Jon, 32, moved back—along with his wife and daughter—two years ago. That way, he could train for a job change and his wife could be a full-time mother while they saved up to buy a home.

Keith says he doesn't mind that his adult kids have returned home, and has even encouraged it. "In each case, they wouldn't have been able to save for a down payment if they'd had to rent an overpriced apartment," he explains. "We wanted them to buy a home rather than rent, so the best solution all around was for them to come back and live with us."

The Parental Toll

Permaparents suffer potential financial and emotional repercussions. The empty-nest years are a crucial time for adults to bone up for retirement, rather than payoff their child's credit cards or feed another mouth. Keeping the kids also prevents couples from reconfiguring their lives in a post-parenting marriage, when, historically, many marriages break up. When marriages do end in divorce, or when one spouse dies, parents may be especially inclined to reconnect with their adult kids.

Avoiding the empty nest and yearning for youth, many of today's parents (the original Peter Pan generation) just don't want their adult children to grow up.

"The empty nest is doubly empty when you don't share it with a partner," says Betty Frain, who sees close relationships between single mothers and their adult children so often that she labels it a phenomenon. Nevertheless, as Roberta Maisel explains, "For women who find themselves widowed or divorced in their 50s or 60s, being too involved in adult children's lives can be a big mistake. They have decades ahead and need to find a way to approach their lives as individuals."

Married or not, adults who re-feather the nest past its prime postpone their own personal development. During the late 1990s, a spate of books with titles like *Give Them Wings* or *As You Leave Home: Parting Thoughts From a Loving Parent* appeared to address the challenge of accepting children's adulthood. But despite the temptations—pleas for help from adult children, the desire to pitch in financially, the urge not to let go—experts agree that having kids at home is generally a bad idea. Unless the child is suffering from a crisis, adult children belong on their own; empty nest parents have their own lives to attend to. Jeffrey Arnett, author of the upcoming book *Emerging Adulthood: The Winding Road from the Late Teens Through the Twenties,* believes boomeranging home may not be best for parents. "Parents like being in a position to help their kids, and they like the fact that they get along well enough to live together," he says. "But parents are usually ready by then to move on with their own lives."

Indeed, many psychologists believe the post-parenting period is one in which people have the opportunity to reconfigure their identities—to relocate, downshift or change a career, become more involved in the community, take continuing education courses or learn new creative skills. Carl Jung in particular emphasized the importance of this last stage of development. Having an adult child lurking around the house and feeding off the parental nest egg robs parents of some of this latitude. "These parents end up impeding their own transition into a new period of adulthood," say Furedi. "It's a flight from life." Permaparents, perhaps it's time to grow up.

PAMELA PAUL is the author of *The Starter Marriage and the Future of Matrimony.*

Being a Sibling

The purpose of this descriptive exploratory study was to explore the meaning of being a sibling using Parse's human becoming perspective. Twelve children between 5 and 15 years of age with a younger sibling with a cleft lip and palate or Down Syndrome participated. Through semi-structured interviews and the use of art children talked about their experiences. Major themes portrayed the complex and paradoxical nature of being a sibling. The themes also revealed that having a sibling with special circumstances includes some unique opportunities and challenges. The finding of this study is the descriptive statement, being a sibling is an arduous charge to champion close others amid restricting-enhancing commitments while new endeavors give rise to new possibilities. *Implications for nursing are discussed in the context of understanding being a sibling.*

STEVEN L. BAUMANN, RN; PhD
Associate Professor, Hunter College, The City University of New York, New York

TINA TAYLOR DYCHES, EdD
Associate Professor, Brigham Young University, Provo, Utah

MARYBETH BRADDICK, MS
Ingram Visiting Nurses, Lansing, Michigan

The sibling relationship can be one of the longest and most important relationships in a person's life. Having a sibling can be very formative for children and instrumental in life. In an age when many people choose not to marry, marry later in life, and many marriages end in divorce, a sibling tie can provide stability and consistency. A sibling can provide fulfilling child-rearing experiences for people who do not have their own children. Yet for many, having a sibling fails to fulfill this potential. Despite years of research on the sibling relationship it is still not well understood (Dunn, 2000). Like being a parent, being a sibling includes much that is not in our control (Baumann & Braddick, 1999). This is particularly evident when a family has a child with special circumstances, or what most of the current literature describes as a child with *special needs*. The phrase *special needs* is avoided here because it imposes meaning, and labels, on the person. In the words of one participant from this study, siblings with special circumstances are *just different*. The authors of this study do assume that siblings of children with a cleft lip and palate (CL&P) or Down Syndrome (DS) in particular, can teach us not only about their personal experiences of being a sibling, but also about being a sibling in general.

Some researchers have said that having a sibling with special circumstances is stressful and problematic for the other children in the family (Murray, 1998, 1999, 2000; Senel & Akkok, 1995; Terzo, 1999). Others have reported that there is not much difference between having a sibling with special circumstances and having a sibling in general (Benson, Gross, & Kellum, 1999; Stawski, Auerbach, Barasch, Lerner, & Zimin, 1997). Still others have identified some benefits for siblings of children with special circumstances (Derouin & Jessee, 1996). It remains unclear what it means to children to have a sibling, with or without special circumstances. Therefore, the purpose of this descriptive exploratory study was to explore what it means to be a sibling. The primary aim of this inquiry was to add to the current understanding about being a brother or sister from the perspective of Parse's (1998) theory of human becoming. Parse holds that children, like adults, live situated freedom as full participants in the cocreation of their lives.

Relevant Literature

The word *sib* is thought to be derived from an Old English word *sib*, meaning relative, and from the Germanic word *sibja*, which means both blood relation and "one's own" (American Heritage Talking Dictionary, 1994). In everyday use, the word *sibling* refers to having one or both parents in common, or having a common ancestry. The terms *sister* and *brother* have numerous meanings, mostly related to close association or shared background (American Heritage Talking Dictionary, 1994).

Family psychoanalytic theory, on the other hand, focuses primarily on parent-child family processes and attributes both the closeness and tensions among family members to conscious and unconscious dynamics (Nichols & Schwartz, 1998). Families and social groups tend to impose expectations on siblings.

Sociologists, such as Mendelson, de Villa, Fitch, and Goodman (1997), have said that adult role expectations for siblings differ with age and gender of the sibling.

A family systems theory (Nichols & Schwartz, 1998) which views the family as an interactive system where what happens to one member affects all members, posits that the siblings represent a subsystem. Some family systems theorists hold that sibling position is very important to both the family and the child development. From this perspective, sibling experiences are shaped by birth order and gender (Silver & Frohlinger-Graham, 2000), and sibling relationships cannot be understood apart from other family relationships and events.

Most social scientists now view being a sibling as both a relationship and a family role (Dunn, 2000). It is likely that this dual nature of being a sibling contributes to the conflict that is common among many siblings. Pollack (2002) suggested that expecting older children to be the primary caregivers of their younger siblings contributes to intersibling tension and can lead to long-term resentment. Family size and the age differences of siblings may also influence sibling relationships, but this effect varies with the age of the siblings, proximity of one to another in the sibling constellation, and gender (Newman, 1996). Larger families may demonstrate both more affection and conflict, whereas wider age spacing between siblings has been observed to be related to less closeness and conflict (Newman, 1996).

Parents and researchers are generally impressed with how different siblings are from one another (Dunn, 2000). These differences are particularly evident in families with a child with special circumstances. As mentioned above, some authors have reported that siblings of children with special circumstances have more stressful lives, exhibit fewer competencies, have more psychopathologies, and may have more unrealistic housework and caregiving demands than siblings in general (Fisman et al., 1996; Fisman, Wolf, Ellison, & Freeman, 2000; Murray, 1999; Williams, 1997). These children are also described as having more limited playtime and opportunities to be with their friends (Seligman & Darling, 1997). Age is considered to be an important factor in understanding how children experience the circumstances of their siblings; older siblings of children with special circumstances have been reported to have more behavioral problems than younger siblings of children in the same situation (Morrison, 1997; Skidmore, 1996; Stawski et al., 1997).

Siblings of children with special circumstances have also been described as harboring intense emotions, such as anger and guilt (Meyer, Vadasy, & Vance, 1996). In addition, unequal parental attention, insufficient information, and ineffective communication between parents and children have been associated with misunderstandings, resentment, and conflict (Brody & Stoneman, 1996; Kowal & Kramer, 1997). Dunn (2000) reported that this pattern is also common in families stressed by separation or illness.

Siblings of children with special circumstances may also face comments by others who equate differences with moral inferiority (Goffman, 1963). These siblings must then make sense of incorrect assumptions, over generalizations, and insults, and have to respond in awkward social situations. Some siblings have been observed altering their thinking or frame of reference

in relation to these family members to mitigate their emotional involvement and negative feelings (Andersson, 1997). This shift in frame of reference could be seen as a defense, which minimizes the differences among the siblings, or it could be that they appreciate underlying likeness and the gifts that their siblings possess. Some health professionals judge the quality of life of persons with special circumstances as more negative than the individuals report themselves (Albrecht & Devlieger, 1999). This *disability paradox* can be explained by the pathological orientation of many biomedical-oriented health professionals, and their failure to appreciate factors which account for health and well being, such as how all individuals cocreate meaning with their values and choices (Parse, 1998).

Cuskelly, Chant, and Hayes (1998) found no significant differences between siblings of children with DS and a comparison group of siblings from the general population in relation to parent-reported behavioral problems. In addition, siblings of children with special circumstances have been found to demonstrate greater sensitivity and nurturing behaviors (Seligman & Darling, 1997), closer family relationships, more independence, and greater satisfaction in seeing improvement in their ill sibling than children without siblings with special circumstances (Derouin & Jessee, 1996).

The contributions of children with special circumstances to the family and community have also been described. Teachers have reported that siblings of children with special circumstances were more cooperative and had greater self-control than other children (Mandleco, Olsen, Robinson, Marshall, & McNeilly-Choque, 1998). Dunn (2000) suggested that sibling relationships offer children opportunities to learn about and better understand people and themselves. Vanier (1997) referred to the family as places where *lessons of the heart* can be learned, and children with special circumstances as particularly attentive to this dimension of human and family life. For Vanier, the heart is the affective core of the human being and its most fundamental reality (Downey, 1986). Being a sibling of a child with special circumstances can contribute to the sibling's identity and career direction (Seligman & Darling, 1997).

In summary, being a sibling is a significant experience for children and the literature is mixed regarding the experience of being a sibling of a child with special circumstances. Clearly unrealistic parenting roles assigned to siblings can contribute to sibling conflict and resentment. Further information is needed to explore the meaning of being a sibling, especially from the child's perspective. Therefore, through this study the authors sought to better understand the experience of being a brother or sister from the child's own perspective.

Conceptual Framework

The human becoming theory (Parse, 1998) views individuals and families as in mutual process with the universe. It represents a synthesis of selected existential phenomenological tenets and Rogers' science of unitary human beings (Parse, 1981). Three major themes emerging from Parse's assumptions are meaning, rhythmicity, and cotranscendence. In Parse's (1998) terms, meaning is cocreating reality through the languaging of valuing

Table 1 Demographics of Participants

Participant	Age	Gender	Number of Siblings	Birth Order	Special Circumstance
Mary	5	Girl	2	Oldest	Cleft Lip and Palate
Joe	6	Boy	1	Oldest	Cleft Lip and Palate
Marvin	8	Boy	7	3rd youngest	Cleft Lip and Palate
Marie	9	Girl	2	Middle	Cleft Lip and Palate
Jane	10	Girl	7	4th youngest	Cleft Lip and Palate
Peter	12	Boy	2	Oldest	Cleft Lip and Palate
Bob	13	Boy	2	Middle	Cleft Lip and Palate
Rebecca	14	Girl	7	Oldest	Cleft Lip and Palate
Mark	15	Boy	2	Oldest	Cleft Lip and Palate
Maura	9	Girl	1	Oldest	Down Syndrome
Sue	10	Girl	1	Oldest	Down Syndrome
Barbara	11	Girl	1	Oldest	Down Syndrome

and imaging. In other words, individuals, including young children, choose personal meaning in situations based upon their values. Rhythmicity is explained by Parse (1998) as patterns of relating which are paradoxical in nature, such that in the process of revealing something, one is also concealing, and likewise with enabling-limiting and connecting-separating. This view shows appreciation for the many levels and complexities that unfold in relationships of all kinds. It acknowledges that possibilities and limitations arise from choice-making. Cotranscending with the possibilities describes how one continually transforms one's view of the world based on life experiences (Parse, 1981). The theory holds that children, like adults, define what health and well-being is for them. Parse's theory guided the researchers in focusing on how siblings construct language to make sense of their experiences, how siblings live their patterns of relating, and how they participate in constructing their view of the future. The research question is, *What does it mean to be a sibling?*

Method

This descriptive exploratory study used the philosophical assumptions and the framework of the human becoming theory (Parse, 1998) to guide the researchers in viewing the participants, being with the participants, and designing objectives and questions to ask the participants. The objectives were: (a) to describe the meaning of being a sibling, (b) to describe changing relationship of living with a sibling, and (c) to describe views of the future in light of having a sibling.

Participants

Twelve biological siblings (ages 5–15), from eight families with a child with cleft lip and palate or DS participated in this descriptive exploratory study. Eight were the oldest children in their family, four were middle children, and all were older than their sibling with special circumstances (see Table l). Most participants were recruited after their parents responded to notices in newsletters of support groups in the northeast or midwestern

United States; three were referred by others. All of the participants were Caucasian, but they represented several different cultures and religions. The human subjects institutional review board of a university approved the study; steps to safeguard minor-age participants' rights for self-determination and confidentiality were taken. The use of informed consent/assent and all other guidelines for protection of human subjects were followed, including the right to withdraw at any time. Each participant was given a pseudonym.

Procedure

Children were asked to describe (a) what it means to be a brother or sister, (b) how their relationships with others were different because they had a brother or sister, and (c) how their view of the future or what they wanted to be when they grew-up, had been altered by being a brother or sister. The special circumstances of their siblings were not mentioned in the questions used by the researchers, but it was in the consent. Specific questions included, What is it like for you to be a brother or sister? What is most important for you about being a brother or sister? How has being a brother or sister changed the way you relate to the people who are most important to you? How has it changed your relationships with others? Do you feel you relate differently to people because of your experiences as a brother or sister? What do you want to be when you are older, and has that changed because you are a brother or sister? Have your dreams changed? How has your view of life been changed by your experience of being a brother or sister? Tape-recorded interviews, guided by the open-ended questions, were conducted in a private area of the participants' homes. After being interviewed, participants were invited to draw or use a laptop with art software (Adobe Illustrator 7.0 or Microsoft Paint) and talk about their artwork. Children's art has been used with human becoming theory by the primary researcher in two previous studies (Baumann, 1999a, 1999b). From this perspective, the interpretation of the art is left to the participant. The children

Table 2 The Findings Reflecting the Human Becoming Theory

Objectives of the Study	Theoretical Concepts	Participants' Language	Researchers' Language
To describe the meaning of being a sibling.	Structuring meaning multi dimensionally	Being a brother or sister was a big responsibility, especially when they have something like Down's, "because yon have to watch out for them," "you have to be there for them, defend them, protect them, or stand up for them."	An arduous charge to champion close others
To describe the changing relationship of living with a sibling.	Cocreating rhythmical patterns of relating	Having a sister or brother had "not changed their relationships with others much," they had less time to play with their friends, "learned how to treat others, to share, take care of people, and be nice to people who are different."	Restricting-enhancing commitments
To describe the views of the future in light of having a sibling.	Cotranscending with the possibilities	"Plans for the future had not changed," "interested in what their siblings like to do," "wanted to do things differently than their siblings had done," "careers where they would protect or care for others."	New endeavors gives rise to new possibilities

were asked to talk about their drawings. The interviews and art sessions with each participant lasted 30-60 minutes.

Data Analysis

In a process Parse (2001) referred to as analyzing-synthesizing, major themes were identified according to the objectives of study. In this study, all interviews were transcribed and major themes of what being a brother or sister was like for the participants were determined by reading and contemplating participants' comments and artwork (Parse, 2001, 1987). These data contained answers to the specific questions asked by the researchers. Themes arose directly from the language of the participants, and were then synthesized to construct a descriptive statement in the language of the researcher, reflecting Parse's theory (Parse, 1998, 2001). All of the analysis-synthesis in this study was conducted by the primary researcher (SB). An earlier work by two of the authors on fathering used a similar methodology (Baumann & Braddick, 1999).

Findings

The finding of this study is the descriptive statement: *being a sibling is an arduous charge to champion close others amid restricting-enhancing commitments while new endeavors give rise to new possibilities*. The process of going from objectives to findings is outlined in Table 2. In Table 2, column 1 contains the objectives of the study and column 2 contains the themes of the human becoming theory. Column 3 presents participants' comments and column 4 presents the researchers' synthesis of being a sibling in the researcher's language.

Discussion

The Meaning of Being a Brother or Sister

Although the participants' comments clearly identified who is older, or *bigger* using their words, and the gender of each sibling, they were less likely to refer to the special circumstances of their brother or sister. One participant's comment regarding a sibling's special circumstances demonstrates this relative lack of attention to the special circumstance: In Barbara's (age 11) words, "I kind of forget that he has DS and I just see him as a boy." Some authors see this inattention to details as related to siblings' lack of information and awareness about the medical and other special circumstances of their sibling (McHale & Pawletko, 1992).

The participants' comments could also be seen as part of their way of "constructing reality through assigning significance to events" (Parse, 1998, p. 35). For example, when asked about being a sister, Mary (age 5) talked about her cousin, who was older than her, and about her brother who died without coming home from the hospital (at age 7 days), and not much about her two sisters with whom she lived. She also named one of her favorite stuffed animals after her brother who had died, which can also be seen as her defining of the membership of her family and how she is keeping her deceased brother present in her life.

For most of the participants in this study, being a sister or brother is a "big responsibility," which at times is fun. Participants said they have to "be there for their sibling, to stand up for them and protect them." Jane (age 10) said, "It's tough, you have to watch out for the others." Peter (age 12) said,

If someone is pushing my brother I have to be there, or if my sister gets into trouble I have to be there, I have to defend them. That's what being a brother or sister is all about. If I'm a big brother I have to defend littler kids than me, like the kid next door, I'll do that. One time I saw these kids go over to this kid and say, "Do you want to play Power Ranger?" The kid was little, he picked him up and threw him on the ground, so I went over there and stared at him and told him not to, he just stared right back at me. You kind of pester these kids or they don't listen.

Rebecca (age 14) said, "Well, it's hard sometimes because there are things to be taken care of, and you have to help them, but its still fun, because they help you and they can be fun. So it's fun, but it's hard." Rebecca's comments reveal that being a sibling is both a duty and a source of enjoyment or amusement.

The participants in this study described the role of older sibling as being *fill-ins*. One participant said that when her mother was not around she had to tell her siblings what to do and what not to do. Mark (age 15) said, "for me as the oldest, I always felt that I had to look out for Dan, like when my mother has to go out." Bob (age 13), the middle brother in that same family, said, "I have to fill in for Mark, when he is not around, in looking out for Dan." Pollack (2002) referred to the caregiving role of older siblings as *auxiliary parents*. She said that in the United States since the 1970s older children spend less time in this role, than in earlier generations. She stated that this has reduced the resentment and conflict that can arise when older children's own needs and education were to some degree shortchanged because of their caregiving responsibilities.

Several participants discussed the moods and behaviors of their siblings, which they described as *difficult*. Sue (age 10) said, "Well, it gets kind of annoying sometimes, but if you don't have a really restless sister, it can be kind of fun. My sister, as she is younger than me, she's kind of restless and sometimes it bothers me, she bugs me so much. Sometimes I wish she was not even there." Maura (age 9) said, "Well, I think it is sort of a responsibility, because you have to look after your brother. I think it is a little harder with a kid having DS, but its not that much harder. It's a big responsibility." She described him as "rough" and having a "tough build," and that used to bother her until she realized that this is "the way he is." Peter (age 12) created a computer image of an oval face and described it as his brother when he gets mad—he gave him concentric red circles in his eyes. He also drew himself offering his brother who fell while skating on the sidewalk a band aid from a first aid kit.

When asked what was the most important thing about being a brother or sister, several participants again mentioned having to be responsible. Others mentioned caring, listening, and "cheering each other up." Maura (age 9) said, "I think it's really important for me to listen to him and understand what he's saying, not to ignore him, to understand that he has feelings too." While none of the participants focused on the learning differences of their siblings, this comment by a very articulate sibling of a child with DS, hints at the effort she has to make to understand what her brother is saying and her choice to see it as important. Rebecca (age 14) said, "to be able to help them and care about them." Sue (age 10) said what was most important for her was when her sister was there for her, "Like when my grandpa died…she pats you on your back. It's like when you cry, she cries." Peter (age 12) said,

Being there for them when they are sad or depressed, or mad about something, I go there and talk to them, I sought out the problems that they are having, like when Jim got mad at something, I got mad at him, I gave him a piece of gum, and he was happy again, he came downstairs and we went outside. I help Marie (age 9) sometimes, when Mom yells at her, I comfort her.

The synthesis of the participants' comments related to the first objective, which was to describe the meaning of being a brother or sister, in the language of the researcher is: *an arduous charge to champion close others*. Being a sister or brother is a mix of feelings, including feeling dutiful, antagonism, and enjoyment, from which a mutually nurturing presence can arise. This synthesis also exemplifies the complexity of being a sibling. Longitudinal studies of sibling relationships have suggested that close relationships between siblings can become closer as siblings provide assistance and support for each other (Dunn, 2000). The participants' comments also suggest that courage and commitment is required when being a brother or sister, particularly when *being there* for a younger sibling with special circumstances. This finding is related in this study to the first principle of human becoming theory (Parse, 1998), structuring meaning multidimensionally is cocreating reality through the languaging of valuing and imaging (p. 35). Being a sibling is a paradoxical rhythm of confirming-not confirming that one is neither alone nor without obligations.

The Way Relationships Unfold

Several participants said they did not think having a brother or sister changed their relationships with others very much. However, others said their mothers spent more time with younger siblings than they did with them. Mary (age 5) said her youngest sister (who has a cleft lip and palate) slept in her mother's bed, "because she could suffocate." She also said, "My daddy used to be home more. He used to buy me rainbow cookies, but when my sister was born he had to work all the time." Some participants said being a brother or sister decreased the time they had to be with and play with their friends.

Several participants described how being a brother or sister had altered their relationships with other people. As mentioned above, some participants reported that there had been times when having to take care of their sibling reduced the time they could spend with their friends. A few reported incidents when their sibling's *difficult* behaviors were directed at their friends, or were embarrassing. What they said also suggested that having a sibling, especially one with special circumstances, can deepen relationships with others. Peter (age 12) said,

Sometimes my friends tease my brother, so I say, "Don't do that;" but I am not too harsh on them. My friends have been there for Marie and my brother too, they like them and care for them too. When I baby sit my brother, and Linda comes over and she helps me, or Tracy, they come over and help me with my brother and Marie. They help out, almost like they are part of the family.

In this way several participants came to value and appreciate their friends who had shown understanding and helpfulness to their siblings. Several said that they had looked out for the well-being of other young children as well, recalling how their own brother or sister had been treated by other people. Having a sibling at times interfered with their plans. Having a sibling also served to encourage children to try things, they might not have done alone, such as a pair of brothers in this study who chose to be in their school plays.

The way relationships unfold when being a sibling was stated in the language of the researcher as the paradox: *restricting-enhancing commitments*. At times participants had to forego their own plans because they had a sibling, but most times this was not without satisfaction and learning. While the conflict and tensions evident in some of the participants' comments could be related to their perception of having less time to be with their parents or friends, it can also reflect their annoyance that siblings wanted what they had. Marie's (age 9) drawing of being a sibling was very similar to her brother's (Peter, age 12) which she had seen, but she was happy to point out the differences. The annoyance of having younger siblings imitate them was evident in Sue's (age 10) comment that her sister "loves every single thing that I have." Girard (1996) saw rivalry for the same object as a basis of most social conflict, and he said such conflicts arise because a person wants to be like their model. He called this phenomenon *mimetic desire* and he saw this in most cultures and religions. Girard (1996) did not see this as a bad thing, because imitating ultimately involved "opening oneself out" (p. 64).

One participant (Sue, age 10) mentioned how unfair some children are to children with DS. She described children with DS as "just different." Her use of the word *just* suggested that to her they were essentially like other children, despite their obvious differences. She was also referring to the importance of including all children, and this reveals her growing awareness of the importance of being sensitive to the feelings of others. Some participants also found ways to cheer up their siblings when they were feeling down, and learned how to accept their anger without needing to retaliate. The second principle of human becoming theory (Parse, 1998) is: Cocreating rhythmical patterns of relating is living the paradoxical unity of revealing-concealing and enabling-limiting while connecting-separating (p. 42). For example, Peter's computer graphic of one of his brother's anger, could be seen as his revealing, while concealing, his own differences and difficult feelings. The second part of the finding of this study, restricting-enhancing, can be described as reflecting the enabling-limiting of connecting-separating of being a sibling. Being a sibling involves decisions which alter one's view of the past, and living out of one's present and future possibilities.

How One's View of Life Has Changed When Being a Sibling?

Several participants said being a brother or sister had not changed their view of their future or the world, but some children said they had learned from their sibling's mistakes. Others identified their own interests by trying and liking things their siblings liked. For example Bob (age 13) got involved in school plays like this older brother Mark (age 15), and both wanted to continue to be in plays in high school and maybe go into acting.

Several participants were able to connect their thoughts about their future with their current family situation. Peter (age 12) said he wanted to be a police officer so that he could "be responsible to take care of other people." Another said she wanted to be a pediatrician to take care of children. One participant planned to go into business with her siblings. Dunn (1999) observed that in sibling interactions, play, and conversations, there is evidence that children read each other's feelings and intentions and explore their abilities and differences. Most participants' comments suggested that they accepted their situation as siblings of children with special circumstances, and accept these children for who they were. This appeared to be a transformative process for them.

The concept of psychosocial adjustment as applied to the situation of siblings of children with special circumstances (Murray, 2000), fails to appreciate the transformative possibilities in the experience. In the present study, the researchers, led by the assumptions of human becoming theory, synthesized these comments as the theme: *new endeavors give rise to new possibilities*. Children participate in cocreating their world by their choices in given circumstances. Often children are particularly imaginative in their envisioning of new possibilities.

The possibilities that arise for young children reflect their exposure to various experiences and to close others, including parents, siblings, and teachers. The personal meanings and imaginations of children also reflect this cocreating process. For example, they and their siblings are from time to time transformed into various characters from their favorite stories. The special circumstances of siblings in this study did not hamper these participants' abilities to make choices, to play, or to use their imagination; however, it did give them some different options to consider. The third principle of the human becoming theory is cotranscending with the possibles is powering unique ways of originating in the process of transforming (Parse, 1998, p. 46). The tasks and challenges of being a sibling faced by the participants of this study were different from most of their friends and it gave rise to personal uniqueness, if not distinction.

Conclusions and Implications

Like all qualitative research, the findings of this study are not meant to be generalized to other groups or suggest causal relationships. This study is also limited because it did not include children of color. It also did not include enough varied participants to explore the differences between the experiences of siblings of children with CL&P and DS and those without siblings with special circumstances. The reader is also encouraged to keep in mind that most of the participants were the oldest child in these families.

For the most part, the participants of this descriptive exploratory study talked about being a brother or sister in general, but some of their comments related to having siblings with special circumstances. The participants' comments suggest that the *special circumstances* of their siblings were generally accepted and relatively unimportant to them. Only one participant said there were times she wished her sibling "wasn't even there." All participants found both challenges and opportunities in having a sibling, for example, they generally understood that younger children need more attention from their mothers, and they realized that some children require special arrangements. The participants generally took their responsibilities very seriously, and for the most part, felt it gave them a sense of purpose and direction. Many admitted their experiences contributed to how they were with other people. There were three sets of participants from the same family in this study. These sibling pairs seemed to share much in common and be cohesive, perhaps in part because of their relationship and duties with their sibling with special circumstances.

The findings related to Parse's (1998) theory suggest being a sister or brother is *an arduous charge to champion close others amid restricting- enhancing commitments while new endeavors gives rise to new possibilities.* Being a sibling is a complex, paradoxical and ever-changing experience. It includes making choices and being responsible. This investigation also uncovered a definition of being a sibling that reflects shifting rhythms and changing perspectives of what is possible.

Parents and nurses should provide opportunities for children to talk about their feelings and thoughts regarding being a sibling in general and in particular about being a sibling of a child with special circumstances. The use of art can be a particularly helpful means of communicating with such children. It may also be helpful if nurses can get to know children's favorite stories and toys, to explore new meaning in difficult situations, such as discovering that a child's favorite stuffed animal was named after a family member who had died. The tendency of many children, especially older children of siblings with special circumstances, to feel overly responsible can interfere with their ability to enjoy the pleasure of being a child (Pollack, 2002). Childhood is the secret place where imagination, uniqueness, and hope are most alive. This place is a vital resource not only for them but also for their families and close others. Some families with unexpected birth events and children with special circumstances have a difficult time finding new meaning. For them there is incongruence between what they had previously hoped and dreamed for and their present lives. This is a particularly good opportunity for nurses who practice nursing in a way which is "illuminating meaning, synchronizing rhythms and mobilizing transcendence" (Parse, 1998, pp. 69-70).

This study also suggests that nurses can help families find ways to understand the difficult behaviors of children, especially those with special circumstances. These behaviors can be difficult for siblings to understand and live with. While providing siblings with more information may be needed at times,

each child's view of his or her family and sibling's circumstances should be respected. Longitudinal studies of being a sibling, and a sibling of children with special circumstances would provide valuable understanding of this important and common life experience.

References

Albrecht, G. L., & Devlieger, P. J. (1999). The disability paradox: High quality of life against all odds. *Social Science & Medicine, 48,* 977-988.

The American heritage talking dictionary of the English language (3rd ed.). (1994). New York: Houghton Mifflin.

Andersson, E. (1997). Relations in families with a mentally retarded child from the perspective of the siblings. *Scandinavian Journal of Caring Sciences, 11,* 131-138.

Baumann, S. (1999a). Art as a path of inquiry. *Nursing Science Quarterly, 12,* 106-110.

Baumann, S. (1999b). The lived experience of hope: Children in families struggling to make a home. In R. R. Parse, *Hope: An international human becoming perspective* (pp. 191-210). Boston: Jones & Bartlett.

Baumann, S., & Braddick, M. (1999). Out of their element: Fathers of children who are not the same. *Journal of Pediatric Nursing, 14,* 369-377.

Benson, B. A., Gross, A. M., & Kellum, G. (1999). The siblings of children with craniofacial anomalies. *Children's Health Care, 28,* 51-68.

Brody, G. H., & Stoneman, Z. (1996). A risk-amelioration model for sibling relationships: Conceptual underpinning and preliminary findings. In G. H. Brody (Ed.), *Sibling relationships: Their cause and consequences* (pp. 231-247). Norwood, NJ: Ablex.

Cuskelly, M., Chant, D., & Hayes, A. (1998). Behaviour problems in the siblings of children with Down Syndrome: Associations with family responsibilities and parental stress. *International Journal of Disability, Development & Education, 45,* 295-311.

Derouin, D., & Jessee, P. O. (1996). Impact of a chronic illness in childhood: Siblings' perceptions. *Issues in Comprehensive Pediatric Nursing, 19,* 135-147.

Downey, M. (1986). *A blessed weakness: The spirit of Jean Vanier and l'Arche.* New York: Harper & Row.

Dunn, J. (1999). Making sense of the social world: Mindreading, emotion and relationships. In P. D. Zelazo, J. W. Astington, & D. R. Olson (Eds.), *Developing theories of intention: Social understanding and self control* (pp. 229-242). Mahwah, NJ: Lawrence Erlbaum.

Dunn, J. (2000). State of the art: Siblings. *The Psychologist, 13,* 244-248.

Fisman, S., Wolf, L., Ellison, D., & Freeman, T. (2000). A longitudinal study of siblings of children with chronic disabilities. *Canadian Journal of Psychiatry, 45,* 369-375.

Fisman, S., Wolf, L., Ellison, D., Gillis, B., Freeman, T., & Szatmari, P. (1996). Risk and protective factors affecting the adjustment of siblings of children with chronic disabilities. *Journal of the American Academy of Child & Adolescent Psychiatry, 35,* 1532-1541.

Girard, R. (1996). *The Girard reader* (J. G. Williams, Ed.). New York: Crossroad.

Goffman, E. (1963). *Stigma: Notes on the management of spoiled identity.* Englewood Cliffs, NJ: Prentice-Hall.

Kowal, A., & Kramer, L. (1997). Children's understanding of parental differential treatment. *Child Development, 68,* 113-126.

Mandleco, B., Olsen, S., Robinson, C., Marshall, E., & McNeilly-Choque, M. (1998). Social skills and peer relationships of siblings of children with disabilities: Parental and family linkages. In P. Slee & K. Rigby (Eds.), *Children's peer relations: Current issues and future directions* (pp. 106-120). London: Routledge.

McHale, S. M., & Pawletko, T. (1992). Different treatment of siblings in two family contexts: Implications for children's adjustment and relationship evaluations. *Child Development, 63*, 68-81.

Mendelson, M. J., de Villa, E. P., Fitch, T. A., & Goodman, F. G. (1997). Adult expectations for children's sibling roles. *International Journal of Behavioral Development, 20*, 549-572.

Meyer, D. J., Vadasy, P., & Vance, R. S. (1996). *Living with a brother or sister with special needs: A book for sibs* (Rev. ed.). Seattle, WA: University of Washington Press.

Morrison, L. (1997). Stress and siblings. *Pediatric Nursing, 9*, 26-27.

Murray, J. S. (1998). The lived experience of childhood cancer: One sibling's perspective. *Issues in Comprehensive Pediatric Nursing, 21*, 217-227.

Murray, J. S. (1999). Siblings of children with cancer: A review of the literature. *Journal of Pediatric Oncology Nursing, 16*. 225-234.

Murray, J. S. (2000). Attachment theory and adjustment difficulties in siblings of children with cancer. *Issues in Mental Health Nursing, 2*, 149-169.

Newman, J. (1996). The more the merrier? Effects of family size and sibling spacing on sibling relationships. *Child Care, Health and Development, 22*, 285-302.

Nichols, M. P., & Schwartz, R. C. (1998). *Family therapy: Concepts and methods* (4th ed.). Boston: Allyn & Bacon.

Parse, R. R. (1981). *Man-living-health: A theory of nursing*. New York: Wiley.

Parse, R. R. (1987) Parse's man-living health theory of nursing. In R. R. Parse, *Nursing science: Major paradigms, theories, and critiques* (pp. 181-204). Philadelphia: Saunders.

Parse, R. R. (1998). *The human becoming school of thought: A perspective for nurses and other health professionals*. Thousand Oaks, CA: Sage.

Parse, R. R. (2001). *Qualitative inquiry: The path of sciencing*. Sudbury, MA: Jones and Bartlett.

Pollack, E. G. (2002). The children we have lost: When siblings were caregivers, 1900-1970. *Journal of Social History, 36*, 31-61.

Seligman, M., & Darling, R. B. (1997). *Ordinary families, special children: A systems approach to childhood disability* (2nd ed.). New York: Guilford Press.

Senel, H. G., & Akkok, F. (1995). Stress levels and attitudes of normal siblings of children with disabilities. *International Journal for the Advancement of Counseling, 18*, 61-68.

Silver, E. J., & Frohlinger-Graham, M. J. (2000). Brief report: Psychological symptoms in healthy female siblings of adolescents with and without chronic conditions. *Journal of Pediatric Psychology, 25*, 279-284.

Skidmore, K. L. (1996). Childhood cancer, families and siblings. (Doctoral dissertation, Loyola University, 1996), *Dissertation Abstracts International, 56*(12B), 7056.

Stawski, M., Auerbach, J. G., Barasch, M., Lerner, Y., & Zimin, R. (1997). Behavioral problems of children with chronic physical illness and their siblings. *European Child and Adolescent Psychiatry, 6*, 20-25.

Terzo, H. (1999). Evidence-based practice: The effects of childhood cancer on siblings. *Pediatric Nursing, 25*, 309-311.

Vanier, J. (1997). *Our journey home: Rediscovering a common humanity beyond our differences* (M. Parham, Trans.). Maryknoll, NY: Novalis.

Williams, P. D. (1997). Siblings and pediatric chronic illness: A review of the literature. *International Journal of Nursing Studies, 34*, 312-323.

Aunties and Uncles

JOHN TYLER CONNOLEY

When Mom was a kid, her nuclear family consisted of her mom and dad, one sister, two brothers, one cousin and his wife, and Grandpa and Grandma. They all lived together in an Indiana farmhouse, where 40 relatives (the extended family) would arrive each Sunday afternoon for chicken and dumplings. Family holidays, like Thanksgiving and Christmas, included even more people, many of whom were not strictly relatives but were "church family." Like a quilt, Mom's childhood family was constructed from many pieces sewn together with love.

When Mom grew up and left home, she became a missionary and moved to Africa with her husband and two kids, but she took her family values with her. Family in our house meant all the people we cared about. Of course, we had relatives in the United States, but we also had our missionary family.

My sister and I called all the missionaries Auntie and Uncle, which I suppose made their children our "cousins." When I think of my earliest memories, I think of eating Auntie Eleanor's cheesecake, being scared by Auntie Rosemary's funny faces, and visiting Uncle Ora and Auntie Linda in South Africa.

The first time we came back to the United States, the terms grandma and grandpa confused my sister and me: We kept calling them Auntie Grandma and Uncle Grandpa because that's how one referred to relatives.

These aunties and uncles who made up my familial world are the people I learned to depend on. They're the ones who taught me what it meant to be a grown-up. Their children were the kids I wrestled with and fought with and played Star Wars with. Later they would become the people I'd pick up the phone and call for help if I needed it. It never occurred to me that family should be related by blood or marriage, or that familial responsibility might extend only to the people to whom you are legally bound.

I've grown up and moved away, but I've taken my mom's inclusive definition of family with me. Like my grandparents in their Hoosier farmhouse and my parents on their mission station, my partner, Rob, and I have a door that's always open. We intentionally moved to a small town here in New Mexico so we could afford to buy a big house with lots of space for guests and where we would have a close community of people we cared about. We don't have kids yet, but we know when we do they'll be raised in an extended family that includes lots of relatives and lots of friends.

We believe children should be raised by a community—of aunties and uncles, of friends and relatives, of all the people we love. And we trust that if our child's immediate household doesn't include a mother and a father, well, that's OK, because the quilt is bigger than our little corner. And there will always be adult role models around.

Rob and I have embraced a traditional meaning of family that is expansive enough to include the whole world. And this family tradition of inclusiveness has made us wary of "traditional family" rhetoric. Why would anyone want to limit the definition of family to a mother, father, and two kids? It's like substituting a quilted place mat for a warm bedspread.

The way we understand it, family is just another word for the people we love, and the nuclear family is everyone we can fit under our roof. If one of our friends loses his job and needs a place to stay, he might become part of the nucleus. If Rob's mom decides to move to New Mexico, she might join the nucleus too. It doesn't matter how or if we're legally related; what matters is that family takes care of each other.

Instead of limiting the legal definition of family, we would like to expand it. Let the patchwork connections we make with one another be reflected in the way the government treats us. Let people choose their families, and then write the laws to support those choices. To do anything else seems contrary to my family's values.

JOHN TYLER CONNOLEY cowrote *The Children Are Free: Reexamining the Biblical Evidence on Same-Sex Relationships*. He lives in Silver City, N.M.

Roles of American Indian Grandparents in Times of Cultural Crisis

Abstract: This study examined the roles of contemporary American Indian grandparents in the lives of their grandchildren. Structured interviews were conducted with 20 American Indian grandparents. Analysis of interviews followed a sequence of strategies traditionally identified with the process of data reduction and analysis using qualitative methodologies. Participants reported enculturative responsibilities for their grandchildren in regard to traditional tribal values and knowledges such as tribal spirituality and protocol, cooperative interaction, tribal language and appreciation of nature. Methods of enculturation took the form of stories, modeling, direct teaching and playful interaction.

Key Words: American Indian, American Indian Grandparents, Cultural Crisis

ROCKEY ROBBINS, PHD, AVRAHAM SCHERMAN, EDD,
HEIDI HOLMAN, MS, AND JASON WILSON, MS

Given the dearth of articles about American Indian grandparents in psychological journals, it is necessary to briefly review relevant articles in order to provide an enriched context for this study. In many cultures, grandparents are seen as "fun relatives," offering treats and activities that parents were unable or unwilling to provide, such as social games, companionship, community events and domestic help (Kennedy, 1992). Grandparents are also seen as the designated repository of family histories, culture and memories (Williams, 1995). In some cultures, grandparents are viewed as community leaders, mediators and to some extent, lawgivers (Bahr, 1994). Grandparents are also seen as transmitters of family values, such as morality, altruism, social identity, a sense of accomplishment, competency and affiliation (Timberlake & Chipungu, 1992).

Grandparents are frequently mentioned as providers of emotional and tangible support for their grandchildren (Scherman, Goodrich, Kelly Russell, & Javidi, 1988; Scherman, Beesley, & Turner, 2003). However, this varies, due in part to the grandparents' health, geographical proximity and financial ability. Grandparents often provide support for their children who have young children of their own. The support can be monetary, advice giving, baby sitting or emotional support. This role changes depending on the perceived needs of the family, and the grandparents situation. The grandparents may become the ones needing care and support due to health problems (Creasey & Kahiler, 1994, Sander & Trygstad, 1993). The frequency and quality of contact between grandparents and grandchildren also affect the roles adopted by the grandparents, as well as the level of perceived support (Creasey & Kahiler, 1994).

Few articles have been written specifically about American Indian grand parenting. Those have focused primarily on grand-

mothers, changing status, and social culture (Barr, 1994; Nahemow, 1987; Schweitzer, 1987; Williams, 1995) and their place in the American Indian extended family (Coleman, Unau, & Manyfingers, 2001). They have also been described as storytellers (Barnett, 1955) and mentors (Elmendorf & Kroeber, 1960). Weibel-Orlando (1990) conducted interviews with 28 American Indian grandparents to determine grand-parenting styles. She found five basic styles: ceremonial, which entails grandparents acting as models of appropriate ceremonial behavior; fictive, which entails older persons nurturing children as an alternative to the lack or absence of biological grandchildren; custodial, which entails grandparents taking on full child care responsibilities for their grandchildren; distanced, which entails almost complete lack of contact with grandchildren; and cultural conservator, which entails grandparents and ways of life.

Williams (1995) differentiated the roles American Indian grandfathers and grandmothers played. Grandfathers are more likely than grandmothers to view grand-parenting as an opportunity to share information with grandchildren and to take pride in grandchildren's accomplishments. Noor Al-Deen (1997) lists American Indian women's traditional roles as life-givers, healers, caregivers, mothers, guardians, nurturers, family counselors, providers, and sources of wisdom and knowledge to their nations, including council decisions and participation in battle. She noted that female American Indian elders experience conflict that may result from divergent tribal and dominant culture's pressures and expectations regarding their grand-parenting roles. Noor Al-Deen proposes three factors which contribute to these conflicts: 1) cultural deprivation caused by prejudice from Euro-American mainstream populations; 2) restricted traditionalism from governmental and societal pressures coupled with the loss of tribal lands; and 3) federal bureaucratic health care from Indian Health Services.

According to Coleman, Unau, and Manyfingers (2001), the extended family plays a central role in raising Indian children. Grandparents and community elders are considered potent sources of influence for children, families, and communities as a whole. It is common for grandparents to willingly assume childcare responsibilities for their grandchildren and for parents to seek advice from community elders. This study attempts to explore and explicate the specific contents of the roles of American Indian grandparent's roles in the enculturation process of passing down values, stories and songs, as well as the cultural costumes, and their function as a nurturer and protector.

Methodology

Three American Indian and one Euro-American interviewers met with 20 American Indian grandparents. Interviews were conducted in American Indian mental health centers and in the homes of participants. A structured interview schedule was used to conduct the interviews (a copy of the structured interview is available from the first author). Information was collected on contents of grandparents roles play in lives of their grandchildren., the relationships between grandparents.[sic] Each interview was summarized and transmitted electronically to the person analyzing the data.

Eighteen of the twenty participants in this study were from Oklahoma. The tribes represented were: Cherokee, Creek, Chickasaw, Commanche, Lakota, Pawnee, Pottawatomi, Seminole, and Shawnee. Participants included seven grandfathers and thirteen grandmothers, ranging in age from 42 to 79, averaging 59. Eight participants reported that they spoke their tribal language fluently and two participants reported they could understand their tribal language, but could not speak it fluently. Two other participants reported being able to speak their tribal language as young children but could not speak it now. Ages of participants ranged from 42 to 79, averaging 59. The grandchildren participants described ranged in age from 2 to 18 years and averaged 11. Seven participants reported that the grandchild they described lived with them. Six participants reported that the grandchild they described lived over 30 minutes away from them. Six grandparents reported that they and their families participated in the Relocation Program for American Indians during the 1960's. Three grandparents had attended Indian Boarding Schools and none of the grandchildren described attended Indian Boarding Schools.

Participants were asked to describe the roles they played in the lives of one of their grandchildren. The questions were open-ended, and throughout the interview each grandparent was provided as much time and autonomy to answer the questions as she needed. The interviewer was allowed to rephrase or probe as a way to elicit clarification, additional information, detail, or elaboration (Bodgan & Biklen, 1992; Survey Research Center, 1982). When supplemental questioning occurred, nondirective probing techniques (Survey Research Center, 1982), whereby the interviewer's response is only a simple acknowl-

edgement using a neutral follow-up question or comment (such as "could you tell me more," or "what do you mean by that"), were used to insure that the interviewer did not influence the grandparents' responses.

Analysis of the interviews followed a sequence of strategies traditionally identified with the process of data reduction and analysis using qualitative methodologies (Bogdan & Biklin, 1992; Creswell, 1998; Huberman & Miles, 1994; Lincoln & Guba, 1985). The analysis began by independently reviewing the transcripts through multiple readings, taking a micro analytic perspective, and using grounded theory methodology to identify concepts and generate potential categories to represent participant responses (Strauss & Corbin, 1994, 1998). Categories and themes that existed across all interviews, as well as those within the context of specific questions, were identified. A series of meetings were then held where identification and discussion of potential concepts, their properties and constructions, and metaphors to realistically represent grandparents' responses were shared. Over the course of these meetings, initial themes and coding conventions were established, resulting in a process often referred to as "open coding" (Strauss & Corbin, 1998). It was also determined that in most cases the level of coding would anchor on phrases or sentences (Strauss & Corbin, 1998), and that frequency counts (Huberman & Miles, 1994) would be collected to aide in the representation of themes and concepts.

Having identified the coding conventions, two raters independently returned to the transcripts and coded the responses to each question. The process of coding and data analysis in qualitative research is one that is fluid and dynamic, and can often result in intuitive modifications regarding the labeling and meaning of themes and categories (Criswell, 1998; Straus & Corbin, 1998). Therefore during this phase of the coding process, the raters continued to document new or alternative constructions of themes and concepts. Huberman and Miles (1994) view data analysis as an interactive process where data reduction, data display, and conclusion drawing interact with one another. These components do not occur in a single linear sequence, rather they revolve around each other, indicating that the process of data analysis can go through a number of iterations. Subsequent to independent analysis, the raters held a second set of meetings, and applied procedures consistent with the principle of multiple investigator corroboration (Lincoln & Guba, 1985) and the value of employing multiple perspectives during analytic interpretations (Strauss & Corbin, 1998). They reviewed and compared their analyses, held additional discussion, and combined their interpretations, finally reaching a consensus regarding how each participant's responses were coded for each question.

Results

In many ways contemporary American Indian grand-parenting roles are similar to grand-parenting roles in general. For instance, participants in this study frequently reported partaking in general custodial and care taking responsibilities such as babysitting, transporting, disciplining, coordinating extended family gatherings and cooking for their grandchildren (Sherman, 2003). They also emphasized their role of cultural conservator through telling traditional and family stories (Sherman, 1988). The styles with which they performed these roles were also often commensurate to the styles described in previous studies. For instance, participants spoke of "spoiling," "giving more space," and offering unconditional love to their grandchildren (Sherman, 2003). Nonetheless, contemporary American Indian grand-parenting roles and styles emerge from unique socio-economic and cultural conditions that dress them in unique costumes.

All of the participants expressed feelings of enculturative responsibilities, in greater and lesser degrees. Only one person was tentative, stating that he would not take an assertive role in this area, but would wait to respond to his granddaughter's own interest to discuss tribal history and beliefs. All other participants reported that they engaged in active efforts to pass on American Indian traditional knowledge. Nineteen of the twenty grandparents interviewed expressed grave fears about the possibility of tribal culture being lost. One grandfather said, "Our ways are dying out with the death of every elder."

The most commonly mentioned strategy of cultural preservation took story form. Sixteen participants mentioned that they told stories to their grandchildren. The stories that were retold during the interviews might be categorized as nature, prudence, historical and ghost stories. In one story a duck rescues a man from drowning and in another a reed offers life saving air to a girl who is hiding from a fight at home. Stories such as these seem to imply that if nature is respected it will provide human beings with survival. Several participants told stories suggesting a prudence theme, recommending that children should think before acting. For instance, one interviewee related a story about Indian boys thoughtlessly playing a game of shooting arrows straight up into the air. One day an arrow came down onto the head of one of the boys, injuring him. Another person told a story of how "White people" came onto their land wanting to set up a trading post, which many feared would disrupt their way of life, and were directed to locate on a hill away from the Indian community. Some told stories of spirits. One warned of not telling ghost stories to grandchildren until they "grew older" and another warned not to tell ghost stories after dark. The stories suggest that many Indian grandparents are intent on their grandchildren knowing that the world consists of more than its material surface and that traditional rules function as forms of protection.

American Indian grandparent participants almost unanimously provided active support in their grandchildren's' participation in both tribal and pan-Indian activities, ceremonies, and ways of interacting. The list of these activities include facilitating grandchildren's participation in pow-wows, gourd dances, sweats, Indian church, dressing out in appropriate traditional regalia, Indian games, naming ceremonies, adoption ceremonies, stomp dances, bread dances, making tribal foods, crafts, and drumming. Several grandparents expressed great concern that their grandchildren know the differences and protocol regarding tribal dress at pow-wows, understanding different perspectives regarding "stomp dancers" and "pow-wow people," and distin-

guishing between stomp dance beliefs and Indian church beliefs. Another grandmother claimed to be so concerned that her son learn to drum and sing his tribal songs that she had taken the lead to teach him rather than leaving it to males in her tribe. Also, the majority of the participants mentioned that it was important to teach at least some words of their tribal language to their grandchildren. Their language teaching ranged from teaching their grandchildren to be fluent to teaching them basic introductions, words for relatives, and songs. Almost all participants spoke of tribal language being an important element or their tribal culture.

Every American Indian grandparent interviewed stressed a concern for passing down values, which she believed to be colored by their ethnicity. Thirteen participants discussed their desire to teach their children a love and respect for nature. For some an ecological mindedness for clean water and respect for plants and animals was expressed, while for some it was an appreciation for nature's beauty. Just under half the participants said that "respect" was a value they wished to pass on. When asked to define this word it was usually defined as "honoring your elders." Other values mentioned at from three to six times were: showing appreciation, courage, unselfishness, hard work, giving, quietness, kindness, pride in being Indian, balance, and regular prayer. Participants said they taught these values by role modeling and through direct verbal communication. Several participants complained that their children were not teaching the above values to their grandchildren.

Acting as a facilitator in "bringing the family together" was another role participants believed that they regularly performed to help grandchildren. This idea was expressed in the following ways: "I feel a responsibility to bring the family together for meals. My grandchild can get to know his family this way." "I bring him to Indian church and show him off." "I look forward to the day I can bring her to my tribal pow-wow. When she gets old enough, her white father won't be able to stop me. My tribal people know she is alive and they will be so happy to meet her." "It is important for me to have her mix with her cousins and aunts. She will need them for support." "It is great to get the nephews and nieces together to fish and play softball." "Our land has been in our family for 150 years. We clean it up and I get everybody together there. My grandchild fishes there with his cousins." "My grand daughter sits right there next to me and her family at the pow-wows. The preceding remarks reflect the grandparents' values of regular interaction and closeness across generations and among extended family members. While one does not detect a law like regularity that governs interactions, there appears to be an expectation of continuous exchanges. Grandparents also appear to view this role as a source of self-worth.

All participants expressed the belief that as grandparents they had unique offerings for their grandchildren. Several mentioned the love, support and interaction that they had with their grandchildren as more egalitarian and less structured, characterizing it as "less directive," "more imaginative" and "more flexible" than parent/child interactions. One grandmother described her role with her granddaughter as being a "playmate." Others spoke again of their responsibilities to transmit "old ways" and "family history" and to gather the extended family together.

One person reflected comments several others made when she described herself as a "safety net" when problems arose with her grandchild's parents. One grandparent said his unique contribution to his grandson's life was starting a drum group for his grandson to participate in.

When asked about what they would prefer to do as a grandparent, comments reflected desires to be useful and attached, yet not overused and inextricably bound to their grandchildren everyday. Several wished for greater proximity in order to interact more frequently with their grandchildren. One grandfather wished his granddaughter lived with him, while three, who had custodial care of their grandchildren, expressed a desire to live separately and to have fewer obligations, including financial responsibility. Two participants suggested that their interactions contrasted with mainstream grandparents because they lacked financial resources. They were proud to offer their grand children "stories," "histories" and "good cooking" rather than "finances." Two said that they "just wanted to be there to soothe" their grandchildren emotionally when they needed it, contrasting this relationship with parents' interactions which one described as "picky or critical." Another's comment reflected many of the comments when she said, "I just want to be useful, you know, to be needed, like to be asked for something. I can give good advice because I have lived a lot."

Discussion

The status of American Indian grandparents has until recently been of an exalted nature. Today there are traces or this past reverence in speeches made about grandparents at pow-wows and other ceremonies, but as indicated in the above fragments of interviews the deferential attitude shown is often a matter of form and devoid of power. Many elders feel the wisdom they believe they possess is too often unappreciated. The grandparents in this study often expressed low levels of antagonism toward their children for not working to preserve tribal culture. Still they reported that they continue to transfer tribal values and knowledge to their grandchildren through telling stories, modeling, direct communicative teaching, and playful interaction.

Almost all of the American Indian grandparents interviewed in this project felt great responsibility for mediating American Indian religion and culture. They felt they were at a crossroads at which they could let the old ways go forever or try to pass some of the ways down to their grandchildren. For some the possibility of preserving heritage was seen as remote. In spite of the cultural bombs dropped to annihilate beliefs and tribal unity by the American government, almost all participants in this study took active roles to pass down at least a few of the old ways. Nonetheless, there appeared to be an anxious awareness among participants that their present predicament was not purely a matter of personal choice but it arose from a historical situation. They were all too aware that economic, political, cultural, psychological and military pressures have quite a strangle-hold on tribal culture.

Such responses indicate that American Indian grandparents want the cultural needs of their grandchildren met despite the fact that they themselves were taught by educators who were probably emphatic assimilationists. American Indian elders have lived through periods when tribal customs and ways were either disregarded or vehemently opposed as uncivilized and anti-Christian (Szasz, 1984). Nonetheless, the grandparents in this study expressed the desire to teach aspects of American Indian culture to their grandchildren. But because of past and present, covert and overt discrimination and assimilation policies they are limited. It is no accident that grandparents in this study frequently mentioned language and love of the land, values often used to define American Indian peoples (Sue & Sue, 2003), as two of the most important gifts they might impart to their grandchildren.

The interviewers in this study could not help but be cognizant of the contradiction of having American Indian grandparents define their roles in terms of a language (English) of imperialist imposition. Possibly the most meaningful information offered regarding the grandparent's relationship to their grandchildren came when they used the Indian names of their grandchildren. One musically breathed, "My grandson's Indian name is Onsehoma … Red Eagle." From such tribal words, phrases, and names one can glean norms, attitudes and values of tribal grandparents in regard to their grandchildren. Some researchers contend that language is the primary factor of cultural identity because it connects persons to their cultures' traditions, customs, unique styles of humor, history, and understandings of ceremonies (Eastman, 1985; Dividoff, 2001). Unfortunately, while many American Indian grandparents wish to pass on their tribal language, many are limited by their own lack of fluency that comes as a consequence of having had it forbidden for generations. Some grandparents expressed despair about having lost their tribal language. Stealing language from a people is the bullet of spiritual subjugation. Many of the participants in this study are attempting to pass down tribal language with all its cultural attachments to their grandchildren.

For American Indians love of the land and nature in general (Highwater, 1982), is one of the most essential values because, unlike many values, it is concrete and bound up with history and contemporary politics. The valuing of land and the protection of natural sites is a passionate concern for many American Indians. In fact, many claim that the Great Spirit has given American Indians a special vocation to model respect and love Mother Earth for other races (Highwater, 1982). But tribal lands were taken away by conquest, unequal treaties, or by genocide. American Indian grandparent participants in this study wished to teach their children about the importance of the unique historical character of American Indians' connections to their land and nature. Tragically, for many of the participants, tribal land has been wrested from their families, which has had devastating consequences. For example, American Indians are now the most poverty stricken of all races in the United States (Sue & Sue, 2003), which undermines cohesiveness among tribal members who find themselves fighting against each other for limited resources. In Oklahoma, where all the land was taken from tribes and redistributed according to checkerboard plans (farms given to Whites to separate American Indian families) in the early twentieth century, American Indians find themselves separated from other tribal members, as well as from their historical and spiritual connections to their land (Sue & Sue, 2003), Nonetheless, though the American government robbed American Indians of their land, they were not successful in stealing their dignity. In heroic fashion, the participants in this research project expressed a profound love of the land and a passionate desire to pass this love of land on to their grandchildren.

Grandparents also asserted that telling stories to their grandchildren was important. Stories act as mechanisms through which grandparents can teach succeeding generations how to live life consistent with tribal values (Robbins, 2002). Both traditional and personal stories were told by participants to add meaning and coherence to their grandchildren's lives and to offer structures with which to frame their experiences. They were told to grandchildren to help clarify their cultural and personal self-concepts and to unravel confusing rules, ceremonial expectations and relationships. Many of the traditional stories had animals as main characters. While sometimes small and weak, they were full of wit and cunning when claiming victory over stronger enemies or saving someone from hostile nature. The stories appeared to reflect past and present real life psychological and political struggles. Dances, songs, and ceremonies taught and promoted by grandparents served similar purposes. But for participants in this study, storytelling roles no longer could be assumed in the same fashion as they were historically. For instance, many grandparents in this study were separated geographically not only from their grandchildren, but also from tribal gatherings where they might have told their grandchildren seasonally appropriate stories. The grandparents in this study told their stories in situations when the opportunity presented itself.

In addition to the values often taught indirectly through stories, there were many taught directly and others were demonstrated through modeling. Spiritual and community values appeared to be the most cherished. Grandparents taught grandchildren to pray and continue customs as well as to show appreciation, to be generous, and unselfishness) as the ultimate good their communities. Grandparents taught values that might provide the foundation for tribal renewal and cooperative communities. It is not easy for American Indians to maintain traditional values in the wake of years of gradual accumulation of Euro-American values, which easily over time become almost self-evident truths governing what is right and wrong, and good and bad. Still, the grandparents in this study expressed a commitment to preserve and renew traditional tribal values.

Lastly, the grandparents in this study repeatedly expressed the complex predicament of being somewhat marginal in their grandchildren's' lives, yet also in better positions to joke and laugh with their grandchildren. Their marginality was typically explained as being the result of living at a distance from grandchildren, lack of mobility, feelings of a decline in influence and loss of culture. Their "special" intimacy was often either directly or indirectly explained as being the result of being freed from the disciplinarian role. Those who had not been forced to become custodial described teasing, kind, close, playful and affectionate relationships with their grandchildren. Some grandparents' descriptions of their interactions contrasted with the severity of the parents' involvement with their children. While custodial grandparents complained of the tension associated with establishing rules and enforcing punishments on their

grandchildren, non-custodial grandparents could indulge their grandchildren, being in positions where they were free from the taboos of parental discipline.

Recommendations, Limitations, and Further Directions

The recommendations of this study are for democratic initiatives and human liberation. They directly address the deepest fears of many of the grandparents' of this study who feel they are at a dramatic crossroads that requires nothing less than fundamental social and political transformation. It is a call for rediscovery and for regenerative reconnections. This begins with the resumption of tribal languages. Tribal governments should employ American Indian grandparents who speak their tribal languages to teach their grandchildren their tribal languages before those languages, with their unique cultural nuances, are irrevocable erased. To lose one's tribal language is to lose, to a large extent, a tribal sensibility and to be alienated from much of one's tribal culture. Language is an enormous carrier of culture, and many American Indian grandparents have this part of culture to share. Secondly, tribes could employ grandparents to teach tribal arts and crafts, tribal religions, and tribal history to their grandchildren. All this must be done soon, taking into account that many elders are taking traditional tribal culture with them and that children must be taught early in life before the values of Euro-American society become implanted and nearly impossible to eradicate. Thirdly, there must be a systematic effort to reclaim tribal lands. Many tribes are already attempting this. Grandparents might lobby for this sort of political directive. Without a doubt the reacquisition of tribal lands would provide renewed dignity and greater cohesiveness among tribal members. Support in these endeavors from culturally sensitive, non-American Indians is welcomed.

Due to the fact that almost all of the participants in this study live in Oklahoma and do not live on reservations, the generalizability of the study is limited. There was a profound commitment Researchers expected a lower level of commitment to the transference of tribal values among this non-reservation sample. One might expect an even greater commitment among American Indians living on reservations. A replication of this study might bear this hypothesis out.

Future research might also explore the impact of American Indian grandparents' efforts in the role of cultural conservator in specific areas such as story telling, participation in tribal activities and in the transference of tribal values on their grandchildren. Such a study may entail interviewing grandchildren as well as grandparents. Efforts to develop reliable and valid acculturation instruments might facilitate further research.

References

Bahr, K. S. (1994). The strength of Apache mothers: Observations on commitment, culture and caretaking. *Journal of Comparative Family Studies, 25,* 233–248.

Barnett, H. (1955). *The Coast Salish of British Columbia.* Eugene, Oregon: University of Oregon.

Bogdan, R. C., & Biklen, S. K. (1992). *Qualitative research for education.* Boston: Allyn & Bacon.

Coleman, H., Unau, Y.A, & B. Manyfingers, (2001). Revamping Family Preservation Services for Native Families. *Journal of Ethnic & Cultural Diversity in Social Work, 10* (1), 49–65.

Cooney, T., & Smith, L. (1993). Young adults relations with grandparents following parental divorce. *Journal of Gerontology Services B: Psychological Sciences and Social Sciences, 51B,* 591–595.

Creasey, G. L., & Kaliher, G. (1994). Age differences in grandchildren's perceptions of relationship quality with grandparents. *Journal of Adolescence, 17,* 411–426.

Creswell, J. W. (1998). *Qualitative inquiry and research design: Choosing among five traditions.* Thousand Oaks, CA: SAGE Publications.

Elendorf, W. W., & Kroeber, A. (1960). *The structure of Twona with notes on Yurals culture.* Pullman, WA: Washington State University.

Gladstone, J.W. (1988). Perceived changes in grandmother-grandchild relations following a child's separation or divorce. *The Gerontologist, 28,* 66–72.

Highwater, J. (1982). *The primal mind.* Hammondsworth: Penguins Books.

Huberman, A. M., & Miles, M. B. (1994). *Data management and analysis methods.* In N. K. Denzin, & Y. S. Lincoln, Handbook of qualitative research (pp. 428–444). Thousand Oaks, CA: SAGE Publications.

Jaskowski, S., & Dellasega, C. (1993). Effects of divorce on grandparent-grandchild relationship. *Issues in Comprehensive Pediatric Nursing, 16,* 125–133.

Kennedy, G. E. (1992). Shared activities of grandparents and grandchildren. *Psychological Reports, 70,* 211–227.

Lincoln, Y. S., & Guba, E. G. (1985). *Naturalistic inquiry.* Newbury, CA: Sage Publications.

Nahemow, N. O. (1987). Grandparenthood among the Baganda: Role option in old age. In Sokolovski, J. (ed.). *Growing old in Societies.* Belmont, CA: Wadsworth.

Noor Al-Deen, Hana S. (Ed.) (1997). *Cross-cultural communication and aging in the United States.* Mahwah, NJ: Lawrence Erlbaum Associates.

Robbins, R. R. (2002). The role of traditional American Indian stories and symbols in counseling adolescents with behavior problems. *Beyond Behavior, 16,* 12–19.

Sander, G. F., & Trygstad, D. W. (1993) Strengths of grandparents and grandchildren relationships. *Activities, Adaptation and Aging, 17,* 43–53.

Scherman, A., Beesley, D., & Turner, B. (2003). Grandparents' involvement with grandchildren during times of crisis in the family. *Oklahoma Association of Teacher Educators, 7,* 47–61.

Scherman, A., Goodrich, C., Kelly, C., Russel, T., & Javidi, A. (1988). Grandparents as a support system for children. *Elementary School Guidance and Counseling Journal, 37,* 16–22.

Schweitzer, M. M. (1987). The elders: Cultural dimensions of aging in two American Indian communities. In Sokolovski, J. (ed.). *Growing old in Societies.* Belmont, CA: Wadsworth.

Strauss, A., & Corbin, J. (1998). *Basics of qualitative research: Techniques and procedures for developing grounded theory.* Thousand Oaks, CA: SAGE Publications.

Sue, D. W., & Sue, D. (2003). *Counseling the culturally diverse.* New York: John Wiley & Sons.

Survey Research Center (1982). *General interviewing techniques.* Ann Arbor, MI: Institute for Social Research.

Szasz, M. C. (1984). *Education and the American Indian.* Albaquerque: University of New Mexico.

Timberlake, E., & Chipungu, S. S. (1992). Grand motherhood: Contemporary meaning among African American middle class grandmothers. *Social Work, 37,* 216–222.

Weibel-Orlando, J. (1990). Grand parenting styles: Native American Perspectives. In Sokolovski, J. (ed.). *The cultural context of aging* (pp 109–125). Westport, CT: Greenwood Press.

Williams, E. (1995). Father and grandfather involvement in childrearing and the school performance of Ojibwa children: An exploratory study. (Doctoral dissertation, University of Michigan, 1995). *Dissertation Abstracts International, 56* (4-A), 1530.

ROCKEY ROBBINS, PHD (Cherokee/Choctaw), is in the Counseling Psychology Department at the University of Oklahoma in Normal, OK 73019. **AVRAHAM SCHERMAN, EDD**, is also in the Counseling Psychology Department at the University of Oklahoma. **HEIDI HOLEMAN**, MS and **JASON WILSON**, MS are doctoral students in the Counseling Psychology Department at the University of Oklahoma. Dr. Robbins may be reached at 405/325-8442 or E-mail: Rockey@ou.edu.

From *Journal of Cultural Diversity,* Vol. 12, no. 2, Summer 2005, pp. 62–68. Copyright © 2005 by Tucker Publications, Inc. Reprinted by permission.

Aging Japanese Pen Messages to Posterity

Heartfelt 'Ending Notes' Give Elderly a Voice in Traditionally Reticent Society

ANTHONY FAIOLA

TOKYO—Living alone in a tidy little house on the outskirts of Tokyo, 75-year-old Tomohiro Ishizuka spends hours dwelling on things unsaid. There are, he recalls, the stories he never told his two adult children—such as the horror of finding the charred remains of boyhood friends after the U.S. firebombing of Tokyo in 1945. And then there are stories half-told—such as the depth of his pain after the sudden death in 2002 of his wife of 45 years.

In a society where the expression of innermost thoughts is considered awkward or self-indulgent, Ishizuka was never able to find the right moments to share such personal things with his family. So last month he joined the growing ranks of elderly Japanese who are writing down what they cannot manage to say.

"Ending notes" is what the resulting works are called. An estimated 200,000 seniors have taken to composing these often candid autobiographical reflections, in the hopes that family members will read them after the authors' deaths. A few of the works have gone on to be published posthumously and sold in bookstores. Ranging from synopses a few pages long to book-length epitaphs, they all serve as records for posterity of things too important to be lost at death.

The advent of ending notes, experts here say, reflects changing notions of old age and death in Japan, which has the longest average life expectancy on Earth—now 81.9 years, more than four years longer than the average in the United States.

Seniors are living longer even as centuries-old family traditions are eroding. Many grandparents no longer live with their children or grandchildren, for instance, as housing becomes more affordable, due to a protracted recession in the 1990s, and society places greater emphasis on privacy. In 2003, almost half of Japanese over 65 lived alone or with a spouse, compared with only 37.7 percent in 1991.

"For years, senior citizens in Japan let their emotions and histories be known to younger generations through everyday gestures or simple words around the house," said Haruyo Inoue, who last year published an updated version of her best-selling book on how to write ending notes, now one of about a half-dozen available in Japan.

"But as many are no longer living with their families, it has reduced the ways in which they can share their feelings or pass on their personal histories to their children or grandchildren," she said. "That is one important reason they have turned to writing ending notes."

Ishizuka is composing his note in his straw-matted living room, writing in a lustrous purple notebook. "When my wife died, I realized that there was nothing tangible for me to remember her by…. I lost so much, all her stories, all her memories," he said. It would have been different had she left an ending note.

Indirectness is highly prized in Japanese conversation; to avoid embarrassment, husbands and wives or parents and children often use the word "like" instead of "love" to express their affection for one another.

"It is easier for me to write it down so they can read it when I am gone," Ishizuka said of his grown children. "That way they will know what their father and mother were really like… and understand why we made the choices in life that we made."

In his draft, he writes of his deep depression after his wife succumbed to a brain hemorrhage in 2002 and his hopes that his children will someday come to understand his eccentricities.

"You often tell me, 'Father is greedy,'" he says in the draft. "But the truth is I love you all dearly. I want to be with you forever and see my grandchildren grow, to feel your kindness, a kindness that has been handed down to you from your late mother.

"I want you to understand that, when I spend time alone, to draw, to go listen to music, to go watch a movie or go for a drive in the mountains, it is to confirm the bond I had with your mother. To reflect on my life, and understand what it means to be me."

Living so long—often while remaining in extraordinarily good health—can force older Japanese to confront death often. In the five-year period ending in 2003, for instance, Ishizuka lost his wife, his mother and his son-in-law.

For Ishizuka, writing his autobiography proved cathartic, a way to come to grips with such massive loss. "There was so much death around me that I felt I needed to write about life," he said.

The many changes in what it means to be old have led to a surge of so-called late-life crises in Japan. Analysts say more senior citizens are making pilgrimages, often mostly by foot, to the 88 holy sites on the island of Shikoku, for example, or engaging in metaphysical experiences such as standing under bitterly cold waterfalls in search of enlightenment.

Japan's record-low birthrate, a result of women choosing to stay single or couples deciding not to have children, has meant that many elderly people here do not have grandchildren, which in Japanese culture poses practical problems for the aged.

New generations—almost always eldest sons, but sometimes daughters—are expected to financially maintain hereditary tombs, mostly inside Buddhist temples. If, after the sons and daughters die, there is no grandchild to assume the responsibility, cremated remains are often removed and placed in common rooms, a fate that is now troubling many older Japanese.

One study conducted by Inoue showed a massive boom in so-called independent cemeteries, where people can make an advance payment ensuring that their bodies will be kept indefinitely in a marked burial compartment. In 1989, there were only four such cemeteries in Japan; last year there were more than 500.

"Japan is not like the United States, where the aged have a culture of self-dependency," said Sumire Nohara, who offers seminars on aging and wrote a how-to book on ending notes. "The Japanese have long depended on their children. But lifestyles are changing here, and that is no longer possible, or desired, in many cases. So the elderly, especially as they live longer and longer, are searching for new ways to leave their legacy."

Enter the ending note. The practice began, experts say, in the 1990s, part of a similar trend in the United States and Europe for people to write extended wills or leave detailed instructions regarding funerals or medical care in case they become mentally or physically incapacitated.

But in Japan, the concept took a broader form because of traditional inhibitions about sitting down and talking intimately. "There are some things that are just easier for me to write than to say," said Juniko Kuriyama, 62, who began writing her ending note last year. She is older than her husband, Junichi, who is 57, and admitted she was writing it as much for him as for her childless adult daughter. "There are so many things that he and I have never spoken about," she said—and, she added, probably never would.

Inside the cozy uniform store that the couple runs near Yokohama, their third attempt at a business after two previous enterprises failed, her husband shook his head as his wife spoke.

"We've made it this far precisely because we don't talk so much," he said. "There are things I don't want to know. It would only make me feel worse to know that I did or did not do something and I can't make up for it anymore."

"You say that now," she replied. "But there are still things I want you to know.... And this is also about what I want. I feel as if I need to leave behind evidence of my life."

Special correspondent Akiko Yamamoto contributed to this report.

UNIT 4

Challenges and Opportunities

Unit Selections

Key Points to Consider

- How does an abusive relationship develop? What, if anything, can be done to prevent it?

- What are the risk factors for child abduction? Why do we hold the belief that it is strangers who are more likely to abduct children? What can be done to protect children from family abduction?

- If you felt your intimate relationship was troubled, how would you act? Would you discuss it with your partner? Would you hope that it would correct itself without you doing anything?

- What is the best way to work out the competing demands of work and family?

- Discuss how the breakup of a relationship or a divorce affects the people involved. Is it possible to have a "good" divorce? What would that good divorce look like? What are the particular issues related to remarriage and the family dynamics associated with it?

- What is the relationship among loss, grief, and care?

Student Website

www.mhcls.com/online

Internet References

Further information regarding these websites may be found in this book's preface or online.

Alzheimer's Association
http://www.alz.org

Caregiver's Handbook
http://www.acsu.buffalo.edu/~drstall/hndbk0.html

National Crime Prevention Council
http://www.ncpc.org

Widow Net
http://www.widownet.org

Stress is life and life is stress. Sometimes stress in families gives new meaning to this statement. When a stressful event occurs in families, many processes occur simultaneously as families and their members cope with the stressor and its effects. One thing that can result is a reduction of the family members' ability to act as resources for each other. Indeed, a stressor can overwhelm the family system, and family members may be among the least effective people in coping with each other's behavior.

In this unit, we consider a wide variety of crises. Family violence is the initial focus. "Hitting Home" argues that greater awareness of the cycle of violence and the complexity of an abusive relationship can only benefit us as a nation. "The Myths and Truths of Family Abduction" confronts commonly held, but incorrect, beliefs about child abduction. Stranger abduction is much rarer than abduction by family members. With this in mind, the article suggests several tips for anticipating and preparing children for the risk of family abduction.

Next, "Love But Don't Touch" addresses emotional infidelity, a form of unfaithfulness that many see as less serious than sexual infidelity, but others view as just as damaging to a couple's relationship. In this article, Mark Teich addresses a variety of ways of spotting emotional cheating as well as ways of strengthening a relationship after or in anticipation of its happening.

The subsection that follows looks at the work/family connection, with interesting results. The other side of employment is explored in "For Better or Worse: Couples Confront Unemployment." Involving the whole family and maintaining communication are found to be essential to helping the family to survive the crisis of unemployment. "Keeping Work and Life in Balance" looks at the stress working women face, balancing home and work…and the effects of some companies to facilitate the balance. The final article discusses the necessity of careful preretirement planning. The 21st century poses new crises for investment and insurance. Jane Bryant Quinn offers advice on how to develop a plan to assure that retirement savings will be sufficient for one's needs.

In the next section, the crisis of war is portrayed in "Home Alone." Military personnel, many of them single parents, must find child care when they are called up and sent to war. The strain of the service person facing death as the children also must deal with disruption of their lives is depicted. A related phenomenon, terrorism, is addressed in "Terrorism, Trauma, and Children: What Can We Do?" How do we, as caring adults, respond to questions children have about the dangers of terrorism

and war? Because children personalize the threat, the suggestions for how to respond to a child's concerns are highly pragmatic and focused on building a sense of safety and comfort for the child.

Divorce and remarriage are the subjects of the next two subsections. In the first article of the first subsection, E. Mavis Hetherington presents an overview of "Marriage and Divorce American Style." One of the life skills that newly divorced individuals may have gotten rusty on is discussed in "Dating After Divorce." The other side of divorce—remarriage—is the focus of the next articles. A particular concern of blended families is finances and financial management. How do they blend their financial houses? Should they? "Managing a Blended Family" addresses these concerns and provides tips for merging two different financial systems. Similarly, "Stepfamily Success Depends on Ingredients" details characteristics of successful stepfamilies, paying particular attention to ways of building resilience into the family system.

The nature of stress resulting from loss and grief is the subject of the final subsection. In "Death of One's Partner: The Anticipation and the Reality," Florence Kaslow discusses the effect of one of the most devastating losses one can experience in adulthood. The final article, by Neris Diaz-Cabello, discusses the Hispanic way of dying and points out the importance of family and religion during the process of dying and after the event of death.

Hitting Home

Domestic violence is the issue that embarrasses traditionalists. Today, despite greater awareness and a variety of model programs, partner abuse is still far too prevalent.

CARA FEINBERG

A leathery woman with a darkening black eye smokes cigarettes through the spaces of her missing front teeth and tells the police how her boyfriend slapped and bit her because he didn't like her grandchildren. Another woman tells a counselor at a shelter that she's tried to leave her husband 15 times in the two years that she's been married to him. Still another can't speak at all, her moans incoherent as she's wheeled out of her house on a stretcher covered in blood, her cheek slashed into two loose flaps from the corner of her mouth.

These graphic details of domestic abuse come to us courtesy of documentary filmmaker Frederick Wiseman, whose camera has been mercilessly recording the often unpleasant aspects of our social reality for three decades. In the years since 1967, when his first documentary, *Titicut Follies*, garnered artistic awards and journalistic respect—and an injunction from the Massachusetts Superior Court, which banned the film in the state for the next 24 years—Wiseman has captured everything from the crumbling walls of a housing project to the locker-lined hallways of a high school, from a ballet company to a state prison for the criminally insane. Using his signature cinema verité style—there is no narration, music, or overt editorializing in his films—Wiseman has become a barometer of our values and mores, revealing our culture and progress by observing our social organizations, institutions and institutional practices.

It is therefore telling that Wiseman has chosen to take on the issue of domestic violence at precisely this moment. While the scenes from his latest film, *Domestic Violence*, are explicit, we've seen these types of images before. Hardly a news cycle goes by nowadays without a domestic-violence story. The media attention is a salutary development; not long ago, domestic violence didn't exist as a legal or social concept.

Yet while we've come incredibly far in our struggle to recognize domestic violence as a national, public problem, battered women now face a new set of challenges—preeminent among them, the religious right's efforts to portray marriage as the panacea for all social and moral problems. If only we could all just pair up in happily heterosexual matrimony and stay that way, the logic goes, social ills such as violence, crime, and poverty would simply wither away.

While ample data suggest the social and personal benefits of a happy marriage, the get-married-and-stay-married-at-all-costs ethos often ignores the damage that bad marriages can do both to adults and to children. And domestic abuse? Social conservatives often pretend that the problem would disappear if only more people got and stayed married. They make it more difficult for women to leave abusive relationships—not only by steeling social attitudes against divorce but by making it contractually harder (through such vehicles as "covenant marriages") for domestic-violence victims to escape.

> **"Everyone asks why she continues to stay; no one thinks to ask, 'Why does he hit her in the first place?'"**

Moreover, social conservatives tend to confuse marriage policy with welfare policy; indeed, they would like to replace the latter with the former. This is the "get-married-and-stay-married-and-you-won't-need-welfare" argument. Robert Rector, a senior fellow at the Heritage Foundation, argues that marriage incentives must be built into Temporary Assistance for Needy Families (TANF)—the basic federal welfare program, designed to provide assistance and work opportunities—and that divorced and out-of-wedlock mothers should get diminished levels of welfare assistance for not being married. This is a typical conservative argument that not only gets the relationship between poverty and welfare backward—and this is a great source of liberal-conservative argument generally—but also makes it much harder for wives to leave their abusive husbands, for fear of being financially penalized.

Domestic Violence and the Law

It is this sort of rhetoric that threatens to roll back the heroic—and remarkably recent—achievements of the battered-women's movement. As late as the 1960s, if you looked at American newspapers, police reports, medical records, and legal texts, you would find little mention of domestic violence anywhere. "In the last few decades, there has been a great surge in attention to this issue," says Clare Dalton, Northeastern University's Matthews Distinguished University Professor of Law, who is a leading feminist legal scholar and a pioneer in the development of legal education about domestic violence. A founder of Northeastern's domestic-violence clinical program and the Domestic Violence Institute (an interdisciplinary educational, research, and service organization), Dalton served as a consultant on Wiseman's film and led discussions about the issue at several showings of *Domestic Violence* in the Boston area.

"Right up into the 1980s, we still had states in the Union with out-of-date immunity laws based on common law from the 1800s, protecting men who beat their wives," Dalton says. "It was only 10 years ago now that the Supreme Court was even ready to recognize the severity of domestic violence in our country—only eight years ago that Congress addressed it on a federal level with the Violence Against Women Act [VAWA]."

... the number of women dying in domestic-violence situations hasn't changed. The problem is as widespread as ever.

That legislation, passed initially in 1994 and renewed by Congress in 2000, was a milestone: It was the first federal law ever to address the issue, and it came at the problem with a variety of solutions, including funding for women's shelters, a national domestic-abuse hot line, rape education-and-prevention programs, training for federal and state judges, new remedies for battered immigrants, and criminal enforcement of interstate orders of protection.

As Dalton points out, VAWA would have been impossible without the work that began with the feminist movement of the 1960s and 1970s. "Our latest campaign against domestic violence grew directly out of the movement," she says. "For the first time, women were getting together and talking about their experiences and discovering the great prevalence of these unspoken terrors. Emerging feminist theory allowed women to connect with each other and to the ideas that feminists had been arguing for all along: that women's legally sanctioned subordination within the family was denying them equality."

Taking their cue from the civil-rights and antiwar movements earlier, feminist activists began to see the law not only as an important tool for protecting victims but as a way to define domestic violence as a legitimate social problem. Local legal groups and grass-roots advocacy organizations began to develop legal remedies based on the link between sexual discrimination and violence. Starting in the sixties, lawyers began to seek civil-protective or restraining orders to keep batterers

away from their victims. Courts began to create special rules for domestic-violence cases and custody cases involving children from violent homes. And by the mid-1990s, Congress had passed VAWA. Today, feminist advocates for battered women have begun to draw important interconnections among battering, poverty, welfare reform, homelessness, immigration, employment, gun control, and many other areas of concern. They are working with all sorts of organizations to step up education and reform.

The Psychology of Abuse

While the stories of domestic violence in Wiseman's film are horrifying, even the most compassionate viewer's sympathy can run thin when victims shun opportunities to abandon their own torture chambers. Of the three women in the opening scene who have called the police, not one is prepared to listen to advice about legal options or free social services. Rather, each one simply continues recounting her abuse, speaking as if she had never even heard the officers' recommendations.

"We have always looked at the victim and said, 'Well, why doesn't she just leave?'" says Lynn Rosenthal, executive director of the Washington, D.C.-based National Network to End Domestic Violence. "We've got cops and judges and lawyers who get upset when victims don't flee, or fail to report their abusers, or don't show up in court to press charges." This past January, a judge in Lexington, Kentucky, sparked outrage among victims' advocates when she fined two women for contempt of court because they returned to their alleged abusers despite having obtained protective orders against them. "But this attitude places the burden on the victim, not the abuser," Rosenthal says. "Everyone asks why she continues to stay; no one thinks to ask, 'Why does he hit her in the first place?'"

Dr. Judith Lewis Herman, an associate clinical professor of psychiatry at Harvard Medical School and the training director of the Victims of Violence Program at Cambridge Hospital, has been fighting to change this perception of victims for more than 30 years. "The tendency to blame the victim has always influenced the direction of psychological study," Herman said in an interview in her office at Harvard. "Research had always looked at what the woman did to provoke her batterer, or it focused on her own 'personality disorders.'" In 1964, for example, researchers conducted an egregious study of battered women called *The Wife-Beater's Wife*, in which the inquiries were directed toward women simply because the men refused to talk. The clinicians identified the women as "frigid" or "indecisive" and went on to *treat* the women so they would stop "provoking" their husbands.

In the mid-1980s, when the diagnostic manual of the American Psychiatric Association came up for revision, this misdiagnosis of victims—and the tendency to blame them for their partners' violence—became the center of a heated controversy. A group of male psychoanalysts proposed that "masochistic personality disorder" be added to the manual to describe any person "who remains in relationships in which others exploit, abuse, or take advantage of him or her, despite opportunities to alter the situation"—a proposal that outraged women's groups around the country. Herman was one of the leaders in the fight to formulate a new diagnosis that accurately described the psychological conditions of battered women. Herman proposed "complex post-traumatic stress disorder," which describes a spectrum of conditions rather than a single disorder, and is now listed as a subcategory of post-traumatic stress disorder in the latest edition of the standard diagnostic manual.

Although wiseman recounts none of this political or legal history explicitly in *Domestic Violence*, the evidence of these years of struggle pervades every frame he shoots. In the opening sequence, a lean, tattooed, middle-aged man wearing only his undershorts asks, "Why do you always take the woman's word?" as police officers cuff and arrest him.

"When it comes to domestic violence," they respond, "that's the way it is. If she says you hit her, you hit her."

This brief exchange may not seem particularly significant—after all, if a stranger had assaulted a woman in a parking lot, we would expect the police to haul him away. But the very fact that the Tampa, Florida, officers responded immediately to a call for domestic violence and then removed the batterer from his home without hesitation or an arrest warrant is a testament to the progressive laws, police training, and legislative reform developed and implemented in the past 30 years.

According to Elizabeth M. Schneider, a professor at Brooklyn Law School and the author of *Battered Women and Feminist Lawmaking* (2000), one of first and most important legal issues to come to the attention of the feminist movement in the 1960s was the failure of police to protect battered women from assault. By the 1970s, class-action lawsuits were filed in New York City and Oakland, California. All of a sudden, domestic violence was considered a crime against the public and the state, not just the individual.

Yet even these victories and others like them initially made little headway in police attitudes and practices. Nineteen years ago, a woman named Tracey Thurman was nearly beaten to death in Torrington, Connecticut, before the police came to her aid. Though Thurman had reported her estranged husband's threats and harassment to the police repeatedly for over a year, it wasn't until she called in utter desperation, fearing for her life, that the police responded. They sent only one officer, however, who arrived 25 minutes after the call was placed, pulled up across the street from Thurman's house, and sat in his car while Thurman's husband chased her across the yard, slashed her with a knife, stabbed her in the neck, knocked her to the ground, and then stabbed her 12 more times.

Permanently disfigured, Tracey Thurman brought what became a landmark case to the Supreme Court, which found that the city police had violated her 14th Amendment right to "equal protection of the laws" and awarded her $2.3 million in compensatory damages. Almost immediately, the State of Connecticut adopted a new, comprehensive domestic-violence law calling for the arrest of assaultive spouses. In the year after the measure took effect, the number of arrests for domestic assault increased 92 percent, from 12,400 to 23,830.

"We'd all like to look at our progress and be optimistic," says Clare Dalton. "But if you look at the most recent statistics from the Justice Department, the number of women dying in domestic-violence situations hasn't changed. The problem is as widespread as ever.

"But there is one interesting thing here," Dalton notes. "While the number of deaths among women hasn't changed, fatalities among men have dropped significantly. This, in truth, is our first real triumph. If women feel they can get help—if they believe the police will come when they call them, if they understand they will get support and have a place to go where they will be safe with their children—then fewer are pushed to the wall. Fewer will resort to killing or dying at the hand of their abuser."

The Tampa Example

Such wisdom has not been lost on the City of Tampa Police Department, whose progressive, community-wide response to the problem Frederick Wiseman chose to film for *Domestic Violence*. Tampa's network of coordinated, cooperative services—from law enforcement, to social services, to the legal system—is a model example of similar programs around the country.

"We now have a zero-tolerance policy toward domestic violence here in Tampa," said Lieutenant Rod Reder, a 24-year veteran of the Hillsborough County Sheriff's Office in Tampa, when reached by phone. A former supervisor for the Sex Crimes Division and onetime member of the Governor's Domestic and Sexual Violence Task Force, Reder is now widely considered to be an expert in the field of domestic and sexual violence. Under the auspices of the U.S. Department of Justice, he runs training sessions for law-enforcement officers at conferences nationwide. "We discovered there were so many simple things we weren't doing... to help victims of domestic violence," Reder said. "And we found there really is only one way to make things work. All the community players have to come to the table; otherwise, it's the victim's safety that gets compromised."

> **"In the past, many officers looked at domestic-violence calls as a waste of time or a private family matter. Now we consider them some of the most dangerous calls there are."**

The catalyst for Tampa's adoption of community cooperation was a woman named Mabel Bexley, who in 1981 pushed Reder to bring police practices in line with new domestic-violence laws, and who two years later became the director of a women's shelter called the Spring. In her 19-year tenure there, Bexley, now 65 and recently retired, expanded the Spring—which is the focus of much of Wiseman's documentary—from a three-bedroom house with more than a dozen women and children huddled inside to a 102-bed facility with 120 employees and a $4-million budget.

Reder and Bexley teamed up again in 1995, when Tampa hit an all-time high in domestic-violence-related homicide, to work alongside members of the state attorney's office and the 13th Judicial Circuit Court to form the zero-tolerance campaign against domestic abuse. Reder and the Hillsborough County police then formed a special domestic-violence unit and developed a three-day training seminar for all seven local law-enforcement agencies.

"We do all sorts of things now to make the system work," said Reder. "When police answer a domestic-violence call, they are required to file a report—even if there is no arrest—just so the incident is documented. We had deputies who would walk away from incidents saying, 'No harm, no foul,' and would leave with no report," he recalled. "But now officers are required to document domestics by state law. You start dinging a few deputies and taking disciplinary action, and word gets out real quick: If you go to a domestic, write a report."

According to Reder, Tampa officers have also become very aggressive about arrests: "We used to think we were doing the right thing by not arresting the man—we didn't want to get him any angrier than he already was. In the past, many officers looked at domestic-violence calls as a waste of time or a private family matter. Now we consider them some of the most dangerous calls there are."

Hillsborough County has also addressed other gaps in the system. "We've sent advocates to go pick up victims at their homes so they'd be sure to get to court," said Reder. "We used to have communal waiting rooms in the courthouse, but now we have separate ones so victims won't have to face their abusers before their trial begins. To file an injunction, you used to have to fill out a complicated 25-page form that was only available in English. This alone used to scare people away, so now we have bilingual advocates and lawyers available to help people fill them out."

This is where the Spring comes in. Though most victims who arrive at the shelter are running for their lives and have no desire even to consider legal action against their abusers at that point, the facility employs an on-site attorney to help them navigate the judicial system and pursue the available options. In addition, each one of the Spring's hot-line operators is a deputy of the court who can file injunctions at any hour of the day or night. This is crucial, because the most dangerous time for abuse victims actually begins the moment they choose to leave their homes. "The Bureau of Justice statistics say that one-third of all women murdered in the U.S. are killed by an intimate," says Jennifer Dunbar, who works at the Spring. "But of those 30 percent, 65 percent are murdered when they leave. It's our job to make sure [victims are] protected at this point."

Nearly 40 years after the first feminist activists in the women's movement brought domestic violence to the nation's attention, the policies have largely been set and the laws are finally on the books. Now it's a question of making sure that the systems work and helping the larger community to understand, recognize, and accommodate the needs of battered women. "Right now, we're working on expanding efforts into other systems, like job placement, affordable housing, welfare reform, and child-protective services," says Lynn Rosenthal of the National Network. "A number of states now have special domestic-violence provisions within their welfare systems and housing programs. For instance, under the original job-placement programs in the TANF program, people who showed up tardy three times to the program would lose their benefits. A battered woman might have tremendous problems meeting these criteria—her husband could still be sabotaging her efforts." Rosenthal adds: "It's easy to see how our own well-intended programs could send her right back to her batterer."

... in communities where awareness of partner abuse remains limited... reform movements lag well behind their counterparts in more progressive places.

Throughout the country, states have begun to integrate their systems and have developed new, progressive programs to deal with domestic violence. Though they vary in their specific reforms, many have expanded their legal definition of domestic violence to include nonmarried and nontraditional couples. And some, shifting their focus from punishment to rehabilitation, have begun to examine the root causes of violence in the first place. Programs like EMERGE in Cambridge, Massachusetts, work with batterers to find nonviolent ways to express their anger; many others educate children and teens—ideally, before any battering starts. A number of states have created specialized domestic-violence courts so that the judges hearing these cases are not only familiar with and sympathetic to the special circumstances surrounding battering cases but can follow them from start to finish.

Yet for all the progress that has been made in addressing domestic violence, Wiseman's film makes clear that there is a long way yet to go. One problem is how practically and psychologically difficult it can be for a victim to leave her batterer. But another is the complexity of the political environment itself. As elected officials come and go, their varying agendas affect the winds of legislative change and shift fiscal priorities along with idealistic convictions. According to Robin Thompson, the former executive director of the Florida Governor's Task Force on Domestic Violence, in order for a state to stay vigilant in its fight against domestic abuse there must be "a bedrock of political commitment"—be it a designated task force or a group of grass-roots activists invested in educating and uniting their community. Awareness alone is not enough.

And while states may have implemented great judicial and law-enforcement reforms, if these are not closely monitored and coordinated, they can still fall short of their goals. For instance, if an accused batterer is arrested right away but then must wait six months for a trial, the victim is still largely unprotected. Or if a judge orders a defendant to participate in an intervention program but no one checks to see if he complies, the sentence may be useless.

Obstacles to reform certainly don't fall neatly along partisan lines. A liberal judge might opt for a surprisingly lenient sentence for a defendant, while a conservative judge might make an equally counterintuitive ruling, viewing the court as the woman's traditional protectorate. Yet in communities where awareness of partner abuse remains limited—and partisan issues such as welfare, gun ownership, and "family values" remain entwined with domestic violence—reform movements lag well behind their counterparts in more progressive places.

So far on a national level, what little government funding there is for community-based programs like the community courts or the Spring has not been cut by the Bush administration. But Rosenthal remains worried about the potential for an "unholy merger" between social conservatives and the growing movement for fathers' rights. Though she respects much of the work that fathers' rights groups have done in calling for more paternal responsibility and accountability, she fears that some men will latch on to the claims of right-wingers who resent gains by the battered-women's movement—and by the feminist movement generally—and will seek to cripple these movements' effectiveness by demanding their defunding.

In a tableau that echoes the opening scene of *Domestic Violence*, Wiseman returns at the end of his documentary to police officers responding to a call. This time, it seems, the outcome will be more hopeful: The call was placed not by a battered woman but by a potential batterer seeking intervention—a last-ditch effort to stave off the violence brewing in his household. But when the police arrive, the couple refuses to listen to their suggestions or take any steps to change the situation. When neither the man nor the woman agrees to leave the premises, the police ultimately return to their squad car shaking their heads, leaving behind only words of advice and a volatile couple "afraid of what they might do." It is an ominous ending to a celebration of progress—an eerie mirror of the problem we continue to face.

Prospect assistant editor **CARA FEINBERG** writes the "World Responds" column for *Prospect Online*.

The Myths and Truths of Family Abduction

Nancy B. Hammer

The very idea of child abduction is met by parents in equal measures of fear and disbelief—it can't happen to us. The series of high-profile abductions of children in 2002 raised the country's awareness. The kids spanned the ages of two to 15 and came from all types of families and environments, both urban and rural, across the U.S. In the more horrific cases, the abductor was someone the child did not know. Yet, a recently published study by the U.S. Department of Justice confirms that, compared to the frightening, but relatively rare, kidnappings by strangers, family abductions are commonplace.

In 1988, the Federal government first attempted to count the number of children who become missing each year. In 2002, the Second National Incidence Studies of Missing, Abducted, Runaway, and Thrownaway Children (NISMART-2) was published. The study confirms, once again, that offspring taken by a family member without the knowledge or consent of the custodial parent continues to represent the second-largest category of missing children, with a total of 203,900 youngsters abducted by a family member, as opposed to 115 stereotypical kidnappings by a stranger. Indeed, in your lifetime, you are likely either to experience within your own family or know someone who has gone through some type of family abduction.

Despite the fact that so many kids are abducted by a family member, many people do not fully understand this issue. The public generally views these incidents as infrequent, minor occurrences best handled privately. "After all," people believe, "the child is with a parent; it can't be that bad." Or can it?

On a clear autumn day, John Cramer (name changed) did not return his daughter, age 11, or son, age nine, from his scheduled weekend visitation. John and his wife Sandy (name changed) had separated several months earlier and had begun divorce proceedings. After Sandy contacted police, John's car was found inside a storage locker with a hose running from the tailpipe to the driver's side window. Inside, police found the lifeless bodies of John and the two children. Although it was known that he was unhappy about his failing marriage, no one suspected the level of John's despondency or that he was capable of taking his children's lives as well as his own. While the typical incident of family abduction does not end in death, every time it occurs there is the potential for horrible consequences.

Though the public believes the incidences of these kidnappings are infrequent, they rank as the second-largest category of missing children in the U.S.

In family abduction cases, kids typically are taken by a parent, although in a few cases, a grandparent or other relative may be the abductor. Parents who abduct often do so when they feel their relationship with the child somehow is threatened. Research indicates that fathers, who are slightly more likely to abduct than mothers, often flee before a custody order is issued, perhaps spurred on by the fear that they are about to lose meaningful contact with their offspring. Mothers, however, typically kidnap after a custody order has been issued, perhaps reacting when the terms of the custody and visitation don't meet their expectations. Regardless of who the abductor is, the overriding motivation is a desire to control the child's relationships and hurt the other parent. The abducting parent often is unable to consider the effects on the youngster and thinks only of his or her immediate situation. One father, after the eight-year abduction of his children, reflected that his actions were motivated by his own inadequacies and need to control, not for the love of his kids.

The public has a tendency to minimize the risk to offspring involved in a family abduction in the mistaken belief that a child is safe in the hands of a parent. A simple scan of the headlines of any major newspaper reveals stories of child abuse, neglect, and even death of kids at the hands of their own parents. In this way, abduction is no different from any other crime committed against a child—kids often are at risk from those they know. Official statistics may not fully reflect the danger inherent in family abduction situations. Some cases resulting in death may be counted as murder or suicide, without reference to the family abduction incident that started it all.

This oversight may leave family abduction out of the crime statistics, yet abduction of a child, even if perpetrated by a parent, is a felony in every state. The state laws often are referred to as "custodial interference" statutes and, if charged as felonies, carry a jail sentence of one year or more and allow the abducting parent, when caught in another state, to be extradited for prosecution in the state from which he or she fled. A conviction of child abduction can have a serious effect on subsequent custody decisions in family court. The FBI can become involved under Federal law if the abducting parent flees with the child across state lines. Further, if the abducting parent takes the child outside the U.S., he or she has violated the Federal international parental kidnapping law, thus involving the FBI and other Federal resources to locate and prosecute the abducting parent.

Research conducted on the consequences of family abduction confirms the seriousness of these cases. In the best-known study of this issue, researchers Geoffrey Greif and Rebecca Hegar interviewed 371 parents whose kids were abducted by a noncustodial parent and found a seven percent incidence of sexual abuse, 23% incidence of physical abuse, and five percent incidence of both physical and sexual abuse.

In addition to statistical information, adults who were parentally abducted as children have begun to raise their collective voices through a new organization called Take Root. This group formed after an initial meeting hosted by the National Center for Missing & Exploited Children (NCMEC) and provides an online venue (**www.takeroot.org**) for the sharing of stories—in addition to hosting a newsletter called "The Link." One of the members of the organization chronicles her own struggle for identity and self-awareness after having lived on the run and under many aliases during the period of her abduction. She writes, "I have had many [names] in my life. The first, my birth name, the name lovingly bestowed upon me as a newborn child, was Cecilie ... until my abduction at age four I was called Sissi or Sisselina, in the sweet custom of nicknaming a young child. After my abduction my father changed my name to Sarah Zissel, the first of many aliases, and for all intents and purposes my birth name was no more."

It can be very difficult to locate the abducting parent and captive child. An abductor can find many hiding places. While some abductors simply adopt new names, others seek to alter their identities illegally. Information on forging birth certificates and creating assumed identities is only a click away on the Internet. Other abductors get assistance from relatives willing to hide a child in violation of the law, or from more formal groups, sometimes known as underground networks, which help abductors violate the law by providing funds and housing. Many abducting parents seek refuge in a foreign country. Not all international abduction cases involve parents of two nationalities. Often, American parents choose to flee to a foreign destination in order to better hide their crime or to be with a new partner.

Parents as Abductors

Regardless of the method or the destination, parents considering abduction must realize that, one day, they could be found. NCMEC's nationwide poster distribution program leads to the recovery of one in six children featured. A growing awareness of missing children and an increasingly vigilant public shed light into the dark corners where abducting parents once hid their children from the other parent, extended family, friends, and law en-

forcement. In the past year, the U.S. has seen several recoveries of children who had been missing for more than five years. Abducting parents find, upon their return, that the problems they tried to run away from still exist. In addition, their actions have created new ones. Facing the issues now, however, requires being honest with the child about the left-behind parent, often for the first time since the abduction, and may result in a sense of betrayal in the child who does not know whom to trust. Moreover, the child frequently suffers emotional confusion and depression, as he or she is left to wonder what will subsequently happen. The irony for some parents is that the same child they fought so hard to keep for themselves can become estranged once he or she learns the full truth of the abduction.

If you are concerned about the potential of family abduction, there are steps that can be taken to lessen the risk. Every parent should strive to reduce the tension with the other parent throughout the separation, divorce, or custody process. As difficult as it may be to go through divorce and resolve the custody issues, children need both parents in order to become the individuals they were meant to be. For some families, seeking help from a mediator to define custody and visitation helps both parties to feel as though their concerns have been addressed. A resolution reached together may help prevent one side from feeling like he or she "lost," and therefore, prevent a potential "lashing out" through abduction. In addition, a mediator can talk openly about how parents should strive to remember that their child's need for access to both parents must come first.

Parents should take any threats of abduction seriously and evaluate the risk. Additionally, lawyers should encourage the court handling custody issues to do the same. Recently, California enacted legislation requiring courts to consider whether such a risk exists. The law is modeled on a Department of Justice report, "Early Identification of Risk Factors for Parental Abduction," and can be obtained at **www.ojjdp.ncjrs.org**. If the court finds a risk of flight, it is required to consider certain measures designed to prevent the abduction from occurring. They include:

Child custody bond. The court may require parents to post a financial bond or give some other guarantee that they will comply with its order. Such a bond may be obtained from an insurance carrier or bail bonding company. The Professional Bail Agents of the U.S. maintains information on how to find a company able to write this type of bond and may be reached at 1-800-883-7287.

Supervised visitation. The terms may allow visits only at certain places, such as the custodial parent's home or a visitation center to be supervised by a professional or other intermediary. This may be appropriate in cases in which an abduction has occurred previously; where there is violence in the relationship; or when threats of abduction have been made.

Restrict child's removal from state or country. The court may require either parent to obtain legal permission prior to removing the child from the state. If there is a risk of international abduction, the court will issue a bulletin with the U.S. Department of State's "Children's Passport Issuance Alert Program." It requires a written request to enter the child's name and enables the Department of State to notify a parent before issuing a U.S.

passport for the child. Information can be obtained at **www.travel.state.gov.**

Parents also should take certain practical steps to reduce the risk of family abduction and ensure swift action to locate the child:

- Keep a current photograph of your offspring.
- Maintain a complete description of your child, including height, weight, birthmarks, and other unique physical characteristics. Fingerprints also are provided by most law enforcement agencies. All copies of the fingerprints should be turned over to the parent for safe keeping.
- Teach kids to use the telephone. Make sure they know their home phone number, including area code, as well as emergency numbers such as "911" and "0."
- Notify schools, babysitters, and day care centers of the terms of your custody order and who is permitted to pick up the child.
- Maintain identifying data about your former spouse, including description, date of birth, social security number, and contact information for friends and relatives.

Once it is determined that the child is missing, a parent immediately should take the following steps: Contact the local law enforcement agency to make a missing child report; ask that the child be entered into the National Crime Information Center computer as missing (NCIC is the national law enforcement database, operated by the FBI, that allows law enforcement in other states access to information about the child's disappearance); call NCMEC at 1-800-843-5678 and report the child as missing; ask local missing child organizations for assistance; aid law enforcement's search by providing all information available to help locate the child and the abductor; and obtain temporary or sole custody if it was not already court-ordered.

Family abductions are real crimes with real child victims and no winners. If you are considering abducting your child or are concerned that your child might be abducted, help is available. Besides maintaining a 24-hour hotline, NCMEC provides information on family abduction and other child protection issues on its website, **www.missingkids.com.**

Despite the frequency of these cases and the trauma caused to the families involved, there is hope in every child recovery. The public's understanding of this issue and awareness in looking at the pictures of missing children and reporting suspicious circumstances involving children will yield even more happy endings.

NANCY B. HAMMER is the director of the International Division of the National Center for Missing & Exploited Children, Alexandria, Va.

Love But Don't Touch

Emotional infidelity is intense but invisible, erotic but unconsummated. Such delicious paradoxes make it every bit as dangerous as adultery.

MARK TEICH

She was the first girl Brendan ever kissed, the first he made love with, the first he truly loved. They'd lost their virginity together on a magical trip to Amsterdam. He felt they were soul mates and believed that their bond would never he severed. But she had suddenly broken up with him after eight months, and they lost touch until 2000, when he paid her a visit. Their exchange was unremarkable, but they traded e-mail addresses. At first, they merely sent an occasional message, chatting superficially. But the correspondence became more frequent and personal. It was easy—she was sunnier and more passionate than Brendan's wife, Lauren, who was bleary-eyed from caring for their sick son while working full-time to pay the bills. Without the burden of these responsibilities, his old love divided her days between visits to the gym and e-mails to him. Yes, she had a husband: but while Brendan was "witty and creative," she said in her lustful notes, her husband was a drone. What a high it was for Brendan to see himself through this complimentary lens after Lauren's withering view of him: hypercritical, angry, money-obsessed.

At the same time, Lauren found herself drawn to a love interest with roots in *her* past: a man she met through a Web site devoted to the neighborhood she grew up in. In short order, Lauren was deeply involved in an Internet relationship that kept her mood aloft throughout the day. In every way, her new companion was superior: While Brendan had set out to be a novelist, he now worked for a little health newsletter. It was Lauren's online friend, a research biologist, who spent his free hours writing a novel, and what a gifted writer he was! While Brendan talked about bills past due and criticized everything from her clothes to her weight, her online partner was fascinated by her thoughts and the minutiae of her day. He abounded in the type of wit and imagination Brendan had lacked for years. Sure, her online partner was married, too; he described his wife as remote and inaccessible—a scientist like himself, but so involved with her work that she left the child-rearing to him and almost never came home.

The New Anatomy of Infidelity

Brendan and Lauren never slept with or even touched their affair partners. Yet their emotional involvements were so all-consuming, so blinding, that they almost blew off their marriage for the disembodied fantasies of online love. Infidelity, of course, is older than the Bible. And garden-variety cheating has been on the rise for 25 years, ever since women swelled the workforce. But now, infidelity has taken a dangerous—and often profoundly stirring—new turn that psychologists call the biggest threat marriage has ever faced. Characterized by deep emotional closeness, the secret, sexually charged (but unconsummated) friendships at issue build almost imperceptibly until they surpass in importance the relationship with a spouse. Emotional involvement outside of marriage has always been intoxicating, as fictional heroines such as Anna Karenina and Emma Bovary attest. But in the age of the Internet and the egalitarian office, these relationships have become far more accessible than ever before.

The late psychologist Shirley Glass identified the trend in her 2003 book, *Not Just Friends*. "The new infidelity is between people who unwittingly form deep, passionate connections before realizing they've crossed the line from platonic friendship into romantic love," Glass wrote. Eighty-two percent of the unfaithful partners she'd counseled, she said, had had an affair with someone who was at first "just a friend." What's more, she found 55 to 65 percent of men and women alike had participated in relationships she considered *emotionally* unfaithful—secret, sexually energized and more emotionally open than the relationship with the spouse.

Glass cited the workplace as the new minefield for marriage; 50 percent of unfaithful women and 62 percent of unfaithful men she treated were involved with someone from work. And the office has only grown more tantalizing, with women now having affairs at virtually the same rate as men. Factor in the explosive power of the Internet, and it's clear that infidelity has become an omnipresent threat. No research exists on how many affairs are happening online, but experts say they're rampant—more common than work affairs and multiplying fast.

> "You go on the Internet and ask, 'Whatever happened to so and so?'" Then you find him. As soon as you do, all of those raw emotions flood back.

The Slippery Slope

An emotional affair can threaten any marriage—not just those already struggling or in disrepair.

"No one's immune," says Peggy Vaughan, author of *The Monogamy Myth* and creator of the Web site, DearPeggy.com, where surveys and discussion reflect the zeitgeist. Although those with troubled marriages are especially susceptible, a surprising number of people with solid relationships respond to the novelty and are swept away as well.

Because it is so insidious, its boundaries so fuzzy, the emotional affair's challenge to marriage is initially hard to detect. It might seem natural to discuss personal concerns with an Internet buddy or respond to an office mate having trouble with a spouse. But slowly, imperceptibly, there's an "emotional switch." The friends have built a bubble of secrecy around their relationship and shifted allegiance front their marriage partners to the affair.

Web of Deceit

The perfect petri dish for secret, sexually charged relationships is, of course, the Internet. The new American affair can take place right in the family room; within feet of children and an unsuspecting spouse, the unfaithful can swap sex talk and let emotions run amok.

Often, it's the anonymity of online encounters that invites emotional disclosure, says Israeli philosopher Aaron Ben-Ze'ev, president of the University of Haifa and author of *Love Online*. "Like strangers on a train who confess everything to an anonymous seatmate, people meeting online reveal what they might never tell a real-world partner. When people reveal so much, there is great intimacy." But the revelations are selective: Without chores to do or children to tend, the friends relate with less interference from practical constraints, allowing fantasy to take hold. Over the Internet, adds Ben-Ze'ev, the power of imagination is especially profound.

In fact, says MIT psychologist Sherry Turkle, author of *Life on the Screen: Identity in the Age of the Internet*, it's particularly what's *withheld*—the "low bandwidth" of the information online partners share—that makes these relationships so fantasy-rich and intense. She compares the phenomenon to that of transference in psychotherapy—where patients, knowing little about their therapists, invest them with the qualities they want and need. Similarly, the illicit partner is always partly a fantasy, inevitably seen as wittier, warmer and sexier than the spouse.

So is online love real? "It has all the elements of real love," says Ben-Ze'ev: obsessive thoughts of the lover, an urgent need to be together and the feeling that the new partner is the most wonderful person on earth. You experience the same chemical rush that people get when they fall in love.

Are You an Emotional Cheat? 7 Telltale Signs

Ever since Scarlett O'Hara flirted in front of Rhett Butler, the jury has been out on extramarital friendships that are sensual, even intimate, yet don't cross the line to actual sex. With emotional affairs so prevalent, psychologists studying the issue have finally drawn some lines in the sand. You may be emotionally unfaithful, they say, if you:

- Have a special confidante at the office, someone receptive to feelings and fears you can't discuss with your partner or spouse.
- Share personal information and negative feelings about your primary relationship with a "special friend."
- Meet a friend of the opposite sex for dinner and go back to his or her place to discuss your primary relationship over a drink, never calling your partner and finally arriving home at 3 A.M.
- Humiliate your partner in front of others, suggesting he or she is a loser or inadequate sexually.
- Have the energy to tell your stories only once, and decide to save the juiciest for an office or Internet friend of the opposite sex.
- Hook up with an old boyfriend or girlfriend at a high school reunion and, feeling the old spark, decide to keep in contact by e-mail.
- Keep secret, password-protected Internet accounts, "just in case," or become incensed if your partner inadvertently glances at your "private things."

"But the chemicals don't last, and then we learn how difficult it is to remain attached to a partner in a meaningful way," points out Connecticut psychologist Janis Abrahams Spring, author of *After the Affair*.

Blasts from the Past

People may be exceptionally vulnerable to affairs when they reconnect with someone from their past, for whom they may have long harbored feelings. "It's very common online," says Vaughan. "You go on the Internet, and the first thing you say to yourself is, 'What happened to so and so?' Then you go find them."

Lorraine and Sam had been high school friends during the Sixties, and even camped out together at Woodstock in 1969. In love with Sam but "awed by his brilliance," Lorraine remained too shy to confess. Then he went off to the University of Chicago while she stayed in New Jersey. She married and had a family, but the idea of Sam still smoldered: If only she had admitted her love!

One day she Googled him and located him in Chicago—and they began to correspond by e-mail. He was a partner in a law firm, had a physician wife and coached his daughter's Little League team. "Originally I e-mailed just to say, 'hi,'" she explains. But after a few friendly notes, Sam sent a confession. He'd always been in love with her. But her beauty had daunted

Inoculating Your Relationship

The biggest mistake couples make is taking monogamy for granted. Instead, they should take affairs for granted and protect themselves by heading infidelity off at the pass.

As part of a proactive approach, psychologist Barry McCarthy suggests couples discuss the importance of fidelity from the outset, identifying the type of situation that would put each at greatest risk. Is drinking on a business trip your downfall, or the novelty of an exotic individual from a far-off locale? Whatever your weakness, work together to make sure you help each other walk past it.

As for Internet relationships, Peggy Vaughan says the safest way to protect the primary relationship is to "make sure that no online interactions are secret. This means having your partner agree that neither of you will say anything to someone online that you aren't willing for the other one to read. If they resist and invoke privacy rights," she adds, "it is probably because they already have something to hide."

Miami Beach psychologist M. Gary Neuman recommends that in addition to setting limits, you actively build the bond with your partner every day. Among the protective strategies he suggests are exchanging "five daily touch points," or emotional strokes, ranging from bringing your partner a cup of tea to a kiss and hug. He also suggests that partners talk for 40 minutes, uninterrupted, four times a week and go on a weekly date. "It's so easy," Neuman says, "to forget why we fell in love." — MT

him, so he'd settled for a plain, practical woman—his wife—instead. E-mails and then phone calls between Lorraine and Sam soon became constant, whipping both of them into a frenzy of heat and remorse. "I can't stop thinking about you. I'm obsessed," one of Sam's e-mails said. But Sam could never get away, never meet face-to-face. "I feel so guilty," he confessed.

That's when Lorraine stopped sending e-mails or taking his calls. "He was a coward," she says, adding that he disappointed her even more by "begging to continue the affair over the phone."

What kind of person chooses to remain immersed in fantasy? It could be someone who "compartmentalizes the two relationships," psychologist Janis Abrahms Spring suggests. "The person may not want to replace the marriage partner, but may want that extra high."

A woman may languish for years in the throes of her "special friendship," while her male counterpart considers it a nice addition to his life.

Women in Love

Frank Pittman, author of *Private Lies*, says that Lorraine lucked out. If she's like most of those involved in Internet affairs, "the face-to-face meeting would have killed it." And if she'd run off with Sam, it probably would have been far worse. "In the history of these crazy romantic affairs, when people throw everything away for a fantasy, the success rate of the new relationship is very low," he explains.

But Lorraine was just acting true to her gender. It is the woman who typically pushes the relationship from friendship to love, from virtual to actual, says Pittman. It's the woman who gets so emotionally involved she sees the affair as a possible replacement for her marriage—even if her marriage is good—and wants to test that out.

American University professor of psychology and affair expert Barry McCarthy explains that for men, "most affairs are high opportunity and low involvement. For women, an affair is more emotional. President Clinton and Monica Lewinsky are the prototypes," he says.

How does this translate to emotional infidelity, where opportunity may be thwarted but emotion reigns supreme? Some men have begun following female patterns, placing more emphasis on emotion than in the past, while women are increasingly open to sex, especially as they achieve more financial independence and have less to fear from divorce.

Even so, says Peggy Vaughan, women are usually far more involved in these relationships than men. A woman may I anguish for years in the throes of her "special friendship," while her male counterpart considers it a nice addition to the life he already has. As a result, men and women involved in emotional dalliances often see the same affair in different ways. The woman will see her soul mate, and the man will be having fun. Sometimes, says Ben-Ze'ev, a woman will feel totally invested in an affair, but her partner will be conducting two or even four such affairs at once. (The pattern holds for consummated affairs, too.)

For women, the dangers are great. When an emotional affair results in sex, the man's interest usually cools instantly, says Pittman. Meanwhile, husbands are less forgiving than wives, making it more likely for a woman caught up in such an entanglement to be slammed with divorce.

Total Transparency?

With easy access to emotional relationships so powerful they pass for love, how can we keep our primary relationships intact? Psychotherapist M. Gary Neuman of Miami Beach, author of *Emotional Infidelity*, draws a hard line, advocating a rigorous affair-avoidance strategy that includes such strictures as refusing to dance or even eat lunch with a member of the opposite sex. Vaughan suggests we put transparency in our Web dealings—no secret e-mail accounts or correspondence a partner wouldn't be welcome to see.

Others say such prescriptives may be extreme. "Some Internet relationships are playful," Turkle comments. "People may take on different identities or express different aspects of self; an introvert can play at extroversion, a man at being a woman." The

After Infidelity: The Road Back

An emotional affair can deliver a body blow to a marriage, but it rarely results in divorce. Instead, couples can navigate recovery to make their union stronger than before.

The first step in recovery, says psychologist Barry McCarthy, is honesty. "It is secrecy that enables affairs to thrive. The cover-up, for most people, is worse than the actual infidelity," he says. "So it's only by putting everything on the table that you'll be able to move on."

"The involved partner must be honest about all aspects of the affair," says author Peggy Vaughan. Moving on too fast usually backfires, leaving the injured party reeling and the problem unresolved. "Many people believe that too much discussion just reopens the wound; but, in fact, the wound needs to be exposed to the light of day so that it can heal." The involved partner must answer questions and soothe the injured partner for as long as that person needs.

Psychologist Janis Abrahms Spring says the ultimate goal is restoring trust and suggests couples make a list of the trust-enhancing behaviors that will help them heal. Both partners may need compassion for their feelings, she says, but "the hurt partner shoulders a disproportionate share of the burden of recovery and may require some sacrificial gifts to redress the injury caused." These may range from a request that the unfaithful partner change jobs to avoid contact with the "special friend" to access to that partner's e-mail account.

McCarthy, meanwhile, emphasizes that sexual intimacy should resume as soon as possible, as part of the effort to restore closeness and trust.

"In the course of an emotional affair, you open the window to your affair partner and wall off your spouse," McCarthy says. "To repair the marriage, you must open your windows to your partner and wall off the affair." *—MT*

experience may be transformative or casual. "Someone may want just a chess partner, and the technology allows for that."

But if you're going to permit some leeway in the context of your marriage, where do you draw the line? "It's a slippery slope," says Ben-Ze'ev. "You may set limits with your spouse—no phone contact, don't take it off the screen. But people can break the deal. It is a profound human characteristic that sometimes we cross the line."

At best, notes Turkle, a serious emotional affair can alert you to problems in the primary relationship. The injured partner can view it as "a wake-up call" that needs are not being met.

It was perhaps no more than the glimmer of that alarm that enabled Brendan and Lauren to navigate back home. For both, that happened when fantasy clashed with reality—especially when they needed to pull together and care for their sick son. Brendan told Lauren he wanted to take some time to "visit his dad," when his intent was to see his old girlfriend. "I'm so exhausted. Please don't go," Lauren had said, finally asking for help. Using the excuse of a book deadline, she soon began answering e-mails from her online partner only sporadically, then hardly at all.

The illicit partner is always partly a fantasy, she or he is inevitable seen as wittier, warmer and sexier than the spouse.

What had caused them to pull back? On one level it was the need to care for their child, but on another, it was the realization that their online affairs had been a diversion from intimacy, not intimacy itself.

"The idea of actually meeting made me feel ill. I was relieved when Lauren asked me to help at home," Brendan confesses.

"There was so much about my life I never discussed in those e-mails," says Lauren. "In the end, all that witty, arch banter was just a persona, and another job."

MARK TEICH is publications manager of the Skin Cancer Foundation.

For Better or Worse: Couples Confront Unemployment

When the pink slip arrives, it signals changes not only in employment, but also in a marriage.

MARILYN GARDNER
Staff writer of The Christian Science Monitor

SOMETIMES IT'S BEST not to count certain things.

Just ask Marilyn and Tom Middleton. They no longer tally the number of times he's been laid off when companies have merged, restructured, or failed. Nor do they keep precise track of the job-related moves they've made—15? 16?

They're not even sure how many years they've spent working in separate cities, commuting to see each other on weekends. She thinks it's about seven. He guesses closer to 10.

What they do know with certainty is that the job losses, moves, and separate addresses have strained their marriage almost to the breaking point at times. Like many couples dealing with unemployment, they have struggled with economic and emotional challenges. They even went through bankruptcy.

"Our marriage has had such incredible highs and lows," says Mrs. Middleton. "But we've hung in there. Now we're enjoying some of the good things."

"Hanging in there" is a skill more couples are honing these days as joblessness rises. More than three-quarters of unemployed Americans say family stress has increased since they lost their job, according to a new study by the National Employment Law Project.

Last month the unemployment rate rose to 6 percent—an eight-year high. In the past three months alone, more than half a million jobs have disappeared. Nearly 2 million people have been searching for at least six months.

In the first rush of pink-slip blues, a couple's concern is typically financial: how to keep the family afloat. As they settle into routines involving résumés, interviews, and rejections, other challenges may test a marriage.

"Work is so important to men in particular that when they lose that, they lose a pretty important part of their life. It affects relationships," says Larry Flaccus of Lexington, Mass., founder of a job-search group for executives called WeWantWork-Boston.com.

'How Many Résumés Did You Send?'

At work, he explains, people get positive feedback. But during unemployment, feedback may be negative.

"It's critical for the spouse to fill in some of the feedback that might be missing and say, 'I still love you,'" Mr. Flaccus says. "But it's also difficult for them." Almost no support groups exist to let spouses talk about unemployment issues.

Those issues can include loneliness, a lack of communication, changes in the balance of power, housework, too much togetherness, and not enough money.

When the Middletons exchanged wedding vows in 1970, the promise to stay together "for richer, for poorer; for better, for worse" seemed easy enough to make. Love conquers all, right?

That's the fairy-tale version. What they hadn't counted on was unemployment. In 1987, the company where Mr. Middleton worked merged with another company and laid off 95 percent of its staff. The couple had just bought a "dream house," and their two daughters were attending private school.

"It was devastating," he says. "You ask yourself, How am I going to provide for my family, a role I take very seriously?"

His wife remembers it as "a really rough time for us as a couple. You just don't think anything like that can ever happen to you."

For nine months Mr. Middleton looked for work. Eventually, they began an odyssey that took them from Toledo to a job in Colorado Springs. But that job disappeared before the moving van arrived from Toledo. Desperate, Mr. Middleton, a health-insurance executive, drove a taxi in Colorado Springs, while his wife worked two jobs at the mall. "We were barely making it," she says.

Family Involvement

At one low point, the couple separated. But her father intervened, she recalls. "He told Tom to get his act together. He

Job Loss Is a Family Affair

By Judy Lowe

Some years ago, when experts began saying that wage earners would probably be employed by a number of different companies in their lifetimes, I wondered just how that would work.

The predictions were right: Rarely these days do people stay with the same company their whole careers. But my apprehensions were correct, too. No one explained—or planned for—a process by which someone could easily change professions several times.

Now we know that working for multiple companies and reinventing our careers often involves stretches of unemployment. And that can be demoralizing not just for the former job holder but also for the spouse.

When my husband's job was in peril through downsizing, and again when it ended, our marriage went through plenty of ups and downs.

Some of his fellow employees got divorces. I've often wondered what made the difference for us. Several things stand out, although they wouldn't necessarily be the same for others. We had always been used to discussing and sharing every aspect of our lives, including finances. How to allocate funds became a real problem for husbands and wives we knew who were used to keeping their earnings separate.

We have found, as did the couples Marilyn Gardner interviewed, that the lessons we learned during that period continue to strengthen our marriage. But if given a choice, I would rather have learned them some other way.

• *E-mail the Homefront at* **home@csps.com**.

came to me and said, 'You have no business leaving.' I was mad at him for several years. But we took his advice to heart and were grateful."

Still, challenges—and moves—continued. A business partnership failed. Their daughters faced serious problems, and Mr. Middleton dealt with major illness.

How did the couple manage? Mrs. Middleton began a career as a foster-care therapist, which provided essential income. Their families and close friends gave emotional support. Their church and their faith also sustained them.

In one moment of despair, Mrs. Middleton remembers looking out the window and thinking, "You are going to make a commitment to go through this, and in the process you're going to learn to be joyful and content." She adds, "I've learned that that is not based on my husband."

Later she started a "gratitude journal," each day listing something she was thankful for.

Efforts like these paid off. After their earlier rocky patches, Mr. Middleton now calls his wife his "biggest cheerleader," explaining that she constantly reassured him that everything would be all right.

Now they are optimistic about a new chapter. Last month they moved from San Antonio to Baltimore, where he took up an executive position. They hope this job will take them to retirement.

When the Wife Is Unemployed

For working women, unemployment brings many of the same challenges, with an added factor: domestic responsibilities. Lucille Wilson of Waltham, Mass., a software developer, was laid off 19 months ago. She has 3-year-old twins and a husband she describes as "wonderful."

Yet household tasks intrude. "Now that I have 'so much free time,' I'm given all these other jobs that need to be done," says Mrs. Wilson, who, like others in this story, was interviewed by phone. "How am I supposed to look for a job, keep my skills up, clean the house, and do all the other things on the 'honey-do' list?"

Housework also becomes an issue when a man is jobless. Monica Leahy of Los Angeles avoids asking her unemployed husband to cook or clean, even though she works full time.

"He's going through such a tough period," she says. "To add this would be much more of a burden on him than it is on me." At the same time, she appreciates the help he gives. "He has done the dishes without me asking. He's helped with the laundry. He's kept the apartment very clean."

Then there is the essential issue of communication. At a time when couples need to air concerns and consider solutions, an out-of-work husband may become defensive or silent, while a wife may pepper him with too many questions. Mrs. Leahy emphasizes the importance of avoiding an interrogating tone.

Honest Communication

Her husband, she says, "was appreciative that I wasn't badgering him each day or asking him, 'Did anyone call? Do you have any interviews?' If he does, he'll let me know. I know how hard he works to find a job. I would never question that."

In the networking groups Flaccus leads, members complain about pressure at home. "Spouses say, 'Why don't you just go get a job?' There seems to be a difficulty in understanding that when there are no jobs available, you can't just go get a job."

Communication is a two-way street, of course. "You have to be able to vent your feelings, telling him once in a while, 'I'm scared, I'm upset,'" says Donna Birkel of Winston-Salem, N.C., whose husband, Damian, has been out of work twice.

Mr. Birkel, now the author of "Career Bounce-Back!" suggests that couples meet weekly to update their situation, rather than face daily grilling. He also urges them to focus on abundance wherever they can, instead of scarcity.

Sometimes dual-career couples find themselves sending résumés and reading want ads at the same time. A couple in Lee, N.H., who wish to be identified only as Elizabeth and Patrick, lost their jobs in quality assurance at separate companies a year and a half ago. Now both are "totally reinventing" themselves, trying to start new businesses.

With three children, money is tight. "Sometimes we sit there and think, 'If only you would find a job. Why aren't you looking for a job at this very moment?'" she says. "We don't say it, but that's the undercurrent."

To gain fresh perspectives, Elizabeth and others emphasize the value of getting out of the house regularly, enjoying free or low-cost activities. Cabin fever is not conducive to family harmony.

When Birkel was unemployed, he and his family went to the art museum on the day admission was free. They also enjoyed picnics and "one-tank" trips. The Middletons like to take walks and talk along the way. Elizabeth and Patrick often head for their networking group, which offers a change of scenery and a welcome upbeat mood.

"Trying to stay positive is really key," Elizabeth says. "If you can find people to help you stay positive, it's important."

No one pretends that staying positive is easy. But Susan and Larry Flaccus, who have been married 32 years, find that a long-term perspective helps.

"There have been better times, and you know there will be better times again," Mrs. Flaccus says. "You have faith that somehow, together, you'll work something out. Which is not to say that I don't have terrible days. It isn't easy, but it isn't all bad."

While her husband job-hunts in Boston, she runs the couple's bed and breakfast in Shelburne, Mass. She thinks the fact that her income is secondary makes her husband's unemployment easier. "He doesn't have the feeling, 'Oh, I'm not making the money, she's making the money.'"

NOW EMPLOYED: Billy Skinner was laid off from his job just before young Will was born, so Rachel had to return to work right away.

Young couples face different challenges. Two weeks before Rachel and Billy Skinner's baby was born in 2001, Mr. Skinner lost his job in public relations in Austin, Texas. Suddenly Mrs. Skinner's plan to take 12 weeks of maternity leave changed. To bring in needed income, she returned to work when their son, Will, was 6 weeks old.

"It was very difficult," he says. "My wife obviously felt torn, as most mothers do, about going back." Yet he praises her for being supportive and encouraging during his job search, which he describes as "a real roller coaster." At 28, he was competing with experienced 45-year-olds who were willing to take a big pay cut just to get a job.

Encouraging Words

For her part, Mrs. Skinner focused on "getting through each day in the most supportive way." She thought of positive things in their lives—their baby, their health, their abilities. And she reminded her husband that he is smart, confident, capable.

"Sitting home and being mean to each other isn't going to change the situation," she says.

The couple also received encouragement from their parents. "They were reminding us to love each other and continue supporting each other, and were reinforcing our abilities."

After Mr. Skinner was turned down by several employers, the couple theorized that having a job would help him get a job by imposing a routine. He took a minimum-wage post at the Gap.

"Going to my mall job and working with 18- and 20-year-olds put a lot of things in perspective for me."
—Billy Skinner of Austin, Texas, who was laid off from a public-relations job and temporarily took a minimum-wage position just to get back into the workforce.

"Going to my mall job and working with 18- and 20-year-olds put a lot of things in perspective for me," he says. He began interviewing for positions paying considerably less than the $50,000 he had been earning.

Eventually, he received two job offers. He now works as marketing director for an auto-leasing company in Austin.

Looking back, he reflects on how they made it. "There was lots of prayer from lots of people, and a lot of effort on my wife's part. We had to be cheerleaders for each other."

Humor, philosophy, and gratitude help couples live through unemployment. It's good to realize it's not the end of the world.

The experience has also given him a reminder: "All of us forget to be as thankful as we should be when things are good."

Humor helps couples get through jobless periods, too. "We joke about all the character-building experiences we've had," says Teri Nelsen of Fort Collins, Colo., a mother of four, explaining that her husband declared bankruptcy after a franchise failed.

She would tell him, "You're a good person, and we'll get through this." He is graduating this spring with a master's degree in family therapy, which is her field as well.

Other job-seeking families also grow philosophical. "It's a phase," Leahy says. "This isn't permanent. This, too, shall pass."

HAPPY DAYS: In the 32 years Marilyn and Tom Middleton have been married, they have seen many job-related ups and downs. These have strengthened their bonds.

Elizabeth looks at the larger picture, saying, "This isn't the end of the world, and it shouldn't be the end of the marriage either. Keep track of what's important. You didn't marry this person just to be rich. Marriage is hard work whether you're out of work or not."

As the Middletons settle into their latest home, she calls these the "gift years," their reward for staying together. In San

Antonio they even gave premarital seminars called Building a Solid Foundation at their church to help other couples avoid problems they faced.

"I would not for the world trade where we are as a couple," she says. "Is it perfect? No. Do I wish we could settle down?

Yes. Life hasn't gone the way I would have chosen, but I've been blessed. Tom tells me daily that he loves me and that he's glad I'm a part of his life. We feel that if we can make it, there are few people out there who can't."

Keeping Work and Life in Balance

Many organizations understand how critical it is to provide work-life balance for retaining employees, encouraging job satisfaction, and improving productivity. Flexibility will soon be business as usual rather than an employee perk. Learn how Lancaster Laboratories and Ernst & Young tailor their programs to meet employees' changing needs.

VICKI POWERS

Flexibility is not a working mother's issue as some people seem to think. Rather, it relates to "how and when work gets done and how careers are organized," according to the Families and Work Institute. Everyone has the need for flexibility in the workplace—whether it's to care for an elderly parent, take college classes, take a sick child to the doctor, or get a haircut. More and more, work is "interfering" (as some people would say) with life and is creating overscheduled, stressed people.

"Flexibility isn't going to be an option in the future," says Lois Backon, co-director of When Work Works, a Families and Work Institute project on workplace effectiveness and workplace flexibility. "It's just going to be the way good, competitive businesses operate." Fortunately, many large and small organizations have adopted and perfected innovative programs and opportunities that encourage employees to better balance their work days with their home and family life.

Lancaster Laboratories: Intergenerational

Young children and older adults smiling and laughing during "Show & Tell." Children blowing kisses to mom from the playground while she works in her office window. Parents sharing lunch with their kids in the middle of the workday. Those are some of the opportunities that Lancaster Laboratories offers its employees and their families through on-site, intergenerational child and adult daycare centers in Lancaster, Pennsylvania.

"Founder Earl Hess always believed that if you take care of your people, the bottom line will always take care of itself," says Margaret Stoltzfus, manager, human resources and safety, at Lancaster Laboratories. "He would often state that a decision he made with his heart was one of the best business decisions he ever made."

With annual sales of approximately US$50 million, Lancaster Laboratories—a provider of chemical and biological lab-

oratory services in the environmental and pharmaceutical industries—has grown since its beginnings in 1961, when Hess, his wife, and a technician started the company on the family farm with the Hess children right in the workplace. Even as the organization has grown to more than 700 employees, it still operates with a people-first approach.

By the mid-1980s, Lancaster Labs recognized a need for its young workforce, made up of more than 60 percent women. Twenty-five percent of its 100 employees surveyed at the time said they expected to start a family within five years. Lancaster realized that it needed to do something quickly to ensure retention of those employees and not risk losing the chemists and biologists it had relocated, employed, and trained. Employees expressed an interest in on-site child care, which at the time was pioneering and bold.

"Certainly, a lot of companies questioned what we were doing when we started [on-site child care], based on concerns about liability and keeping employees focused on work with their kids here," Stoltzfus says. "Those same companies several years later were calling us."

Lancaster Laboratories provided the space and partnered with an external provider that ran other child-care centers. Lancaster renovated the front part of its original building for the center and moved the president, vice president, and other administrative offices to another area. Lancaster Laboratories Child Care Center opened in August 1986, with a license for 29 children. Early on, the community filled most of the spots, but that gradually changed as employees started their own families. Stoltzfus says Lancaster Laboratories was the third company in the United States to provide on-site child care. Now, it offers a licensed program for 161 children from infants to school age, along with a full-day kindergarten program and summer daycare. Employees receive a discount averaging 25 percent. Lancaster Labs subsidizes the center each year and paid approximately $141,000 in cash and in-kind services in 2003.

Lancaster Laboratories made another pioneering decision, in the late 1980s, by surveying employees about the issue of adult daycare. Though there wasn't an immediate need, there was a planned need. With adult daycare, Stoltzfus notes, many people find out they need it and then that they need it immediately. Lancaster Generations Adult Day Care Center opened in late 1991, with space for up to 40 individuals. This center has served more of the community population enrollment rather than employees, but it is providing a necessary niche and partners with the child-care center in several activities and events. "It's neat for those in the adult daycare center because they look forward to the kids coming over," Stoltzfus says. "Their eyes light up when these kids come in and do activities with them. That's an unbelievable benefit for both."

Jill Wolgemuth, senior specialist in Lancaster's Environmental Client Services, believes the organization's generous and diverse employee benefits have given her family a level of comfort and confidence. Her son began on-site daycare at age two months, which gave her comfort knowing he was close by. Wolgemuth can work 30 hours a week and be considered "full-time," which lets her take advantage of benefits as well as have more "mommy" time. Says Wolgemuth, "Rather than feeling like I should be more 'ambitious,' the support makes me feel proud in my role as a mom and as an employee."

Stoltzfus says that the child-care/adult daycare centers go well beyond the people who want to start families or want care for their aging parents. The centers demonstrate the character of the company and make people want to work there. What's more, turnover is 8 percent company-wide, absenteeism is lower, and 96 percent of its new moms return to work in three months.

"For us, it has been terrific to get the caliber of people we're looking for and to get that retention," says Stoltzfus. "It's having happy and satisfied employees who are going to focus and work hard to get their jobs done because they appreciate what we do."

Lancaster has earned a spot on *Working Mother's* "Top 100 Companies for Working Mothers" list for 11 years.

Ernst & Young: Advancing Women

"Corporations that aren't already 'in the game' of actively working to recruit, advance, and retain women [employees] won't be able to catch their competitors who are," says Roslyn Duda, co-founder of CorporateHOPE, a Pennsylvania-based, genderspecific talent development and consulting business. "Those companies that heeded the warning signs and have made it a priority to develop their female talent are already reaping the rewards."

Studies—such as the 2004 Catalyst report, "The Bottom Line: Connecting Corporate Performance and Gender Diversity"—show a positive correlation between the increased number of women in senior leadership and bigger profits. Ernst & Young's strong efforts in developing and advancing women, as well as nurturing a culture of flexibility, have helped save the organization about $12 million annually by reducing turnover.

"We've never presented our work-life issues as women's issues," says Wendy Hirschberg, Ernst & Young's Americas Gender Strategy Leader. "They are issues for men and women, and flexibility is something everyone needs. It doesn't just ap-

Workplace Perks: Hot and Not

According to John Challenger, CEO, Challenger, Gray & Christmas, the Chicago-based "original outplacement firm," employee perks are beginning to reemerge. But today's perks, according to Challenger, are vastly different from those of the 1990s. "The perks that remain popular with employers *and* employees are those that help workers stay healthy, career focused, and financially stable," says Challenger. "Perhaps the most appreciated perks are those that help workers maintain work-life balance."

What's Hot	What's Not
Free shuttle rides	Leased automobiles
On-site fitness centers	Fully paid health benefits
Quiet rooms	Game rooms
Investment seminars	Pension plans
Event tickets	Cash bonuses
Extra day off around holidays	Three-month sabbaticals
Concierge services	Stock options
Matching charitable contributions	Matching 401(k)
Education assistance/ tuition reimbursement	Retiree benefits
Flexible scheduling	Bringing pets to work

www.challengergray.com

ply to working mothers, though it's critical for us to keep our women [here] so we can continue to diversify our leadership."

Ernst & Young, a New York-based professional services organization, provides a complete solution to help ensure advancement opportunities for women and that all employees achieve balance between their professional and personal lives. That includes providing flexibility to help employees navigate how, when, and where their work gets done. This strong commitment, begun in 1994, came straight from the chairman at the time, Phil Laskawy, who understood the value and diversity that women brought to the firm and wanted to keep their ideas and experience. Several issues resulted from the organization's high turnover among women: lost productivity, higher recruiting costs, disruptions in client service, and organizational knowledge loss. In response, Laskawy created the Gender Equity Task Force comprising business unit leaders and key partners. That group commissioned Catalyst, a New York-based nonprofit firm working to advance women in business, to study the female retention issue across Ernst & Young.

"The underlying issues that cause women to leave our firm—such as access to leadership, appreciation for life balance, the availability of role models and mentors —are, of course, people issues," said Laskawy in the "1998 Office for Retention Annual Report."

Laskawy put "people issues" as a priority and created the Office of Retention to address the challenges and specifically focus on retaining and advancing women. OFR, headed by Deborah

Holmes (whom Laskawy recruited from Catalyst), reported directly to Laskawy in 1996, and provided central support for locally owned efforts relating to gender and work-life issues. OFR evolved into the Center for the New Workforce in 2001, and continues to focus on implementing and supporting local change. Ernst & Young focuses on a variety of initiatives to support women's leadership development, including group and one-to-one mentoring for women pursuing partnership or leadership in the support ranks, mentoring for key women leaders by executive board members, an annual gathering of top women with key business leaders and executive management, women's forums, and 41 networks within Ernst & Young to raise women's stature in the business world, both inside and outside the organization.

Strategy focuses on initiatives that align with the firm's values, norms, and culture.

Leverage the power of partnership. Ernst & Young brought men into the process as champions for change around gender equity, which continues to be a strength of the organization's efforts to advance and retain women. "We've developed great rapport with our business leaders and learned a lot with them," Hirschberg says.

Create local focus and ownership. A key element in Ernst & Young's success is its annual goal-setting meetings between the Center for the New Workforce, top leadership in each business unit, and the local Gender Equity Task Force member. This gathering promotes discussion around the past year's progress and future goals regarding women's development and advancement in that location. Ernst & Young created a Balanced Scorecard that reveals enterprise-wide goals and the leaders accountable for each goal. Business units maintain their own scorecards with information and accountability at the business unit level.

Educate staff about the issues, reward contributions. Hirschberg says that Ernst & Young has initiated some innovative aspects around its Women's Leadership Conference that stand out from other organizations. One is including the reverse percentage of men at the event to put men in the minority in the same percentage that women represent in partnership as a whole.

"We've brought in interactive discussions between men and women and have been notably honest and very candid," says Hirschberg. "It breaks down a lot of myths of what people harbor as slight doubts about the reality of what 'flexible work arrangements' can mean."

To reward contributions, Ernst & Young created the Rosemarie Meschi Award in 1997, to honor men and women in the organization who are doing the most to create a level playing field for women.

Technology helps drive Ernst & Young's flexibility options through its Flexible Work Arrangement database. This Website has a variety of tools to help employees brainstorm and navigate how to complete their work in a flexible manner. One component features profiles of more than 700 employees who are actually using flexible work arrangements. People can look up those individuals from a specific region or practice area and find out how they negotiated a flexible arrangement.

Research from Families and Work Institute says that flexibility is linked to engagement, retention, job satisfaction, and employee well-being. Flexibility represents one ingredient to an effective workplace. The others are

- job autonomy
- learning opportunities
- decision-making involvement
- co-worker and supervisor support.

"I believe flexibility is a common-sense, obvious way to manage a lot of the changes that our culture has gone through," says Backon. "Flexibility needs to be more accepted by business and more understood that it's an option to offer employees that doesn't really cost anything but that companies can gain from. The data consistently shows that people with flexible options tend to be happier employees and give back to their companies."

Hirschberg believes that opening up conversations between leaders and their staffs is one of the greatest benefits of Ernst & Young's work-life efforts. That's one reason she favors the profiles in the Flexible Work Arrangement database, which puts people in touch with others directly to have real conversations about day-to-day challenges.

Ernst & Young's dedication to work-life integration has enabled it to create a variety of flexible work arrangements. More than 2300 (83 percent of that number are women) participate in a formal flexible work arrangement. As of July 2003, 44 people (43 women and one man) have been promoted to the level of partner, principal, or director while in a flexible working arrangement.

The strategic focus and efforts to advance and retain women have paid off, which is critical when women account for half of Ernst & Young's head count. Currently, women represent 16 percent of all partners, principals, and directors, a figure that has doubled since 1996. Women represent 25 percent of the partner promotion class. The presence of women in top executive management positions has increased from zero to 14.5 percent. Twenty percent of the Americas executive board are women, which is higher than the 12 percent average, according to Catalyst's recent study of corporate boards in the *Fortune* 500. Over the past three-year period, 84 percent of women professionals who took a maternity leave returned to work.

Ernst & Young is one of only five companies to appear five consecutive times on both *Fortune* and *Working Mother's* "Best Companies" lists.

"While there are still challenges ahead given the nature of our business, I think we've made some real headway making 'real life' feel different for our individual women—and our men, to some extent," says Hirschberg. "The more these things are acceptable for women, the more acceptable they become for men."

VICKI POWERS is a Houston-based freelance writer focusing on a variety of business issues, including knowledge management, information technology, and customer relationship management; vpowers@houston.rr.com.

Your Retirement

How to Land on Your Feet

Your golden-years lifestyle depends more and more on investing smarts, luck and timing. Time to understand the new risks, and develop a plan to deal with them.

JANE BRYANT QUINN

Steve Griggs was feeling flush. In a perfect, late-'90s bull-market moment, his investments reached $1.6 million, mostly from the Texas Instruments stock in his 401(k). High on his luck, he retired at 50 from his job as a TI manager—planning to have some fun, try new businesses and spend time with his ailing parents. Then . . . well, you know the rest. TI plunged from $84 a share to $23, sending Griggs back to work. He now teaches special education in a Houston school and saves half his $38,000 salary to rebuild his nest egg. Griggs likes his job, but says, "If I had to do it all over again, I probably would not have retired."

On his drive to school, Griggs might pass the Witkowskis, Kathleen, 61, and Ron, 53, tooling around town on their bikes. Retired for three years from technical jobs at Southwestern Bell, they garden, read, surf the Internet and practice their fox trot at a ballroom-dancing class. "We don't have to get up at 5 a.m. And we think nothing of staying up until 3 in the morning to watch a great movie," a gleeful Kathleen reports. Like Griggs, they invested their 401(k) entirely in company stock (SBC Communications), which is down a third in price. But they had a safety net: old-fashioned pensions, which they took as a lump-sum payout of $553,000. A financial planner diversified it into bonds and dividend-paying stocks to complement their cash savings and other income. Says Ron: "We're not worried at all."

Two early retirees, two similar plans, but outcomes that are poles apart. As the boomer generation leaves work, some surprising differences will emerge among people who think of themselves as pretty much alike. Some of you won't have saved enough (you know who you are!). But to a degree you may not be prepared for, your retirement standard of living will also be driven by timing, investment skills and luck. Call it the new "market based" retirement, with more winners and losers than before and a widening gap between them. The winners will enjoy good health, employer-paid pensions and health insurance, investment success and the skill to stretch their savings over a long lifetime. The losers will empty their bank accounts on medical bills, see their pensions slashed because their company failed, lose assets in divorce, retire from small companies that don't pay benefits or invest their retirement savings badly. If Social Security switches to private accounts, the gap will widen between those who make it and those who don't.

Earlier generations faced retirement risks, too, when companies failed or inflation struck. But collectively, the system strove to minimize uncertainty. In 1972, Congress raised Social Security benefits by 20 percent; two years later it passed ERISA, the law that put guarantees under shaky company pensions. Contrast that with the "ownership society" hailed today. Guaranteed pensions are on the decline in favor of investment accounts, such as 401(k)s. The age for claiming full Social Security benefits is going up, which translates into smaller checks for those who retire at 62. (Current full retirement age: 65 and 6 months, gradually rising to 67 for people born in 1960 or later.) Increasingly, boomers will be expected to live on whatever money they've saved themselves. Winners will step around the losers on the street.

Happily, you've gotten a good start. This generation is better prepared for retirement than their parents were. You're in better health, with more job opportunities and a substantially higher net worth ($239,000 at the median for people 55 to 64, says Zhu Xiao Di, a city planner with Harvard's Joint Center for Housing Studies).

But how well are you managing your money? The news is mixed. The Employee Benefit Research Institute (EBRI) recently surveyed people in the 64-to-74 age group, typically retired. During the prior 10 years, 52 percent saw their financial wealth grow by more than half. But 30 percent *lost* half or more of their wealth. Nearly 10 percent lost everything (mainly those with few assets). EBRI estimates that more than one third will eventually be wiped out. Part of the money went for medical bills or living expenses, but a substantial amount was lost in bad investments. A 401(k) can yield more than a traditional pension, but only if you play it right. Given control of our finances, half of us haven't a clue what to do.

Even if you're dumb about money, you might win one of life's lotteries—stock options, shares in a successful new company, a big inheritance (for "lucky sperm"). Conversely, money smarts can't protect you if your luck turns bad. Americans like to think that everyone makes his or her own fate. But some risks are out of our control, and you need to factor them into your retirement hopes. For example:

Health surprises. When Pat and Margaret Brickman, both 62, retired four years ago, medical bills were one of the last things on their minds. Then disaster struck. Pat, a former cop with the Miami-Dade police force, needed two heart bypass operations and suffered a stroke. While their medical bills climbed toward $250,000, the police union's insurance company, the National Public Employees Trust, sank into insolvency. Collection agents for doctors and hospitals called five and 10 times a day. Eventually, the county arranged for plan members to buy other insurance. The state settled some bills, and the Brickmans are chipping away on 18 others. When they retired, their planner told them they'd die before they could spend all their money. Now they've pared expenses and worry a lot.

Pension and benefit risks. Public employees' retirements are pretty safe. They leave their jobs with higher average pensions than other workers get, and taxpayers pick up any shortfalls in the plan. In the private sector, most traditional pensions are also guaranteed up to certain ceilings, but that's far from a total safety net. Just ask Karl Farmer, 56, an electrical engineer, who took a Polaroid buyout in late 2001. He was promised health benefits and six months of severance pay. Then Polaroid filed for bankruptcy and the benefits stopped. His Employee Stock Ownership Plan, worth nearly $250,000 at its peak, paid him just $300. He received a $200,000 lump-sum pension payout, but is chewing through it for living expenses, including $400 a month for health insurance. He'd planned to pay golf. Instead, he's a mechanic at Patriot Golf Course in Bedford, Mass., earning $14.60 an hour.

Outliving your resources. For 65-year-old men, life expectancy runs to 81. But do you really know what that means? Half of all men are likely to die before 81, while half live on, some to 100 or more. Life expectancy stretches to 84 for 65-year-old women, with half living longer than that. Over such lifetimes, savings run down, especially if they're meager to start with. Social Security's special value is that it lasts. If you're 65, entitled to $1,500 a month, and live 30 years with inflation at 3 percent, your total benefit is the equivalent of $352,808 today, in cash.

Having no husband. For women, "spouselessness" is tough. (For men, too, —but not as drastically.) Typically, a widow suffers a drop in income—losing her husband's Social Security benefit, as well as his portion of any joint pension they received. Single women often labor at mediocre wages, so they can't put a lot of money aside. Divorced women may have kids at home without enough support. Carole Engeman, 67, works at a small roofing company in Cleveland. She's happy there, which is lucky because she can't afford to retire. Two of her grown children live with her—a daughter in school (paying nominal rent) and a married son recently unemployed. "Kids sometimes need help," she says. "People like me do the best we can."

Retirement timing. You probably think that you can decide how long you'll work ("I'll work till I drop"). But exits often come upon us unawares. Nearly 40 percent of retirees left for reasons beyond their control—mainly, illness, disability or job loss (downsizing, plant closing, getting fired).

Investment luck. Good investing depends partly on using your common sense to diversify among U.S. and international stocks and bonds. But what if you have no common sense (or forget to practice it when stocks run up)? What if you blank on investing and turn to an adviser? A good one can save you; a bad one may wipe you out.

Skills aside, success also depends on market conditions in the few years right after you leave your job. If the markets move up, you can draw on the gains to pay your bills while leaving your capital intact. If the markets tank, your withdrawals will slice your nest egg even more—leaving you with less to build on when prices turn back up. Timing is all, and you're not in control.

When dealing with so much uncertainty, your best defense is having a pot of spare money on hand. Pat Brickman, the Miami cop, raised his automatic savings deduction to $200 from each biweekly check ($5,200 a year) when he was 51 and left it there until he retired at 58. Margaret worried that there wouldn't be enough left to pay the bills but, she says, "there always was." That's the magic of sliding money into savings before it hits your checking account. Your life somehow fits around the cash you have, even without budgeting. All the retirees NEWS-WEEK spoke with wished they'd started saving money earlier, even just $20 or $50 a week. If you haven't increased your IRA or 401(k) contributions lately, do it now.

After saving more money, here's how to prepare, for both the best and the worst:

> **Money smarts can't protect you if your life turns bad. Americans like to think that everyone makes his or her own fate. But some risks are simply out of our control.**

Pay off your house. Getting rid of the mortgage was "the first step, the acid test," Ron Witkowski says, because it showed that he and Kathleen had the discipline to save. Most of our interviewees lived in paid-up homes, and are glad of it.

They appear to be throwbacks. Mortgages are in style among retirees today. About 39 percent of people 65 to 75 are carrying loans against their homes, compared with only 28 percent in 1989, says Harvard's Zhu. Home values have soared, so even with higher loans, today's seniors possess more home-equity wealth than prior generations. But they also need higher retirement incomes to make their payments—one of the reasons more older people are working today. They're not locked in. If forced to retire, they could sell the house, pay off the loan and buy something smaller for cash (assuming they have enough equity left). In the end, however, income and asset security lie in a paid-up house, combined with a home-equity line to tap for emergencies.

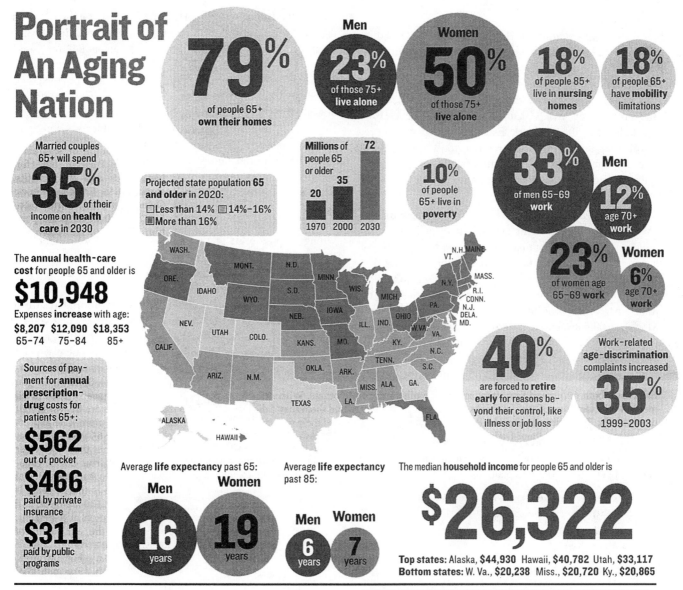

Portrait of An Aging Nation

79% of people 65+ **own their homes**

Men **23%** of those 75+ **live alone**

Women **50%** of those 75+ **live alone**

18% of people 85+ live in **nursing homes**

18% of people 65+ have **mobility** limitations

Married couples 65+ will spend **35%** of their income on **health care** in 2030

Projected state population **65 and older** in 2020:
☐ Less than 14% ☐ 14%–16% ■ More than 16%

Millions of people 65 or older
20 — 1970
35 — 2000
72 — 2030

10% of people 65+ live in **poverty**

33% of men 65–69 **work**

Men **12%** age 70+ **work**

23% of women age 65–69 **work**

Women **6%** age 70+ **work**

The **annual health-care cost** for people 65 and older is
$10,948
Expenses **increase** with age:
$8,207 — 65–74
$12,090 — 75–84
$18,353 — 85+

40% are forced to **retire early** for reasons beyond their control, like illness or job loss

Work-related **age-discrimination** complaints increased **35%** 1999–2003

Sources of payment for **annual prescription-drug** costs for patients 65+:
$562 out of pocket
$466 paid by private insurance
$311 paid by public programs

Average **life expectancy** past 65:
Men 16 years
Women 19 years

Average **life expectancy** past 85:
Men 6 years
Women 7 years

The median **household income** for people 65 and older is
$26,322
Top states: Alaska, $44,930 Hawaii, $40,782 Utah, $33,117
Bottom states: W. Va., $20,238 Miss., $20,720 Ky., $20,865

SOURCES: AARP, BUREAU OF LABOR STATISTICS, CDC, CENTERS FOR MEDICARE & MEDICAID SERVICES, CENTER FOR RETIREMENT RESEARCH, EMPLOYEE BENEFITS RESEARCH INSTITUTE, EQUAL EMPLOYMENT OPPORTUNITY COMMISSION, U.S. CENSUS

Work longer. The age you retire is your "primary portfolio decision," says economist Eugene Steuerle of the Urban Institute. The longer you work, the fewer assets you'll need, at any level of spending. An early departure requires bigger bucks.

Consider the Schroder brothers, who, like Karl Farmer, spend most of their retirement days on golf courses. Pat, 62, quit his TV ad-sales job five years ago, and plays almost daily. He built his current lifestyle on a $12,000 pension, $16,800 from Social Security, an Individual Retirement Account (IRA) now worth more than $1 million and a wife who earns "well into six figures." Meanwhile, Mark, 53, does maintenance work on a course while others golf. He quit a warehouse job at Procter & Gamble at just 46, with nearly $700,000 in P&G stock. His financial adviser diversified his money into other investments, which Mark thought would set him up for life. But his regular withdrawals, plus some poor stock choices (WorldCom, Cisco Systems), have slashed his

savings in half. What looked like a fortune actually wasn't enough. Mark's advice? "Work till you die."

Manage expenses. "Those who pitch their standard of living one degree below their means will be OK in the long run," says planner Matthew Kelley of Broomfield, Colo. "Overspenders have trouble retiring."

Manage your kids. "The retirement failures I've seen have almost always been related to overspending or to bailing out kids," says planner Kathleen Day of The Enrichment Group in Miami. Some parents support adult children who live better than they do. Some drain their savings for children with serious illnesses or problems with substance abuse (note to yourself: buy health insurance for any child who can't afford it). Some will back any business venture, even if it's a lousy idea, or pick up restaurant checks that the kids should be reaching for. "It's an ego thing," Day says. If your assets look too meager to retire on, take your children off the dole—and don't feel guilty about it. They'll get by.

Do a retirement calculation. Half of all workers 45 and up haven't even made a stab at figuring how much money they'll need when they retire, EBRI reports. That's a calculation you ought to make before reaching "company buyout age" (50-plus). Typically, those who do the math get a reality shock, and raise the amount they save. Calculators abound on the Web. A good, simple one: the Ballpark Estimate at www.asec.org. When projecting future investment returns, don't be tempted to bump up the numbers just to make the calculation look good. That's like seeing a shadow in your lungs and asking the doctor to touch up the X-rays.

Manage your assets to last for life. You thought saving was hard? Wait until you try to figure out how to make your money last for life. For success, nothing matters more than the rate at which you dip into your savings to cover your expenses. It's your key decision—far more important than how much you allocate to stocks or bonds. You're generally safe if you spend no more than 5 percent of your financial assets the first year you retire. After that, take just enough to cover each year's inflation—say, an additional 3 percent. If your investments lose value, take less (and postpone your vacation). Minneapolis planner Jerry Wade advises his clients to "stress test" their investments once a year, to see how long their money will last at various withdrawal rates.

For a free estimate of how much you can afford to spend from your savings every year, check out T. Rowe Price's online Retirement Income Calculator at troweprice.com. For $500, you can get a personally tailored plan.

See a planner. Beverly Glass, 65, a former chief news assistant for the Lexington, Ky., Herald-Leader, got a buyout offer four years ago. Her first thought? "Oh, goodie!" Her second: what did her accountant and longtime financial adviser think? They both told her she could afford it, which gave her the confidence to jump. With Social Security, pensions from the newspaper and her late husband, $130,000 in investments she doesn't have to touch, and new, blond highlights, she figures she's set. (There are always those pesky health risks, but that's what her untouched investments are for.)

Retirement preparation is my Number One reason for seeking advice. Find a planner who charges for his or her time (not one who sells products). Get a savings and spending projection, so you'll know where you are. Your planner should also show you, in numbers, what could happen if something went wrong—a possibility that do-it-yourselfers rarely consider, says Ray LeVitre of Net Worth Advisory Group in Salt Lake City. You don't have to plan for the worst, but it's helpful to know where it lies.

Who'll be the luckiest retirees? Those who underestimate their resources, says Miami planner Day. Then, when you lay out your options, you'll have fallback positions built in. And, on the upside, more possibilities than you thought. You can't control everything in this new market-based retirement world. But the more attention you pay to risk, the better your chance of winding up on the winning side.

With Temma Ehrenfeld; Ace Atkins; Jennifer Barrett Ozols; Pat Crowley; Le Datta Grimes; Nadine Joseph; Joan Raymond; Jamie Reno; Hilary Shenfeld; Ken Shulman and Catharine Skipp

Family

Home Alone

Single parents in the armed forces face some special problems as they ship out for the Gulf

ADAM PIORE

Master Sgt. Sue Harper stands in her kitchen clutching a drawer so tightly her knuckles turn white. Oblivious to the dinner chatter in her dining room, the rail-thin blonde with the ponytail and glasses presses a telephone to her ear. "Master Sergeant Harper, sir. I was told to check in every couple hours," she says. After a moment, she hears what she was hoping for. "Well, good! Thank you, sir." Harper hangs up, relieved. There will be no deployment to Turkey tonight. Instead, she can sleep at home in the same bed with her 12-year-old daughter, Maria, on the Kaiserslautern military base in Germany. From her smile, you'd think she won the lottery. But this simple reprieve is better than money. Harper is a single mom, and living alone with Maria has forged an unusually strong bond between mother and daughter. Saying goodbye is never easy; saying goodbye as she heads off to war is almost more than Harper can bear. "Every parent feels they are the only person who understands their kid and can do things for them," says Harper, 39, a public-affairs officer with the 21st Theater Support Command, a logistics unit. "I worry that other people just won't get her like I do." Then she asks the question that haunts her most: "What if I don't come back?"

These are lonely times for parents like Harper. Those familiar media images of husbands and wives bidding each other tearful farewells on docks and airfields tell only part of the story. According to the Pentagon, the number of single moms and dads in the military has nearly doubled since the last gulf war from 47,685 in 1992 to almost 90,000 today. Despite the dramatic increase, however, the Pentagon has no special programs in place for them. Military officials aren't even sure why the numbers are up. "That's not something we could speculate on," says Lt. Col. Cynthia Colin, a Pentagon spokeswoman. "We recruit people, and the people in the military reflect society."

While there are no hard data to explain the jump, it's clear that jobs in today's much smaller forces are more demanding than in the past. Between 1992 and 2002, the military shrank from about 1.8 million to 1.4 million active-service members;

those who remain have seen their burdens increase. "Certainly, frequent deployments and long separations are challenging for marriages," says Shelley MacDermid, a professor and co-director of the Military Family Research Institute at Purdue University. "One hypothesis is that as the tempo has gone up, it's been harder to stay married."

The prospect of war brings parents agonizing choices. Perhaps the most difficult of them all: what to do with your children while you're gone?

Raising a child in the military—moving from base to base, surviving on a paltry government salary—has never been easy. But life as a single military parent these days poses special challenges. The prospect of war brings agonizing choices: How to explain to your child the need to leave? How much to reveal about the danger ahead? Perhaps most difficult of all: What to do with your kids while you're gone?

FAMILY MATTERS: Sgt. Gatson sent her sons, Cori and Dashon, to stay with her ex-husband, Elton, in Louisiana

For Sgt. Shala Gatson, 24, also stationed in Germany, the solution lay about 5,000 miles away. In January, Gatson delivered her two young sons, Cori, 7, and Dashon, 5, to her ex-husband (and Dashon's father), Elton, in Alexandria, La. Because the Army doesn't pay the cost of flying children back to the United States, Gatson, a supply specialist also with the 21st who makes roughly $2,000 a month, had to borrow from friends to come up with the $800 airfare. During the all-too-brief time with his mother in Louisiana, Dashon one day nonchalantly asked, "Mama, are you going to die?" "No," she told him. "I'm going to do my best to come back. Mommy has to go and protect the other people from the bad guys. Mommy is going to go work on computers." After she left, the boys struggled to adjust. They were happy to be spending time with Elton, but their mother was ever in their thoughts. "My mama is fighting a war," Cori told his teacher one day, "and after the war we're all going back to Germany."

Harper chose to bring a friend from Arkansas to Germany to care for Maria. Theresa Snuffer, or "Ms. Theresa," is a silver-haired former stay-at-home mom whose husband served five tours in Vietnam. She understands the needs of children like Maria. "I don't think a kid should be uprooted," says Snuffer, who arrived in Europe last month. "It's OK for summer vacation. But during the school year, they should be around their own things." In addition to a tight-knit group of military neighbors to help Snuffer look after Maria, there is a school staff experienced in handling deployments. In recent weeks counselors at Kaiserslautern Middle School have been gathering the names of students whose parents are deploying. They will be watching for several telltale signs. "Some children start acting out," says counselor Harriet Scofield. "We often see grades falling, uncompleted homework. Other children will start having problems with peers, picking arguments."

Ironically, the increase in the number of single parents in the military may be in part the result of recent Pentagon successes. In 1989, Congress created a new network of mostly five-day-a-week child-care centers for parents in the military, and offered subsidies based on family income. The moves made the military a more viable career option for all parents, singles and couples alike. Still, there are gaps. Child care is usually available only weekdays from 9 to 5 and soldiers are fined if they are late picking up their kids. More broadly, no consideration is given to the special needs of single parents. "We have a lot of different people in different situations," says the Pentagon's Colin. Providing more assistance for single parents being sent to the Gulf is "really not feasible," Colin says. "It would just be way too much work. Each situation is different, depending on where you are stationed and what your situation is. Some people might live near a grandparent. Others may live in another country."

While they were still together in Germany, Sue and Maria made the best of it. Maintaining the ordinariness of life, the little daily rituals, seemed to bring the most comfort. There were dinners at their favorite restaurant, Alt Landstuhl, where waitresses still wear traditional German costumes, and where Maria and her mother like to order "the grossest things" on the menu. "That's how I fell in love with snails," says Maria. In those precious final days, special events took on new meaning. In an auditorium festooned with balloons, men and women in camouflage sat among students for an awards ceremony that was likely to be the last school event many of the parents would attend for a long time. Maria was called to the stage three times: for good citizenship, for making the honor roll and, most important, for winning the school competition in the National Geographic Geography Bee. She received a medal on a ribbon and placed it squarely over her mother's shoulders. Sue won't be able to attend the regional finals, to be held this month. But for a little while, at least, things were as they should be. Mother and daughter shared a moment of celebration together, and Iraq and the looming thunder of war seemed far, far away.

Gatson and Harper finally shipped out to Turkey the last week of February. It was easier for Gatson—by the time she left, she could barely stand the sight of her sons' rooms. "The house is so empty," she said. "Nobody fussing, nobody coming in and saying, 'How you doing?'" Harper found it difficult. Every morning before school, she said a tearful goodbye, never knowing if she would be there when Maria came home. Finally early one morning a little past 4 a.m., Harper kissed her sleepy daughter and slipped away.

With ARIAN CAMPO-FLORES

Terrorism, Trauma, and Children: What Can We Do?

LINDA GOLDMAN

"I never knew grief could feel so much like fear."
—C. S. LEWIS

On September 11, 2001, our children, either directly or vicariously, witnessed the terrorist assault upon our nation, watching over and over again as fanatics crashed American planes into the World Trade Center, the Pentagon, and the fields of Pennsylvania. Our young people witnessed adults running frantically out of control, jumping blindly out of windows, screaming, crying, and appearing bewildered—through black smoke-filled skies and burning buildings—as an insidious and non-locatable enemy emerged to wreak pandemonium and panic upon their lives. The media acted as a surrogate parent and extended family *before* this horrific event, and shared with our children *during* this event visually, aurally, and viscerally. These were sounds and images so graphic that they will forever be imprinted upon their psyche and ours. This unprecedented horror is now a traumatic overlay, potentially triggering all of the pre-existing grief-related issues that our children were carrying before September 11.

Death-related tragedies involving suicide, homicide, and AIDS, and non-death-related traumas such as bullying and victimization, divorce and separation, foster care and abandonment, violence and abuse, drugs and alcohol, and sexuality and gender identification had left many youth living their lives with overwhelmed feelings and distracted thoughts. After September 11, these issues still prevail, infused with the paradigm of terrorism, war, biological destruction, and nuclear annihilation—ideas that are entirely new for our children, for whom "war" is part of a history lesson. In the adult world our children look to for security and comfort, they now see or sense a world of terror, panic, and anxiety, with too many questions and too few answers about their future.

Children processing their grief and trauma may not necessarily progress in a linear way through typical grief phases. The four phases of grief are shock and disbelief, searching and yearning, disorganization and despair, and rebuilding and healing (*Life and Loss,* 2002). These phases may surface and resurface in varying order, intensity, and duration. Grief and trauma work can be messy, with waves of feelings and thoughts flowing through children when they least expect them to come. Kids can be unsuspectingly hit with "grief and trauma bullets" in the car listening to a song or the news, seeing or hearing an airplane overhead, or watching the video of the New York devastation or the Pentagon crash. A fireman's siren, a jet fighter, a soldier in military uniform, a letter in the mailbox, or a balloon bursting can trigger sudden intense feelings without any warning.

Children's Voices

Children's reactions to terrorism, war, anthrax, and the perceived loss of safety and protection provide a window into their psyches and help suggest ways the adults around them can help. Our ability to listen to questions, thoughts, and feelings is paramount in creating a safe zone for our children to process these life-changing times.

Children normally assume they live in a friendly, safe, and caring world. The terrorist attacks of September 11 amplified the pre-existing signs that their world is unprotected, scary, and contains an uncertain future. This deepened loss of the assumptive world of safety for our children creates a new set of voices that all parents, educators, and health professionals must heed.

Five-year-old Tommy, after sitting and listening to his Mom's careful explanation about the terrorist attack, explained why he was really upset about the terrorism: "This is a real tragedy, because I kept searching and searching all day and couldn't find any of my cartoons on TV."

Talking to Children About Terrorism, Trauma, and War

One question weighing heavily on the minds of parents, educators, and mental health professionals is "How do we talk to our children about war, terrorism, prejudice, biochemical attack, and nuclear destruction?"

Sometimes it may help to ask children if they have been "thinking about world events" and if they are, open a dialogue. Some children don't want to talk about it. Some live in fear they will be killed, others say there is nothing to worry about. Some may want to know the facts; therefore we need to choose words

"If the terrorists can crash into the World Trade Centers and the Pentagon, they can crash into a regular house like mine!"

Darian, age 6, illustrates his fear for his own safety after September 11.

that will help them understand what is happening around them. Because so many of us feel "it's just too big," we need to be able to discuss each piece of this huge experience a little at a time. The following are examples of definitions helpful to initiate dialogue with children.

Terrorism is an act or acts of violence, abuse, murder, or devastation against unsuspecting people and countries by a person or group of people that believe their cause is more important than human life or property. Their feeling of "being right" is sometimes more important to them than their own lives. Terrorists can be big or small, black or white, or any color, American or foreign. Their goal is to create terror, disruption, and vulnerability.

Trauma is an experience that can be scary and difficult. It may create feelings of fear, anger, rage, and revenge. A trauma can be a death of someone close to use, caused by a car accident or a terrorist bombing. It can also be from knowing something scary that happened on TV, or to someone we know, or even to a stranger we see on a news video.

Creating Dialogues

When creating dialogues with children, use accurate, real, and age-appropriate language, avoiding clichés or denial of their experience. Concentrate on giving the facts, and keep responses to questions simple and age-appropriate. This helps adults follow the lead of children as to how much information they choose to

take in. Especially with young children, minimize the scope of the tragedy, without contemplating with them what did or may happen.

Keeping explanations developmentally appropriate allows children to process this experience at their own level. Young elementary school children need simple information balanced with reassurance that trustworthy adults are bringing stability to their day-to-day life. Middle school children may seek out more facts and want to know more about what is being done to keep them safe and healthy at home, school, and in the community. High school students may outspokenly voice opinions about what happened and why, and may need to develop ways to combat terrorism, rationalize war, and prevent world annihilation. (Adapted from National Association of School Psychologists, NASP, www.nasponline.org.)

Telling children the truth in an age-appropriate way is very important. They often have a conscious or unconscious knowledge of events happening around them and can sense the impact of the terrorist trauma on the adult world. One mom shared just such an experience in the car with her four-year-old son, Andy. She was "sneaking" a listen to the news on the day of the attack. As the reporter began talking about the destruction of the World Trade Center, she quickly turned it off so Andy couldn't hear. Andy immediately explained his level of awareness: "Mommy, they are talking about the plane crash that blew up buildings today."

He just knew about it. If Andy had then been told his experience wasn't real, he may have begun to doubt himself and/or the adult world and question his mother's truthfulness. If Andy felt his mom was hiding the truth about what happened, he might worry more, thinking his mom was too afraid to tell him what really happened. Either way, Andy may have another loss—the loss of the trust in the adult world. Teachable moments for all children can evolve with teachers and parents on subjects such as bullying, violence, prejudice, sexual discrimination, and conflict resolution.

It's OK to let children know you are upset and worried too. Using mature modeling of this upset and worry can create examples for children to follow. It's often hard for them to reconcile a message of "Don't worry; everything is fine" with the enormity of anxiety they may feel coming from the adult world. Find out what they may know about the traumatic event, remembering that they may process what they see and hear inaccurately. Search for faulty perceptions and replace these with simple truths. Young children usually worry about their immediate environment, their family and friends and pets, and their ongoing day-to-day routine. Kids may worry something will happen to their dog, their home, or their friend.

Prepare Children for Dialogue

Reassure children that what they are feeling is very common. Emphasize to them that adults are feeling the same things that they are. Remind them that everyone has different ways of showing their feelings and that is OK. Restore confidence by reassuring them that problems are being handled, people who were hurt are being cared for, buildings are being cleared, and that things are getting a little better each day.

Helping our children grieve can only help the grieving child in each one of us.

Mature modeling guides children to create responsible ways to be helpful during the crisis. Emphasize ways that adults can help. Parents can volunteer to give blood, food, time, and money. Relief agencies such as the Red Cross issued appeals for help. Contributions of needed goods and family money can be taken to needy areas. Children can be included in planning ways families can help and joining in delivering food and clothing. Families and schools may want to join together in saying a prayer for the victims that were attacked, for their families, and for world leaders to bring about peace.

Accept Children's Reactions

While there are several commonly seen reactions to trauma in children, these reactions range widely. Some children will listen to your explanation and then go out to play. Others will want to stay near you and talk about it for a length of time, or maybe ask you to drive them to school instead of taking the bus. Still others may be angry that adults can't immediately fix the problem.

Children can use many activities to safely tell their story. Props like firefighter and police hats, doctor kits, toy soldiers, and hand puppets can be used to reenact the tragedy and war. Toys, puppets, art, clay modeling, collage, letter writing, journaling, and other projective play can be used for role-play and expression of emotions. Positive visualizations and breathing exercises can help kids to relax.

Activities to Help Children Participate in World Events

Children can create rituals that allow commemoration and avenues to voice feelings. Lighting candles, planting flowers, writing letters, raising money for victims, or saying prayers for survivors or world peace allow children to be recognized mourners. Thirteen-year-old Helen lived in a New Jersey community where many families, especially those of firefighters and police, had been deeply affected by the World Trade Center disaster. "Let's make brownies," she told her younger brother and sister, "and sell them to raise money for the firefighters. Everybody likes brownies."

Communities can involve children in participating in fundraisers for the survivors of terrorist attacks. Making patriotic pins and selling them to raise money to help victims and survivors, creating Web sites for world peace, or having a poster contest at school on "What We Can Do to Feel Safe" are ways to give children back a sense of control and participation in their own lives.

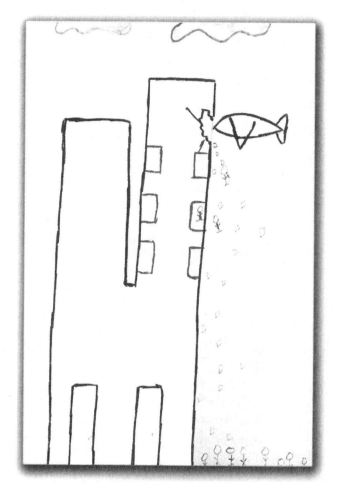

With this recreation of the World Trade Center destruction, 13-year-old Tiara illustrates her grief over the horrific footage she viewed on TV.

What Kids Can Do About Terrorism

1. Talk about their feelings. Allow children ways to tell their story as much as they need to. Draw pictures, create poems, write letters, or offer suggestions about ways to help.

2. Make a fear box. Cut out pictures from newspapers and magazines about what frightens them and paste these around the box. Write down their fears and put them inside.

3. Create a worry list. Make a list of worries from 1 to 5; number 1 is the biggest. Suggest that children talk about this list with someone they trust, like their mom or dad, their sister or brother, their guidance counselor, or a good friend.

4. Put together a "peaceful box." Ask kids to find toys, stuffed animals, and pictures that make them feel safe and peaceful, and keep these items in the box.

5. Help others. Help boys and girls give food or clothing to people who need it. Suggest that the family donate money to a good cause, like the Red Cross, the fund for victims and survivors of terrorist action, or the children in Afghanistan.

6. Display an American flag and create an original global flag. Children can place these flags together outside their house to remind everyone of their support for their country and their hope for world peace.
7. As a family, say a nightly prayer and light a candle for world peace.

Helping Our Children Grieve

We are now a nation and a world of grieving, traumatized children, and the terror of bullying lives inside most of us on this planet and threateningly looms over our everyday life. Our children fear terrorism from foreign strangers and bullying from well-known classmates, siblings, and adult figures. If we can help our kids to see the relationship between terrorist attacks, bullying behaviors, and issues of power and control, we can begin rooting out the behaviors that create oppression, prejudice, misguided rage, and destruction of people and property as a justification for a cause or self-serving purpose.

Responsible adults need to help children cope with trauma and loss and grief from the terrorists outside their country and the bullying within their homes, schools, and community. Providing information, understanding, and skills on these essential issues may well aid them in becoming more compassionate, caring human beings and thereby increase their chances of living in a future world of inner and outer peace.

When the crisis interventions have passed, we will need extensive training in schools and universities to prepare to work with kids in the context of a new paradigm of trauma and grief. Educators, parents, health professionals, and all caring adults must become advocates in creating understanding and procedures to work with our children facing a present and future so different from their past. Our task is to help our children stay connected to their feelings during the continuing trauma of terrorism and war.

The terrorist attack has transformed us all into a global community joining together to re-instill protection and a sense of safety for America and for the world. Helping our children grieve can only help the grieving child in each one of us.

Read more about children and complicated grief issues in Linda Goldman's book *Breaking the Silence: A Guide to Help Children With Complicated Grief/Suicide, Homicide, AIDS, Violence, and Abuse* (Taylor and Francis, 2002). To contact Linda Goldman, e-mail her at lgold@erols.com or visit her Web site at **www.erols.com/lgold**.

Marriage and Divorce American Style

A destructive marriage is not a happy family.

E. Mavis Hetherington

On average, recent studies show, parents and children in married families are happier, healthier, wealthier, and better adjusted than those in single-parent households. But these averages conceal wide variations. Before betting the farm on marriage with a host of new government programs aimed at promoting traditional two-parent families and discouraging divorce, policy makers should take another look at the research. It reveals that there are many kinds of marriage and not all are salutary. Nor are all divorces and single-parent experiences associated with lasting distress. It is not the inevitability of positive or negative responses to marriage or divorce that is striking, but the diversity of them.

Men do seem to benefit simply from the state of being married. Married men enjoy better health and longevity and fewer psychological and behavioral problems than single men. But women, studies repeatedly have found, are more sensitive to the emotional quality of the marriage. They benefit from being in a well-functioning marriage, but in troubled marriages they are likely to experience depression, immune-system breakdowns, and other health-related problems.

We saw the same thing in the project I directed at the Hetherington Laboratory at the University of Virginia, which followed 1,400 divorced families, including 2,500 kids—some for as long as 30 years—interviewing them, testing them, and observing them at home, at school, and in the community. This was the most comprehensive study of divorce and remarriage ever undertaken; for policy makers, the complexity of the findings is perhaps its most important revelation.

Good Marriages, Bad Marriages

By statistical analysis, we identified five broad types of marriage—ranging from "pursuer-distancer" marriages, (which we found were the most likely to end in divorce), to disengaged marriages, to operatic marriages, to "cohesive-individuated" marriages, and, finally, traditional marriages (which had the least risk of instability).

To describe them briefly:

- Pursuer-distancer marriages are those mismatches in which one spouse, usually the wife, wants to confront and discuss problems and feelings and the other, usually the husband, wants to avoid confrontations and either denies problems or withdraws.
- Disengaged marriages are ones where couples share few interests, activities, or friends. Conflict is low, but so is affection and sexual satisfaction.
- Operatic marriages involve couples who like to function at a level of extreme emotional arousal. They are intensely attracted, attached, and volatile, given both to frequent fighting and to passionate lovemaking.
- Cohesive-individuated marriages are the yuppie and feminist ideal, characterized by equity, respect, warmth, and mutual support, but also by both partners retaining the autonomy to pursue their own goals and to have their own friends.
- Traditional marriages are those in which the husband is the main income producer and the wife's role is one of nurturance, support, and home and child care. These marriages work well as long as both partners continue to share a traditional view of gender roles.

We found that not just the risk of divorce, but also the extent of women's psychological and health troubles varies according to marriage type—with wives in pursuer-distancer and disengaged marriages experiencing the most problems, those in operatic marriages significantly having fewer, and those in cohesive-individuated and traditional marriages the fewest. Like so many other studies, we found that men's responses are less nuanced; the only differentiation among them was that men in pursuer-distancer marriages have more problems than those in the other four types.

The issue is not simply the amount of disagreement in the marriage; disagreements, after all, are endemic in close personal relations. It is *how* people disagree and solve problems—how they interact—that turns out to be closely associated with both the duration of their marriages and the well-being of wives and, to a lesser extent, husbands. Contempt, hostile criticism, belligerence, denial, and withdrawal erode a marriage. Affection, respect, trust, support, and making the partner feel valued and worthwhile strengthen the relationship.

Good Divorces, Bad Divorces

Divorce experiences also are varied. Initially, especially in marriages involving children, divorce is miserable for most couples. In the early years, ex-spouses typically must cope with lingering attachments; with resentment and anger, self-doubts, guilt, depression, and loneliness; with the stress of separation from children or of raising them alone; and with the loss of social networks and, for women, of economic security. Nonetheless, we found that a gradual recovery usually begins by the end of the second year. And by six years after divorce, 80 percent of both men and women have moved on to build reasonably or exceptionally fulfilling lives.

Indeed, about 20 percent of the women we observed eventually emerged from divorce enhanced and exhibiting competencies they never would have developed in an unhappy or constraining marriage. They had gone back to school or work to ensure the economic stability of their families, they had built new social networks, and they had become involved and effective parents and socially responsible citizens. Often they had happy second marriages. Divorce had offered them an opportunity to build new and more satisfying relationships and the freedom they needed for personal growth. This was especially true for women moving from a pursuer-distancer or disengaged marriage, or from one in which a contemptuous or belligerent husband undermined their self-esteem and child-rearing practices. Divorced men, we found, are less likely to undergo such remarkable personal growth; still, the vast majority of the men in our study did construct reasonably happy new lives for themselves.

As those pressing for government programs to promote marriage will no doubt note, we found that the single most important predictor of a divorced parent's subsequent adjustment is whether he or she has formed a new and mutually supportive intimate relationship. But what should also be noticed is that successful repartnering takes many forms. We found that about 75 percent of men and 60 percent of women eventually remarry, but an increasing number of adults are opting to cohabit instead—or to remain single and meet their need for intimacy with a dating arrangement, a friendship, or a network of friends or family.

There is general agreement among researchers that parents' repartnering does not do as much for their children. Both young children and adolescents in divorced and remarried families have been found to have, on average, more social, emotional, academic, and behavioral problems than kids in two-parent, non-divorced families. My own research, and that of many other investigators, finds twice as many serious psychological disorders and behavioral problems—such as teenage pregnancy, dropping out of school, substance abuse, unemployment, and marital breakups—among the offspring of divorced parents as among the children of nondivorced families. This is a closer association than between smoking and cancer.

However, the troubled youngsters remain a relatively small proportion of the total. In our study, we found that after a period of initial disruption 75 percent to 80 percent of children and adolescents from divorced families are able to cope with the divorce and their new life situation and develop into reasonably or exceptionally well-adjusted individuals. In fact, as we saw with women, some girls eventually emerge from their parents' divorces remarkably

competent and responsible. They also learn from the divorce experience how to handle later stresses in their lives.

Without ignoring the serious pain and distress experienced by many divorced parents and children, it is important to underscore that substantial research findings confirm the ability of the vast majority to move on successfully.

It is also important to recognize that many of the adjustment problems in parents and children and much of the inept parenting and destructive family relations policy makers have attributed to divorce actually are present *before* divorce. Being in a dysfunctional family has taken its toll before the breakup occurs.

Predicting the aftermath of divorce is complex, and the truth is obscured if one looks only at averages. Differences in experience or personality account for more variation than the averages would suggest. A number of studies have found, for instance, that adults and children who perceived their pre-divorce life as happy and satisfying tend to be more upset by a marital breakup than those who viewed the marriage as contentious, threatening, or unfulfilling. Other studies show that adults and children who are mature, stable, self-regulated, and adaptable are more likely able to cope with the challenges of divorce. Those who are neurotic, antisocial, and impulsive—and who lack a sense of their own efficacy—are likely to have these characteristics exacerbated by the breakup. In other words, the psychologically poor get poorer after a divorce while the rich often get richer.

The diversity of American marriages makes it unlikely that any one-size-fits-all policy to promote marriage and prevent divorce will be beneficial. Policy makers are now talking about offering people very brief, untested education and counseling programs, but such approaches rarely have long-lasting effects. And they are generally least successful with the very groups that policy makers are most eager to marry off—single mothers and the poor.

In their recent definitive review of the research on family interventions, Phil Cowan, Douglas Powell, and Carolyn Pape Cowan find that the most effective approaches are the most comprehensive ones—those that deal with both parents and children, with family dynamics, and with a family's needs for jobs, education, day care, and health care. Beyond that, which interventions work best seems to vary, depending on people's stage of life, the kind of family or ethnic group they are in, and the specific challenges before them.

Strengthening and promoting positive family relationships and improving the many settings in which children develop is a laudable goal. However, policies that constrain or encourage people to remain in destructive marriages—or that push uncommitted couples to marry—are likely to do more harm than good. The same is true of marriage incentives and rewards designed to create traditional families with the husband as the economic provider and the wife as homemaker. If our social policies do not recognize the diversity and varied needs of American families, we easily could end up undermining them.

E. MAVIS HETHERINGTON is a professor of psychology at the University of Virginia and the co-author (with John Kelly) of *For Better or for Worse: Divorce Reconsidered.*

Dating After Divorce

5 Tips for Navigating the Singles Scene

The rate of divorce in America remains high, leaving many adult men and women alone, available and wondering how to maneuver on the playing field. After years of being in a relationship, putting yourself back in the singles market can be a daunting endeavor. Here, David A. Anderson, Ph.D., offers advice gleaned from his own research and that of other experts to help you get back into dating mode.

DAVID A. ANDERSON AND ROSEMARY CLANDOS

After 19 years of waking up next to the same person, 44-year-old Yolanda*, a marketing consultant, suddenly found herself greeting mornings alone. Recently divorced, she was overwhelmed by the mere thought of dating again. Yolanda's self-esteem was so damaged by her tumultuous breakup that she worried about her ability to start a new relationship, not to mention her rusty dating skills. And the pool of single men looked more like a droplet compared with the ocean available to her during her younger years.

Approximately nine in 10 people will marry, but about one half of first marriages end in divorce.

Yolanda may have felt alone on the playing field, but she was far from it. According to the U.S. Census Bureau, approximately nine in 10 people will marry, but about one half of first marriages end in divorce. Between 1970 and 1996, the number of women living alone doubled to 14.6 million, and the number nearly tripled for men, jumping from 3.5 million to 10.3 million.

With so many single adults out there, one might guess that there's also a lot of dating going on. Instead, it seems that the older we get, the less we date. In one study conducted at the University of Michigan Institute for Social Research, social psychologist Jerald G. Bachman, Ph.D., found that nearly 50 percent of 18-year-olds go out at least once a week, compared with only approximately 25 percent of 32-year-olds.

While it's true that some people simply choose not to date, others want to but don't know how to go about it or can't overcome their negative self-thoughts. So how can those who are struggling with these obstacles successfully and healthfully re-enter the dating arena? First, it's important to set appropriate personal standards. In particular, will you play hard to get or be an easy catch? I call the manifestation of these standards one's "social price." The more you have to offer in a relationship, the more you can expect in return, thus increasing your appropriate

social price. Factors that help determine your social price include your ability to bring desirable traits such as inner strength, kindness, intelligence and affection to a relationship.

Working with Shigeyuyki Hamori, an economist at Kobe University in Japan, I researched methods for estimating the qualities and contributions of marriage prospects. We hypothesized that singles seeking relationships assess unseen qualities in others based on social price as it is reflected in actions, body language and verbal communication. We concluded that those exhibiting self-confident assertions of dating standards are perceived as holding relatively more promise as marriage partners. Conversely, those who appear insecure and desperate, call a love interest excessively or engage in sexual activity too soon send signals that they hold inferior unseen traits.

Abby, 31

"I started dating the day my divorce was final. I found myself desperate for confidence and I thought I might find it by dating. But nobody really wants that kind of burden. However, a little later, nobody measured up to my standards. I've met people on buses and airplanes and in airports, even walking down the street. I don't think I ever had a date that resulted from a bar experience. I dated some real morons. I jumped in too quickly. My first few relationships were definitely physical. They weren't the kind of people who, in my right mind, I would have dated. I'm still dating. And now I've met somebody really great online. We e-mailed back and forth for two weeks before we started talking on the phone. It's a fun and great way to get to know someone. I think it's a whole lot more honest. You get a better view of a person when you start off corresponding."

> ### Alex, 28
>
> "After my divorce, I had to face dating. I didn't know what dating was. I had never dated. I came from France with my girlfriend whom I married. Dating is a process and there are rules. Every time I met with someone, I was thinking of my wife—where she was, what she was doing. Dating was a decision, not a random encounter. I started using the Internet. But even when the criteria were right, the people were wrong. When I did meet someone through the Web, it didn't work. In France, one could sweet-talk with a complete stranger, without a phone number exchanged. Here, even a gentle smile across the train platform is not well received. Maybe I tend to overanalyze things. I should seize the day and stop asking questions."

So just as we tend to assume that expensive cars are better than similar, cheaper ones, we may also conclude that those demonstrating high social prices have unobserved qualities superior to those with lower social prices. But be wary: Overselling also occurs. For instance, individuals with a substantial income but little else to offer may exaggerate their social price. And as with any type of price misrepresentation, true quality eventually surfaces. In the dating market, this can translate into a broken relationship.

Those who believe they have a lot to offer set higher standards for potential partners

At the core, inaccurate social pricing is a by-product of low self-esteem and other negative self-emotions. "Fear absolutely devastates some people," says clinical psychologist Michael S. Broder, Ph.D., a former radio-talk-show host and author of *The Art of Living Single*. "It can be the fear of being hurt, rejected or involved, and it can stem from a history of having been hurt or of traumatic relationships. People can be very proficient in other parts of their lives, but the fear of dating can make them stay alone—or pine for the relationship they left."

Others rebound or get involved in another relationship too soon. Their desperation usually stems from sadness, guilt, anger or anxiety about being alone. "You get this feeling that you're in the worst possible situation in your life," Broder explains. "Then you may do what you later consider desperate: a one-night stand, calling the ex or ignoring intuitive warnings and jumping into a bad relationship you would never choose if you weren't feeling reckless."

Fortunately, it is possible to avoid these and other pitfalls when seeking out a new partner. If you're ready to get back in the saddle again, here are five key tips to help you on your way.

1 Develop a (New) Support Group

It's natural to turn to old friends for support. They know and care about you, and they typically have your best interests in mind. But more often it's new friends who will better help you adjust to your new life. That's because friends shared with your ex often unwittingly take sides, and either alliance can prove a hindrance when introducing someone new into your life. Old

> ### Patricia, 38
>
> "I've been divorced for 10 years. And since then, I have been focusing on raising my teenage daughter as well as on my career in commercial real estate. So it leaves no time for dating. I tried the Internet, but it is so time-consuming. It was work. You have to get online and check your messages and then figure out who these people were. I got tired of looking at the computer too. In the end, I don't think I lasted for more than a week. The best way to meet people, I find, is through friends. I ask them, 'Do you know anyone?' Still, it is very difficult to meet people. I met the man I am spending time with now at my daughter's school. I've also been introduced to other people through friends and work. What's really important, though, is maintaining a positive outlook."

friends may lack the proper interest or compassion, and they may even be jealous of your newfound freedom.

"My divorce split our extended families and friends," says Yolanda of her and her ex-husband. "But my new friends had a fresh perspective that helped my self-esteem. Those who were single had confidence that was contagious; that really helped me when I started going out again as a single person. And sometimes they offered good advice."

Do use discretion when listening to others' words of wisdom, advises Broder. "Solutions that worked for a friend may be a disaster for you. If you don't want advice, be assertive and let people know that advice giving is off-limits unless it's requested."

For the most part, however, friendship is a vital ingredient in the recovery process. "Facing things alone can take a toll on you," says Broder. "Friends can help you see that dating doesn't have to be so serious."

2 Assess Your Self-worth

People with low self-esteem tend to create relationships with others who evaluate them negatively, suggests one study on self-concept done by William B. Swann Jr., Ph.D., a University of Texas psychology professor. If you're suffering from a negative self-image, it's vital you take steps to create a positive, healthy self-concept.

Begin by making a list of your positive qualities, then hang it in your home where you'll see it regularly, suggest Bruce Fisher, Ed.D., Robert Alberti, Ph.D., and Virginia M. Satir, M.A., in their book *Rebuilding When Your Relationship Ends*. Sharing your list with your support group and asking for honest feedback will help you to work on clearing up any discrepancies between your self-image and the real you. Broder also recommends making a list of new beliefs and affirmations that you'd like to incorporate into your thinking system. Read aloud these new self-concepts often, regardless of how you're feeling, to help solidify them in your mind.

"It can be the fear of being hurt, rejected or involved, and it can stem from a history of having been hurt or of traumatic relationships. People can be very proficient in other parts of their lives, but the fear of dating can make them stay alone—or pine for the relationship they left."

For Yolanda, a brief relationship five years after her divorce made her realize she had to adjust her mind-set. "I felt ashamed about all of the times I'd say yes when my answer was really no," she says now. "The consequences were painful, but I didn't believe I could completely change the pattern. Then I took the advice you hear about in 12-step programs and turned it over to God—my higher power. Moving forward and forgiving myself became easier."

People who feel victimized after a breakup may do well to develop a bold—or even defiant—attitude. Psychologists at the University of Washington and Canada's University of Waterloo recently found that feelings of resignation and sadness make people with low self-esteem less motivated to improve their mood. "When you feel defiant you become excited, confident and ready to take action," says Broder. "You take care of yourself, making it pretty clear that you are not going to be ruined by divorce. It's a very healthy thing to do."

3 Plan Activities

You won't find a new mate—or even a new friend—while sitting on the couch, your television on, curtains drawn. Consider your post-relationship time as an opportunity to do the things you couldn't do while you were with your ex. Create a list of 20 activities you would enjoy doing with a perfect partner, then give the list a second look. "Rarely do people have more than three or four things on their list that they cannot do if they're not in a relationship," says Broder. "Be active; don't feel like your whole life is on hold."

Today's singles are finding luck—and love—in nonconventional ways. After her 17-year relationship ended, Lili*, a 43-year-old writer, re-entered the dating arena by joining a telephone dating service. Instead of meeting men for dinner, she invited them for daytime walks in a well-populated park. "They weren't dates; they were interviews," says Lili, who admits that taking the first step was difficult. "If I liked them, we went for coffee." Laura*, a 49-year-old financial adviser, also missed companionship after her 24-year marriage dissolved. "I don't sit with problems for very long," she says. "I knew what I wanted and went after it." Laura joined an online dating service and eventually met her soon-to-be second husband.

Brian*, 35

"Soon after my wife and I were separated, I felt it was very difficult to be alone. I forced myself to go out almost every night, just to be out of the house. I did a lot of things, such as listening to music at clubs, going to bars. I was being open to the world—it was almost a Renaissance. It wasn't a matter of getting back into the scene—I was never in the scene. I had never been aggressive about dating. So I really didn't know what I was doing. I wanted to go out and meet people. After a relationship ends, though, loneliness is the hardest thing. It's important to learn how to be with yourself and not force a new relationship to compensate for that loneliness. I've also learned that it's important to know how to accept help. Before my divorce, I never felt the need to rely on friends for emotional support. It had been more difficult for me to accept support rather than give it. For the first time, I reached out."

Joseph Walther, Ph.D., an associate professor of communication, language and literature at Troy, New York's Rensselaer Polytechnic Institute, found that people who use Internet dating services such as Match.com may achieve more beginning-stage emotional intimacy than they do in face-to-face situations. Single surfers don't have to worry about common first-impression concerns such as bad-hair days and wrinkled clothes, Walther points out. Plus, they don't see body-language cues such as shrugging and smirking that can create barriers in communication. Currently, cyber researchers believe that as much as 33 percent of friendships formed online eventually advance to face-to-face meetings.

4 Curb Unhealthy Cravings

When we are in emotional pain, our feelings often don't coincide with our intellect and instead manifest themselves as cravings that can prove unhealthy and self-destructive. Cravings usually plague people who have zero tolerance for a single lifestyle and want to jump into a new relationship as soon as their breakup is final. Also susceptible are individuals with low self-evaluation who are convinced they can't make it alone. Fortunately, while such cravings may feel overwhelming and unavoidable, Broder asserts that they don't have to be.

Take Julie*, a 42-year-old college student in Southern California whose need for immediate passion led her to make decisions despite intuitively knowing they were unwise. "I kept going out with men who did not have the potential for a long-term relationship," she confesses. "One had problems with his ex-wife, another wouldn't marry outside of his religion. After getting hurt many times, I finally decided to be more careful when choosing men. I'm still prone to my old behavior, but I'm more apt to say no to men who are a poor match for me."

People with low self-esteem tend to create relationships with others who evaluate them negatively in turn

To short-circuit cravings, Broder suggests doing something that actively breaks the pattern and makes you approach the situation in a healthier way. Call someone in your support group, share your unwanted tendencies and ask that he or she invite you out when you fall into bad habits. And consider keeping a journal of the things that successfully distract you from your urges, such as renting a funny movie or going for a long walk, that you can turn to the next time cravings crop up.

5 Prepare for Pitfalls

Certain times of the year—holidays, anniversaries and birthdays, for instance—are harder to navigate than others because they are loaded with expectations and memories. After a separation or divorce, social configurations change, making feelings of loss and loneliness more intense. Perfectionists tend to struggle most during the holidays, according to Broder. High expectations lead them to dwell on favorite memories of their past and compare them with current situations.

Garrett*, an optometrist in his mid-40s, remembers that his first Christmas alone was a tough one. "Weeks prior to the holidays were extremely difficult because the traditions were highly disrupted," he says. "Not being in my own home and not having a closeness with someone was difficult, and I felt very much afraid of not finding someone again."

Ultimately, the best tip for re-entering the dating game is to explore various action strategies and choose those that are most comfortable for you

To cope, Garrett stuck close to his family. "You stitch together the connections that you have," he says. "It was piecemeal and patchwork, but it was critical for me. I also looked for other ways to divert my attention. I organized a staff party, participated in a musical and cooked at other people's homes."

Garrett got it right, according to Sally Karioth, Ph.D., R.N., an associate nursing professor at Florida State University and an expert on stress, grief and trauma. Karioth points again to planning as the key to reducing stress and meeting new people. Don't be afraid to ask for help organizing new activities, and break tasks into smaller chores to fend off feelings of being overwhelmed. Broder also suggests avoiding holiday comparisons and focusing instead on the enjoyable aspects of current and future ones. "You'll get through, and then you won't fear it

Elli, 65

"There have been some periods in my life when I couldn't find a match—I would fall for someone who didn't want me or reject someone whom I didn't want. But I never had a problem with dating after my divorces. I met my first husband on the second day of college when I was 18 years old, and I abandoned my studies to marry him—this was the kind of choice women made in those days. Immediately after we were separated, I moved away to resume my studies. Coincidentally, I met my next guy on the second day of classes. When we broke up, I immediately began dating again."

anymore," says Broder. "It may not be the best of your life, but it may not be the horror you thought it would be."

Ultimately, the best tip for re-entering the dating game is to explore various action strategies and choose those that are most comfortable for you. For some, getting into the right frame of mind before taking the leap is essential. For others, simply trying something new or even uncomfortable works. You know yourself best, so trust your inner wisdom. If you are ready to find new love, take heart: More than 40 percent of weddings in America are remarriages. But don't feel obligated to rush into another marriage, either—the U.S. Census Bureau reports that 60 percent of second marriages end in divorce. Now that you're single it's perfectly acceptable to remain so if that's what you prefer. As Broder says, "What you do with your life now is up to you."

Learn More About It:

The Courage to Love Again: Creating Happy, Healthy Relationships After Divorce
Sheila Ellison (Harper San Francisco, 2002)

Resilient Identities: Self Relationships and the Construction of Social Reality
William B. Swann Jr. (Counterpoint Press, 1999)

Rebuilding When Your Relationship Ends
Bruce Fisher, Robert E. Alberti and Virginia M. Satir (Impact Publishers, 1999)

www.Match.com
www.Lavalife.com

* Identities have been changed.

DAVID A. ANDERSON, PH.D., is an associate professor of economics at Centre College in Danville, Kentucky. **ROSEMARY CLANDOS** is a freelance science writer in Calabasas, California.

Managing a Blended Family

Crafting a financial plan for two *families* that merge through marriage is serious business. Here's how to do it right.

SHERYL NANCE-NASH

From the outset, Kofi and Yvette Moyo Firmly believed that their union would add value to all members of their growing brood. Combining his eight children and her one child could have easily led to emotional upheaval and financial discord—but the Moyos had a plan.

First, they adopted the concept of a village raising a child. Yvette and Kofi needed unity to raise nine children (who now range in age from 18 to 33) over their 15-year marriage. The couple garnered support from both sets of grandparents as well as Kofi's former wives and Yvette's former partner. Some of the children stayed with the Moyos full time for a stretch, but Kofi and Yvette didn't have primary custody. The children would journey from Cincinnati to join them in Chicago for the summer months, weekends, holidays, and birthdays. "We had a commitment to harmony," maintains Yvette.

So, how did the Moyo's keep their financial house in order? Yvette, 50, an advertising sales and marketing executive, and Kofi, 64, a photojournalist, author, and amateur chef, quit their jobs to start Resource Associates International (PAI), a marketing firm best known for its Real Men Cook for Charity fundraising events, and the Marketing Opportunities in Business and Entertainment (MOBE) conference series. The company grossed annual revenues of approximately $600,000, generating enough income to support the growing clan and pay for everything from summer camp and family trips, to child support and the first year of college tuition for everyone. (By the second year, the children have to pay for their tuition by working or gaining scholarships or other forms of financial aid.)

Next, the family went on an austerity program. "I shopped at Burlington Coat Factory instead of downtown at Lord & Taylor," Yvette explains. Furthermore, Kofi is a frugal and savvy shopper. For example, he drives a mint condition 1988 Land Cruiser that he purchased online. (Yvette owns a 1971 Mercedes, which is also in excellent condition.) Over the years, they have been able to realize more savings since Kofi makes repairs around the house. "We gave up luxuries like new suits and expensive stuff and settled for what mattered," says Yvette. "[The children] knew we cared for them. If one of them had a prom, they'd go and I'd do without if necessary. The priority was to expose them to a variety of things and make them feel good about themselves."

How to Blend Your Family's Finances

Re-evaluate all of your insurance needs. Review your policies—health, property, auto, and, especially, life. Your expanded family will likely mean you need to increase coverage. Consult with your financial adviser.

- **Update all financial documents.** Any paperwork that named your previous spouse as a beneficiary should be changed.
- **Create a budget and stick to it.** With a bigger family, there is less wiggle room for money mistakes if you want to achieve your financial goals. Be sure that budget includes a fund for emergencies and savings for the short and long term.
- **Rethink your asset allocation.** Before it was just you and now it's you and your spouse. Look at both portfolios closely. You don't have to merge accounts, but it's important to note, for example, if you both have shares of the same stock or if your respective portfolios are heavily weighted in a particular asset class or sector. In all cases, think diversification.
- **Develop a will or living trust.** If you already have one, it will need to be changed to reflect your current situation. If you don't have one, by all means complete one. In the document, name guardians for your children. This is a tough issue for any parent, but particularly when there are different sets of children and possibly multiple guardians.

As the Moyos demonstrate, bringing two households together—each with its own culture, traditions, financial habits, and values—is no small matter. Entering a new relationship with children, former spouses, and expanded financial responsibilities can be downright daunting. But many couples are willing to take on the challenge. According to the Lincoln, Nebraska-based Stepfamily Association of America (SAA), about 75% of divorced people eventually remarry and about 65% of those remarriages involve children from prior unions.

While the divorce rate is nearly 62%, blended families can and do succeed. Making it work, however, requires a strong commitment from the couple—to each other and to the newly formed family.

Poor planning and disagreement on goals can quickly unravel recently constituted stepfamilies. For one thing, the second or third time around, finances can be an even greater issue since both spouses usually have more assets, more debts, and contradictory money-management styles. Also, asserts Marilyn Bergen, a certified financial planner with CMC Advisers in Portland, Oregon, "the children may have very different spending habits and values. How will you get everyone on the same page?

Achieving Financial Harmony

Few things are as unromantic as finances. Before you get too deep into the prospects of marital bliss, you must engage in straight talk about money. There are a myriad of issues to deal with, including child support, prenuptial agreements, property ownership, retirement finances, and estate planning. First, you need to gain a full accounting of your loved one's assets, debts, legal issues, and tax liabilities. "You want to know what sort of verbal agreements they may have, say to help pay their parent's prescription drug costs, or to buy a child a car," says SAA President Margorie Engel.

Take a good look at each other's spending habits. "Poor spending habits are often what caused the first marriage to break up. You should work to come up with a common financial plan and a debt-elimination plan," advises Pierre Dunagan, president of The Dunagan Group, a Chicago-based financial services firm. "Commit your plan to paper. Having a document that you both agreed on and signed makes a huge difference. It's a little hard to dispute."

Dunagan says once couples are married, they should schedule weekly or monthly meetings to review the family's finances. The two need to determine whether financial goals are on track or, if not, factors that have stalled progress. Other issues include deciding how money will be managed. You should answer the following questions before you take the plunge: Will you have separate accounts, joint accounts, or a combination of the two? How much will each contribute to household expenses?

Commit your plan to paper. Having a document that you both agreed on and signed makes a huge difference.

Dunagan says there's another important matter to address: What will the combined financial needs of the children be? Maybe you already made plans for college financing for two children, but how do you now make adjustments for your spouse's other two? Or, what if you and your new spouse are contemplating having a child together? Have you considered the expenses of daycare, larger living quarters, and the like?

Making Adjustments

These are matters that the Moyos had to take into account when their family expanded. In fact, the entrepreneurs made some rather smart financial moves along the way. They bought a house with a four-car garage, which was spacious enough to provide living quarters for Yvette's mother, an office for a staff of four, and the family's living quarters. "It's a major resource," says Yvette. "We've used the equity to assist the business, make home repairs, and otherwise keep the family going."

Another decision they made early on was to get substantial life insurance for each other ($1 million for Yvette, and $1.5 million for Kofi) and for their children ($10,000 per child). However, some would argue that life insurance is about income replacement, so it's not necessary to obtain it for a child. But when tragedy struck—one of Kofi's daughters was killed in a car accident—they realized that it was a wise decision.

All stepfamilies have to make major adjustments to their lifestyles and to their spending habits. Take the Hales of Long Branch, New Jersey.

When Kim, 37, and William, 39, were married seven years ago, they had six children between them. Since then, they've added one foster child from Guatemala, Kim gave birth to another, and one more is on the way. Initially, the family moved into a three-bedroom apartment in Kim's building because she didn't want to live in the home that William had rented with his former wife. The newly formed family was a bit cramped, and within a couple of years, the Hales purchased a four-bedroom home.

Resources for Stepfamilies

Websites:

Family and Stepparenting Tips:
www.blended-families.com

Stepfamily Matters:
www.step-family-matters.com

The Stepfamily Association of America:
www.saafamilies.org/index.htm

Books:

Blending Families: A Guide for Parents, Stepparents, and Everyone Building a Successful New Family (Berkley Books, $14.00)

Money Advice for Your Successful Remarriage: Handling Delicate Financial Issues Intelligently and Lovingly (iUniverse.com, $14.95)

The Complete Idiot's Guide to Step-parenting (Alpha Books, $16.95)

Largely due to Kim's influence, the Hales have learned to be frugal in their spending. Concedes William: "I made some bad financial decisions in my first marriage. We were over-spenders. I thought I could work overtime and make it work, but that wasn't the case."

In fact, when William and Kim married, he didn't have a checking or savings account. Kim proved to be a good teacher and he was a willing student. They opened joint accounts and William has learned from her thriftiness. "Saving is hard with a big family," says Kim, who spends as much as $250 each week on groceries. "I learned from my mom to save on small stuff. When you have a family this size and everybody saves a dollar here and there, it adds up. I shop with coupons."

They have also spent considerable time teaching their children to have respect for the value of a dollar. When the children were younger, they received allowances of $5–$10 a week, but now the teens must earn their money—especially since they have developed a taste for FUBU, Sean John, and other designer goodies. The older children have jobs and the Hales require them to fork over 10% of their paycheck as a tithe, another 10% for long-term savings, and the remainder for personal items such as school clothes, cell phones, and leisure activities.

These days, the Hales have been forced to batten down the hatches. Before William lost his job 18 months ago due to a legal complication with his employer and Kim was unable to handle the physical demands of nursing as a result of her pregnancy, their household income was $120,000. Today, their household income has been downsized to $35,000. To make ends meet, William sells health plans for AmeriPlan USA and Kim sells real estate. The two also generate limited income from Pure Word Ministries (William is a licensed and ordained evangelist). Over the past two years, they have tapped William's entire 401(k) account—roughly $40,000—to maintain living expenses.

The good news, however, is that William will return to the electric company as well as gain 18 months in back pay. He plans to use the money to pay off debt that the family has accumulated, build up retirement savings, and develop a fund to help their children finance their college education. Kim and William hold life insurance policies but admit that they have yet to complete their wills. "With a blended family, it's more than a notion about what to do about the kids," says Kim. "Somebody's not going to like the decisions you make, like the children's mother. It's a sticky situation because we haven't legally adopted each other's children though we have custody."

Making household finances work will mean that couples must pay attention to details and diligently handle legal and financial matters. But in order to truly secure their family's future, each spouse must embrace the planning process as a joint venture.

Stepfamily Success Depends on Ingredients

One in three Americans is part of a stepfamily, each with its own flavor. How can psychologists help them thrive?

Tori DeAngelis

I f Tolstoy were alive today, he might have penned his famous line like this: Happy families are all alike—and every stepfamily is complex in its own way.

Take one example. If a stepparent is frequently battling his former spouse, research shows that his children suffer. But if he is *close* with his ex-partner, his new spouse may feel anxious and insecure. On top of this, say experts, many children don't view their stepparents as "real parents" for the first few years—if ever—and parents in second marriages may treat their biological children differently from their stepchildren.

"Stepparents once were viewed as 'replacing' biological parents, thus recreating a two-parent family," notes University of Virginia (UVA) psychology professor Robert E. Emery, PhD, author of "The Truth about Children and Divorce: Dealing with the Emotions So You and Your Children Can Thrive" (Viking/Penguin, 2004). "Economically, there may be some truth to this, but psychologically, that is not the reality. Remarriage and stepparenting are new, tricky transitions for children, the stepparent and the biological parents."

Fortunately, researchers and clinicians today better understand the common pitfalls of such "blended" families and how they can overcome them. That's important because one in three of us is a member of a stepfamily, according to the Stepfamily Association of America, and that number is likely to grow as traditional family bonds grow more fragile (see sidebar, page 61). The demographics of stepfamilies are as complex as the psychological ones: About a quarter are headed by unmarried parents, for example, and stepfamilies make up the full spectrum of our nation's citizens, according to the association.

The Role of Children

Given the complexity of the subject matter, researchers and clinicians are looking at stepfamilies through many lenses. A major one is via the children, who often suffer the most through divorce, remarriage and stepfamily situations. They are particularly at-risk if their biological parents are in conflict (see box, next page), the divorce situation is protracted, they receive less parenting after the divorce or they lose important relationships as a result of the divorce, according to a 2003 article in *Family*

Relations (Vol. 52, No. 4, pages 352–362) by Emery of UVA and Joan B. Kelly, PhD, a psychologist and divorce expert in Corte Madeira, Calif.

> **"When the kids aren't happy, they'll say things like, 'I don't like your new husband—he's mean to me.' That creates conflict in the marriage. In a first-marriage family, if a kid says, 'I don't like my dad,' the mom says, 'So?'"**
>
> James H. Bray
> Baylor College of Medicine

Indeed, children of divorce—and later, remarriage—are twice as likely to academically, behaviorally and socially struggle as children of first-marriage families: About 20 to 25 percent struggle, compared with 10 percent, a range of research finds. They're also more likely to get divorced themselves, reports University of Utah sociologist Nicholas H. Wolfinger, PhD, in his book, "Understanding the Divorce Cycle" (Cambridge University Press, 2005). Adults whose parents divorced but didn't remarry are 45 percent more likely to divorce than adults whose parents never divorced, he notes, and 91 percent more likely to divorce if their parents divorced and remarried.

Furthermore, children often "calls the shots" on the emotional trajectory of family life, says psychologist and stepfamily expert James H. Bray, PhD, of the Baylor College of Medicine.

"When people get married for a second time, the biological parent really feels they need to attend to the kids," explains Bray, author with writer John Kelly of "Stepfamilies" (Broadway, 1998). "And when the kids aren't happy, they'll say things like, 'I don't like your new husband—he's mean to me.' That creates conflict in the marriage. In a first-marriage family, if a kid says, 'I don't like my dad,' the mom says, 'So?'"

That said, UVA psychologist and professor emeritus E. Mavis Hetherington, PhD, found in a much-publicized 20-year study that the vast majority of children of divorce do well. As adults, many still feel pain and sadness when they think about

Containing Conflict in Divorce Battles

As a parent coordinator who helps to resolve custody disputes in divorce cases, Bruce Copeland, PhD, JD, has seen his share of high-drama conflict.

"I had one case involving the father's infidelity with a close relative of the mother's," the Bethesda, Md., psychologist and attorney recalls. "You can imagine the level of intensity around that issue."

Despite the high-octane feelings between the couple, Copeland acted as a conduit so they could exchange information about their two young children. The process went well enough that six months later, "They were able to have a conversation, to make some decisions and to coordinate their children's care," he says.

Parent coordination—a growing niche for qualified psychologists (see the September 2004 *Monitor*)—addresses an important research finding: The level of conflict between parents is one of the key predictors of children's long-term adjustment following a divorce.

"Children in these cases are often caught in a tug of war," says Michelle Parker, PhD, a clinical psychologist and parent coordinator in Washington, D.C. "Much of the energy of the family is being diverted toward the conflict, which doesn't leave an appropriate level of energy and space for the children to grow and develop."

Parent coordinators are meant to help create that space. Unlike mediators and custody evaluators, they have, in many instances, quasi-judicial clout allowing them to make binding recommendations to the courts about parenting arrangements, even if the parents can't agree. Often their work centers on helping parents create specific, developmentally appropriate schedules and plans for their children and teaching them communication skills so they can eventually co-parent without intervention.

Because of the complexity of the work, parent coordinators need special backgrounds, including expertise in child psychology, dispute resolution, marital conflict and legal issues, says Copeland. They also need a solid emotional foundation, since their task is to remain neutral vis á vis the parents, while ensuring—and enforcing if necessary—that children receive the best possible arrangements.

"You need all your clinical skills and more," he says.

The role is gaining in importance, Copeland adds: Courts are calling in coordinators at increasingly early stages of the process to help contain conflict before it gets too toxic for children. Such early intervention also can serve a reporting function, he notes, where coordinators are able to give courts useful psychological information if the case ends up litigating.

–T. DeAngelis

Parenting Plans with Kids in Mind

Many courts still order a one-size-fits-all custody arrangement in which fathers see their children every other weekend, and mothers assume parenting duty the rest of the time.

However, psychological research suggests families fare better with individualized custody plans tailored to fit children's developmental stage and individual circumstances, as well as the particular relationship between children and their parents.

That research shows that children experience cookie-cutter plans as confusing and arbitrary, notes clinical psychologist and divorce expert Joan B. Kelly, PhD. Especially affected are children who have good relationships with their fathers and those so young they "have no cognitive capacity to understand why this abrupt decrease in their contact with the object of their affection occurred," she notes.

Other research she cites in a paper in press at the *Journal of the American Academy of Matrimonial Lawyers* finds that:

- About half of children want more contact with their noncustodial fathers than they have.
- Children are rarely asked about living arrangements, but when they are and their input is used, they report high levels of satisfaction with postdivorce living arrangements.
- Children whose fathers are more involved with them postdivorce generally do better socially, behaviorally and academically than those whose fathers are less involved.
- Children in joint-custody arrangements have better emotional, behavioral and general adjustment than those living only with their mother, according to a 2002 meta-analysis of 33 studies.

University of Virginia psychology professor Robert E. Emery, PhD, co-author with Kelly of a 2003 paper in *Family Relations* (Vol. 52, No. 4, pages 352–362) on children's postdivorce adjustment, puts some of these findings into concrete and user-friendly terms on his Web site at **http://emeryondivorce.com/parenting_plans.php**. Using a review of the developmental literature, Emery spells out specific custody schedules for children in six developmental periods from birth to 18 years old. He further separates them into categories for angry, distant and cooperative divorce situations.

Meanwhile, APA has embarked on a number of projects to aid the work of psychologists working in the child-custody area. These include collaborative ventures with a range of children-and-law organizations, including the Family Law Section of the American Bar Association (ABA), says Donna Beavers of APA's General Counsel's Office. APA and the ABA section have joined on a number of projects, including a successful joint conference on children, divorce and custody in 1997. Now, the two groups are establishing an interdisciplinary committee aiming to develop projects to ease child-custody conflict.

–T. DeAngelis

their parents' divorce, but they still build productive and satisfied lives, and they don't experience clinical levels of depression, anxiety or other mental health disorders, Hetherington concludes in her and writer John Kelly's book, "For Better or For Worse: Divorce Reconsidered" (Norton, 2002).

Fostering Resilience

Indeed, many researchers are focusing on these young people's resilience and how to build on it. Psychology professor Allen Israel, PhD, of the University at Albany of the State University of New York, for example, has been developing and evaluating a model of family stability that he believes has special relevance to children in divorce and stepfamily situations.

Family stability, he and his team are finding, isn't contingent on whether you live in a first-marriage, stepfamily or single-parent family, but more particularly on the environment that parents create for their kids, such as the presence of regular bed- and meal-time hours.

That's heartening, Israel believes, because it suggests intervention potential: "You can't always prevent the big things that are causing stress in these kids, such as parents moving or parents who have periods of low contact," he says. "But you might be able to affect the little things that are happening in the home."

In a related 2002 study in the *Journal of Marriage and Family* (Vol. 64, No. 4, pages 1,024–1,037), Kathleen Boyce Rodgers, PhD, a child and family studies researcher at Washington State University, found that outside influences like friends and neighbors can help youngsters undergoing such transitions cope better.

Analyzing data on 2,011 children and adolescents in first-marriage families, stepfamilies and single-parent divorced families, she found that teens who lived with a single, divorced parent and who said they received little support from that parent were less likely to have internalizing symptoms like depression, suicidal ideation and low self-esteem if they had a friend to count on.

In addition, Hetherington has found that consistency in school settings helps predict positive adjustment in children, especially when their home lives are chaotic.

Successful Stepfamilies

Bray examined factors that may predict stepfamilies' success in a nine-year, National Institute of Child Health and Human Development-funded study of 200 Texan stepfamilies and first-marriage families.

Classifying stepfamilies into categories of neotraditional, matriarchal and romantic, he found that neotraditional families fared the best. These parents formed a solid, committed partnership so they could not only nurture their marriage, but effectively raise their children. They didn't get stuck in unrealistic expectations of what the family should be like.

Relatively successful were matriarchal families, headed by strong, independent women who remarried not to gain a parenting partner, but a companion. While their husbands were devoted to these women, the men had fairly distant relationships with the children, Bray found.

Matriarchal families functioned well except in parenting matters, Bray found. Conflicts arose, he says, either when the men decided they wanted to play a greater role in parenting—in which case the women were loathe to relinquish their parenting

---

A Sea Change in Family Values?

Researchers consistently find that children of divorce do as well as their nondivorced peers on academic, social and behavioral measures.

But what about their internal lives? And how will their experiences shape their future family choices?

In a March paper in the *Journal of Sociology* (Vol. 4, No. 1, pages 69–86), Katie Hughes, PhD, a senior lecturer in the department of communication, culture and languages at Victoria University in Melbourne, Australia, explores those questions via in-depth interviews with 31 gen Xers, ages 29 to 44–all children of divorced parents who grew up in single-parent or stepfamily homes.

These young adults demonstrated:

- An emphasis on individual growth, as opposed to a family or couple focus. "They argue very strongly that personal and intimate relationships are about personal growth," Hughes notes. "They've almost completely replaced old-fashioned notions about gender roles, obligation and duty, and sticking to things, with notions of self-actualization."
- The willingness to abandon a relationship if it turns sour or is not promoting growth.
- The use of subliminal "exit strategies," such as deciding not to have children or declining to pool resources with one's partner.

When Hughes probed the interviewees on their transient views of relationships, many expressed a strong belief that all relationships would inevitably end.

"That's where the divorce patterns kick in," she notes, "because people from intact families don't have that belief."

Reasons they held this notion, interviewees told her, included their own bad memories about their parents' breakup, and their observations that if their parents did remarry, their second marriages often were happier than their first, Hughes says.

While Hughes' study lacks a control group, her subjects' demographics parallel the quantitative literature on children of divorce, she notes. In her sample, 36 percent lived alone, 18 percent cohabited only with a partner, 10 percent lived in stepfamilies and 15 percent lived in shared-house arrangements, she notes.

–T. DeAngelis

---

power—or when the women decided they wanted their partners to get more involved. In one common scenario, the woman asked her husband for parenting help but he prevaricated. "She'd ask him to pick up the kids, for example, and he'd forget," Bray says. "That created a lot of conflict."

Romantic families were the most divorce-prone, Bray found. Couples in these families had unrealistic expectations, wanting to immediately create the perfect family atmosphere, and they took their stepchildren's ambivalent reactions to the family transition personally instead of seeing them as normal reactions to a stressful situation.

Tips for Clinicians

Bray and others also have put their heads to creating research-based clinical suggestions for those working with stepfamilies (Bray's suggestions, called "Making Stepfamilies Work," are summarized at **www.apahelpcenter.org/articles/article.php?id=41).**

These include encouraging second-marriage parents to:

- Discuss and decide on finances before getting married.

- Build a strong marital bond "because it will benefit everybody," says Bray.

- Develop a parenting plan, which likely will involve having the stepparent play a secondary, nondisciplinary role for the first year or two. "Otherwise, even if you're doing a good job, the children will rebuff you," he says.

Family psychologist Anne C. Bernstein, PhD, author of "Yours, Mine and Ours: How Families Change When Remarried Parents Have a Child Together" (W.W. Norton, 1990), additionally advises parents to:

- Take time to process each transition.
- Make sure that big changes are communicated adult-to-adult, not via the children.
- Work with therapists who are specially trained in stepfamily dynamics.

Finally, parents in these families need to "take the long view," Emery advises. "You're going to be a parent forever," he says. "For the sake of the kids, you want to at least make that a working relationship."

TORI DEANGELIS is a writer in Syracuse, N.Y.

Death of One's Partner:
The Anticipation and the Reality

FLORENCE W. KASLOW

Florida Couples and Family Institute, Kaslow Associates,
Florida Institute of Technology, and Duke University Medical Center

"Till death do us part." This statement of commitment has long been and still is a cornerstone of the marriage vows taken by the majority of couples entering what they hope will be long-time connubial bliss. The covenant of matrimony is sacrosanct to many as they embark on their life's journey together.

If the couple is young, they soon tend to focus on the creation of new life and either bringing children into the world or adopting a child that needs a home (Babb, 1999; Schwartz & Kaslow, 2003). They tend not to be concerned about their partner's eventual death in the early years of being together. Their savings are for purchasing cars, a home, and consumer goods, taking vacations, and providing for their children's education. Little thought is given to the senior years, retirement, or the ultimate death of each other in this stage of the life cycle, especially if each partner is relatively young and healthy, physically and emotionally. With life expectancy now extended into one's 70s and 80s, death seems a long way off—barring a fatal accident or a natural or people-made disaster. Optimism tends to run high as couples are in their expansive building years. Worries about the end of life are more apt to be centered on what is happening to their respective parents. However, with the passage of the years and the approach of retirement or onset of arthritis, chronic illness, or other problems associated with the normal aging process, and the increasing number of deaths of their own peers, concerns about the inevitability of their own deaths are likely to surface, perhaps to be ignored, only to return to consciousness periodically.

Occurrence of Prolonged Illness

However, for some, their optimistic dreams (Seligman, 1991) all too soon can be darkened by various shadows. Their partner can be diagnosed with multiple sclerosis, muscular dystrophy, or Lou Gehrig's disease. He or she may be incapacitated by a serious stroke, have cardiac failure or require quadruple bypass surgery, need kidney dialysis, have some kind of cancer, or be seriously injured in an accident. All of these conditions tend to have some life-altering consequences and to be very sobering occurrences.

Relevant Family Systems Concepts

Family systems theory has numerous basic precepts that have evolved and been refined and elaborated in the past approximately 60 years since the emergence of the family psychology/psychiatry therapy field. I present those principles most pertinent for the purposes of this treatise on the death of a spouse, viewed within a family systems perspective, which I have updated and synthesized, with a brief explanatory comment added for each.

1. All members of the family system are interconnected and interdependent, and the behavior of each affects all of the others. (This particularly applies to the nuclear family unit, and often to the extended and intergenerational family as well [Bowen, 1988].) Because of this interconnectedness, therapists can encourage the surviving spouse to turn to other members of the nuclear and close extended family unit so they can reminisce and grieve together, for emotional support, to help with tasks that need to be executed immediately, and to plan for the future.

2. Families strive to maintain their homeostatic balance and to resist major challenges to their values, lifestyle, and overall equilibrium. A patient can be reassured that not wanting to make drastic changes immediately, like moving into smaller living quarters, is normal and that decisions to undertake such actions probably can be postponed until one feels more ready to consider these.

3. When one member of the family experiences pain (or distress), all members of the family experience some form of pain (Satir, 1964, 1967), discomfort, or anxiety. These feelings may provide the leverage for getting the significant others of the originally identified or index patient into family treatment. Children are also affected by the death of a parent and, if the family is close, will resonate to the surviving parent's grave sense of loss, as well as experiencing their own. Sharing the pain and

bewilderment about the future can provide solace and mutual comfort and should be encouraged.

4. Each member of the family has their own narrative to tell (White & Epstom, 1990) and should be listened to empathically. It is their version of their family's story, and their place, role, and status within their family. Each person in treatment, or assembled anywhere, should be encouraged to tell his or her story and share memories with one another, which can have a curative effect in the opportunity reminiscing provides for catharsis; this can also optimize feelings of "bonding" and attachment.

5. As any one member of the family system changes, this will trigger changes in the other members of the system, as they will ultimately have to respond differently. As the surviving parent regains composure and starts to function more competently and independently, this sets grown children free to deal with their own changed world and worry less about their parent. If the children are young when their Mom or Dad dies, the remaining parent will have to tend to their needs, also, so their rates of reequilibration will be intertwined.

6. Each person is responsible for his or her own behavior and should be held accountable for changing it in accordance with the tasks to be mastered and goals set in treatment. Clinically, despite their recent tragedy, each person should be treated in an age- and stage-appropriate way and gently guided to resume responsibilities. For example, children should be expected to return to school after a lapse of time devoted to active grieving, and adults to work, or their other activities after sufficient time has been allotted for the first phase of the mourning process. Yet they should be reassured that periods of being sad, lonely, teary, or angry will recur for a while to come, and they should allow themselves to feel what they feel while still attempting to resume their normal activities. (These principles are alluded to later in the Z case summation.)

Bentovim (1992) talked about trauma-organized systems, that is, how the family organizes itself differently than before the illness set in, or the accident or other traumatic event(s) occurred, to deal with the immediate crises or series of events. Initially, the majority of families shift into a crisis mode, which first entails dealing with what must be done immediately, like getting someone to the doctor or hospital, arranging for surgery, visiting daily, or setting up nursing, physical therapy, rehabilitation, or other needed services. They may also be confronted with the need to reapportion roles in the family, like chauffeuring children to activities and making meals. Filing insurance claims may be another time-consuming task with which the partner may be unfamiliar, yet that needs to be done. Financial concerns may mount, driving everyone's stress level higher. The sick person needs empathy and understanding and is likely to get it, at least initially, from family and friends. However, the well partner, who is often on overload and feeling distraught in the caregiver and general manager roles, may get little of the sympathy and support he or she requires, especially if the illness becomes chronic and drawn out. The needs of all change over

time, so it is important that the system continue to be flexible and make new adaptations (Olson, 1996) and longrange plans, rather than stay in the crisis mode that was appropriate in the beginning and acute phases of the illness. Children may be baffled and frightened, their sense of security threatened by one parent's plight and possible diminished accessibility at the same time the other parent has become preoccupied and therefore also less available.

Death Following a Long-Term Illness

As an acute illness becomes chronic and then is viewed as terminal, the anxiety level is likely to escalate, and if death seems to be hovering near, everyone's dread may mount. Under these circumstances, fear of death may exact as much of a toll as the illness itself, and the caretaker/partner may feel overwhelmed by the burden of all the responsibilities and resentful or saddened by the multiple losses devolving from no longer having a capable, cheerful, and contributing partner (Rainer & McMurry, 2002). When a person dies after a prolonged illness, the remaining partner, if still young and with children at home, often feels an admixture of new apprehensions about managing as a single parent and relief that the ordeal has ended.

If the person is in a financially solvent position, it is likely to be easier to pay attention to the children and their dilemmas about the loss and other needs, as well as do their own mourning and subsequent reequilibration. If they are impoverished or financially strapped, their grief and often a sense of aloneness are complicated by yet another layer of serious concerns about mounting bills and having to earn a living, thus not being available to the children much of the time. For many, this is a bleak scenario for an extended period of time, and the comfort of neighbors, family, and friends is essential during the most difficult months following the death. If they can be guided to enter individual or family therapy or go to a support group with others who are also dealing with bereavement issues, they can receive assistance for coping with the grief and exhaustion and planning for the present and future. Their coping capacities and sense of well-being can be enhanced. For those who have a strong religious or spiritual faith, talks with their minister, priest, or rabbi, as well as prayer and church attendance, may help them regain strength, courage, and perspective and to find a way to move forward (Close, 2002b).

In older couples who have been together for many decades and who still like being married to each other, the bonds of friendship, companionship, and love deepen over the years (Sharlin, Kaslow, & Hammerschmidt, 2000). They become interdependent, and although they may maintain separate and well-individuated identities, their couple identity is vitally important and significant to their sense of being and well-being. While they are still well, it is advisable that future threats to this vital bond be discussed and tentative plans made, including the preparation of advance directives stating each one's wishes in the event one becomes seriously ill (Rainer & McMurry, 2002). However, many couples harbor a silent fear of the demise of their spouse that neither cares to broach in open discussion. Both hope the inevitable end to life will not come for many years. The Z case, which follows, is illustrative of the second type of older couple.

Clinical Vignette 1: The Z Case

[1]Mrs. Z was referred to me by her primary care physician. She and her husband had been married about 45 years and lived an affluent lifestyle in Palm Beach, Florida. They had been on vacation in Europe when Mr. Z suffered a moderately severe stroke. He was flown back to the United States and provided with the best care available. Mrs. Z felt terribly stressed and agitated; she was accustomed to her husband being a competent, take-charge kind of person, and she rarely had had to make major decisions. Seeing him unable to ambulate easily and hearing his slurred speech were initially incomprehensible. She had been somewhat pampered and enjoyed their country club existence; now he could no longer handle their daily affairs, play golf, or go to social functions with her. She had little understanding of their complex investments and other aspects of their finances. She knew it was important to him that he be treated with dignity and respect and to remain at home.

Her physician recognized her confusion and depression, and thus the referral to me. She was pleased to have someone to talk with who empathized with her plight and who could provide support and guidance. She was able to form a strong therapeutic alliance, which she sustained over many years. Over time she expressed strong resentment and great anger (not unusual reactions) that her husband's stroke had interfered with their wonderful lifestyle and that she felt adrift. Because her husband's mind was still functioning well at this point, I suggested she ask him to set up meetings with their accountant, banker, lawyer, and stockbroker so she could become better acquainted with these key people who affected her life and could learn to understand the trusts and will he had set up, how to monitor their investments, and what it was she had to manage. A bright woman, she followed through on this and learned fairly rapidly so she became well versed in their financial affairs.

Friends, as well as her husband's brother and sister-in-law, visited and sometimes went out to dinner with them the first few months after his initial stroke. However, in the next year he suffered several mini TIAs (transient ischemic attack), and his condition deteriorated visibly. People stopped calling and were reluctant to accept her invitations to come visit and play bridge (he still could) or meet them for dinner. He was using a walker and slobbered when he ate. I sympathized with how cruel this "desertion" by long-time friends must feel and then explained that being around a dear friend who is declining forces others to face their own vulnerability and mortality, and many shy away from situations that serve as a reminder. In addition, I indicated that some of their friends had already decided life for them was short and they wanted to have fun, which may have excluded being exposed to the unhappy sight of a friend who was debilitated. She protested, disliking this idea, but after pondering it, realized she would not like to go out with someone in his condition either, if she did not have to.

One day she came into her therapy session quite sheepishly, which was unusual for her. She said she was afraid and ashamed to say what she was thinking and feeling and yet to talk about anything else seemed trivial. I asked if she wanted help in articulating her feelings, and with tears in her eyes, she nodded. I asked if, after 4 long years of living with her husband while his condition worsened and her own existence revolved increasingly around his illness, she wished the end would come quickly. She nodded again, and asked if she were a terrible person for wishing this for the husband she had once loved so much and who had been so good to her. I provided the reassurance she needed that feeling this way when one has been the caretaker for a person who is chronically ill and is not expected to improve is frequent and that it did not make her a horrible person. She heaved a sigh of relief, and we were able to proceed with discussing other issues during the session. About a month later she was able to finalize arrangements for her husband to enter a nursing home and for private duty nurses, when needed. He had become incontinent, and she and the at-home nurses could not change his diaper or move him easily. This fact helped her justify "breaking" the promise she had made years earlier not to place him in a nursing home. His residing outside of the home allowed her more free time, so she felt less confined and resentful, and she knew he was getting good care. She visited daily and then did whatever else she wanted to.

With encouragement from her therapist and some preparatory role rehearsals on how to do so before he died a few months later, she was able to say her goodbyes and thank him for what he had contributed to their life together, and for their children. She had kept them apprised of their father's declining health, but both had come to visit from their homes up north infrequently, indicating they were just too busy.

In treatment we processed her feelings of abandonment and her regrets that they had not paid more attention to their father (as sometimes happens). Her son, daughter, and grandchildren did come to Florida for his funeral, and did find time to fly down again when his will was being probated (Klein, 2000) to see what personal items, like jewelry and cars, they might be getting and could take back with them. She was disappointed by their selfishness and calloused behavior. Yet in many ways, relief was her predominant emotion, and she was ready for the closure death brought.

Z Case Summation

Mr. Z's illness led to a change in the Z's marital interaction; it necessitated Mrs. Z becoming much more self-sufficient and taking on the major decision-making and caretaking roles. Their grown children's neglect of both of them during this time, while they continued to expect their usual annual tax-free $10,000 checks per person, plus other major gifts, forced Mrs. Z to recognize that she and her husband had indulged their children and had failed to teach them appreciation and mutuality. My psychodynamic therapeutic interventions facilitated ventilation and catharsis and promoted greater insight into herself, her husband, and their children. Cognitive-behavioral techniques used for goal-oriented planning (Kaslow & Patterson, 2002), plus systemic and narrative approaches, were included. (The principles alluded to herein were explicated earlier in this article.) These included the following:

- Encouraging Mrs. Z to tell their life story; listening attentively, sympathetically, and empathically; and interjecting responses as she related her memories and interpretations. (Principle 4: Retelling one's personal narrative.)
- Helping her become aware of her strengths, which included her intelligence (previously underutilized), her astuteness and perceptiveness, her competence to learn about and later to manage their affairs, and her considerable energy. (Principle 6: Encouraging independence, responsibility, and mastery.)
- Giving "permission" to her to find ways to resume enjoying her own life, including taking occasional mini vacations, without feeling guilty once she had devised and implemented good plans for his care in the nursing home. (Principle 1: Helping her extricate slightly from feeling too interconnected and losing any sense of being a separate self.)
- Encouraging her to articulate her thoughts and feelings about him to her husband, thank him for their life together, and say her goodbyes—while he was still coherent and could respond and give her loving feedback, too. As they had not been prone to being emotionally expressive of deep sentiments, engaging in this kind of behavior had seemed alien to her, and yet she knew intellectually that it was something she would like to do. We did several role enactments to ready her for what proved to be a very dramatic and touching interaction. (Principle 2: Here we attempted to disrupt a long-term homeostatic balance that had had negative consequences.)
- Gently guiding her to assess her children and grandchildren more realistically so she was not repeatedly disappointed in and hurt by their inattentiveness and lack of concern. (Principle 5: As Mrs. Z changed, it was anticipated there would be a concomitant change in the reactions and behaviors of her children and grandchildren.)
- Once Mr. Z had died, and she had had time to mourn, I refocused treatment on what she wanted to do with her life in the immediate future, and she was able to ponder this and make some decisions, like how much she wanted to move back to a beachfront condominium, increase her travel, renew neglected friendships, and take appropriate actions to implement her plans. (Principle 6: In using this type of intervention, I encouraged Mrs. Z to take charge of her own life—in the present and for the future—and free herself of her husband's remaining vestiges of control, which she had abhorred.)
- Suggested bringing many years of therapy to closure, as she was capable of managing quite well on her own, thereby supporting her recently acquired sense of her own self-sufficiency. (Principle 6: She had achieved her goals and needed to be off on her own, by mutual agreement. It was an excellent, liberating final session, like a graduation.)

Sudden, Unanticipated Death

This scenario is quite different from what is apt to occur when someone is confronted with the sudden, (almost) instantaneous death of their partner. This can result from an airplane or car crash, a drive-by shooting, a hurricane or flood, a fatal coronary, or a horrendous event like the terrorist attack of 9/11 that quickly destroyed thousands of lives. All of these occurrences seem inexplicable and incomprehensible and are overwhelming to deal with. There is no time for emotional preparation, no time to work through problems, no time to say goodbye and bring any sort of emotional closure to the relationships, and no time to ask for or offer forgiveness (Close, 2002a). Instead, there probably is disbelief, shock, incredulity, numbness, grief, rage, and bewilderment about how this happened, and myriad questions that one may obsess over such as: Did he or she suffer? What could I have done to prevent it? How am I going to go on? What is going to happen to me, the children, and his/her (dependent) parents? Given the quandary and quagmire in which they may perceive themselves to be caught, and all of the uncertainties that beset them, it is not unusual for people to try to give some meaning to their terrible loss by seeking someone to blame. It can be the doctors (in the case of a partner's fatal coronary or not being able to save their life after an accident), God for allowing such a disaster to occur, or the airline or government for not properly protecting its passengers or citizens.

Rather than seeking someone to blame, others turn to their faith for comfort and believe that somehow what happened is part of God's plan and they must accept it and pray for guidance, strength, humility, and understanding. They may turn to family, friends, and the community for succor and solace. Still others dull the pain with antianxiety or antidepressant medication, illegal drugs or alcohol, gambling, or overeating. But sooner or later they must face the loss and its implications and attempt to deal with the present and future—for at least a while—alone, as a widow or widower. Loneliness may be pervasive and paralyzing. It may be many decades since they lived alone and were not part of a couple. The solitude and emptiness can cause despair and a feeling of not knowing where to turn, what to do, how they will survive, and whether they want to go on without their partner. Clinically, we see a myriad of other feelings also, such as guilt and remorse expressed in such statements as "I should have been a better husband [or wife]," "I did not realize how much I cared for him [or her]," "I'm so sorry for all the missed opportunities."

Here attentive listening, loads of support and encouragement, and "permission" to grieve, be angry, and generally "feel what you feel" can be given. Later, suggestions can be made about how to pick up the pieces. Discussion about whether to move or stay put in the marital home, how to reach out to old and new friends, and resuming activities may be warranted. The therapist should pace interventions to the rhythm of the patient's ability to hear and perhaps use the suggestions.

The therapeutic approaches and strategies recommended earlier are also applicable when death has been sudden. But first a safe sanctuary or holding environment (Winnicott, 1986) must be provided by the therapist so the person can do his or her grieving. Occasionally, we hear relief expressed when a fatal accident occurs. This seems to be particularly true where a situation has been abusive and the partner's death sets the spouse free, when divorce was perceived as untenable or dangerous to pursue.

Clinical Vignette 2: The C Case

Bob C was 39 years of age. His wife, Lira, was 35 years old, and they had twin daughters, age 3. Bob, a CPA, worked hard and put in long hours at the office and with clients. Although he was devoted to his family, he saw his main role as providing well for his family financially, just as his dad had done. Lira agreed, since she wanted to be a stay-at-home mom and devote her to time to raising the children. Both considered the marriage and their life together quite happy and fulfilling, until tragedy struck suddenly.

One day when Lira had a babysitter she went to do some shopping in the nearby mall. While she was driving, another car rammed into her and she was thrown out onto the road. By the time the paramedics came and got her to the hospital, she was pronounced dead on arrival. Her injuries had been fatal.

When Bob received the phone call at his office telling him there had been an accident and he should come to the hospital immediately, his heart began to pound. With barely a word of explanation, he raced out of his office. When he got to the hospital and was told the horrific news, he went into a state of disbelief saying, "It can't be true; you must have the wrong person." But when they showed him her wallet and identification and described her mangled car, the truth became undeniable.

What he later described to me in therapy (which one of the nurses had urged he seek right away) was that disbelief turned to shock, horror, fury, and then uncontrollable tears. His whole life had changed instantaneously, and he had no idea of what to do or where to turn. A social worker in the emergency unit suggested that the few things he needed to do immediately were (a) call his office, tell them what had occurred and arrange for others there to cover his accounts and paperwork for the next week; (b) notify his wife's parent and his, and see who could help with the children immediately and until other arrangements could be made; and (c) think about funeral arrangements and decide if he wanted to handle these or delegate them to someone else. Through his tears, he nodded, but he was so dazed he felt like a "dead man walking." He realized he had to decide quickly whether to take the twins to the funeral, which he was reluctant to do. In the initial emergency therapy session, I suggested that even though the twins might not understand what death and a funeral really signified, it was probably better to take them, for them to symbolically say goodbye, and conveyed that this memory probably would become increasingly important as they got older.

For weeks afterward, he went through the motions of conducting his life, handling what seemed most pressing at the moment. Both sets of parents set up a schedule of shifts to help with the children when he was not available and agreed to do this for 4 to 6 weeks, and thereafter when other arrangements could not be made. One of the greatest dilemmas for him was how to tell the

children that their mommy was not coming back and to communicate how fatal accidents occur without frightening them so that they would still be willing to go in a car. We dealt with this in his second and third therapy sessions, as this was a pressing matter. Despite having gone to the funeral, the girls kept asking, "Where is mommy?" "Why isn't she coming back?" He explained about death as best he could and found that their longing for their mommy and anger at her disappearance just added another huge layer of despair to his own distress. The demands of his daily life felt overwhelming; he could not concentrate; he could not show his grief and upset to the children, and his talks with his clergyman left him feeling even more frustrated and distraught. Being told "it is part of God's mysterious plan for you" was an anathema. He tried to come to therapy twice a week, as this was the only place he felt he could pour out his heart, get some sincere empathy for his pain and plight, and also receive some rational help with step-by-step procedures for accomplishing the tasks that needed to be done. He was able to follow through and implement the plans and actions we had devised jointly.

Fortunately, his parents and in-laws were wonderful to him and the children, and they all loved each other dearly. Their constancy helped the children stay in their prior routine and enabled them to be tucked into bed each night by their daddy or an adoring grandparent. Bob went back to work part time a month after his wife died. He made arrangements to set up a complete office in his home where he could continue to work part time. He found an excellent "nanny/housekeeper" whom he hired for 30 hours a week. The rest of the time he chose to be Mr. Mom, and the two sets of grandparents remained actively involved.

Six months later the household was running smoothly and Bob enjoyed spending more time with his twins. He still desperately missed his wife, and the children still occasionally asked, "When is mommy coming back?" Fortunately, the nanny was reliable, affectionate, and kind. In therapy Bob had asked all of the unanswerable "why" questions, cried over his loss and the enormous changes it had wrought, deliberated over how to handle his children, and decided to take one day at a time. Eventually, it became clear that the "Why did this happen" question has no answer, unless one has deep faith and can accept that the death was God's will and their loved one is happy in heaven.

The Aftermath

As in the Z case, therapy here used an integrative approach (Kaslow & Lebow, 2002), each strategy tailored to what was most pressing in the moment. Initially I used crisis intervention or critical stress debriefing by "being with him" as Bob sobbed, screamed out in fury at the driver of the car that killed his wife, and poured out his confusion and desperation. Then I structured the interventions to help him focus on:

- What needed to be done immediately regarding the funeral and child care.
- Establishing a longer term plan for the children's parenting, what to tell them, and how.
- Calling upon and relying on their extended family support system as a key resource network.

- Emphasizing how much the children needed to be able to rely on his resiliency.
- Rearranging his work schedule and setting up an auxiliary office at home.
- How to continue loving and remembering his wife, and yet slowly begin to move on in his life without her presence by renewing friendships and occasionally going out for a social evening.
- Setting a realistic timetable and expectations for his own and the children's recovery.

Phase 1 of treatment lasted for about 3 months, and then he felt he could "go it on my own." We agreed to hold a follow-up session every 3 months for a year, and that he could call as needed. He adhered to the plan and actually called only one time for guidance when the twins insisted he had to "make mommy come back." He was stymied, like most parents would be, posed with this request. I helped him elaborate on what he had originally told the children, to reassure them of her continuing love, but that much as he would like to, he could not bring her back. Such moments are always poignant and highlight the impermanence of relationships and of life itself.

Other Variables to Be Considered

Many variables influence the kind of death that is apt to occur and the grief, mourning, and healing process that ensue. Age is a significant one, and it seems that younger people are more apt to die of sudden, accidental deaths as they are more likely to take such risks as riding motorcycles or driving cars at high speeds, sky diving, bungee jumping, and drag racing. Also, they may serve in the armed forces and may die on the battlefield. Younger surviving partners may go into temporary shock, as Mr. C did, yet recuperate more swiftly because they know their children need them to be healthy and competent, and they have more options available in terms of job opportunities, friendships, and activities in which to participate than their older counterparts usually do. They are likely to have more social resources to call upon and to be more resilient.

It is in the over-65 age range that long-term chronic illness is likely to prove debilitating and culminate in death. In this age cohort, one rarely has healthy parents still alive to turn to, and they will already have lost some of their friends who have relocated for their retirement, or to death. Often their own health is no longer robust, and they view their world as no longer dynamic and expansive but rather as dull and shrinking. In therapy, the components of this pessimistic view needs to be reframed, new alternatives generated, strengths underscored, and hope for a bright future instilled (Seligman, 1991).

When the death occurs through suicide (see earlier article in this section by N. Kaslow and Aronson for fuller discussion), it is devastating to the survivor spouse, unless the spouse has long been terminally ill and this action is perceived as a self-chosen "mercy killing." Given that statistics in the United States show that White men between 75 and 85 years of age have a higher suicide rate than any other age group and that both elderly men and women commit suicide three to four times more than younger

adults of the same sex (Saul & Saul, 1988–1989), it is reasonable to assume that a significant portion of these individuals are married and leave behind a bereaved partner. It has been found that elderly people who commit suicide have a strong intent to die (Miller, 1979), and the means they use are more lethal and lead to death more frequently than with younger attempters. A study by Lund and his colleagues (Lund, Caserta, & Dimond, 1986) found that the highest levels of depression and bereavement-related symptoms in the surviving partner were manifested "in the first few months after the loss, and that the symptoms lessened over time"; nevertheless, the loss was often not resolved within 2 years (Balter, 1993).

Most, if not all, of the great religions have rituals for helping people deal with death, and these involve loved ones in the process for support, comfort, and reassurance. The prevailing rituals may entail prescribed ways of handling the preparations for the funeral, the actual funeral ceremony in a chapel and at the gravesite, and what is to happen after the burial. The rituals serve as road maps that prescribe a structured way that things should be handled, and sometimes even how people should behave. Following these rituals means the grieving and beleaguered survivors do not have to figure out the details for themselves; there is a predetermined and widely accepted template for doing so within their personal reference group and community of origin (Imber-Black, Roberts, & Whiting, 1988). Thus, for example, whether one is Catholic and there is a wake and a mass, or is Jewish and is expected to "sit Shiva" for anywhere from 3 days to 1 week followed by, in orthodox Judaism, a mandated, prolonged period of 1 month of heavy mourning and then another 10 to 11 months of lighter mourning until the ceremonial unveiling of the tombstone, the expectations are familiar. This familiarity and link to past and future generations of relatives and mourners provide a modicum of comfort and succor. Friends are also expected to be around to take over to temporarily relieve the bereaved individual (and immediate family) of some pressing chores. In the event that no funeral or burial arrangements have been made, and doing so would be exceedingly stressful for the new widow or widower in the immediate aftermath of their loss, others can execute these tasks. The presence of neighbors, friends, and relatives for the days and weeks following the death not only provides some reassurance and soothing but also can serve as an intermittent distraction from one's grief and sense of woe. They may also be able to offer some counsel, guidance, wisdom, and assistance in problem solving as to next steps to be taken and the handling of myriad financial concerns.

In a summary of the literature, Balter (1993) found that those who have strong social support networks fare better than those who are isolated and feel lonely, and that they are able to adapt to bereavement without excess physical or psychiatric problems. Clinically, what we see when a senior adult has been widowed by the death by suicide of a spouse is that the living partner goes through the gamut of emotions, from all the self-doubts as to their contribution to precipitating the deadly act to fury that it was committed, leaving them alone and humiliated. They are extremely distressed by what has transpired and its sequelae.

Pitta (2002) and Sanders (1992) have identified tasks that need to be accomplished in the *healing* and *renewal* phases of recuperation from grieving the loss of a loved one. These seem applicable to someone mourning the loss of a spouse, and therefore are listed here, with amplifications, because they incorporate and extend what has been discussed earlier in this article and have practical utility for the clinician involved with helping patients heal.

The healing phase—the turning point after recognition of loss and frequent withdrawal:

- Relinquishing roles (particularly that of spouse)
- Forming a new identity (as a widowed person)
- Assuming control (and responsibility for one's own decisions)
- Self-care (like exercising, eating well, socializing)
- Centering, including self-soothing (perhaps meditating, doing relaxation breathing and exercises)
- Forgiving (the loved one for dying)
- Searching for meaning (in the loved one's death, perhaps from a spiritual relationship with a higher power)
- Closing the circle (possibly through a ritual or special event, and then embarking on new pathways and opening new circles of friends and activities)
- Renewing hope (remembering both the sad and happy times realistically)

The renewal phase (Sanders, 1992):

- Keeping loneliness in perspective (learning to live without the partner)
- Enduring the anniversaries (and other special couples events, and knowing they may bring about some temporary resurgence of grief and longing)
- Accepting responsibility for and living for oneself (establishing emotional independence and enjoying one's newfound freedom)
- Focusing (putting one's energies into meeting new challenges and goals)
- Reaching out
- Understanding the long process of grieving

Smith (2003) cautioned that it is important to differentiate between mourning and melancholia, and to recognize the difference between bereavement and sadness over the loss and clinical depression, which is more serious and longer lasting. The first response of mourning, sorrow and sadness, is normal and reactive. The second is marked by a greater number and more severity of symptoms, plus a sense of worthlessness experienced by the depressed survivor. It is this "sense of worthlessness … possibly accompanied by corollary guilt and suicidal ideation, that sets depression apart from grieving" (p. 3). It is imperative that therapists recognize the difference and predicate treatment on an astute differential diagnosis.

Footnote

1. All case illustrations have two or more similar cases intertwined. Nonetheless, all identities have been carefully camouflaged to protect the privacy and confidentiality of the actual patients.

References

Babb, L. A. (1999). *Ethics in American adoption*. Westport, CT: Bergen & Garvey.

Balter, R. (1993). The elderly suicide: Those left behind. In D. Lester & M. Tallmer (Eds.), *Now I lay me down: Suicide in the elderly* (pp. 163–178). Philadelphia: Charles Press.

Bentovim, A. (1992). *Trauma organized systems: Physical and sexual abuse in families*. London: Karnac Books.

Bowen, M. (1988). *Family therapy in clinical practice* (2nd ed.). Northvale, NJ: Jason Aronson.

Close, H. T. (2002a). *Becoming a forgiving person*. Unpublished manuscript, Atlanta, GA.

Close, H. T. (2002b). A ceremony for grieving. *Journal of Pastoral Care and Counseling,* 56 (1), 65–68.

Imber-Black, E., Roberts, J., & Whiting, R. (1988). *Rituals in families and family therapy*. New York: Norton.

Kaslow, F. W., & Lebow, J. (Eds.). (2002). *Comprehensive handbook of psychotherapy: Vol. 4. Integrative/eclectic*. New York: Wiley.

Kaslow, F. W., & Patterson, T. (Eds.). (2002). *Comprehensive handbook of psychotherapy: Vol. 2. Cognitive/behavioral approaches*. New York: Wiley.

Klein, S. (2000). Wills and trusts: Family planning. In F. W. Kaslow (Ed.), *Handbook of couple and family forensics: A source book for mental health and legal professionals* (pp. 426–438). New York: Wiley.

Lund, D. A., Caserta, M. S., & Dimond, M. F. (1986). Gender differences through two years of bereavement among the elderly. *The Gerontologist,* 26, 314–319.

Miller, M. (1979). *Suicide after sixty*. New York: Springer.

Olson, D. H. (1996). Clinical assessment and treatment interventions using the family circumplex model. In F. W. Kaslow (Ed.), *Handbook of relational diagnosis and dysfunctional family patterns* (pp. 59–80). New York: Wiley.

Pitta, P. (2002, Fall). Journey through grief. *The Independent Practitioner,* 259–264.

Rainer, J. P., & McMurry, P. (2002). Caregiving at the end of life. *Journal of Clinical Psychology/In Session,* 58, 1421–1431.

Sanders, C. (1992). *Surviving grief and learning to live again*. New York: Wiley.

Satir, V. (1964). *Conjoint family therapy*. Palo Alto, CA: Science & Behavior Books.

Satir, V. (1967). *Conjoint family therapy* (Rev. ed.). Palo Alto, CA: Science & Behavior Books.

Saul, S. R., & Saul, S. S. (1988–1989). Old people talk about suicide. *Omega,* 19, 237–251.

Schwartz, L. L., & Kaslow, F. W. (2003). *Welcome home: An international and cross-cultural adoption reader*. New York: Haworth.

Seligman, M. E. P. (1991). *Learned optimism*. New York: Alfred A. Knopf.

Sharlin, S. A., Kaslow, F. W., & Hammerschmidt, H. (Eds.). (2000). *Together through thick and thin: A multinational picture of long term marriages*. Binghamton, NY: Haworth.

Smith, E. W. L. (2003). Mourning and melancholia—bereavement and depression. *Bulletin of the American Academy of Clinical Psychology,* 9 (1), 3–4.

White, M., & Epstom, D. (1990). *Narrative means to therapeutic ends.* New York: Norton.

Winnicott, D. W. (1986). *Home is where we start from: Essays by a psychoanalyst.* New York: Norton.

FLORENCE W. KASLOW received her PhD from Bryn Mawr College and is director of the Florida Couples and Family Institute and president of Kaslow Associates, PA, in Florida. She is a visiting professor of psychology at both Florida Institute of Technology in Melbourne and Duke University Medical Center in Durham, North Carolina.

CORRESPONDENCE CONCERNING THIS ARTICLE may be addressed to Florence W. Kaslow, 128 Windward Drive, Palm Beach Gardens, FL 33418. E-mail: drkaslow@bellsruth.net.

From *Professional Psychology: Research and Practice,* Vol. 35, No. 3, June 2004, pp. 227-233. Copyright © 2004 by the American Psychological Association. Reprinted by permission.

The Hispanic Way of Dying: Three Families, Three Perspectives, Three Cultures

Recent statistics, including the latest census, demonstrate a rapid increase in the growth of the Hispanic population of the United States. In some cities, they are the largest population group. While it is important to note that Hispanic, as a label, does not wipe out the uniqueness of different countries, their customs and traditions, and those of the families, this article highlights the fear and celebration as death approaches, the role of the family and the extended family, the significance of social and familial ritual, the spiritual implications of faith and loss, and the religious presence throughout.

NERIS DIAZ-CABELLO

Six Feet

How did you dare to go to the isolated cosmos of the dead?
With a one way ticket escaping from the body at dawn
With your soul open to the immensity of the eternal light
From an aching body that dwells in darkness without a sight.

And I went out to see you with others
My human compass was my mother,
And she had forgotten were the wake took place,
Saying: "if her tombstone is not in the valley, it most be at the hill"
And she whispered: "now-days, no one has mercy of the dead"
We walk and walk … and I walked with tears on my face
crying her memories, seeing her lost memory
And in my grandmother's diary were found,
The virtue of her reality compounded.

And I visited your place.
There you were in your silent cosmos
Six feet under earth without a word to say
Not even thoughts my mind produced,
No words my mouth had to say,
Only silence, birth silence,
And in the sequence of quietness, loneliness
I wanted for a moment mitigate my need to see you
In the last embrace of the eternal "farewell,"
But, I arrived late, too late to see you.

There, I was crying a river over your cross
With the sweet remembrance breathing on my chest,
Denoting the ache of your absence on my eyes,
Fertilizing my land in the denial of your cosmos

I woke up wanting to see you in our past
The years are the witnesses of what is gone
And in the hallucination of the soul I see you again
Rocking your chair in the breeze, smiling to my love

You are six feet underground from my womb, heart and soon
I will be facing your naked name printed on your tombstone
Embracing my reality in the cruel space and the eternity of the sun
Burning my shoulders, taking away the illusion to breathe next to you

—*Neris Diaz-Cabello*, March 19, 2001

Hispanic people see death with great solemnity. The atmosphere that is circumscribed to the immediate grief incarnates many losses, along with the immediate loss. The physical expression of inner pain is deep sorrow. The dead one does not return to say how the journey went. It is the silence embracing the anguish of the bereaved, the coldness of the event that touches the most sacred feeling, the inner self of our soul, thoughts, and the memories of a life expiring before our eyes that produces emotional distress. The entire being sobs internally and physically. The physical attachment that reaps apart in the process of death draws near a new horizon of new beginnings to walk toward the future.

Some people are comforted by the hope that, one day, they will encounter their loved one in eternity. Others are unable to see their faith as a source of strength and new beginnings.

The Hispanic way of dying is a vast topic and due to the content, religious approach that each family professes, and the variety of cultural diversity within the Hispanic people. This article is limited to some customs and viewpoints from three family traditions because people develop their own hermeneutic when faced with death. I have chosen three patients, three stories, three perspectives, three cultures within the Hispanic culture that correspond to their own family customs and core of beliefs, values, and generational views. In general, I will add other experiences and practices within the wide range of experiences that I have encountered in my life as clergy within a hospital setting.

In general, the Hispanic culture in the United States is the grouping of many entities, nationalities, and cultures as "webs of significance" (Fukuyama and Sevig 1999, 8). In the latest census, there was an affirmation of the Hispanic presence on this nation—more than 30 million people residing in the United States. The common factor is the language and also, within it, there is a diverse indigenous language, idioms, and colloquialisms that differ from region to region. Another aspect is the national dates celebrating the liturgical calendar, a saint's day, and the national celebrations related to our nation's own independence. Each person within his or her own familiar micro-cosmos holds an understanding of the church celebration, the forms of grace, and salvation as it comes to play a part in what the person owns in forms of identity and meaning in his life.

In the topic, Hispanic ways of dying, there is variety and richness in the hermeneutic of how the people conceive God and practice their own spirituality because, in the symbiosis of the culture, the folklore, the language, and the values pass through generations from parents to children. There is a meaning circumscribed to the family that is transmitted, practiced, and lived enriching the sense of identity within the family. The second generation born in this nation will open or close the door to practice these values once learned during childhood.

The great majority of the Hispanic people evolve their spirituality in the structured forms given by the church. These are the sacraments of baptism, first communion, confirmation, for girls *Quinceañeras*, wedding, and the sacramental needs provided through life. There are other people who celebrate and understand their faith differently, based on Bible teachings and the local settlements of practices provided by their local pastor.

People find significance in the process of fulfilling their spirituality in many ways. At the end of life, these expressions produce an echo in the family and friends of the deceased: "S/he was very catholic," "S/he was a person who trusted God," "S/he most be in heaven thanks to the life s/he lived," Many times, the religious legacy practiced once for the deceased helps the survivors in the search of inner peace in the grief process. And if the person was not devoted to church, the family will seek as its responsibility to provide Christian burial "Cristiana sepultura."

Customs in Life with Implications After Death

Every human being grows within his familiar micro-cosmos that teaches him to believe in himself and in certain ways to advance in life. In living his life, and understanding his enigmas and the human implications, the person encounters sickness and death, which are never part of the plans to succeed. The first generation of Hispanic people in this country struggles to survive as immigrants without being caught by immigration. Besides work, paying the bills, and caring for the family, they have the task of thinking about the unique decision that will make a difference throughout their lives. This personal decision will have implications in the long range of goals. One aspect of it is to understand their lives within a new cultural context, acknowledging their own values and customs learned during childhood.

What am I going to do with my family traditions?

What am I going to do with my life, my family, and my money?

Where will I invest my destiny?

These are personal thoughts that people in the street do not speak about, but among family and good friends they are openly spoken. Why is this so important? We take for granted the privilege to think and decide what we want in life, why we came to this country. The immigrant deals with that question from the moment he conceives the idea to leave his native country because it is part of his aspirations in life.

Ada Maria Isasi-Diaz (1993, 35) said,

> Liberation has to do with becoming agents of our own history, with having what ones need to live and to be able to strive towards Human fulfillment. Liberation is the realization of our projecto historico, which we are always seeking to make a reality while accepting that its fullness will never be accomplished in history. Liberation is realized in concrete events, which at the same time point to more comprehensive and concrete realization.

To work introspectively is to find your strengths and weaknesses in order to function, relate, advocate, and live your life. Some people work these internal mechanisms not knowing consciously how they do it, but they survive by deciding what is best for them. The beauty of decision making is that even when you are trapped in your reality, or the structure of this society that suppresses you, you live your life as the projection of inner liberation you need to dignify, who you are. It does not matter what it takes to survive; it matters that you decided how to do it.

The decisiveness will lead the immigrant to actions in the immediate future. To find answers to his existential quest will bring inner peace and a sense of freedom to act within his parameters of actions. The setting up of the questions presupposes interior knowledge, self-awareness, and inner listening to one's own voice. There are many people who are trying to understand their own world and cannot achieve self-encounter, and they survive every day by living it. These people do not decide where to put their roots, dreams, future, and this indecisional riot brings them to the land of desperation of not belonging anywhere. There are many people in this country who only invest in their country of origin. In the same way, there are others whose dream is to stay here, become a citizen, and grow their roots in the United States.

There are always good reasons to go back to the old country. Hispanics make a great deal of economical sacrifices during the year to have the resources for a family reunion, a wedding, and *quinceañera*, a ritual of baptism of a child that was given to a godparent before birth. Even though the immigrant lives, enjoys, and has success in this country where he resides, he always goes back to visit his old country to bring the good news to his own people. The good news begins within the family, in the house of his parents. There, he introduces his wife and children to his parents, and later he introduces his own to his extended family to become acquainted with them and to celebrate the lives that he has developed far from them. It is in family where the center of identification and belonging is reborn.

At the end of life, many people become nostalgic and want to return to their native country. They dream of the sunrises and the sunsets of their town. They dream with their friends and with those who have died long ago. If the wish to go back persists and is not fulfilled for diverse reasons in life, a covenant between father and child takes place: "send my body to Mexico," The child promises to do it and the deal is done. After the person passes away, the child or relative fulfills the promise given, "to ship the body back home."

The sense of family among Hispanics is unique.

Grieving a Wife and a Mother

The spiritual life of the children is the duty of parents. The child is guided in the faith of the parent, in the observance and the practice of the ritual. The child learns from body language how people behave in a holy place until the moment they are ready to go alone and choose their own spiritual path. In the child's heart will stay the footprint of the images taught once by the grandmother, the prayers and the candle veladoras in the altar and the familiar practices of the religious celebrations.

The child will never forget it.

Lupe and Juan are an example of a young Mexican family living and struggling in the United States. Lupe was sick with cancer but she did not know about it. It was after the delivery of her third child that her cancer was detected. Immediately, she pursued an aggressive treatment and it was in counsel with her specialist that she learned that her cancer had metastasized in her whole system. Lupe decided to go back home and spend the time she had left with her children. At her last admission to the hospital she asked to receive the sacrament every day and to speak with the chaplain to look for spiritual direction and comfort. Her fear of death was to leave her children orphans. She said, "Nobody could take care of my children as I do." Her fear of death was that "after they grow I can die in peace, but not now." Lupe fought the good fight with cancer and with God too, to be prepared and be worthy to enter the presence of God. Once she made her peace with God through the sacrament her only concern was her children.

The extended family was attending to the emotional, physical, and spiritual needs of Lupe. Her mother residing in Mexico frequently traveled to take care of her daughter and her grandchildren. The *compadres* (godparents) and friends came more often. They brought whatever the children needed: clothes, food, baby items in a form of a present. The saying, *"mi casa es su casa"* became a truthful affirmation of love and comprehension toward Lupe, Juan, and the children.

A month before Lupe's admission to the hospital, Juan had nightmares in which he saw her vividly agonizing and death coming to her bed to take her from him. He woke up immediately to kiss his wife and the children goodnight. One day, Juan had the courage to share his fears with his mother-in-law and she said to him, "Let us call the priest to give her the last rites, I'm also growing concerned every night but I thought it was my fear as a mother." "God will not abandon my daughter, you or my grandchildren." "God is advising us the time is running near."

In her last week of life, she was admitted to the oncology unit in the hospital. She was known by name and treated with respect and compassion in that place. She was unconscious during her last three days. If she opened her eyes she was unable to respond to simple questions that required yes-or-no answers; only her lips drew a smile if her spouse and children were present. The friends of Lupe continued to visit every day and cry at her side quietly. The godparents dedicated hours at her side in prayer and made an affirmation of the commitment acquired in the ritual of baptism with her children. The priest of the family came several times to provide support and pastoral care. The last day of her agony, her older son was with her in the room, and during my visit he finished his homework by the bedside of "his mommy." He was fearless to accompany his mother in her agony: "My mother taught me that I must be strong and help daddy with my brothers, but I do not want God to take her from us, it hurts," said Manuel, who is ten years old. This young man was able to integrate his mother's teachings and also to identify his own emotional ache. He was aware and mature enough to accept his role as the older brother "to help daddy," but he was not ready "to let her go." He invested two entire years bringing his mom to therapy "and I thought that the chemotherapy would heal her." So that night he was very much frustrated and his little face was saddened. He asked me that night to watch his favorite movie from Walt Disney, and the nurses allowed him to use the unit in the living room. The godparents arrived late that night and after a while asked Manuel to go home with them, reminding him, "Because tomorrow you need to go to school." With great struggle they were able to take him away from his mother's side; it was clear that he didn't want to leave. He reasoned with his father and his godparents, saying, "I don't want to go away. I don't want mommy to die and not to be here." Manuel was not heard.

Juan stayed awake all night saying to his wife, "Dear love, my body aches for you; I don't have an area that doesn't hurt. You are taking with you part of my life and the other will survive because you are leaving me three kids." Juan understood that the anticipation of his wife's death was physically affecting him. Juan wanted to stay at her side witnessing her breathing rhythms in the agony of her last minutes of life. He remembered his nightmares and how at this point he couldn't wake up from it because he was living it. "I want to stay with her until her breath leave her … with her my life goes."

Juan was able to be with his wife "until her breath left her." He held her hand and guided her until she departed from this world to start a new path filled with the promises given to her through the sacrament. Psalm 23:4 says, "Even thou I walk through the darkest valley I fear no evil for you are with me. Your rod and you staff—they comfort me…. Surely goodness and mercy shall follow me all the days of my life, and I shall dwell in the house of the Lord my whole life long."

Lupe did not resist the sweet arms of death. The time came when in her agony she extended her arms to heaven and then expired. The mother said, *"Los ángeles vinieron a buscarla* [the angels came to take her]." The body of Juan ached through the night understanding that it was a manifestation of his grief. He said that after his wife died his body stopped aching to manifest his grief in bitter tears. "She received everything she wanted in life. Even the little baby is the fruit of her familiar project for us; however I had in my plans to grow old with her."

We spoke that night about his plans or thoughts about burial for Lupe. Where did she want to be buried, in Mexico or in a local cemetery? Juan decided to bury his wife in town because the children were still little and to travel as a family nowadays is very expensive. "Lupe will understand what I do, even when she wanted me to ship her body to her brother and sister in Mexico. My kids and I need her near to have a place to go and cry for her." The decision to bury Lupe in town will help Juan and his children to process their grief. It has a therapeutic value: "To cry for her and to talk with her will help me, and even six feet under earth I will need her."

I met a person who remembered vividly images of his father visiting his grandfather's grave at the end of the year and around the holidays. He said that his father talked and cried and after a while lit a candle as a symbol of prayer. This space to go and visit and to have a place to cry helps the bereaved to carry on and survive. The fact that there is a place to go and talk presupposes a relationship, giving the bereaved a sense of transcendence after death, "As a child you don't get it, but after reflecting and interpreting my life, it helped me to know that my father loved my grandfather and even after he died, he did not loose the connection. Dad had a place where to go and visit with us."

I have learned that there is nothing you can do to hold the emotions of a family member suffering the agony of losing a loved one. Why hold the emotions? What is the purpose of containing it? Let the tears flow, let it flow, let the expression of grief reign for a while until the body of the survivor is ready to carry on with the next step, acceptance. Or to ask, What do I do now? The process of grief is a hard path to survive, physically and emotionally. I have lost three of my grandparents, and every time it happened, it was different. One loss does not prepare you for the next. You might learn strategies to help yourself through grief, but every loss is unique, particular because of the intrinsic connections of love and care that are attaching you to the deceased.

Grieving A Stillborn

Galicia is thirty-six years old and having her fifth child. She is an active member of the Pentecostal church, and she believes in miracles. She had thorough prenatal care and attended all appointments and the baby was growing normally. The baby didn't present any anomalies, but in her last appointment, the baby showed no heartbeat. Galicia was sent directly from the doctor's office to the Labor and Delivery Unit after she learned her baby's condition. She said to the chaplain, "My baby is perfectly fine. I'll deliver a healthy baby. I believe God can per-

form miracles." It was explained to Galicia that her baby didn't have a heartbeat, but she was unable to hear her baby's condition; she was in denial. I stayed with her and listened to her journey and needs. Later she requested her pastor to be called because he believed a miracle could be performed.

After two days, the time came when the baby was delivered, and he was dead. She requested her pastor be called immediately, to pray for her dead baby. Her pastor was contacted and came promptly to provide the miracle prayer, but "my baby didn't wake up," she said. "What is wrong with God? Why is God not listening to our prayer, pastor?" The pastor whispered, "I don't know, maybe this baby was not meant to be." Galicia anxiously answered back, "What do you mean, pastor?" He responded, "Your baby, Galicia, is now with God, but you will be able to speak with him every day in prayer." To feed the patient's denial with prayer can be a dangerous ritual for the emotional well-being of the patient; some clergy practice it very often and they don't realize what meaning is given to it by the patient.

Galicia requested for her pastor "to bless her baby," and so he did. She cried, holding her baby and whispering, "I don't know why God took you from me. I'm sorry, baby, why your life was not meant to be. I love you." Galicia and the father of the baby after many hours decided for cremation due to their financial situation. They named, blessed, and grieved their baby, and the time came to say their final good-byes.

Galicia has come several times to the memorial services to commend her baby to God. She continues to hear the voice of her baby crying through the night. "Not the medication, not the advise of my counselors has helped me to overcome my deep grief. I cannot forget my baby as my husband is asking me to do. To forget him will be a betrayal to myself and my little angel."

The bereaved parents do not forget their baby. Parents learn to survive by remembering the baby's album, if there is any. This task is difficult when the baby is born dead because memories are built through the experience of living. Memories are built by the little details produced by the voice of a baby, a special touch, the holding and singing a lullaby, the smile of a baby. Galicia continues to remember her stillborn. She continues to compare the faces of her children. She continues to remember the little fingers and the little toes, and every time she sings a lullaby in remembrance of her little angel that was not meant to be, she cries. The little baby is remembered with love but also with much sorrow. Galicia has a good support system at home helping her and her family to come to term with her loss. To attend the memorial services is helping to let go, although the words of the pastor stayed with Galicia: "I can speak with my baby every day and he listens to me."

Grieving an Uncle

A few days ago, I visited with Don Quijada at the Telemetry Unit. Mr. Quijada is a regular patient in the hospital; he travels every year to treat his cardiac condition. Last year, he couldn't return to his country because his condition got worse. He set high hopes in the treatment that would help him, but a massive heart attack destroyed the little life he had left. Three days before he died, he talked with one of his nieces: "I want to go home. I don't want to continue with this treatment I feel that my health is not improving. I don't want to die alone in this hospital room far away from my wife." His fear became a reality in part; he died in the company of the medical team who tried hard to bring him back and with the chaplain at the door praying for him. All of his relatives where working when he died; the cousins received a call at home. The relatives arrived an hour and half after his death. Mr. Quijada's cousins were with him for a while, and little by little a group of twenty people gathered to accompany the body of Mr. Quijada for one more hour.

Mr. Quijada felt his death near him. He knew that he would die. He stated in several opportunities to his nieces and nephews that he would die alone, but the nieces and nephews couldn't understand his point of view because they were in different stages of grief. While Mr. Quijada wanted to prepare himself with the rites of the church, his nieces were attached to the promises given by the specialists, the hope that "he would get better, and he would return to Mexico with better health."

The afternoon that Mr. Quijada died we prayed for a little while, and later the lay people from the church came to pray the Rosary with them. In the middle of the Rosary, the nieces and nephews cried in an inconsolable way but gradually with the repetition of the Hail Mary and the Lord's Prayer the sobbing decreased. In the last repetitions of praying, "Mary, mother of mercy and compassion," the whole family centered themselves in commending the spirit of Mr. Quijada to God; as they did this, their faces were more serene as accepting the event. The family, who knew the will of Mr. Quijada of wanting to return to his home country, made all the necessary efforts to ship the body to Mexico.

There is a wish to be buried in the land that you were born in. Every reason I have listened to are rooted in human values, in a sense of family belonging. A well-known reason for coming back is, "Our parents are buried in our home town and I want to be buried next to them." "The extended family residing there will fulfill their duty of cleaning the grave and remember me once a year." There is a popular song written by José Alfredo Jimenez that recites like this:

> Mexico lindo y querido, si muero lejos de ti, que digan que estoy dormido y que me traigan aqui. Que digan que estoy dormido y que me traigan aqui. Mexico lindo y querido si muero lejos de ti. [A rough translation is, "Mexico beautiful and dear, if I died far away from you, let them say that I am sleeping and bring me back here. /Mexico beautiful and dear, if I died far away from you."]

The rhyme of the song is known throughout the globe and its verses evoke the nostalgia people have in their hearts when they live and die in exile.

To be part of a Christian structure is to be part of an ethos in which even the dead is part of the liturgical space of the practical devotion of the people in church. This gives sense of ownership and identity and emotional stability to the dying and to the family; it can only be found at home. This has to do with the spiritual understanding that the family has with the soul of the person after they die. It is understood that the person continues to be with them in spirit, the body is buried and is no longer physically present. But the dead person will be remembered for generations, and it is believed that the spirit will return to visit with the family.

Celebrations in Some Religions After the Body Has Expired

There is a series of small rituals done by the family members just after the expiration of a body. The use of holy water or consecrated oil to bless is common, commending the spirit to God. In some families, the adult participation is a priority; like in other families, every member of the family will participate actively in blessing and commending the deceased to God.

There are families that appoint their pastor to commend the body with a prayer and do not use any other physical symbols like water or oil. Another ritual is the blessing of the burial place.

Among other rituals and prayers is the Rosary. For nine days the family and friends will gather in the house of the dearly departed to pray the Rosary. Every day there are different and special emphasis on the mystery of redemption and salvation. The last day the cross is raised, as a symbol of the achievement of one of grief's steps. After the *novena* the family can request a mass once a month, and then one annually. It is not unusual that, if family members were absent from the funeral, burial or *novena* that during their stay another celebration is arranged.

The wake or *velorios* is a tradition practiced once in the house of the deceased, a place where everyone who knew him in society came together to express the condolences to the widow and her children. The wake lasted one whole day (twenty-four hours). Friends and family gathered to talk and grieve together through the night; some activities are drinking hot chocolate, playing dominos or cards, and remembering the anecdotes and jokes of the deceased. The wake is kind of the last social celebration to announce the end of life. The custom has been to leave the coffin open for the people to witness and to come near with reverence to say last words of comfort to the family. This is a time for the family to grieve publicly, receiving support from friends and extended family. Nowadays, the funeral homes provide space and this service under the name of wake with the view of the body.

It is a custom in the Hispanic burial to stay with the family of the deceased until the coffin is lowered six feet underground. This is an emotional time and one of great pain for the ones who loved dearly the deceased. The descending of the body is the realization that the person won't be seen anymore. During this time carnations and roses are thrown over the coffin with a kiss; some people take some dirt and asperse it over the coffin. People stay until the coffin is completely buried. This event will help the bereaved to carry on with the emotional aches and slowly to start another stage in the process, the novena.

Another custom practiced by the Hispanic people that has a metaphysical sense of inspiration born after the death of the loved one is the creation of crosses in the streets. There are people who practice the creation of Christian symbols identifying the local place where the deceased lost his life in an automobile accident. The most common signs are crosses with a wreath of fresh or silk flowers identifying the place of death. These provisional crosses will be a sacred place, where the family gathers to bring flowers, remember anecdotes, cry and grieve to become whole again. It is correct to say that the body of the deceased is not in that place but buried in the cemetery.

Annual Celebrations Also Help the Family to Grieve

In the Christian tradition there are celebrations that offer the believer a space to explore hope within the grief process, Some specific masses are the Candle Mass, All Saints Day, Day of the Death, anniversary of the deceased, and other special events like birthdays. During these festivities mentioned above, the church teaches the promises of God, the meaning of salvation, and the value of believing in a God larger than the finite life we ought to live.

The day of the Candle Mass is a liturgy that invites the people to participate in dressing the newborn Jesus. As the people get ready for a new liturgical calendar focusing in the promise that brings the child, people are able to see the final journey of the child on the cross as he is placed in the center of the altar. The same day people bring candles to bless them during the mass. These candles are taken home to use during difficult times, when things in life get tough, and the expectation of hope requires a miracle. In times of illnesses, and when the agony of death is surrounding life, the candle is lit to claim the presence of God among us and specially to show the new path to walk.

I remember as if it was yesterday that, on the eve of the Day of the Death, my grandmother invited some of my brothers and sisters to remember our ancestors. In childhood your imagination is fresh and ready to engage in anything plausible that will capture your attention and keep you busy. The one task of a child was to hold the candles to remember the family member "now living with God." As my grandmother lit the first candle, a name of a person was pronounced and some memories were recollected as she taught us to remember the life of our ancestors. We were in awe, trying to keep the same reverence as she did. They were people we never met but were part of our past, and as she pronounced the name of the person again, she would commend them back to God and continue with the next one. My grandmother did not have a written list; she just remembered with love those who had died from her family. The night of remembrance is a day of communion and solemnity for the ones you knew or for learning about them. The candles stayed on through the night in a safe place until they were consumed completely. These are unforgettable memories from my childhood. These are valuable impressions rooted in the micro-cosmos of the family and the faith of my ancestors that spring within me as the years pass. As I age, the seed is there ready to sprout. As I configure my own sense of identification, I become more comfortable in exploring "Who am I?"

The Day of the Death is known within the Hispanic culture and perceived in different ways. Some people understand it as superstitious and profane; within the Protestant world it is viewed sometimes as one more festivity within the Roman Catholic calendar. The truth is that some people know about it in depth and practice it. Others just assume it is a bad thing to celebrate. The gray area belongs to the ecumenical hearts and the ones learning about it.

A big population celebrates the Day of the Death, so much so that around the date the media incorporates it as news and part of the people's tradition. A great number of people observe the day as a time to incorporate their loved ones in prayer and to visit the cemeteries. Some churches create a public altar in which the membership participate bringing pictures, fresh flowers, and the bread of the dead, incorporating "the people living with God among us." During the course of the day the names of people are mentioned. Other people make an effort to prepare a family dinner incorporating to the new generation the values and beliefs the family has, passing through the unique practices, hermeneutic, and tradition.

Virgilio Elizondo states in his article, "Popular Religiosity as Core of Cultural Identity,"

> It should be noted that our Dia de los muertos is the very opposite of Halloween. Our "dead" do not come to spook us, but to visit, comfort and party with us. We do not fear them. We welcome their presence and look forward to have a good time with them. Sometimes we even take music to the cemeteries and share with them their favorite song. We celebrate together that death does not have the final word over life and that life ultimately triumph over death. Our family and our pueblo are so strong and enduring that not even death can break it apart.

El Día de los muertos is more than a religious festivity. It is a day when remembering becomes a living reality with a transcendent meaning. It is a day of grieving as it is a day of celebration. It is the day when eating becomes a ritual and a way of communing with the dead, you remember as you taste the favorite meal or drink. It is a day when the cemeteries are most visited to clean and restore the graveyard. Is it a day to celebrate the lives of the ones living with the Eternal God as they once lived among us? The text of 1st Corinthians recovers its meaning; "Where, Death, is your victory? Where, Death, is your power to hurt?" In the understanding of the Hispanics, the deceased continue to visit as they are alive in another dimension.

All Saints Day is the day prior to the Day of the Death, a time when the innocents and those that are considered saints by their parents are remembered in their hearts and prayers. These people are the tender stillborn, the toddler, the youth, and even the fetal demises; all of them have a place in the liturgical calendar to be remembered. The saints of our family have a time and a space in our calendar to be acknowledged among us, and this atmosphere provided to the bereaved family validates the loss and the feelings helping them to heal.

Nicknames Given to Death

The Hispanic people use sarcasm to cope with the emotional tensions in life. From there the creation of nicknames are born and given to the object or individuals whom have made us grieve. In Venezuela, death is commonly called *la pelona*, "the hairless woman." From the Web site **www.acabtu.com.mx/diadelosmuertos/origen.htm,** I collected a list of nicknames given to death; among the many are *la calaca, la huesuda, la flaca*, and *la parca*. Caricaturing the subject is an educated way of poking fun that helps to deal with the inability to cope. Mockery is introduced in poems and popular songs to work artistically with damaged emotions. The radio plays the songs and the listening audience can perceive the grief. Some people even take the risk of dedicating the song to the person who hurt their feelings. This common use of metaphors carries on the issue at hand and helps to deal with the nostalgia of the soul.

Every human being is touched by death in one way or another. Some are better prepared to deal with death than others. Some patients admitted to nursing homes "are waiting for her every day but she never comes." My grandfather always said during the wakes of his friends, "There is something in your life that no one can steal from you, your own death."

Conclusion

As a spiritual caregiver you will notice that the event of death always surprises the affected party, even when the person thinks they are ready to face it. The event of death has a way of making you feel emotionally incompetent, uncomfortable, and uneasy to deal with it. It has to do with the emotional investment you have placed in the person you are losing and the inability to let go.

Each patient brings his spiritual cosmos and his religious preference to the table to guide us as we provide end of life care. We all need to be diagnosed by a doctor to receive medical treatment, but you know to find the spiritual comfort you need to focus in the core of your own values and beliefs. What brings meaning, hope, salvation, and empowerment to your life? It will become the meal of your life as you become unable to express yourself. As the stories unfold before your eyes, you will the patterns of empowerment, hope, guidance, and illumination within the path of the patient and his family. It will become the map of your actions and the goals to achieve on behalf of the dying. As you discover what is important for the family, it becomes easier to focus on your task.

There is a particular thing I have noticed in the Hispanic community, and it is the strong faith the people have in the invisible reality that surrounds them. Hispanic people have a faith based on the crucified Christ. The incarnated God on the cross helps the people in discomfort to overcome the circumstances to lead them to the promise given by God in life.

During the process of death, the icons of the crucified Christ recover a new sense of hope within the people because it is after the trials, after the dark nights that the light of God is waiting for us to see the everlasting light of Christ. This belief in the God that is accompanying us is represented in the resurrection of our Lord Jesus Christ, and the presence of the religious minister coming to provide prayers, anointing the sick with the consecrated utensils helping the people to center their eyes on God.

The process of grief lived by the family in the *novena* is kind of living Holy Week. Days in which the whole family accompany their own dead suffering and agonizing his way to the other side; the dead becomes a figure of Jesus of Nazareth. To walk guiding their family member through the valley of shadows becomes the via cruxes. The intense pain of the agony of death in the deceased and the emotional discomfort the family feels in that moment acquire new meaning for the family. The communion with God in solidarity with your fellow man is acquired. It is the grace of God, which prepares us to see the pain of the crucified Christ in our own flesh. It is the grace of God holding us as we deal with our illnesses, with our dead, in the process to become whole again in the middle of chaos. Without a Good Friday the day of Resurrection would not be as powerful as it is. The agony of suffering, the shame of being emotionally and physically naked before society, helps us to open our eyes to the beauty of life in death. The bereaved will rise from their grief when the time comes. The promises taught by the church acquire new meaning in the figure of the One that rose and left the linens in the tomb. This is the breathing hope and promise when you see your own cross in your dearly departed.

Solomon, a man who was considered a wise king of his time, stated the contrast between grief and happiness in the behavior of the wise and the foolish, Ecclesiastes 7:1-4 reads,

> A good name is better than precious ointment, and the day of death than the day of birth. It is better to go to the house of mourning than to go to the house of feasting; for this is the end of everyone, and the living will lay it to heart. Sorrow is better than laughter, for by sadness of continence the heart is made glad. The heart of the wise is in the house of mourning but the heart of the fools is in the house of mirth.

These words of reflection of King Solomon bring us closer to the cruel reality of life, to the contrasts of sickness and health, and to the dynamics of life and death. The appreciation that the wise man has toward the bereaved is mostly the projection of our own human limitation. There is a beginning and there is an end. Death is hidden within life in an intrinsic way and it appears suddenly through illnesses that finish up with what we know here and now. Mourning and the end of life is the realization of our own finite existence: Our bodies die every day and this affliction prepare us for our own end.

The contribution of hospital institutions, hospice, and religious ministers, the ones that care and interpret our health in terms of diagnosis, prognosis, treatment, and plan of action, continues to grow in identifying the problem, adapting new programs, acknowledging resources to help those who grieve. These institutions help to prepare the path to follow, with the help of local resources for the sake of those who mourn. Religious institutions bring a contribution at a local level, everyday challenges presented by the incarnated theology. Searching for meaning in life, accompanying those in need. They pursue ways to make sense of the gospel in practical terms that free those held captive by pain and understands their spiritual need.

May the God, who embodies the need of the patient and the skills of the one who provides care, help us to find appropriate answers when we are called to serve the needy. May God help us to understand that each patient is a unique and blessed vehicle and that there is not just one formula which provides answers to every one. Seeking the path of meaning in listening, in paying attention to the story that unfolds before us is part of being sensitive and part of the answer. And may the God who unites us in science, love, comprehension, health, and peace help us to develop new answers rooted in the traditions, values, and beliefs of the people we serve. Peace.

Author's Note: This article is part of a forthcoming textbook for Vitas hospice, "The effects of loss and death on health," University of North

Carolina Press, and is shared here with their kind permission. Address correspondence to RGS318@cs.com.

References

Fukuyama, M. A., and T. D. Sevig. 1999. *Integrating spirituality into multicultural counseling.* Multicultural Aspects of Counseling Series 13, Thousand Oaks, CA: Sage.

Isasi-Diaz, A. M, 1993, *En la lucha/In the struggle: Elaborating a mujerista theology.* Minneapolis, MN: Fortress Press.

Steven-Arroyo and Ana Maria Diaz-Stevens, eds, 1994, *An enduring flame: Studies on Latino popular religiosity.* Bilder Center for Wester Hemisphere Studies, Graduate School and University Center of the City University of New York.

From *Illness: Crisis & Loss,* Vol. 12, No. 3, July 2004, pp. 239-255. Copyright © 2004 by Baywood Publishing Company, Inc. Reprinted by permission via Copyright Clearance Center.

UNIT 5

Families, Now and Into the Future

Unit Selections

Key Points to Consider

- After having charted your family's lifestyle and relationship history, what type of future do you see for yourself? What changes do you see yourself making in your life? How would you go about gathering the information you need to make these decisions?

- What is the state of rituals in your family? What rituals might you build in your family? Why? How might you use family gatherings and other traditions to build family integration?

Student Website

www.mhcls.com/online

Internet References

Further information regarding these websites may be found in this book's preface or online.

National Institute on Aging
http://www.nih.gov/nia/

*W*hat is the future of the family? Does the family even have a future? These questions and others like them are being asked. Many people fear for the future of the family. As previous units of this volume have shown, the family is a continually evolving institution that will continue to change throughout time. Still, certain elements of family appear to be constant. The family is and will remain a powerful influence in the lives of its members. This is because we all begin life in some type of family, and this early exposure carries a great deal of weight in forming our social selves—who we are and how we relate to others. From our families, we take our basic genetic makeup, while we also learn and are reinforced in health behaviors. In families, we are given our first exposure to values and it is through families that we most actively influence others. Our sense of commitment and obligation begins within the family as well as our sense of what we can expect of others.

Much that has been written about families has been less than hopeful and has focused on ways of avoiding or correcting errors. The articles in this unit take a positive view of family and how it influences its members. The emphasis is on health rather than dysfunction.

Knowledge is the basic building block of intelligent decisions regarding family. In "Breaking Free of the Family Tree," Jennifer Matlack describes the genogram, a useful technique for mapping out your family history so that you can anticipate, plan, and possibly change the choices you make in relationships and lifestyle. Information is important in planning for our family's future. One way to gather this information is through interviews, and "Get a Closer Look: 12 Tips for Successful Family Interviews" explains just how this can be done. Concluding this volume, family rituals can be a powerful force for family cohesion, and change and the nature of family rituals is described in "Examining Family Rituals."

Relationships

Breaking Free of the Family Tree

Save yourself a lot of bark and spilled sap: Branch out from the usual genealogical charts by mapping your family's behavior tics.

JENNIFER MATLACK

Take a good look in the mirror.

Along with the color of your eyes and the shape of your face, you might also have your mother's quirky sense of humor and your father's artistic flair. And it doesn't stop there. One parent's debilitating depression or peculiar obsession may be as much a part of you as the nose on your face.

All families carry baggage. And when it comes to piling it on, families can be awfully generous. You may have ended up with emotional loads you don't even know you're carrying that will affect important relationships in your life and steer you off course in ways you can't imagine.

Lucinda and Dan (names have been changed), a professional couple in their 30s, were each reliving familiar family patterns—and didn't realize it. They only knew their marriage was in trouble, so they sought help from San Diego marriage and family therapist Sally LeBoy. To LeBoy, Lucinda complained that her husband would agree to do a household chore, such as lock the doors at night, and then forget to follow through. Moreover, he didn't seem to care, and his passivity made Lucinda feel as if she didn't have a partner. Dan, on the other hand, told LeBoy that he thought of his wife as a maddening little Miss Wiz—always taking control and getting things done. He was unhappy because it seemed as if Lucinda was constantly nagging him. "They weren't discussing divorce," says LeBoy, "but they knew they had to work out the problem before it got worse."

LeBoy began, as many therapists do, by exploring the family dynamics in the couple's background. Then she created a family diagram, or genogram, which charts patterns of behavior through several generations of a family. Along with normal behavior, distant or hostile relationships and serious mental or physical problems are diagrammed in symbols that appear on a chart. It becomes immediately clear if history is repeating itself. "We claim that we will never be like our parents and have the same relationships they had," says LeBoy. "But how we define ourselves in an intimate relationship comes from what we have learned in our families."

Your family inheritance may be more than you bargained for. The emotional patterns of families can be handed down in the genes along with physical traits.

Genograms have more details than ancestral trees. They include not only three generations of a family but also live-in partners and other important nonfamily members. In addition to marriages, births, and deaths, genograms record extramarital affairs, miscarriages, abortions, financial problems, serious illnesses, and other major stressful events. The charts also note the personality traits of family members, such as whether someone is emotionally inaccessible, controlling, or passive.

"Think of it as if you're painting a picture of your family," says LeBoy. "The more detail, the better."

Genograms were created by the late psychiatrist Murray Bowen, M.D., developer of the family systems theory in the early 1950s. Bowen's work with schizophrenic patients and their families at the Menninger Clinic in Topeka, Kansas, and later at the National Institute of Mental Health near Washington, D.C., led him to radically depart from previous theories of human emotional functioning. Bowen saw the family as one emotional unit and the individual as part of that unit rather than as an autonomous psychological entity. Through his research, he discovered that an order and predictability in family relationships existed. The recent resurgence of genograms is due in part to New Jersey therapist Monica McGoldrick's use of the charts in family life cycle development and the popularity of her 1999 book, *Genograms: Assessment and Intervention* (W.W. Norton).

Genograms include details not found on the traditional family tree, such as extramarital affairs, abortions, and financial problems.

Behavioral patterns are passed down from generation to generation by parents, who teach their children how to relate to other people. Therapists also believe that learning interpersonal skills occurs on a subconscious level in children, and recent genetics research suggests that some character traits and behaviors, such as shyness and depression, are actually encoded on genes and thus physically transmitted to the next generation.

In Lucinda and Dan's case, the genogram study showed that their behavior toward one another was directly related to how they functioned subconsciously in their respective families. Lucinda came from a line of strong, reliable women and marginally functioning men. In her immediate family, her father was alcoholic and her mother, perhaps to compensate, was extremely reliable. Dan's family was dominated by his rigid, controlling father, who was determined that all his children should be successful. LeBoy also discovered that Dan left his parents' home at age 18 to attend college on the other side of the country, about as far away from home as he could get.

"For people who grow up in a situation where someone in the family didn't pull their weight, the tendency to overfunction is huge," says LeBoy. Clearly, that's what Lucinda was doing in her marriage.

Dan, on the other hand, according to LeBoy, learned to distance himself physically and psychologically from his overachieving, overbearing family. Thus, the more Lucinda demanded of Dan—as her mother had tried to do with her father—the more Dan withdrew, the same way he had always withdrawn from his own demanding father. Both were extremely ingrained in their particular "learned behaviors," that is, how they react in familiar situations.

LeBoy tried to help Lucinda and Dan unlearn some of their programmed behavior. For Lucinda, this meant dropping her mother's overfunctioning style. Dan's job was first to try to change the relationship with his father by relating to him as a responsible adult, rather than a rebellious child. Once Dan "grew up" and began to feel more autonomous, LeBoy believed he would be able to drop his defensive, passive-aggressive style with his wife, and when Lucinda demanded something of him, Dan would be more willing to cooperate. Becoming aware of

the origin of their behavior enabled the couple to set their marriage on a steadier course.

Genograms help people see the big picture, which at times can be scary, and interpreting a baggage-laden lineage is not always easy. Professional guidance is recommended.

"If you do a genogram and discover patterns that you find are negative or disturbing, take this information and work with a therapist," says Ann Kramer, a family counselor in Tampa, Florida. "A professional will help you clarify what you're seeing and perhaps give you some insight you can't see on your own."

Certain key relationship patterns tend to surface repeatedly. One is called "emotional fusion," which occurs when family members fail to establish healthy differences between one another, and function in exclusively codependent ways. "Triangling" is another. It occurs when two people draw in a third person in an attempt to defuse stress and anxiety between one another. A "cutoff" is perhaps the most serious difficulty, which occurs when someone severs ties with his or her family completely. Another important factor to consider in genograms is birth order. Siblings' emotional places in the family are often duplicated in their subsequent intimate relationships. First-borns, for example, tend to be responsible and serious adults, whereas the babies are more carefree and rebellious.

Sorting through past family relationships can be an emotional strain, but the rewards of such a cleansing are great.

As difficult as it is to sort through family dynamics and relationships, the rewards are great indeed. But before you can change a problem, you first must realize one exists. Too often, families live in cycles of despair and anger, feeling that there is no way out, and not realizing the door they seek may be the back door of their past.

JENNIFER MATLACK is a writer based in Wilton, Connecticut.

From *Health*, September 2001, pp. 80, 82, 84, 86. © 2001 by Southern Progress Corporation, with permission of the author, Jennifer Matlack.

Get a Closer Look

12 Tips for Successful Family Interviews

IRA WOLFMAN

How do you get relatives talking? A good family history interview isn't easy to conduct You need to combine the best attributes of caring friend, hard-nosed reporter, and sensitive psychologist. But do it well and you may be rewarded with wonderful stories.

Interviews are different from normal conversations. One person has a goal: to get information from another person (let's call him or her the "talker"). You want the talker to feel comfortable, but you also need to direct the conversation to the points you are interested in.

You also have to be flexible. Sometimes an unexpected topic can turn out to be wonderful. Other times you'll need to lead your talker back to the main point—without hurting his or her feelings. This can be difficult, but you will become better at it as you go along—practice will make you skilled. Be patient with yourself and expect some mistakes. To make things easier, keep these tips in mind:

1. Before any interview, give advance warning. Explain what you want to do, why you want to do it, and why the talker is important to you and your research. You can call or write a letter or e-mail. Here's an example of the kinds of things you should say:

Dear Aunt Gus:

I'm working on a history of our family, and it would be very helpful if I could sit down and talk with you. I'm particularly interested in your memories of my great-grandparents (your mother and father) and the family's early years in Minnesota. I'd also love to look at any old photographs or documents you have.

I won't need much more than an hour of your time and would like to hold our talk at your home. Any weekend day would be fine. Can you let me know a date that is convenient for you?

Thanks so much for your help.

By writing this letter, you've given your relative a chance to start thinking about the topics you're interested in, and you may have even jogged her memory. Of course, not all your relatives will be close by, and your arrangements may be more difficult than "any weekend day." That just makes your writing—and planning—even more important.

2. Prepare before your interview. Find out whatever you can about the talker *before* the interview. Where does she fit in the family? What documents might she have? What other genealogical jewels might she have?

Gather as much information as you can ahead of time about her relationship to everyone in your family. Your parents can probably help you with this.

3. Think out all your questions beforehand. Interviewing requires structure. Write your questions on a sheet of paper, organized by subject. One easy way to organize what you want to ask is by year: Start with your relative's earliest years and then move on from there.

"So, Aunt Gus, you lived in the house in a town outside Minneapolis till you were 10—about 1922, right? Then where did you move?" Or "You say Great-grandpa worked as a tailor in St. Paul. Did you ever visit his shop? Where was it? What years did he have the business there?" As this interviewer did, it's a good idea to summarize what you already know so that your subject can verify your facts. Then move on to a request for more detail.

Sometimes the simplest questions can hit the jackpot. I asked my great-uncle Max, "How old were you when you went from Poland to America?" I didn't get an answer; I got a story:

I must have been about 15 when I went to Warsaw to get a visa to emigrate. I got the visa, but then the counselor at the examination said, "Listen, boy, you are underage. You can't go without your father." He crossed out my stamp.

I went back to our town and told my father. He said, "Don't worry, we'll take care of that."

My father was a religious man, but he also knew how to get things done. He called a policeman from our town and asked him to make me older.

I got new papers. Now I turned from 15 to 18 or 19. I went back to Warsaw, and I was able to leave. And on February 20, 1920, I took the boat Susquehanna *from Danzig to New York.*

Ready, Set, Research ... Your Family Tree

❏ Interview your parents about their family history. Practice interviewing with them.

❏ Make appointments to interview other family members.

❏ Prepare your questions. (For a list of good questions for family interviews, see **www.workmen.com/ familytree**.)

❏ Type up your notes from interviews. Ask the relatives you interviewed to review them and correct or add to them.

❏ Write a thank-you note to every family member you interviewed.

Remember to also ask open-ended questions. "What do you remember most about the apartment on Division Street?" or "Tell me about your relationship with your brothers" may yield something unexpected and wonderful.

4. Bring a video or tape recorder if possible.

A small tape recorder usually doesn't disturb anyone, and it catches every bit of information, including the way your talkers sound and exactly how they answer questions. If you plan to video-tape, be sure someone comes with you to run the camera. You need to focus on your talker.

5. In any case, bring a notebook and a pen.

Even if you have [an audio tape or video] recorder, always take handwritten notes. Recorders can break down.

During the interview, write down names and dates and double-check them with your subject. Facts are important, but the most important information your talkers offer are their stories. Try to capture the way they talk and their colorful expressions: "That ship was rolling on the ocean like a marble in your hand."

There's another good reason to bring pen and paper with you. You won't have to interrupt when you think of a question; just write a note to yourself so you'll remember to ask it at an appropriate time.

6. Start with easy, friendly questions.

Leave the more difficult or emotional material for later in the interview, after you've had time to gain your talker's trust. If things aren't going well, you may want to save those questions for another time.

It's also a good idea to begin with questions about the person you're interviewing. You may be more interested in a great-grandfather if he is the missing link in your family chart. But first get some background information about your talker—your aunt, for example. This serves two purposes. First, it lets her know she's important to you, that you care about her, and that her life is interesting, too. Second, as she talks, she may reveal some other information that you would never have known about otherwise.

7. Bring family photographs with you.

Look for photos, artwork, or documents that will help jog your subject's memory. Bring the pictures out and ask your talker to describe what's going on. "Do you remember when this was taken? Who are the people? What was the occasion? Who do you think took the picture?" You may be amazed at how much detail your relative will see in a photograph and also at the memories that come spilling forth.

8. Don't be afraid of silence.

You might feel uneasy and want to rush in with another question when your talker stops speaking. *Don't.* Silence is an important part of interviewing and can sometimes yield to interesting results. Because people often find silence uncomfortable, they often try to fill it if you don't—and in doing so, they may say something you might not have heard otherwise.

Sometimes silence is also necessary for gathering thoughts. Don't forget—you are asking your subjects to think back on things they may not have considered for years. Calling up these memories may spark other thoughts, too. Allow your subject time to **ponder**. You may be thrilled by what he or she remembers.

9. Ask the same question in different ways.

People don't know how much they know, and rephrasing a question can give you more information. This happens all the time. "I don't know," a relative will tell you, sometimes impatiently. They do know—they just don't know that they know. The most common version of this occurs when an interviewer asks, "What was your father's mother's name?" The relative answers, "I never knew her. I don't know." Then a few minutes later, in response to "Whom were you named after?" this answer comes; "My father's mother."

Try to find a couple of ways to ask important questions. You may feel like you're being repetitive, but you never can be sure what you will learn.

10. Be sensitive to what you discover.

Sometimes people become emotional talking about the past. They may remember long-dead relatives or once-forgotten tragedies. If your talker is upset by a memory, either remain silent or quietly ask, "Is it all right if we talk some more about this? Or would you rather not?" People frequently feel better when they talk about sad things; you should gently give your relative the *choice* of whether or not to go on.

11. Try not to interrupt.

If your talker strays from the subject, let him or her finish the story and then say, "Let's get back to Uncle Moe" or "You said something earlier about ..." By not interrupting, you make the conversation friendlier, and the story may lead you to something you didn't expect.

Of course, there is always the exception to the rule. If a story goes on forever and seems useless, the best way to handle it may be to say, "Gee, Aunt Gus, could you hold the rest of that story for later? I'd like to get the facts out of the way and then come back to that."

12. Ask for songs, poems, unusual memories. You may discover something wonderful when you ask your subject if she recalls the rhymes she used to recite while jumping rope as a little girl or the hymns she sang in church. Probe a little here—ask about childhood games and memories, smells and tastes and sounds.

Examining Family Rituals

GRACE M. VIERE
James Madison University

In this column, the notion of rituals from a historical perspective is provided. The definitions and classifications of family rituals as well as empirical studies are examined.

Family rituals, originating as a belief in mystical powers, have evolved into a vital component of family life that transcends race, culture, and socioeconomic levels. Researchers and practitioners have begun to incorporate family rituals into a variety of studies and therapeutic practices. This article reviews the definition and meaning of rituals and implications of family rituals for the health and well-being of families.

Rituals Defined

Anthropologist Victor Turner (1967) originally defined *ritual* as a "prescribed formal behavior for occasions not given over to technological routine, having reference to beliefs in mystical beings or powers" (p. 19). Turner's definition emphasizes symbols as the building blocks of rituals. The significance of symbols is explained in the following three areas: the ability to carry multiple meanings and thus contribute to the open parts of rituals, the ways symbols can link several disparate phenomena that could not be joined as complexly through words, and the ability of symbols to work with both the sensory and cognitive poles of meaning simultaneously.

Moore and Myerhoff (1977) suggested that the anthropological study of ritual has often been limited to religious and magical aspects of a culture partly because anthropologists have often worked in societies "in which everything has a religious significance" (p. 3). As societies become more secular, they continue to carry within them beliefs that have a similar role in society as religion. Moore and Myerhoff stressed the importance of recognizing the sacredness of these beliefs and the rituals carried out around them. Their definition of *sacred* reaches beyond the traditional religious definition to focus on "specialness" or "something colored with meaning beyond the ordinary."

Rappaport (1971) also suggested that the term *ritual* is not limited to religious practices. He described the following six key aspects to ritual of which family rituals are a part:

1. repetition: not necessarily just in action but also of content and form,

2. acting: not just saying or thinking something but also doing something,
3. special behavior or stylization: where behaviors and symbols are set apart from their usual common uses,
4. order: some beginning and end and containment for spontaneity.
5. evocative presentational style: where through staging and focus an "attentive state of mind" is created,
6. collective dimension: where there is social meaning.

Van Gennep (1960) developed three stages of rituals. In the first stage, separation, special preparations are made and new knowledge is passed on as the frame is set for marking a particular event. This time of preparing for the ritual is as important a part of the ritual process as the actual event itself. The second stage is transitional, in which people actually partake of the ritual and experience themselves in new ways and take on new roles. The third stage is reintegration, in which people are reconnected to their community with their new status. Ritual is not just the ceremony or actual performance but the whole process of preparing for it, experiencing it, and reintegration back into everyday life.

Rituals in Families

Wolin and Bennett (1984) viewed family ritual as a "a symbolic form of communication that, owing to the satisfaction that family members experience through its repetition, is acted out in a systematic fashion over time". They identified six typologies of ritual use in families. First is underritualized, in which families neither celebrate nor mark family changes nor join much in larger societal rituals. This underutilization leaves the family with little access to some of the benefits of ritual such as group cohesion, support for role shifts, and the ability to hold two dualities in place at the same time. Second is rigidly ritualized, in which there are very prescribed behaviors, a sense of "we must always do these things together in this way at this time." There are few open parts in the rituals, and rituals tend to stay the same over time rather than evolving. Third is skewed ritualization, in which one particular ethnic tradition in the family, or religious tradition, or even one particular side of the family has been emphasized at the expense of other aspects of the family. Fourth is hollow ritual as event, not process. This takes place when people celebrate events out of a sense of obligation, with little meaning found in either the process or the event. This may happen because rituals have become too closed or end up creating undue stress for family members. Fifth is ritual process interrupted or unable to be openly experienced. This occurs after sudden changes (e.g., death, moving, and illness) or traumatic events in the family or larger culture (e.g., war oppression and migration). Families may be unable to fully experience the whole ritual process. And finally, flexibility to adapt to rituals is the ability to change rituals over the life cycle, keeping the rituals meaningful for families and reworking roles, rules, and relationships.

Despite differences among families in terms of factors such as socioeconomic status, ethnic background, and religious orientation, the following four types of rituals are universal to nearly all families: family celebrations, family traditions, family life cycle rituals, and day-to-day life events that have become ritualized (Wolin & Bennett, 1984).

Family celebrations are defined as rituals that are widely practiced around events that are celebrated in the larger culture. Through larger cultural expectations, the society to some extent organizes the time, space, and symbols of these rituals. Examples include Passover and Christmas. Family traditions are less anchored in the culture and are more idiosyncratic to the family, based on what might be called an inside instead of an outside calendar. Anniversaries, birthdays, family reunions, vacations, and so on all fall into this category. Although the practice of traditions is influenced to some extent by the culture, the individual family determines which occasions it will adopt as traditions and how these activities will be enacted. Family life cycle rituals include weddings, showers, christenings, graduations, and retirement parties. These are events that mark the progression of the family through the life cycle. Rituals of daily family life, such as dinnertime, bedtime, and recreation, are those events that are infused with meaning as the family creates its roles, rules, and norms. Day-to-day rituals are the least deliberate and consciously planned of the family rituals as well as the least standardized across families, the most variable over time, and the most frequently enacted.

Family rituals provide the family and individual members with a sense of identity by creating feelings of belonging (Bennett, Wolin, & McAvity, 1988; Fiese, 1992). Rituals are the occasions during which family members transmit family values and beliefs (Steinglass, Bennett, Wolin, & Reiss, 1987), reinforce the family's heritage (Troll, 1988), and recognize change in the family (Wolin & Bennett, 1984).

All families experience crisis or stress, and rituals have the capacity to provide families stability during these time (Cheal, 1988). For example, with a funeral wake or sitting Shiva, there are certain prescribed times for mourning. Groups of people meet to support and comfort each other in their sorrow, foods are shared, specific clothes may be worn, and certain words are said. Families draw comfort from knowing they can experience strong feelings of grief with some circumscribed limits and group support (Scheff, 1979).

Rituals can hold both sides of a contradiction at the same time. All individuals live with the ultimate paradoxes of life/death, connection/distance, ideal/real, and good/evil, and rituals can incorporate both sides of contradictions so that they can be managed simultaneously. For example, a wedding ceremony has included within it both loss and mourning and happiness and celebration. Parents give their child away at the same time they welcome another member into their extended family.

Ritual Versus Routine

Steinglass et al. (1987) described the following five types of family rituals that clearly distinguish between family rituals and daily routines: (a) bounded rituals, which are prepared with anticipation and have a clear beginning, middle, and end; (b) identifiable rituals, in which families are aware of their rituals and can clearly describe the organization and patterning of these behaviors; (c) compelling rituals, which families make rigorous efforts to maintain; (d) symbolic rituals, which are associated with meanings and strong emotions; and (e) organizing rituals, which are major regulators of stability for family life.

Although routines are observable and repetitious family behaviors that are important in structuring family life, they lack the symbolic content and the compelling, anticipatory nature that rituals possess (Keltner, Keltner, & Farren, 1990). Routines are activities that family members have to do rather than want to do. Routines have the potential to acquire ritual status if they exceed their functional purpose and become filled with psychological intensity and symbolic meaning (Boyce, Jensen, James, & Peacock, 1983). Conversely, rituals that lose meaning or become mundane may take on routine status for families. Sometimes family members simply outgrow a ritual. Another distinction that can be made between ritual and routine is the capacity of rituals to serve several distinct functions for the family that are symbolically important for the psychological well-being of the family system. Rituals are powerful organizers of behavior within the family system that provide the family with a sense of stability, a unique identity, and a means for socializing children within their cultural context.

Empirical Studies on Family Rituals

Systematic research on family rituals has focused on family risk conditions such as alcoholism and points of family transition such as becoming parents. Beginning in the 1970s, Wolin and Bennett began a series of studies examining the relationship between family rituals and alcoholism. In the first study, the relationship between ritual disruption and alcohol transmission was examined. The researchers hypothesized that families with more intact rituals would be less likely to transmit alcoholism in the next generation. Ritual disruption was assessed using the family ritual interview, focusing on the effect of the alcoholic parent's drinking behavior on family rituals. *Subsumptive* families, in which alcohol use had overridden and effectively controlled the practice of family rituals, were identified, as were *distinctive* families, in which the practice of family rituals remained distinct from alcohol use. The families in which alcohol had subsumed family ritual practice were more likely to have children who developed problematic drinking or married individuals with alcohol problems (Wolin, Bennett, Noonan, & Teitelbaum, 1987). Furthermore, protective factors were identified in the study of individuals raised in alcoholic households. When children of alcoholics chose spouses with highly developed nonalcoholic family rituals, there was less likelihood of developing an alcoholic family identity. The second protective factor was a distinctive dinner ritual in which children from alcoholic families whose parents preserved the dinner ritual had a higher likelihood of a nonalcoholic outcome (Bennett, Wolin, Reiss, & Teitelbaum, 1987).

Fiese (1992) found similar evidence for the role of family rituals in protecting children from the effects of family alcoholism. Using the Family Ritual Questionnaire and self-report measures of problematic drinking and health symptomatology, it was noted that the adolescents who reported meaningful family rituals in addition to parental problematic drinking were less likely to develop anxiety-related health symptoms than adolescents reporting parental problematic drinking and relatively hollow family rituals. The results from these studies suggest that under potentially stressful child-rearing conditions, such as parental alcoholism, family rituals may serve a protective function. In setting aside family gatherings as distinct from alcoholic behavior and in imbuing meaning and deliberateness in the practice of patterned family interactions such as dinnertime, the child may develop an identity of the family that is separate from the disruptions associated with alcoholism.

Family rituals may also serve a protective function during periods of normative family transitions. The transition to parenthood has been identified as a potentially stressful period for couples. A study of 115 married couples found that couples with preschoolers who were able to practice meaningful family rituals reported more marital satisfaction than those who reported relatively hollow family rituals (Fiese, Hooker, Kotrary, & Schwagler, 1993).

Two empirical studies investigated family rituals in families of children with disabilities. Gruszka (1988) examined families of children with mental retardation. She found that mothers of these children perceive that their families engage in fewer family celebrations than mothers of children who did not have any disabilities. Another study (Bucy, 1995) investigated rituals and parenting stress and their relationship to the disability characteristics of preschool children. Bucy (1995) found parents of preschool children with social skill deficits or motor impairments practice more religious and cultural family rituals than families of preschool children with cognitive delays. Furthermore, mothers of preschool children with disabilities that maintained meaningful participation in family rituals evidenced better abilities to cope with parenting stress than did mothers with less ritual participation.

Summary

Rituals both reflect and shape the way people think about themselves and their world. Papp (1983) suggested rituals have a unique ability to "address themselves to the most primitive and profound level of experience" (p. vii)—the level where resistance lies and where real change often begins.

Family rituals provide the family and individual members with a sense of identity by creating feelings of belonging. Rituals are the occasions that serve to facilitate social interaction among family members so that families can transmit cultural and normative information as well as beliefs and values across generations. All families experience crisis or stress, and rituals have the capacity to provide families stability during these times. Rituals may provide a way for people to find support and containment for strong emotions. Families may be encouraged to examine their family rituals and continue those rituals that are working for them as well as to develop new rituals and adapt those that are no longer valued.

References

Bennett, L. A., Wolin, S. J., & McAvity, K. J. (1988). Family identity, ritual and myth: A cultural perspective on life cycle transition. In C. J. Falicov (Ed.), *Family transitions* (pp. 211–234). New York: Guilford.

Bennett, L. A., Wolin, S. J., Reiss, D., & Teitelbaum, M. A. (1987). Couples at risk for transmission of alcoholism: Protective influences. *Family Process, 26,* 111–129.

Boyce, W., Jensen, E., James, S., & Peacock, J. (1983). The family routines inventory: Theoretical origins. *Social Science Medicine, 17,* 193–200.

Bucy, J. E. (1995). An exploratory study of family rituals, parenting stress, and developmental delay in early childhood. *Dissertation Abstracts International, 57*(2A), 575.

Cheal, D. (1988). The ritualization of family ties. *American Behavioral Scientist, 31,* 632–643.

Fiese, B. H. (1992). Dimensions of family rituals across two generations: Relations to adolescent identity. *Family Process, 31,* 151–162.

Fiese, B. H., Hooker, K. A., Kotrary, L., & Schwagler, J. (1993). Family rituals in the early stages of parenthood. *Journal of Marriage and Family, 55,* 633–642.

Gruszka, M. A. (1988). Family functioning and sibling adjustment in families with a handicapped child. *Dissertation Abstracts International, 50*(OB), 748.

Keltner, B., Keltner, N. L., & Farren, E. (1990). Family routines and conduct disorders in adolescent girls. *Western Journal of Nursing Research, 12,* 161–174.

Moore, S. F., & Myerhoff, B. G. (1977). (Eds.). *Secular ritual.* Amsterdam: Van Gorcum.

Papp, P. (1983). Preface. In O. Van der Hart (Ed.), *Rituals in psychotherapy: Transition and continuity* (pp. v–ix). New York: Irvington Publications.

Rappaport, R. A. (1971). Ritual sanctity and cybernetics. *American Anthropologist, 73,* 59–76.

Scheff, T. J. (1979). *Catharsis in healing, ritual, and drama.* Los Angeles: University of California Press.

Steinglass, P., Bennett, L. A., Wolin, S. J., & Reiss, D. (1987). *The alcoholic family.* New York: Basic Books.

Troll, L. E. (1988). Rituals and reunions. *American Behavioral Scientist, 31,* 621–631.

Turner, V. (1967). *The forest of symbols: Aspects of Ndembu ritual.* Ithaca, NY: Cornell University Press.

Van Gennep, A. (1960). *The rites of passage.* Chicago: University of Chicago Press.

Wolin, S. J., & Bennett, L. A. (1984). Family rituals. *Family Process, 23,* 401–420.

Wolin, S. J., Bennett, L. A., Noonan, D. L., & Teitelbaum, M. (1987). Disrupted family rituals: A factor in the intergenerational transmission of alcoholism. *Journal of Studies of Alcoholism, 41,* 199–214.

GRACE VIERE, PH.D., is an assistant professor of counselor education at James Madison University in Harrisonburg, VA. Her current research interests include the examination of the relationship between family rituals and attachments and the use of family rituals by families with children who are adopted.

Index

F

G

H

I

J

K

L

M

Test Your Knowledge Form

We encourage you to photocopy and use this page as a tool to assess how the articles in *Annual Editions* expand on the information in your textbook. By reflecting on the articles you will gain enhanced text information. You can also access this useful form on a product's book support Web site at *http://www.mhcls.com/online/*.

NAME: DATE:

_____

TITLE AND NUMBER OF ARTICLE:

_____

BRIEFLY STATE THE MAIN IDEA OF THIS ARTICLE:

_____

LIST THREE IMPORTANT FACTS THAT THE AUTHOR USES TO SUPPORT THE MAIN IDEA:

_____

WHAT INFORMATION OR IDEAS DISCUSSED IN THIS ARTICLE ARE ALSO DISCUSSED IN YOUR TEXTBOOK OR OTHER READINGS THAT YOU HAVE DONE? LIST THE TEXTBOOK CHAPTERS AND PAGE NUMBERS:

_____

LIST ANY EXAMPLES OF BIAS OR FAULTY REASONING THAT YOU FOUND IN THE ARTICLE:

_____

LIST ANY NEW TERMS/CONCEPTS THAT WERE DISCUSSED IN THE ARTICLE, AND WRITE A SHORT DEFINITION:

We Want Your Advice

ANNUAL EDITIONS revisions depend on two major opinion sources: one is our Advisory Board, listed in the front of this volume, which works with us in scanning the thousands of articles published in the public press each year; the other is you—the person actually using the book. Please help us and the users of the next edition by completing the prepaid article rating form on this page and returning it to us. Thank you for your help!

ANNUAL EDITIONS: The Family 07/08

ARTICLE RATING FORM

Here is an opportunity for you to have direct input into the next revision of this volume.
We would like you to rate each of the articles listed below, using the following scale:

1. **Excellent: should definitely be retained**
2. **Above average: should probably be retained**
3. **Below average: should probably be deleted**
4. **Poor: should definitely be deleted**

Your ratings will play a vital part in the next revision.
Please mail this prepaid form to us as soon as possible.
Thanks for your help!

RATING	ARTICLE
	1. The World Historical Transformation of Marriage
	2. Children as a Public Good
	3. Families and Family Study in International Perspective
	4. Gender Bender
	5. What Makes You Who You Are
	6. This Thing Called Love
	7. Great Expectations
	8. Go Ahead, Kiss Your Cousin: Heck, Marry Her If You Want To
	9. Interracial Intimacy
	10. New Technologies and Our Feelings: Romance on the Internet
	11. Lust for the Long Haul
	12. Reinventing Sex
	13. A New Fertility Factor
	14. The Abortion Wars: 30 Years After Roe v. Wade
	15. Brave New Babies
	16. Barren
	17. Who's Raising Baby?
	18. And Now, the Hard Part: That Sweet Little Thing Is About to Commandeer Your Life
	19. Adopting a New American Family
	20. After the Bliss
	21. Contextual Influences on Marriage: Implications for Policy and Intervention
	22. Marriage at First Sight
	23. Kaleidoscope of Parenting Cultures
	24. Spanking Children: Evidence and Issues
	25. Stress and the Superdad
	26. The Kids Are All Right
	27. What About Black Fathers?

RATING	ARTICLE
	28. Adoption by Lesbian Couples
	29. Are Married Parents Really Better for Children?
	30. The Perma Parent Trap
	31. Being a Sibling
	32. Aunties and Uncles
	33. Roles of American Indian Grandparents in Times of Cultural Crisis
	34. Aging Japanese Pen Messages to Posterity
	35. Hitting Home
	36. The Myths and Truths of Family Abduction
	37. Love But Don't Touch
	38. For Better or Worse: Couples Confront Unemployment
	39. Keeping Work and Life in Balance
	40. How to Land on Your Feet
	41. Home Alone
	42. Terrorism, Trauma, and Children: What Can We Do?
	43. Marriage and Divorce American Style
	44. Dating After Divorce
	45. Managing a Blended Family
	46. Stepfamily Success Depends on Ingredients
	47. Death of One's Partner: The Anticipation and the Reality
	48. The Hispanic Way of Dying: Three Families, Three Perspectives, Three Cultures
	49. Breaking Free of the Family Tree
	50. Get a Closer Look: 12 Tips for Successful Family Interviews
	51. Examining Family Rituals

(Continued on next page)

BUSINESS REPLY MAIL
FIRST CLASS MAIL PERMIT NO. 551 DUBUQUE IA

POSTAGE WILL BE PAID BY ADDRESEE

McGraw-Hill Contemporary Learning Series
2460 KERPER BLVD
DUBUQUE, IA 52001-9902

ABOUT YOU

Name   Date
_____

Are you a teacher? ☐   A student? ☐
Your school's name
_____

Department
_____

Address   City   State   Zip
_____

School telephone #
_____

YOUR COMMENTS ARE IMPORTANT TO US!

Please fill in the following information:
For which course did you use this book?
_____

Did you use a text with this ANNUAL EDITION? ☐ yes ☐ no
What was the title of the text?
_____

What are your general reactions to the *Annual Editions* concept?
_____

Have you read any pertinent articles recently that you think should be included in the next edition? Explain.
_____

Are there any articles that you feel should be replaced in the next edition? Why?
_____

Are there any World Wide Web sites that you feel should be included in the next edition? Please annotate.
_____

May we contact you for editorial input? ☐ yes ☐ no
May we quote your comments? ☐ yes ☐ no